GRAPHIC ARTS PRODUCTION

Lorette C. Dodt

 AMERICAN TECHNICAL PUBLISHERS, INC.
HOMEWOOD, ILLINOIS 60430

1 2 3 4 5 6 7 8 9 - 90 - 9 8 7 6 5 4 3 2

Printed in the United States of America

Library of Congress Cataloging-in-Publication Data
Dodt, Lorette C., 1956–
    Graphic arts production / Lorette C. Dodt.
        p.   cm.
    ISBN 0-8269-2684-3
    1. Printing, Practical. 2. Graphic arts.   I. Title.
Z244.3.D63   1990
686.2—dc20

CONTENTS

Chapter 1
PRODUCTION
OF JOBS   1

Production Process—Communicating Needs—Production of Elements —Assembly of Elements—Final Production—Tools and Equipment— Basic Tools—Measurement Systems—Measurement Devices

Chapter 2
COMPREHENSIVE
LAYOUT   19

Elements of a Comprehensive Layout—Layout Specifications—Layout Elements—Using a Comprehensive Layout—Working with a Comprehensive Layout—Transferring the Layout to the Artboard—Preparing the Artboard for Reproduction—Technical Pen and Ink—Trim Marks— Center Marks—Fold, Score, and Perforation Marks

Chapter 3
RULING   39

Ruling with Ink—Inking Tools and Techniques—Correction Techniques —Ruling with Adhesive Material—Ruling Techniques

Chapter 4
SPECIALIZED
ART ELEMENTS   53

Circles and Curves—Creating Circles—Creating Curves—Borders— Creating Borders—Tint Screens—Adhesive Tint Screens—Film Tint Screens

Chapter 5
TYPOGRAPHY   69

Type Legibility and Readability—Anatomy of a Word—Typographical Layout—Type Arrangement—Type Specifications—Type Classifications —Communicating with the Typesetter—Copyfitting—Type Specification and Proofreading

Chapter 6
INKED AND
HAND-SET TYPE   85

Created Type—Inked Type—Hand-set Type—Layout of Hand-set Type —Adhesive Type—Transfer Type

Chapter 7
TYPE AND
ILLUSTRATIONS   97

Basic Paste-up Procedure—Choosing Correct Adhesive—Applying Adhesives—Production Techniques—Overlay Method

Chapter 8
CAMERA COPY   109

Line and Continuous Tone Copy—Line Copy—Halftone Copy

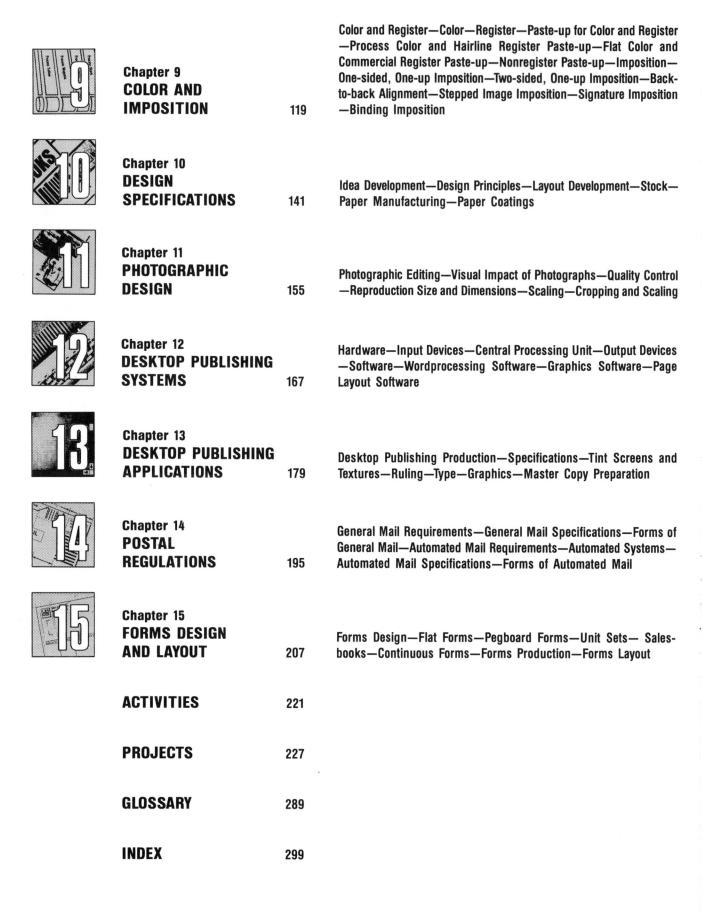

Chapter 9
COLOR AND
IMPOSITION   119

Color and Register—Color—Register—Paste-up for Color and Register
—Process Color and Hairline Register Paste-up—Flat Color and
Commercial Register Paste-up—Nonregister Paste-up—Imposition—
One-sided, One-up Imposition—Two-sided, One-up Imposition—Back-
to-back Alignment—Stepped Image Imposition—Signature Imposition
—Binding Imposition

Chapter 10
DESIGN
SPECIFICATIONS   141

Idea Development—Design Principles—Layout Development—Stock—
Paper Manufacturing—Paper Coatings

Chapter 11
PHOTOGRAPHIC
DESIGN   155

Photographic Editing—Visual Impact of Photographs—Quality Control
—Reproduction Size and Dimensions—Scaling—Cropping and Scaling

Chapter 12
DESKTOP PUBLISHING
SYSTEMS   167

Hardware—Input Devices—Central Processing Unit—Output Devices
—Software—Wordprocessing Software—Graphics Software—Page
Layout Software

Chapter 13
DESKTOP PUBLISHING
APPLICATIONS   179

Desktop Publishing Production—Specifications—Tint Screens and
Textures—Ruling—Type—Graphics—Master Copy Preparation

Chapter 14
POSTAL
REGULATIONS   195

General Mail Requirements—General Mail Specifications—Forms of
General Mail—Automated Mail Requirements—Automated Systems—
Automated Mail Specifications—Forms of Automated Mail

Chapter 15
FORMS DESIGN
AND LAYOUT   207

Forms Design—Flat Forms—Pegboard Forms—Unit Sets— Salesbooks—Continuous Forms—Forms Production—Forms Layout

ACTIVITIES   221

PROJECTS   227

GLOSSARY   289

INDEX   299

ACKNOWLEDGMENTS

The author and publisher are grateful to the following companies and organizations for providing technical information and assistance.

Agfa Compugraphic
Aldus Corp.
American Plywood Association
Ametek, Houston Instrument Division
Apple Computer, Inc.
Armstrong World Industries, Inc.
Bruce Hardwood Floors
Chartpak
Daige Products, Inc.
DFI Diamond Flower International Co. (USA), Inc.
DS America Incorporated
W.W. Grainger, Inc.
Graphic Products Corp.
Heidelberg U.S.A.
Hewlett-Packard Company
Koh-I-Noor Rapidograph, Inc.
Linotype-Hell Company
Mayline Co., Inc.
Mirror Technologies, Inc., Mpls.
Miller Printing Equipment Corp.
Multigraphics, AM International
National Aeronautics and Space Administration
PCW Communications, Inc.
Radius Inc.
Silicon Beach Software, Inc.
J. S. Staedtler, Inc.
Taney Supply & Lumber Corp.

INTRODUCTION

Graphic Arts Production presents tools, equipment, materials, production methods, and design techniques traditionally used in the graphic arts field. Traditional production methods covered include basic paste-up, keylining, inking, applying adhesive type and other graphic elements, halftone treatment, and color separation for flat and process colors. *Graphic Arts Production* also presents information on computers used in graphics, including computer hardware and software, computer terminology, and desktop publishing. The text/workbook provides information essential to the understanding of how traditional production methods tie in with computer graphics programs and desktop publishing.

Chapters 1 through 15 contain review questions at the end of each chapter, which test comprehension of the material covered in each chapter. Review questions include true-false, multiple choice, completion, identification, and matching questions. Always record your answer in the space(s) provided.

True-False

Circle T if the statement is true. Circle F if the statement is false.

T (F)   **4.** The design of a job is the same for all age groups.

Multiple Choice

Select the response that correctly completes the statement. Write the appropriate letter in the space provided.

 1. _____ is the creation of the written message for a job.
  A. Estimating
  B. Copywriting
  C. Typesetting
  D. Wordprocessing

Completion

Determine the response that correctly completes the statement. Write the appropriate response in the space provided.

 **2.** A job _____ is printed on the job ticket, artboards, film, flats, plates, and press sheets.

Identification

Select the response that correctly matches the given word(s). Write the appropriate letter in the space provided.

_____B_____   **1.** Trim mark

_____C_____   **2.** Center mark

_____A_____   **3.** Fold mark

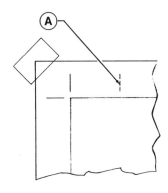

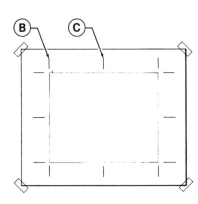

Matching

Select the response that correctly matches the given word(s). Write the appropriate letter in the space provided.

_____B_____   **5.** Perforated

_____C_____   **6.** Scored

_____A_____   **7.** Collated

A. Sections of a job assembled in proper sequence
B. Cut with small slits to facilitate tearing
C. Compressed with dull steel rules

Following the text are 15 sets of activities. The activities correspond with each text chapter and reinforce understanding of information covered in each chapter. Twelve projects follow the activities. The projects are designed to give hands-on, practical experience of the production methods and design techniques covered throughout *Graphic Arts Production*. An illustrated glossary follows the projects.

1 PRODUCTION OF JOBS

A job, or printed piece, goes through a sequence of steps before it is printed on a press. In the initial steps such as copywriting, designing, estimating, typesetting, and the creation of illustrations and photographs, elements for reproduction are produced. The paste-up process is the first step in assembling and creating a reproducible image. A paste-up artist is responsible for the creation of a mechanical. Typeset copy, illustrations, and photographs are combined to create the design agreed upon by the designer and client. The major printing processes including photo-offset lithography, gravure, letterpress and flexography, and screen printing require paste-up or page assembly operations to create the initial reproducible image.

The processes following paste-up, including photographic reproduction, stripping the flats, platemaking, presswork, and bindery, manipulate an image to obtain the finished printed product. The printed image may be a multicolor job or it may need to be die cut or perforated. Paste-up artists should be aware of all operations performed in the creation of a job. This awareness enables them to communicate better with other personnel involved in the production process and provide concise instructions for the production of the job.

PRODUCTION PROCESS

The production of a job involves a sequence of technical processes. A job begins as a need to communicate an idea and follows successive steps including design concepts, presswork, and bindery. Accuracy is required in each step before continuing to the next step.

Proofreading is the procedure of checking a job as it progresses through all phases of production. Proofreading ensures predictable results. The further a job progresses in the production sequence, the more costly mistakes are to correct. For example, a spelling error discovered early in the production sequence results in minimal changes in one or two processes. A spelling error discovered on a press plate results in repetition of many steps in production. Additional costs for labor and materials are also incurred.

Communicating Needs

Communicating needs of a client is the primary purpose of a job. A client approaches an agency, such as a printing company or advertising agency, with the desire to relay a message such as news of a sale or instructions for a product. The agency is responsible for transforming the need into successful communication. The agency also ensures that the message is received accurately by the reader.

The initial task of a printing company or advertising agency is to determine the answers to several questions that define the client's need:

1. What message is to be presented?
2. Who will receive the message?
3. How should the message be presented?
4. Where will the job appear?
5. When is the job needed?
6. What is the total budget for the job?

Once the client's need is defined, copywriting, designing, and estimating begin.

Copywriting. *Copywriting* is creating the written message for a job. A copywriter produces a clear and concise written message, or *copy*. A copywriter works closely with the client to determine what message is to be presented and who is to receive it. When the message is established, a copywriter directs the message at the specific reader such as a child or adult, a man or woman, or any specific group. Each group is approached differently, although the message may be the same.

A copywriter develops *manuscript copy* with double-spaced lines and wide margins. See Figure 1-1. Manuscript copy is proofread then reviewed by the client. When the manuscript copy is approved by the client, it is not altered unless specified. The approved manuscript copy will enable the designer to visualize the job.

Designing. *Designing* is the process in which the job takes on its visual form. The designer uses manuscript copy as an outline to determine what message is to be presented,

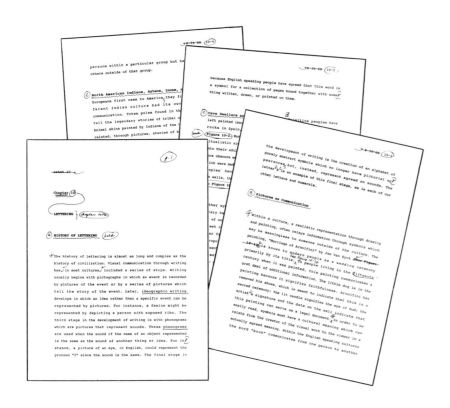

Figure 1-1. A copywriter develops manuscript copy, and a designer uses it to specify typestyles for a job.

who will receive the message, and approximately how much space is required for the job. The designer and client establish where the reader will receive the message such as in a magazine, the mail, or a sign in a store. They also determine when a job is needed and its cost limitations. Additional specifications for the job are compiled, such as colors, typeface, illustrations, and photographs. When all factors have been agreed upon by the client and designer, the designer prepares thumbnail sketches, rough layout, and comprehensive layout.

Thumbnail sketches are rendered by the designer. *Thumbnail sketches* are quick sketches that allow the designer to put initial ideas on paper. These small, proportional sketches include a minimal amount of detail, while allowing the designer to visualize spatial relationships. The approximate space for all elements and copy are positioned without great at-

tention to detail. See Figure 1-2.

A rough layout is developed when the designer is satisfied with the design of an individual thumbnail sketch. A *rough layout* is a full-size pencil drawing of the job with minimal detail. See Figure 1-3. A designer uses a thumbnail sketch as a guide when developing the rough layout. The rough layout allows the designer to visualize the proportion and position of elements of the job. Changes are made as required to alter the proportion and position of elements.

A *comprehensive layout* is a final rendering of the job in full size and color. The completed rough layout is used to finalize the proportion and position of elements before the comprehensive layout is developed. It is used to further define the job and guide the production process. It contains all the information required for production of the job, including stock and ink. See Figure 1-4. Photographs

and body copy are commonly indicated with lines showing the size and position of elements. Art elements and display type are shown in position. The completed comprehensive layout is approved by the client before estimating the price quote.

Estimating. *Estimating* is the process of computing the approximate cost of a job. An estimator analyzes all aspects of the job to determine material and labor costs including art and copy preparation, film, stock, ink, and press time. Possible problems regarding the job are also analyzed, and an approximate total cost of production is determined. The margin of profit is added to the total cost of production, and a price quote is developed. A price quote is final when it is accepted by the client. Unforeseen problems arising during production may result in additional costs. An estimator is responsible for planning a job properly as the additional costs are commonly absorbed by the printing company.

Production of Elements

Elements of a job such as type, illustrations, and photographs are assembled after the comprehensive layout has been approved by the client. An *art director*, or pre-production manager, is responsible for the development and assembly of elements according to the designer's specifications. An art director is also responsible for coordinating the production of elements.

Type, illustrations, and photographs may be produced in-house. *In-house elements* are created by the company that uses them. Many elements may be ordered from a trade shop. A *trade shop* is a company that specializes in one or two production areas of printing. The art director proofreads and approves the elements whether they are created in-house or obtained from a trade shop. The elements are placed in a job folder with instructions and routed to production assembly.

Typesetting. *Typesetting* is the process of producing final type used for

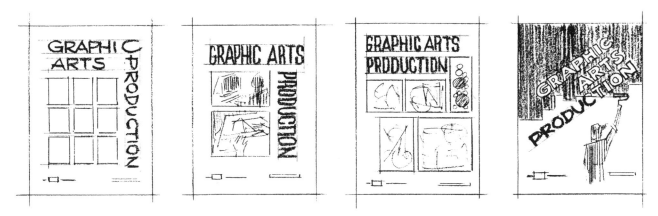

Figure 1-2. Thumbnail sketches are small, proportional sketches of a designer's ideas for a job.

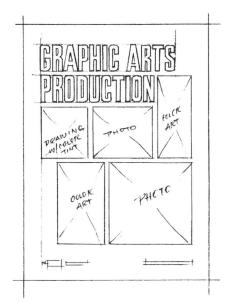

Figure 1-3. Rough layouts allow a designer to visualize how an idea for a job will appear.

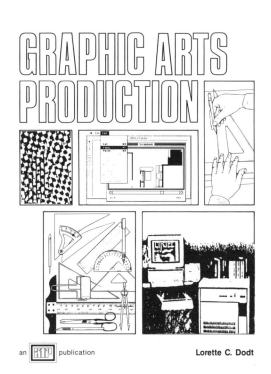

an ▨▨▨ publication   Lorette C. Dodt

Figure 1-4. A comprehensive layout is used to present a design idea to a client and as a guideline for the production process.

reproduction. The manuscript copy and comprehensive layout are used in typesetting. Manuscript copy contains the actual text that is to be included. A comprehensive layout contains specifications for typestyles, sizes, and arrangements.

Type arrangement is indicated on the comprehensive layout. Type may be arranged, or set, as justified, flush right, flush left, centered, run-around, or artistic. Each type arrangement has its individual use, eye appeal, and readability factor. See Figure 1-5.

Typeset material generated from a typesetter is produced on photographic paper as a galley. A *galley* is the final typeset material before it is arranged into final page form. See Figure 1-6. A galley is proofread by the proofreader for typographical errors and also to verify that it fits the comprehensive layout. The galley is then routed to the art director with the manuscript copy and comprehensive layout for final approval.

Illustrations. *Illustrations* are drawings that enhance the communicative ability of a job. An illustrator draws an illustration according to the designer's instructions. Illustrations may be reproduced in a consistent size or in various sizes throughout

Typographical layout is the manner in which type is placed on the printed piece. Typographical layout includes the type and the space surrounding the characters, words, and sentences. Good typographical layout improves the readability of a printed piece while poor typographical layout reduces the readability. A designer determines the typographical layout and the typesetter fits the typographical layout to the comprehensive layout. A paste-up artist occasionally is required to hand set or paste-up type according to a specified typographical layout. Letterspacing is the space between type characters. Each typeface has a specified amount of letterspacing for maximum readability. Letterspacing increases as the size of the type increases. Proper letterspacing facilitates eye movement and recognition of words when read

JUSTIFIED

Typographical layout is the manner in which type is placed on the printed piece. Typographical layout includes the type and the space surrounding the characters, words, and sentences. Good typographical layout improves the readability of a printed piece while poor typographical layout reduces the readability. A designer determines the typographical layout and the typesetter fits the typographical layout to the comprehensive layout. A paste-up artist occasionally is required to hand set or paste-up type according to a specified typographical layout. Letterspacing is the space between type characters. Each typeface has a specified amount of letterspacing for maximum readability. Letterspacing increases as the size of the type increases. Proper letterspacing facilitates eye move

FLUSH RIGHT

Typographical layout is the manner in which type is placed on the printed piece. Typographical layout includes the type and the space surrounding the characters, words, and sentences. Good typographical layout improves the readability of a printed piece while poor typographical layout reduces the readability. A designer determines the typographical layout and the typesetter fits the typographical layout to the comprehensive layout. A paste-up artist occasionally is required to hand set or paste-up type according to a specified typographical layout. Letterspacing is the space between type characters. Each typeface has a specified amount of letterspacing for maximum readability. Letterspacing increases as the size of the type increases. Proper letterspacing facilitates eye move

FLUSH LEFT

Typographical layout is the manner in which type is placed on the printed piece. Typographical layout includes the type and the space surrounding the characters, words, and sentences. Good typographical layout improves the readability of a printed piece while poor typographical layout reduces the readability. A designer determines the typographical layout and the typesetter fits the typographical layout to the comprehensive layout. A paste-up artist occasionally is required to hand set or paste-up type according to a specified typographical layout. Letterspacing is the space between type characters. Each typeface has a specified amount of letterspacing for maximum readability. Letterspacing increases as the size of

CENTERED

Typographical layout is the manner in which type is placed on the printed piece. Typographical layout includes the type and the space surrounding the characters, words, and sentences. Good typographical layout improves the readability of a printed piece while poor typographical layout reduces the readability. A designer determines the typographical layout and the typesetter fits the typographical layout to the comprehensive layout. A paste-up artist occasionally is required to hand set or paste-up type according to a specified typographical layout. Letterspacing is the space

RUN-AROUND

Typographical layout is the manner in which type is placed on the printed piece. Typographical layout includes the type and t   he space surrounding the c   haracters, words, and senten   ces. Good typographical layout i mproves the readability of a printed pi   ece while poor typographical layout red   uces the readability. A designer determi   nes the typographical layout and the typ   esetter fits the typographical layout to the compreh   ensive layout. A paste-up artist occasionally is required to hand set or paste-up type according to a specified t   ypographical layout. Letterspacing is the space bet   ween type characters. Each typeface has a specified amount of letterspacing for maximum readability. Letterspacing increases as the size

ARTISTIC

Figure 1-5. Type arrangement is determined by a designer to enhance the appearance of a job and improve its communicative ability.

the job. Also, type may be integrated into the illustration.

Illustrations are commonly developed to relate to the age group of the viewer. For example, children's textbook illustrations change from lower through upper grades. *Soft art,* incorporating wide lines and simple figures, is used for younger age groups. Illustrations are drawn in more detail for older readers. *Mechanical art,* incorporating thin lines and greater detail, is commonly used for machine parts or in instruction manuals. See Figure 1-7.

Copy-free illustration, or clip art, may be used when a design does not require a specialized illustration. Copy-free illustrations are reproduction-quality drawings available at art stores or through subscription. A variety of illustrations, borders, and decorations are available. The illustration is cut from the original sheet and pasted in position for reproduction.

Computer-aided illustration is another illustration technique. Several quick sketches can be rendered on a computer, integrated with type, and

Agfa Compugraphic

Figure 1-6. Type is set on a typesetter and processed onto photographic paper as a galley.

viewed for aesthetic quality. See Figure 1-8. Modifications to sketches are easily made in preparation for reproduction. The final illustration is then approved, output, and routed to the art director for production assembly.

Photographs. *Photographs* create visual communication and enhance the copy. Black-and-white or color photographs should be handled carefully. Photographs are obtained from a photography studio, freelance photographer, or photographic broker

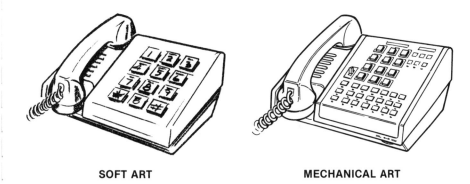

SOFT ART   MECHANICAL ART

Figure 1-7. An illustrator draws soft or mechanical art, depending on the age group of the viewer.

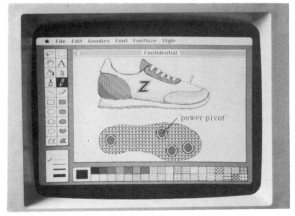

Figure 1-8. Computer-aided illustration enables a designer to visualize a sketch with type.

when not provided by the client.

Photography studios commonly specialize in product and fashion photography. A freelance photographer generally takes on-site photographs or portraits. A photographic broker leases stock photographs, such as a skyline of a city, to the printing company. The art director contacts a broker, chooses the photograph from their stock books, and leases the photograph for a particular job. A photograph is the property of the client unless leased from a photographic broker.

Assembly of Elements

Assembly of elements is the sequence of steps used to prepare a job for production on a press. The time involved in arranging the elements for press is *make-ready time.* Most jobs require similar make-ready steps, although procedures used to print a job vary. Accuracy in make-ready steps helps to ensure a quality job. Copy, including type and illustrations, is pasted up. *Paste-up* is placing copy in the correct position on an artboard for production of a job. The copy is then photographed, and film is generated in a photographic reproduction process. The film is reassembled in the stripping process to conform to the specifications of the stock and plate used to print the job.

Pasting Up Mechanicals. Pasting up mechanicals is the process in which all copy for reproduction is placed in position on an artboard. The completed paste-up, or *mechanical,* involves several make-ready steps. A paste-up artist obtains all the elements of a job, including the comprehensive layout, illustrations, galleys, and other type elements from the art director. The paste-up artist affixes all elements to an artboard according to the designer's layout.

A mechanical is begun by placing keylines and marks for the various elements of the job according to the designer's specifications. *Keylines* are thin black or red lines used to indicate position of elements not directly pasted to the mechanical. A paste-up artist is commonly referred to as a keyliner for this reason. Type elements are pasted in position after all keylines are indicated on the mechanical. Line illustrations are pasted in position and are camera-ready. Photographs are not pasted directly onto the mechanical. Photographs require a different photographic process than type elements and line illustrations. The mechanical is checked for accuracy and debris on the copy.

A tissue overlay is placed over the entire mechanical when all copy is positioned and keylines are indicated. Instructions pertaining to the job, such as trim size, ink color(s), and type of stock are written on the tissue overlay to prevent mistakes during production. A cover sheet is taped over the mechanical and tissue overlay. A *cover sheet* is a heavy piece of paper used to protect the mechanical. See Figure 1-9. The mechanical and photographs are then ready for photographic reproduction.

Photographic Reproduction.
Photographic reproduction for printing includes line photography and halftone photography. *Line photography* is the process used to produce line copy. *Line copy* consists of dense black lines, dots, or solid areas on a white background. Line copy is the simplest form of copy used in production. See Figure 1-10. When line copy is reproduced on negative film, the dense black areas reproduce as clear

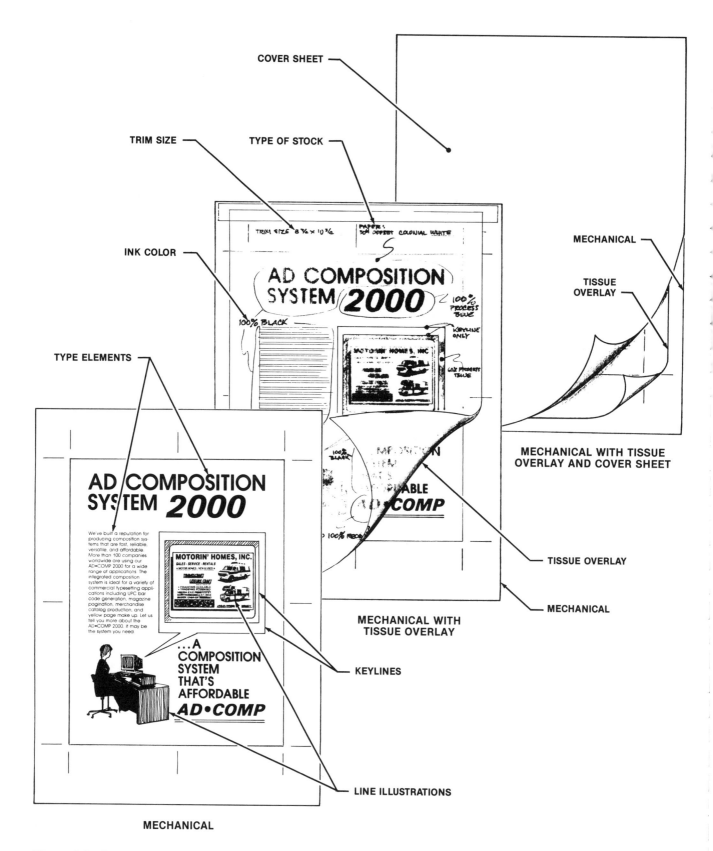

Figure 1-9. A mechanical is covered with a tissue overlay to provide instructions to the printing company. A cover sheet is attached to provide protection against damage to the mechanical.

Kerning is another form of letterspacing. Kerning is the removal of space between certain character combinations. Common character combinations, or kerning pairs, include Yo, We, To, Tr, and Wo. Kerning pairs are kerned to assist in the readability of a word. Wordspacing is the space between words. The size of type and ease of readability are affected by the amount of wordspacing.

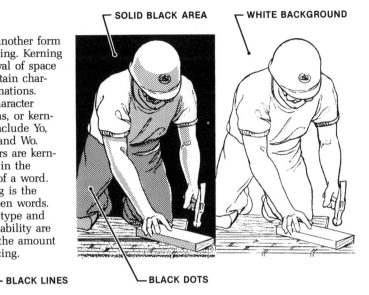

Figure 1-10. Line copy consists of dense black lines, dots, or solid areas on a white background.

images, and the white background reproduces as black images. Film that contains clear images and dense black images is required for the reproduction of most printing plates.

Halftone photography is the process used to create a halftone from continuous tone copy. *Continuous tone copy* is an image that has not been screened. Continuous tone copy includes black-and-white photographs, color photographs, watercolor paintings, pencil drawings, and charcoal renderings. Continuous tone copy is reproduced onto film through the half-tone process, which produces a halftone. A *halftone* is an illusion of continuous tone copy created with dots of varying size and density. When all line and halftone film is completed according to the requirements of the job, it is proofread and sent to the stripper for assembly.

Stripping Flats. *Stripping flats* is the process of assembling all film for a job and taping it to goldenrod. See Figure 1-11. *Goldenrod* is an opaque paper used for positioning the film to create flats. A stripper positions the film on the goldenrod according to the requirements of a job.

Agfa Compugraphic

Figure 1-11. Film produced by photographic reproduction is placed on a flat by the stripper according to page layout.

The size of stock on which a job will be printed, the size and type of press, the trim size, type of stock, page layout, and ink coverage are considered when stripping flats.

Flats are proofed by exposing them to a special proofing paper or acetate. Proofs enable a stripper to visualize how the job will print and ensure that

all film is correctly positioned. Corrections, such as repositioning the film or opaquing, are made before the flats are sent to the platemaker. *Opaquing* is applying a dense liquid substance to negative film to cover cut lines or scratches. Flats are sent to the platemaker after approval for prepress production.

Platemaking. *Platemaking* is the process of exposing film to a printing plate. The procedure used for platemaking depends on the type of press used for a job. All presses print onto a substrate, which is the stock or other material that receives the ink. Some presses, however, accept only certain substrates. The type of press used for a job is determined by the substrate selected for the job.

The primary difference between types of presses is the plate or image carrier. An *image carrier* is the device that applies ink to a substrate. The procedure for creating image carriers is similar for all printing processes. Most printing processes use light-sensitive materials which, when exposed or burned, create an image on the image carrier. The image is generally exposed to the surface of the plate through film.

Four basic image carriers are planographic, intaglio, relief, and stencil. See Figure 1-12. All image carriers have an *image area*, which reproduces copy, and a *non-image area*, which prevents ink from transferring to the substrate. Image and non-image areas are created through various processes. A relief image carrier is created by using acid to etch the non-image surface below the surface of the image area. A stencil image carrier is created by washing in the image with water. Quality of the image and non-image area of image carriers must be closely monitored. The image area must be clean and sharp. The non-image area should be completely free of all ink, allowing only the stock to be visible.

A *planographic image carrier* is used for photo-offset lithographic printing. *Photo-offset lithographic printing*, the most common form of printing, creates sharp images on a

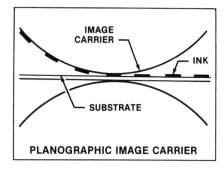

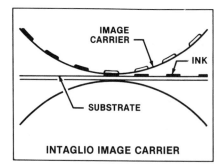

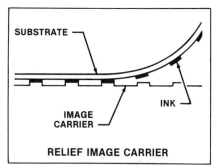

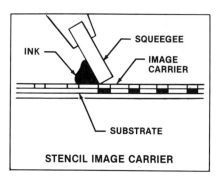

Figure 1-12. Image carriers apply ink to the image area of a substrate.

Final Production

Final production includes all presswork and bindery operations used to complete a job. The plates and all printing instructions are sent to the pressroom after being closely checked. A press proof, or press make-ready, is conducted to check color registration, tone value, and image quality. A *press proof* is a special, low-quantity press run. The press proof for most large jobs is approved by the client before printing finished pieces.

Presswork. *Presswork* is the process of printing ink on stock. A press operator needs excellent mechanical abilities and a keen eye for color. Presses are available in various sizes and complexities. See Figure 1-13. Presses are single-color or multicolor, and they produce 5-, 6-, or 7-color jobs. They may also integrate some bindery operations such as scoring, perforating, and die cutting. A press requires daily maintenance and adjustments regardless of its size. Before starting the press, the operator sets the press for the requirements of the job including ink coverage, stock weight and size, and plates. The press operator also monitors the press for ink coverage and register while the job is running. *Register* is the alignment of the image on the stock and the alignment of various colors with one another. On multicolor printing jobs, each color is created using a separate plate. On single-color presses, one press run is required to produce each color. On multicolor presses, a single press run is required to produce various colors. The plates are cleaned, protected, and stored for future runs as the job is completed. The *press sheet,* or printed job, is sent for finishing in the bindery.

Bindery. Bindery operations manipulate the press sheet to complete the printed product. Although some jobs are trimmed to finished size to complete the printed product, many jobs require specialized operations. See Figure 1-14. A box, for example, may be die cut by using sharp steel rules

variety of stock. Make-ready time and cost for photo-offset lithographic printing are low compared to other printing processes. The image and non-image areas of a planographic image carrier are on the same plane.

The chemical principle that grease and water do not readily mix is applied to separate the non-image area from the image area. The non-image area attracts the water and repels the greasy ink when water is applied to the plate. The image area attracts the greasy ink and repels water. When an ink roller is passed over the plate, ink adheres to the greasy image area and does not adhere to the non-image area.

An *intaglio image carrier* is used in gravure printing. Intaglio refers to the image area etched below the surface of a plate. *Rotogravure* printing uses a copper cylinder in which the image area is etched below the surface. Copper cylinders are costly but are commonly used for long print runs. A *run* is the number of printed images. Reproduction quality of gravure and rotogravure printing is good because of the etching technique used to create the plate or cylinder.

A *relief image carrier* has the image area raised above the non-image area. Letterpress and flexography are printing processes using a relief image carrier. *Letterpress image carriers* are created with hand- or machine-set metal. Make-ready time is short for small quantities of copy. However, reproduction quality is generally poor. *Flexography* uses a raised, flexible rubber blanket. Reproduction quality of flexography is superior to letterpress because of the flexibility of the image carrier. The flexible image carrier of flexography is adaptable to printing on thin cellophane or plastic commonly used in the packaging industry.

A *stencil image carrier* allows ink to pass through a screen in the image area and prevents ink from passing through the non-image area. Make-ready steps for a stencil image carrier are the same as lithography, gravure, and flexography. Screen printing is the most common form of a stencil image carrier. Screen printing may be used to apply several layers of ink to a substrate. It is also used to print on irregular surfaces such as cloth and bottles.

to cut shapes. It is then scored, folded, and glued to produce the printed product. Scoring is the process of using a dull steel rule to compress the stock fiber to facilitate folding or tearing. Sections of a book are collated, gathered, bound, and trimmed. Collating is the process of assembling sections of a job in the proper sequence. A concert ticket is die cut, perforated with small slits to facilitate tearing, numbered, and trimmed. The job is in its final form when it leaves the bindery. The job is then distributed to the client or its final destination.

TOOLS AND EQUIPMENT

Accuracy is required in all aspects of the printing process. High-quality tools and equipment enable a designer, paste-up artist, or stripper to maintain the accuracy of a job. Basic tools such as an art table, a T-square, and triangles allow alignment and positioning operations to be performed. Measurement systems and tools allow accuracy in pasting up a job or stripping film.

Basic Tools

Basic tools for paste-up ensure accurate alignment of the elements of a job. An art table, a T-square, triangles, and measuring devices are commonly used to properly place and align the elements of a job.

Art Table and Light Table. An *art table*, or *drafting table*, is used as a drawing surface for a paste-up artist. An art table has a flat, solid surface with edges that are at a 90° angle to one another. The left and right edges must be smooth and straight to ensure accuracy when pasting up elements of a job.

A *light table* has a frosted glass top that is illuminated by a diffused light source beneath the top. The edges of a light table are at a 90° angle to one another. A light table can be used as a drawing surface and also allows translucent or opaque elements to be accurately aligned. See Figure 1-15.

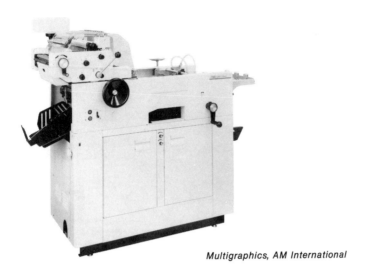

Multigraphics, AM International

DUPLICATOR

Miller Printing Equipment Corp.

MULTICOLOR PRESS

Figure 1-13. Presses are available in various sizes and complexities.

FOLDED SHEETS

Heidelberg U.S.A.

Figure 1-14. Folding machines fold the printed piece as required.

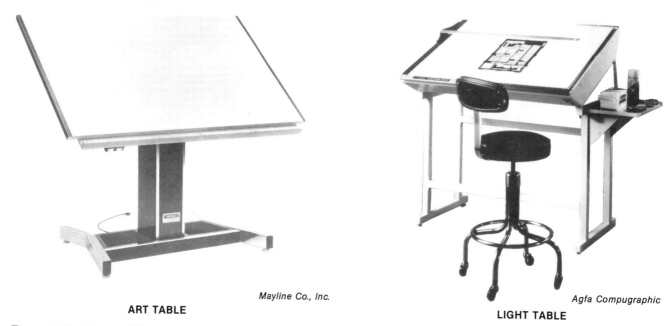

Mayline Co., Inc.
ART TABLE

Agfa Compugraphic
LIGHT TABLE

Figure 1-15. An art table or light table is used as a drawing surface by a paste-up artist. A light table is illuminated by a diffused light source beneath the frosted glass top.

T-Square. A *T-square* is used as a guide to draw horizontal lines and horizontally align elements on an art-board. A T-square should be shorter than the longest dimension of the table. The head of a T-square is at a 90° angle to the blade. The head is guided along the right or left edge of an art table or light table. The blade is the guide for drawing horizontal lines and aligning elements. A blade with a beveled edge allows for a smooth flow of ink without bleeding under the T-square. Stainless steel, wood, and plastic T-squares are commonly available. Stainless steel T-squares are the most practical for a paste-up artist. A T-square should be protected from dents and jarring to ensure smooth, even lines. See Figure 1-16.

The head of a T-square is held firmly against the left edge of an art table or light table for right-handed artists. The head is held firmly against the right edge of the table for left-handed artists. Inward pressure is applied to the head to maintain direct contact with the edge of the table. The blade of a T-square lies flat against the surface of the table. Light downward pressure against the blade

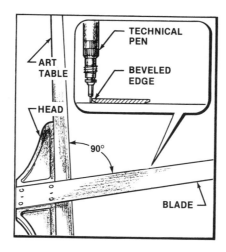

Figure 1-16. A T-square is used to guide a pencil or technical pen when drawing horizontal lines. The edges of the blade are beveled to facilitate the smooth flow of ink.

ensures close contact with the table and artboard. See Figure 1-17.

Triangles. Triangles are used to draw inclined and vertical lines on an artboard. A *45°–90° triangle* and *30°–60°–90° triangle* are used to create

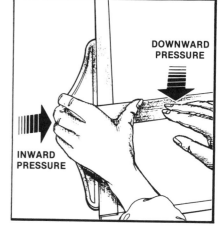

Figure 1-17. The artist holds the head of a T-square firmly against the edge of an art table or light table by applying inward pressure. Downward pressure on the blade ensures close contact with the table.

inclined lines at 15° increments. Both triangles are combined to create 15° and 75° angles. See Figure 1-18. An *adjustable triangle* is used to create inclined lines at any angle.

Triangles are precision drawing instruments and should be protected against damage. Plastic, aluminum,

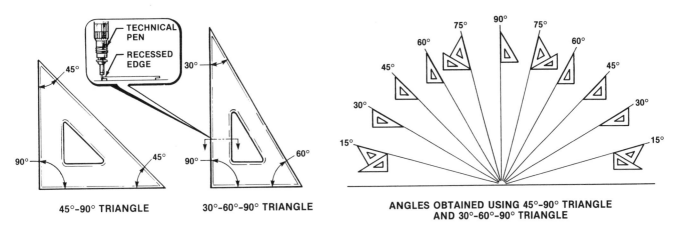

45°–90° TRIANGLE   30°–60°–90° TRIANGLE   ANGLES OBTAINED USING 45°–90° TRIANGLE AND 30°–60°–90° TRIANGLE

Figure 1-18. Triangles are used to draw inclined and vertical lines. A 45°–90° and 30°–60°–90° triangle is used to obtain 15° increments.

and stainless steel triangles are commonly available. Stainless steel triangles are the most practical for the paste-up artist. Triangles are also available in a variety of sizes. Most paste-up jobs can be performed with a 10″ to 14″ triangle.

Artists place one edge of a 45°–90° or 30°–60°–90° triangle tightly against the top edge of the T-square blade when drawing inclined or vertical lines. The T-square head is held firmly against the edge of the art table or light table. The hypotenuse of a triangle should be opposite the T-square head. The *hypotenuse* is the edge of a triangle opposite the right angle. See Figure 1-19. Right-handed artists hold the T-square and triangle in position with the left hand, allowing the right hand to perform drawing or cutting operations. Left-handed artists hold the T-square and triangle with the right hand.

One edge of an adjustable triangle other than the hypotenuse is placed against the top edge of a T-square. The hypotenuse is placed to the left when drawing 0° to 45° angles and to the right when drawing 45° to 90° angles. See Figure 1-20. The *pivot* allows the upper section of the triangle to be positioned at the desired angle. A *lock knob* is loosened to allow movement and adjustment of the upper section. The lock knob is tightened to secure the upper section in position. A *scale* indicates the

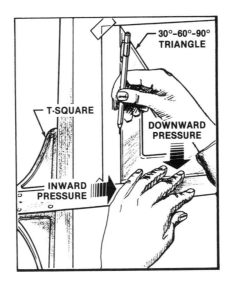

Figure 1-19. One edge of a triangle is placed tightly against the T-square blade. The head of the T-square is held tightly against the edge of an art table or light table.

angle that is created by pivoting the upper section.

Computers. Computers are used in a variety of printing operations such as design, typesetting, paste-up, reproduction of photographs, and platemaking. A computer is capable of storing a large amount of information and performing calculations or tasks quickly.

A *page makeup system* is a computer application that replaces many

of the hands-on operations of a paste-up artist, camera operator, and stripper. The computer's calculating ability and accessibility to information reduce the amount of time required to perform certain operations. See Figure 1-21. Some page makeup systems expose an image directly onto a plate without the use of film. Therefore, the cost of film is drastically reduced, saving the printing company money.

Measurement Systems

Standard measurement systems have been developed to assist in all aspects of the printing industry. A particular measurement system is commonly adopted for use in a specific process. Each measurement system is composed of *increments,* or equal, standardized units.

Greater accuracy is obtained by using a measurement system with smaller increments. The inch, pica, point, and agate are common measurement systems used in the printing industry. See Figure 1-22. An *inch* is the most common measurement system used in the printing industry. An inch is often divided into $1/_{32}$″ or $1/_{64}$″ increments. A *pica* is equal to .166″; 6 picas equal approximately 1″. Twelve *points* equal 1 pica and 72 points equal approximately 1″. An

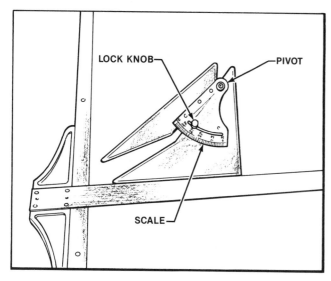
0°–45° ANGLES

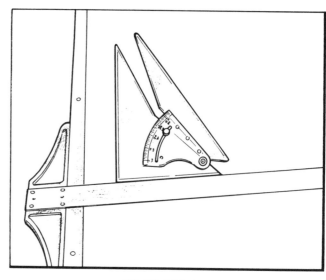
45°–90° ANGLES

Figure 1-20. An adjustable triangle is used to create lines at various angles. The hypotenuse is positioned to the left when drawing lines at a 0° to 45° angle, and to the right when drawing lines at a 45° to 90° angle.

agate is equal to approximately 5½ points; 14 agates equal 1″.

Inch. The inch can be divided into fractional increments, such as ¹/₃₂″ or ¹/₆₄″, or decimal increments, such as .01″ or .001″. A paste-up artist uses ¹/₃₂″ or ¹/₆₄″ increments to align copy. A stripper uses .01″ increments when aligning film. A type designer creating typefaces uses .005″ increments for placing characters.

The inch is also used in a measuring system when describing press size and size of film and stock. A press that accepts a press sheet up to 29″ wide is a 29″ press. Film is available in standard sizes such as 5″ × 7″ and 8″ × 10″. Stock is available and cut by using inch dimensions such as 11″ × 17″ and 25″ × 38″. Trim sizes are commonly designated in inch increments.

Pica. The pica is used primarily in typesetting to measure the width of typeset lines. Some typesetting equipment express the depth of a typeset page in picas. One pica is equal to approximately .166″; 6 picas equal .996″. Since picas do not convert ex-

Aldus Corp.

Figure 1-21. A page makeup system replaces many of the hands-on operations of a paste-up artist, camera operator, and stripper.

actly to inches, inaccuracies may occur when converting picas to inches.

Point. The point is used in typesetting to describe the height of type and the leading. *Leading* is the space between lines of type. One point is a relatively small increment, approximately equal to ¹/₇₂″. There are slightly less than 72 points to an inch. Since points

do not convert exactly to inches, inaccuracies may occur when converting points to inches.

Agate. The agate is used by the newspaper and magazine industry to measure columns of type and space allotted for advertisements. One agate is approximately 5½ points and 14 agates equal 1″.

Measurement Systems

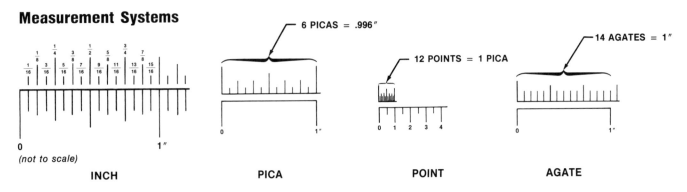

Figure 1-22. Measurement systems ensure accuracy of the printed job. Greater accuracy is achieved using a measurement system with smaller increments.

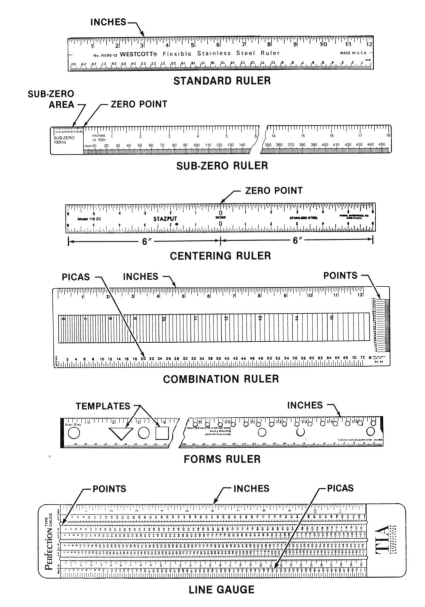

Figure 1-23. Rulers and gauges are used for linear measurements.

Measurement Devices

Measurement devices include rulers, gauges, grids, and scales. *Rulers* and *gauges* are used for linear measurement such as the distance between two points. *Grids* are used to measure vertical and horizontal measurements simultaneously. *Scales* are used to calculate enlargement and reduction percentages and determine the size of an element. A *proportional scale* is used to calculate enlargement and reduction percentages of an element such as a photograph. A *type scale* is used to determine type size.

Rulers and Gauges. Rulers and gauges are used for linear measurement. See Figure 1-23. A *standard ruler* is used for noncritical measurements because the $^1/_{16}$″ increments cannot be used for pinpoint accuracy. Increments start at the end of the ruler and progress in one direction. When accurate measurements are required, a sub-zero ruler should be used.

The zero point for a *sub-zero ruler* is indented approximately $^1/_4$″ to 1″ from the end of the ruler. Sub-zero rulers may have sub-zero increments before the zero point.

A *centering ruler* is used to center elements of a job. The zero point of a centering ruler is located at the center of the ruler with equal increments on both sides. The centering ruler is aligned with the element to be centered and is adjusted until equal increments appear on each side of the zero point.

A combination ruler is used when there is more than one measurement system in a job. A *combination ruler* incorporates several measurement increments into one device. The increments are different on both edges and on the front and back of the ruler.

A *forms ruler* is used to design and paste up business forms. A forms ruler consists of a combination ruler and a template. Increments commonly used to create forms are located along the edges, and template areas are used to lay out holes for binders.

A *line gauge* is used to determine the number of lines of a particular leading. It can also be used to determine leading between lines of type. A line gauge is a type of combination ruler with point, pica, and inch scales printed on both sides. A designer uses a line gauge to determine the number of typeset lines in an area. A paste-up artist uses a line gauge to determine the amount of space between the typeset lines when pasting up copy.

Grids.

Grids are used to make horizontal and vertical measurements simultaneously. A grid is composed of a horizontal and vertical framework of evenly spaced lines. See Figure 1-24. Grids are available with a variety of increments and in several standard sizes. A grid is commonly used in job planning or design to align copy.

Scales.

Scales are specialized measurement devices used in production. See Figure 1-25. A *proportional scale* is a circular slide rule on two concentric disks. A proportional scale is used to calculate enlargement and reduction percentages. The size of the original photograph or illustration, located on the inner disk, is aligned with the

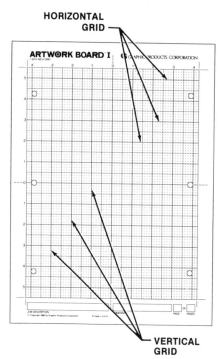

HORIZONTAL GRID

VERTICAL GRID

Graphic Products Corp.

Figure 1-24. A grid is used to make horizontal and vertical measurements simultaneously.

desired size of reproduction on the outer disk. The enlargement or reduction percentage is indicated in the window on the inner disk.

A *type scale*, or *E scale*, is used to identify the type size of copy. It is made of transparent, heavy plastic imprinted with graduated sizes of an uppercase E. The type scale is positioned, preferably over an uppercase E or some other uppercase letter in the copy, and the type size is identified. Various typestyles are sometimes given on the scale because, for example, a 10-point capital E in Helvetica is slightly larger than a 10-point capital E in Times Roman.

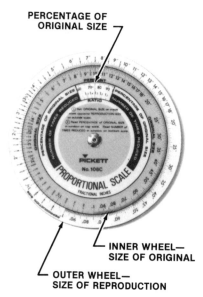

PERCENTAGE OF ORIGINAL SIZE

INNER WHEEL— SIZE OF ORIGINAL

OUTER WHEEL— SIZE OF REPRODUCTION

Chartpak

TYPESTYLE

POINT SIZE OF TYPEFACE

PCW Communications, Inc.

Figure 1-25. A proportional scale is used to calculate enlargement and reduction percentages. A type scale is used to identify type size.

Production of Jobs

True-False

T   F   **1.** Paste-up or page assembly operations are required to create the initial reproducible image for all printing processes.

T   F   **2.** Pasting up the mechanical is the first production process in assembling and creating a reproducible image.

T   F   **3.** Mistakes are more costly to correct in the paste-up process than in the platemaking process.

T   F   **4.** The design of a job is the same for all age groups.

T   F   **5.** Estimating the cost of a job must be completed before the design process.

T   F   **6.** The stripper positions film on goldenrod according to job requirements.

T   F   **7.** The type of press used to print the job is determined by the substrate selected.

T   F   **8.** The image area prevents ink from transferring to the substrate.

T   F   **9.** The printed job is the press sheet.

T   F   **10.** Sharp steel rules are used to cut the required shape when die cutting.

T   F   **11.** Thumbnail sketches are small, proportional sketches that enable a designer to put initial ideas on paper.

T   F   **12.** A rough layout is developed from the comprehensive layout.

T   F   **13.** A designer is responsible for developing and assembling elements according to specifications.

T   F   **14.** A galley is the final typeset material before it is arranged into final page form.

T   F   **15.** Soft art incorporates thin, rigid lines and a great amount of detail.

Multiple Choice

_____   **1.** _____ is the creation of the written message for a job.
    A. Estimating
    B. Copywriting
    C. Typesetting
    D. Wordprocessing

_____   **2.** A _____ is the final rendering of a job in full size and color.
    A. thumbnail sketch
    B. rough layout
    C. comprehensive layout
    D. none of the above

_____   **3.** _____ is the process in which all copy is placed in position for photographic reproduction.
   A. Photography
   B. Paste-up
   C. Stripping
   D. Platemaking

_____   **4.** The final product produced by the stripper is a _____.
   A. negative
   B. goldenrod
   C. flat
   D. positive

_____   **5.** A(n) _____ image carrier is used for photo-offset lithographic printing.
   A. relief
   B. stencil
   C. intaglio
   D. planographic

_____   **6.** The completed paste-up is the _____.
   A. artboard
   B. flat
   C. mechanical
   D. comprehensive layout

_____   **7.** Line photography reproduces _____.
   A. continuous tone copy
   B. line copy
   C. halftone photographs
   D. all of the above

_____   **8.** Stock or other material that receives the ink is the _____.
   A. opaque
   B. mechanical
   C. image carrier
   D. substrate

_____   **9.** A(n) _____ is the device that applies ink to a substrate.
   A. mechanical
   B. comprehensive layout
   C. flat
   D. image carrier

_____   **10.** The glass top of a(n) _____ is illuminated by a diffused light source beneath.
   A. art table
   B. artboard
   C. light table
   D. none of the above

Completion

_____   **1.** A photograph is the property of the _____ unless it is leased from a photographic broker.

_____   **2.** A(n) _____ is drawn by the paste-up artist to indicate the position of elements not directly pasted on the artboard.

_____ 3. A stencil image carrier is used in _____ printing.

_____ 4. A(n) _____ image carrier is used in flexography.

_____ 5. An intaglio image carrier is used in _____ printing.

_____ 6. A copywriter develops _____ copy with double-spaced lines and wide margins.

_____ 7. _____ is the alignment of an image on the stock.

_____ 8. A(n) _____ system replaces many of the hands-on operations of a paste-up artist, camera operator, and stripper.

_____ 9. A(n) _____ is used to draw horizontal lines and horizontally align elements on an artboard.

_____ 10. A(n) _____ is used to draw vertical lines and inclined lines on an artboard.

Matching

_____ 1. Pica

_____ 2. Point

_____ 3. Agate

_____ 4. Inch

A. Graduated in fractional and decimal increments
B. Approximately equal to .166″
C. Approximately equal to $5^1/_2$ points
D. Approximately equal to $^1/_{72}$″

_____ 5. Perforated

_____ 6. Scored

_____ 7. Collated

A. Sections of a job assembled in proper sequence
B. Cut with small slits to facilitate tearing
C. Compressed with dull steel rules

_____ 8. Type scale

_____ 9. Proportional scale

_____ 10. Line gauge

_____ 11. Grid

_____ 12. Centering ruler

_____ 13. Forms ruler

_____ 14. Sub-zero ruler

_____ 15. Combination ruler

A. Composed of a horizontal and vertical framework of evenly spaced lines
B. Used to determine the space between typeset lines
C. Used to determine the size of type
D. Incorporates a template used to lay out holes for binders
E. Used to calculate enlargement and reduction percentages
F. Zero point is located at the center
G. Incorporates several measurement increments
H. Zero point is indented from the end

Identification

_____ 1. Sub-zero ruler

_____ 2. Centering ruler

_____ 3. Combination ruler

_____ 4. Line gauge

_____ 5. Forms ruler

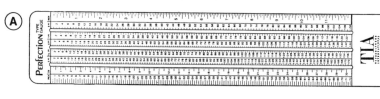

_____ 6. 30°

_____ 7. 45°

_____ 8. 60°

_____ 9. 90°

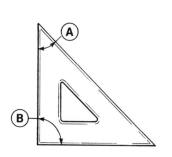

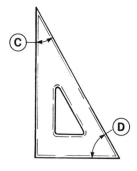

_____ 10. Justified

_____ 11. Flush right

_____ 12. Flush left

_____ 13. Centered

_____ 14. Run-around

_____ 15. Artistic

Typographical layout is the manner in which type is placed on the printed piece. Typographical layout includes the type and the space surrounding the characters, words, and sentences. Good typographical layout improves the readability of a printed piece while poor typographical layout reduces the readability. A designer determines the typographical layout and the typesetter fits the typographical layout to the comprehensive layout. A paste-up artist occasionally is required to hand set or paste-up type according to a specified typographical layout. Letterspacing is the space between type characters. Each typeface has a specified amount of letterspacing for maximum readability. Letterspacing increases as the size of the type increases. Proper letterspacing facilitates eye move

(A)

Typographical layout is the manner in which type is placed on the printed piece. Typographical layout includes the type and t   he space surrounding the c   haracters, wor ds, and senten   ces. Good typogra mproves the readability of a printed pi   ece while poo r typographical layout red   uces the read ability. A designer determi   nes the typogr aphical layout and the typ   esetter fits the typographi cal layout to the compreh   ensive layout. A paste-up artist occasionally is required to hand set or paste-up type according to a specified t   ypographical layout. Lett erspacing is the space bet   ween type characters. Ea ch typeface has a specified amount of letterspacing for maximum readability. Letterspacing increases as the size

(B)

Typographical layout is the manner in which type is placed on the printed piece. Typographical layout includes the type and the space surrounding the characters, words, and sentences. Good typographical layout improves the readability of a printed piece while poor typographical layout reduces the readability. A designer determines the typographical layout and the typesetter fits the typographical layout to the comprehensive layout. A paste-up artist occasionally is required to hand set or paste-up type according to a specified typographical layout. Letterspacing is the space between type characters. Each typeface has a specified amount of letterspacing for maximum readability. Letterspacing increases as the size of the type increases. Proper letterspacing facilitates eye move

(C)

Typographical layout is the manner in which type is placed on the printed piece. Typographical layout includes the type and the space surrounding the characters, words, and sentences. Good typographical layout improves the readability of a printed piece while poor typographical layout reduces the readability. A designer determines the typographical layout and the typesetter fits the typographical layout to the comprehensive layout. A paste-up artist occasionally is required to hand set or paste-up type according to a specified typographical layout. Letterspacing is the space between type characters. Each typeface has a specified amount of letterspacing for maximum readability. Letterspacing increases as the size of the type increases. Proper letterspacing facilitates eye movement and recognition of words when read

(D)

Typographical layout is the manner in which type is placed on the printed piece. Typographical layout includes the type and the space surrounding the characters, words, and sentences. Good typographical layout improves the readability of a printed piece while poor typographical layout reduces the readability. A designer determines the typographical layout and the typesetter fits the typographical layout to the comprehensive layout. A paste-up artist occasionally is required to hand set or paste-up type according to a specified typographical layout. Letterspacing is the space

(E)

Typographical layout is the manner in which type is placed on the printed piece. Typographical layout includes the type and the space surrounding the characters, words, and sentences. Good typographical layout improves the readability of a printed piece while poor typographical layout reduces the readability. A designer determines the typographical layout and the typesetter fits the typographical layout to the comprehensive layout. A paste-up artist occasionally is required to hand set or paste-up type according to a specified typographical layout. Letterspacing is the space between type characters. Each typeface has a specified amount of letterspacing for maximum readability. Letterspacing increases as the size of

(F)

2 COMPREHENSIVE LAYOUT

A comprehensive layout is a set of guidelines for the job. A designer draws a comprehensive layout for a job just as an architect draws a blueprint for the construction of a building. Production personnel, such as a typesetter, paste-up artist, stripper, press operator, and bindery operator, read a comprehensive layout for the specifications of the printed job just as a builder reads symbols and measurements on a blueprint. Symbols and measurements on a comprehensive layout are read and translated into constructive form throughout the printing process.

ELEMENTS OF A COMPREHENSIVE LAYOUT

The elements of a comprehensive layout are information regarding the production steps required to print a job. Elements are commonly indicated on the comprehensive layout and tissue overlay, folding dummy, and job ticket. See Figure 2-1. A *tissue overlay* covering the comprehensive layout allows adequate space for information without marring the appearance of the layout. Information appearing on the comprehensive layout and tissue overlay includes type size and typestyle, art and copy specifications, and photograph and layout requirements.

A *folding dummy* is a sheet of the stock that is folded and marked to indicate how the pages are arranged. The stock used for a folding dummy is the same stock selected for the job. *Folios,* or page numbers, are used to identify the page layout. Type and art elements may be drawn in position. The folding dummy is then

folded, bound, if necessary, and trimmed to final size. A designer uses a folding dummy to ensure that a job fits in an envelope or to determine how much a job weighs. A stripper uses a folding dummy when laying out pages for presswork and the bindery. A folding dummy should accompany the comprehensive layout through all stages of production if folding is required for a job.

A *job ticket* is a form of written communication among people involved in various stages of the printing process. A job ticket is completed by the production manager and accompanies the comprehensive layout through all stages of production. A job ticket is commonly laid out like a business form. It includes information such as the job number, quantity of printed pieces, trim size, ink color, and presswork and bindery operations. The job ticket is compared to the operation performed in each stage and initialed as the operation is completed. Initialing increases quality control throughout the production of the job.

Job tickets are numbered according to a job numbering system. A *job number* is printed on each job ticket and assigned to each job to be printed. Job numbers are placed on all artboards, film, flats, plates, and press sheets. Job numbers increase quality control and assist in recordkeeping, and storage of artboards, flats, and plates after the job is printed.

Layout Specifications

Layout specifications are elements of a comprehensive layout that define the overall appearance of the job. A designer uses a variety of methods to indicate layout specifications. The comprehensive layout, tissue overlay, and job ticket contain symbols and other written information regarding the layout specifications. The typesetter, paste-up artist, and other production personnel use the symbols and written information to define the trim size, gutters and margins, color, stock, and bindery specifications.

19

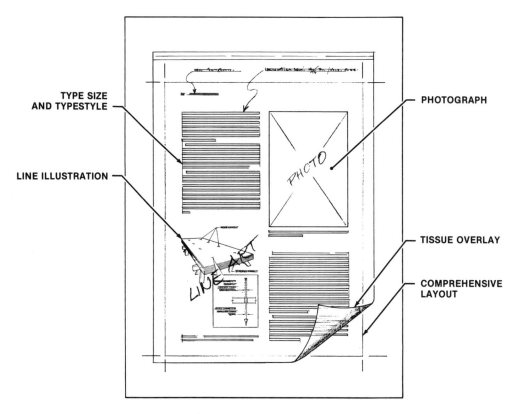

TYPE SIZE AND TYPESTYLE

LINE ILLUSTRATION

PHOTOGRAPH

TISSUE OVERLAY

COMPREHENSIVE LAYOUT

COMPREHENSIVE LAYOUT WITH TISSUE OVERLAY

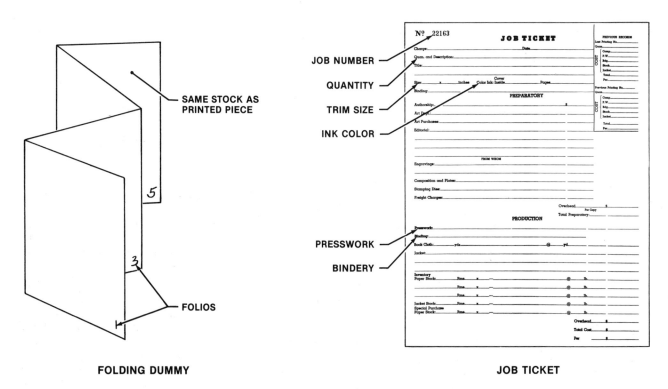

SAME STOCK AS PRINTED PIECE

FOLIOS

FOLDING DUMMY

JOB NUMBER

QUANTITY

TRIM SIZE

INK COLOR

PRESSWORK

BINDERY

JOB TICKET

Figure 2-1. A comprehensive layout with a tissue overlay, folding dummy, and job ticket is used to communicate between stages of the production process.

Trim Size. *Trim size* is the final size of the job after waste has been removed. Accuracy of the trim size must be maintained to ensure that other operations can be performed accurately with the job. A paste-up artist lays out the trim size according to the comprehensive layout, or job ticket. Trim marks are laid out on an artboard and reproduced on film to help the stripper position the negatives for the plates.

Gutters and Margins. Gutters and margins improve the readability of the copy by adding space between and around copy. See Figure 2-2. A *gutter* is the space between columns of copy. A *margin* is the space along the outside edges and at the top and bottom of the copy. A margin is also used between blocks of copy on a single unfolded page. The *back margin,* or gutter margin, is the space between the pages of a job that allows for folding and binding. The amount of space for a back margin is commonly determined by the size of the book and the method of binding. A wide back margin is required for books with a large number of pages. When a margin is not indicated on the comprehensive layout, the image will bleed. A *bleed* is a printed image that extends to at least one edge of a printed piece.

Gutters and margins are indicated on a comprehensive layout with thin lines drawn along the blocks of copy. Gutter and margin indications are laid out after laying out the trim size of the job. Gutter measurements are written on the tissue overlay or indicated on the job ticket. Margin measurements are placed directly on the comprehensive layout and are transferred to the mechanical by the paste-up artist.

Color. Color printing inks are categorized as flat color and process color. *Flat color inks* are composed of premixed inks used to create a variety of colors. Flat color inks are selected by the client or designer from a sample book such as a PANTONE® color book. PMS books, or PANTONE®

Matching System books, are also available in varying degrees of color, or *tints.* The *PANTONE® Color and Black Selector* combines solid colors, tints, and black to indicate the appearance of flat color with black.

Process color inks are transparent inks that print over one another to create a variety of colors. The process colors are magenta, cyan, yellow, and black. Process color inks are commonly used in 4-color reproduction such as color photographs, paintings, and water colors. A paste-up artist transfers all color information from the comprehensive layout to the mechanical regardless of whether flat color or process color is used.

A designer draws the comprehensive layout in colored pencil or marker and indicates a PMS number. The PMS number corresponds to an ink color in a PMS book. A *PANTONE® Color Specifier* may also be used to ensure accuracy in matching color. Perforated squares, or swatches, of ink samples are removed from the swatch book and attached to the lower right-hand corner of the comprehensive layout. The printer uses the swatch number to determine the formula for the PMS ink and checks the swatch for a color match.

Stock. *Stock* is the surface on which an image is printed. Paper is the most common stock used in the printing industry. Paper is described by weight, color, name, surface, and grade. Each characteristic influences the way paper reacts to ink and bindery processes. Paper is selected by a designer based on its brightness, color, ability to accept ink, strength, and durability. A designer uses samples of stock to determine folding, embossing, foil stamping, and durability characteristics. The name and weight of stock are indicated on the tissue overlay covering the mechanical or on the job ticket.

Bindery Specifications. *Bindery specifications* are visual and written instructions indicating placement for bindery processes. Bindery processes indicated on the comprehensive layout include folding, perforating, scoring, die cutting, drilling, and gluing.

Folds, perforations, scores, and die cuts are indicated on the comprehensive layout with a thin dashed line. Drill marks are traced in pencil on a comprehensive layout with a template. Glue areas are indicated on a comprehensive layout with outlined boxes. Written information is often included directly on the comprehensive layout or folding dummy to reinforce these symbols. A paste-up artist measures the position of the bindery specifications on the comprehensive layout and transfers the measurements to the mechanical.

Folds are indicated with a folding dummy. A paste-up artist measures the position of the fold on the dummy and transfers the measurement to the mechanical. The *parallel fold, right-angle fold,* and combination of parallel and right-angle folds are commonly used for 6-, 8-, 12-, and 16-page jobs. A *letter fold*, or gate fold, is a parallel fold created by folding the outside edges of the printed piece inward. An *accordion fold* is a parallel fold created by parallel folds that do not extend over one another. A *French fold* is a combination of a parallel and right-angle fold created by folding the back side inward before making the parallel fold. See Figure 2-3.

Layout Elements

Layout elements are components on a comprehensive layout that represent copy to be positioned on a mechanical. Layout elements include type, illustrations, photographs, and tint screens. A typesetter follows the layout elements to properly set the type size and alignment. A paste-up artist uses the layout elements as a guide to plot the position of copy on a mechanical.

Type. Type is the most common layout element. *Display type*, or headline type, is type that is 14 points or larger. Display type is written out full size on a comprehensive layout. *Body type*, or text type, is type that is 13 points or smaller. Body type is shown as baselines on a comprehensive layout. *Baselines* are lines on a com-

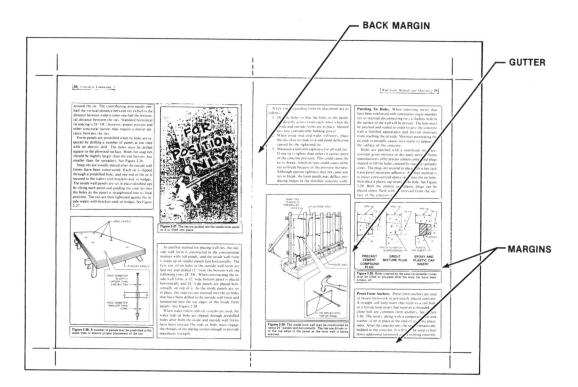

MECHANICAL

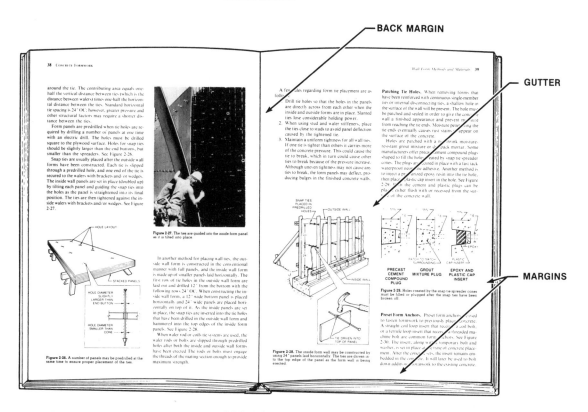

PRINTED JOB

Figure 2-2. Gutters and margins assist in the readability of copy. A back margin allows for folding and binding of the printed piece.

Folds

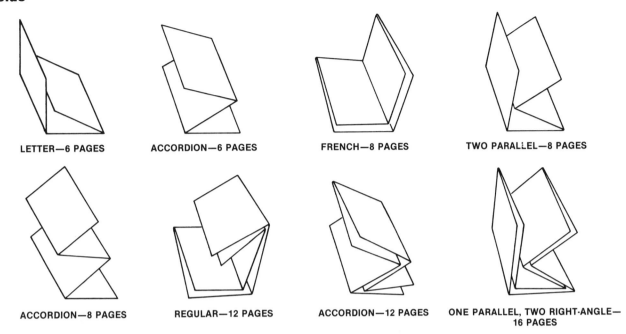

LETTER—6 PAGES   ACCORDION—6 PAGES   FRENCH—8 PAGES   TWO PARALLEL—8 PAGES

ACCORDION—8 PAGES   REGULAR—12 PAGES   ACCORDION—12 PAGES   ONE PARALLEL, TWO RIGHT-ANGLE—16 PAGES

Figure 2-3. Parallel and right-angle folds are used for 6-, 8-, 12-, and 16-page jobs.

prehensive layout that represent the height, width, and vertical spacing of type. See Figure 2-4. A typesetter measures the baselines with a type scale to determine the type specifications for a job. A paste-up artist measures the baselines to determine placement and alignment of *copy block,* or blocks of copy.

Illustrations. *Illustrations* are drawings used to emphasize written information. Illustrations on a comprehensive layout may be simple or detailed. A designer commonly uses simplified illustrations on a comprehensive layout when the illustration is to be provided by an illustrator. A paste-up artist allocates space for an illustration on a mechanical by measuring the comprehensive layout. A line illustration is pasted in position on a mechanical. A continuous tone illustration is indicated on a mechanical with an outlined box.

Photographs. *Photographs* are used to enhance the communicative ability of copy. Photographs are com-

monly simplified on the comprehensive layout by tracing the photograph or indicating its position with an outline. Photocopies of photographs are placed in position when several photographs are used for a job. If photocopies are unavailable, the area to be used for a photograph is outlined and keyed to a letter or number on the photograph. *Keying* is a method of identifying photographs by placing identical numbers or letters on the photographs and the outlined area on the comprehensive layout. See Figure 2-5.

Tint Screens. A *tint screen* is a lighter value of a color created by using a screen pattern. A dot pattern is commonly used, although line, circle, triangle, square, and texture patterns are also available. Dot patterns are identified by percent and line. *Percent* refers to the density of a value created by a tint. A larger percentage indicates a darker color value. *Line* refers to the coarseness of the screen as designated by the number of dots

DISPLAY TYPE

BASELINES

Figure 2-4. Display type is drawn full size on a comprehensive layout. Baselines are used to represent 13-point type or smaller.

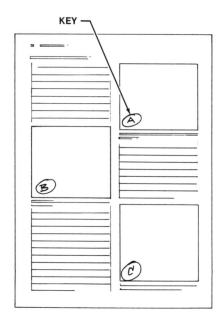

Figure 2-5. Keying a photograph with a number or letter ensures correct placement of photographs on the final job.

per linear inch. A larger line value indicates more dots per linear inch and a finer screen coarseness. See Figure 2-6.

A tint screen is commonly indicated on a comprehensive layout with a lighter shade of colored pencil or marker. *Cross-hatching,* a series of inclined lines, is used to indicate a tint screen in selected areas on a simplified comprehensive layout. See Figure 2-7.

USING A COMPREHENSIVE LAYOUT

Use of a comprehensive layout varies according to the type of layout created by the designer. Ideally, comprehensive layouts are drawn to full size and in full color with great detail. The typesetter and paste-up artist use the comprehensive layout to determine the size and placement of elements. However, the job may not warrant the time and expense of a detailed comprehensive layout. In this case, the designer draws a quick rendering of the job for use as a comprehensive layout. The typesetter uses the layout to fit type as closely as possible. The paste-up artist makes decisions about the placement of copy because not all copy will fit according to the comprehensive layout.

Working with a Comprehensive Layout

A designer draws a comprehensive layout to guide production personnel and define the job. It contains vital information for production of the job from paste-up to bindery. A comprehensive layout should be followed closely to ensure accuracy of the job.

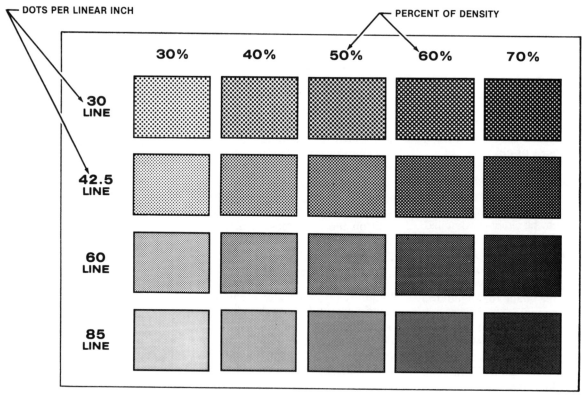

Graphic Products Corp.

Figure 2-6. Tint screens are designated by percent and line values. Percent refers to the darkness of the printed tint and line refers to the coarseness of the tint screen.

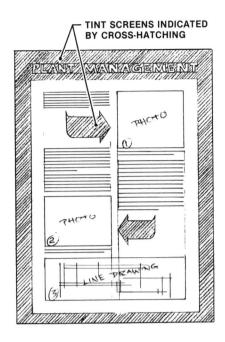

Figure 2-7. Cross-hatching is used to indicate a tint screen on a simplified comprehensive layout.

Using Indicated Measurements.
The designer writes indicated measurements to be used on the mechanical directly on the comprehensive layout or on a tissue overlay. Indicated measurements, whether written or represented by baselines, are not altered by a paste-up artist. The designer should be consulted if indicated measurements are incorrect. A paste-up artist measures and lays out the trim size after squaring the artboard. Baseline measurements are laid out, and measurements for the placement of copy begin at the top trim line and continue toward the bottom trim line. See Figure 2-8.

Altering a Comprehensive Layout.
A paste-up artist alters a comprehensive layout when a designer draws the layout without properly copyfitting the type. The typesetter sets the type according to the specifications designated by the designer on the manuscript copy. The paste-up artist alters the comprehensive layout when the copy does not fit the layout. The paste-up artist is responsible for making decisions to

alter the layout if the copy is illegible or the layout prevents illustrations or photographs from fitting on the page.

Transferring the Layout to the Artboard

A paste-up artist transfers the measurements of the comprehensive layout to the artboard. The paste-up artist begins by assembling all the tools and elements required to complete the job including the comprehensive layout, type, illustrations, and artboard. The paste-up artist compares the type to the comprehensive layout and manuscript copy to ensure proper fit and verify that all copy blocks are represented. The paste-up artist then begins transferring the measurements of the comprehensive layout to the artboard.

Artboards are stock that copy elements are pasted on. Artboards may vary in thickness but should be stiff enough to accept copy elements without buckling. The surface of an artboard should be dull white. Shiny stock may cause glare from the camera lights when photographed. The surface of an artboard should accept ink without spreading. The surface must be kept clean since debris and fingerprints mar the surface and may reproduce on film when photographed. An artboard is cut at least 2″ larger on all sides than the final trim size dimensions. See Figure 2-9. Although detailed mechanicals require a larger artboard, too large an artboard is awkward to work with and may not fit easily onto the process camera copyboard for reproduction.

Squaring an Artboard.
An artboard is squared to ensure accuracy and continuity when aligning copy elements. The art table is cleared of

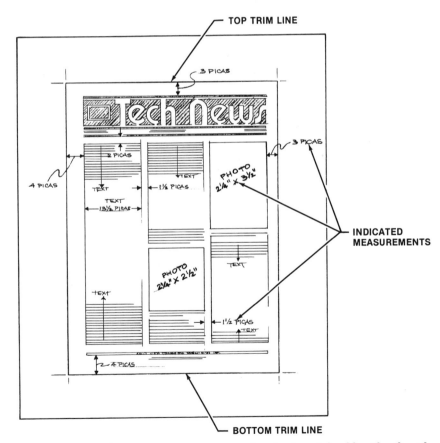

Figure 2-8. Indicated measurements on a comprehensive layout should not be altered by a paste-up artist.

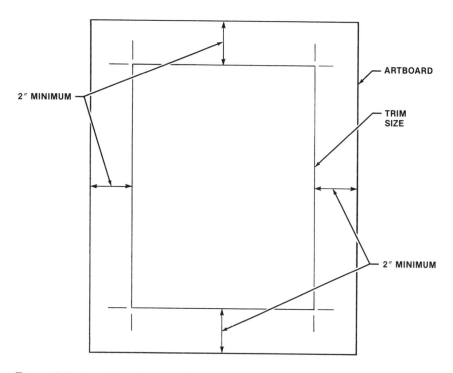

Figure 2-9. An artboard is cut at least 2″ larger on all sides than the final trim size.

everything but a T-square to avoid clutter when squaring the artboard. The position of the artboard is determined by verifying the trim size of the comprehensive layout. The artboard is placed with its longest dimension in a vertical direction if the longest dimension of the trim size is vertical. The artboard is placed with its longest dimension in a horizontal direction if the longest dimension of the trim size is horizontal. See Figure 2-10.

1. Position the T-square on the lower half of the art table. The head of the T-square should not extend beyond the bottom edge of the art table. The blade of the T-square lies flat against the surface of the art table.

2. Position the artboard close to the head of the T-square, and butt it tightly against the upper edge of the blade.

3. Apply tape to the upper corners of the artboard while holding the T-square and artboard securely. Slide the T-square down, and tape the bottom corners.

4. Slide the T-square up to the bottom edge of the artboard to verify its position.

Guidelines are thin, non-reproducible blue lines drawn on the artboard for reference by a paste-up artist. A non-photo blue, or non-reproducing blue, fine-tip marker or pen is used to draw guidelines. *Non-photo blue* does not reproduce on the film used to photograph the mechanical. Non-photo blue pencil leads are not recommended for drawing guidelines. The wax base of the lead causes uneven inking as black ink is applied to the mechanical. See Figure 2-11.

Centering an Image. Centering an image on the artboard ensures that sufficient space surrounds the trim size on all sides. Three methods of centering an image on an artboard are the measurement method, centering ruler method, and diagonal corners method. The method used to center an image depends on the tools or equipment available and the paste-up artist's familiarity with the method.

The measurement method is the most common method of determining the center of an artboard. It is more time-consuming than other methods and requires the ability to

read a standard or sub-zero ruler and divide whole numbers and fractions. See Figure 2-12.

1. Place a standard or sub-zero ruler along the top edge of a T-square. Measure the artboard horizontally.

2. Divide the horizontal measurement by 2. Lay out the horizontal center from one edge of the artboard with a non-photo blue pen or fine-tip marker.

3. Place the ruler along the vertical edge of a triangle, and measure the artboard vertically while intersecting the horizontal center.

4. Divide the vertical measurement by 2. Lay out the distance from the top or bottom of the artboard while intersecting the horizontal center.

The centering ruler method is another method used to determine the center of an artboard. The centering ruler method is a quick and accurate method that does not involve the ability to divide whole numbers and fractions. See Figure 2-13.

1. Place a centering ruler along the top edge of a T-square.

2. Position the centering ruler so that equal increments on each side of the zero point align with the edges of the artboard. Lay out the horizontal center point with a non-photo blue pen or fine-tip marker.

3. Place the centering ruler along the vertical edge of a triangle while intersecting the horizontal center point.

4. Position the centering ruler so that equal increments on each side of the zero point align with the top and bottom of the artboard. Lay out the center of the artboard.

The diagonal corners method is another method of determining the center of an artboard. Accuracy must be maintained when aligning the ruler with the diagonal corners of the artboard. See Figure 2-14.

1. Place the ruler on its face, and position it diagonally across the artboard. Carefully align the edge of the ruler with the corners. Draw a non-photo blue line approximately 2″ long across the center of the artboard.

2. Reposition the ruler across the other two diagonal corners. Draw a

Squaring an Artboard

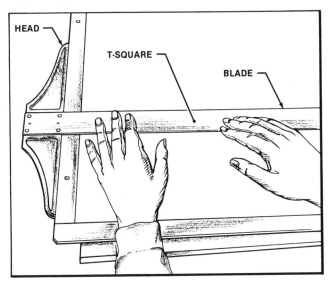

Step 1. Position T-square.

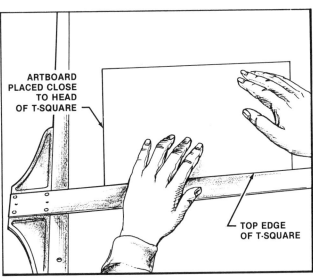

Step 2. Place artboard against blade.

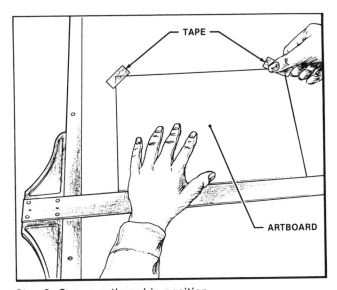

Step 3. Secure artboard in position.

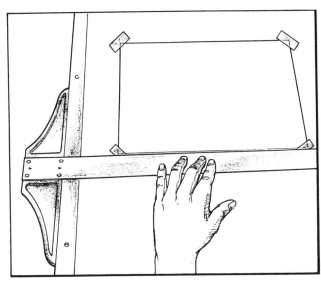

Step 4. Verify position of artboard.

Figure 2-10. An artboard is squared to ensure accuracy and continuity when aligning elements.

non-photo blue line to intersect the initial line to determine the center of the artboard.

PREPARING THE ARTBOARD FOR REPRODUCTION

An artboard is prepared for reproduction by a paste-up artist. The paste-up artist transfers the information from a comprehensive layout, job ticket, and folding dummy to the mechanical. Marks or symbols are drawn on the mechanical to represent written information such as trim size, centers, folds, scores, and perforations used on the job. The marks and symbols are drawn in dense black ink, which reproduces on film and on the final press sheet.

Technical Pen and Ink

A *technical pen* is used to draw marks on a mechanical for reproduction on film. A technical pen must be maintained properly to produce good quality marks and lines. Most manufacturers of technical pens recommend a specific ink and material on which the ink will be used, such as paper or plastic.

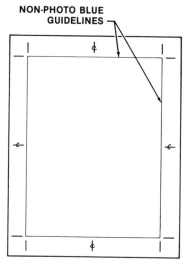

Figure 2-11. A fine-tip, non-photo blue marker or pen is used to draw guidelines on a mechanical.

The primary parts of a technical pen are the cap, nib, needle, air-ink exchange unit, ink cartridge, and barrel. Although most technical pens have a similar design, not all pens have the same parts. See Figure 2-15.

The *cap* of a technical pen protects the end of the nib from damage. A cap is threaded to form an air trap when screwed to the nib. The air trap prevents ink surrounding the writing tip from drying when not in use. Some technical pen caps have an internal moisture reservoir that prevents the ink from drying. The *moisture reservoir* is a small sponge that contacts the writing tip when the cap is screwed in place. A drop of water is periodically placed in the cap to saturate the sponge.

The *nib*, or writing point, is a plastic casing that threads into the air-ink exchange unit. One end of the nib is used for discharging ink to the drawing surface. A weighted needle is housed in the nib and projects a short distance from the end of the writing tip. The *needle* is a plunger that allows the ink to flow smoothly. When the pen is pressed on a drawing surface or shaken vertically, the needle breaks up any dried ink obstruction in the tip of the nib and allows the smooth flow of ink. When the pen is lifted from the drawing surface, the needle repositions itself, stopping the ink flow. A safety screw secures the needle in position.

Nibs are available in various point sizes graduated in decimal or typo-

Determining Center of an Artboard—Measurement Method

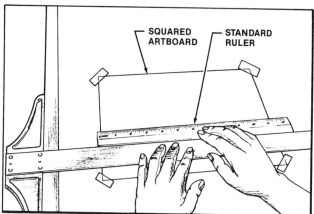

Step 1. Measure artboard horizontally.

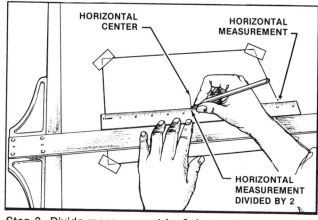

Step 2. Divide measurement by 2. Lay out on artboard.

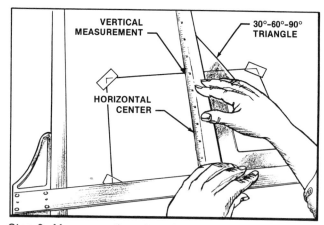

Step 3. Measure artboard vertically.

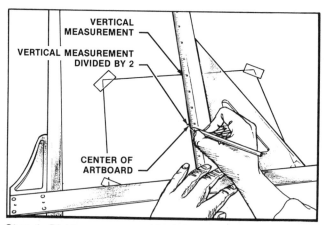

Step 4. Divide measurement by 2. Lay out center of artboard.

Figure 2-12. Horizontal and vertical centers of an artboard can be determined by the measurement method.

Determining Center of an Artboard—Centering Ruler Method

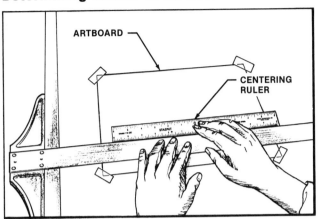

Step 1. Place centering ruler on T-square.

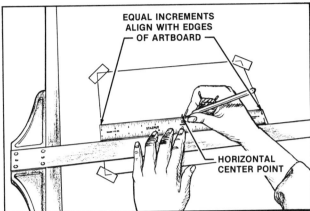

Step 2. Position centering ruler. Lay out center point.

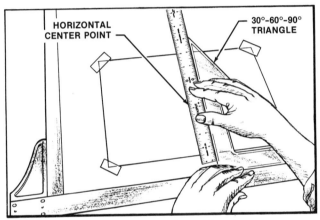

Step 3. Place centering ruler along triangle.

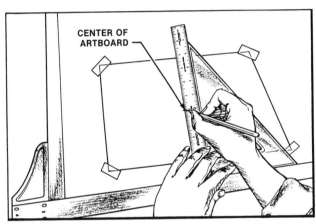

Step 4. Position centering ruler. Lay out center of artboard.

Figure 2-13. A centering ruler is used to determine the horizontal and vertical centers of an artboard.

graphic point increments. Typographic point size represents the width of the line produced by the nib. Nibs are available in typographic point sizes ranging from 6 × 0 to 7 point. A 6 × 0 nib produces a hairline rule approximately .005″ wide. A No. 4 nib produces a line approximately .079″ wide. A nib with a smaller point size is generally more delicate to use and more expensive than a nib with a larger point size.

The *air-ink exchange unit* is a valve that allows air to enter the cartridge of the pen as the ink flows out. The nib is fastened to one end of the air-ink exchange unit, and the ink cartridge is fastened to the other end. Ink flows from the ink cartridge, through the air-ink exchange unit, in-

to the nib, and exits the tip.

The *ink cartridge* is an ink reservoir that fits snugly into one end of the air-ink exchange unit. Ink cartridges are available in a variety of sizes and in empty or prefilled styles. An empty cartridge is filled by removing it from the air-ink exchange unit. The cartridge should be filled to the fill line or approximately three-fourths full when a fill line is not present. The empty space at the top allows for ink displacement when the cartridge is fitted into the air-ink exchange unit. Prefilled cartridges save time, but are more costly than empty cartridges. A prefilled cartridge is opened by pressure when fitted into the air-ink exchange unit.

The *barrel* of a technical pen is

used as a handle and protects the ink cartridge. The barrel of a technical pen is threaded for easy removal. Some barrels contain a hex wrench in the end to loosen the nib of the pen for cleaning.

A technical pen should be cleaned frequently. Use the following guidelines for consistent, quality inking procedures when using a technical pen:

1. Use ink recommended for technical pens only.

2. Store a technical pen vertically with the writing tip down.

3. Clean size 0 or smaller pens daily. If not used on a daily basis, empty the pen and fill it with water.

4. When a technical pen is not used for an extended period of time,

Determining Center of an Artboard—Diagonal Corners Method

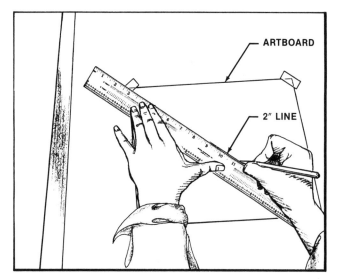

Step 1. Position ruler diagonally. Draw line along center.

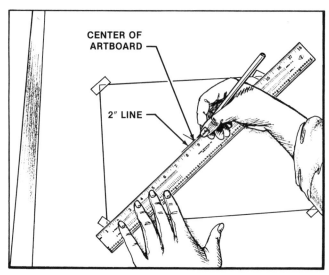

Step 2. Reposition ruler diagonally. Draw line to intersect initial line.

Figure 2-14. A ruler is positioned diagonally across corners to determine the center of an artboard.

Technical Pen Components

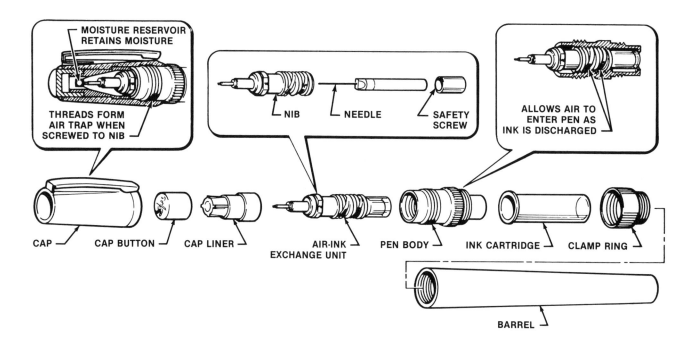

Figure 2-15. A technical pen is used to draw marks such as trim marks and score marks on a mechanical for reproduction on film.

thoroughly clean it, and fill with water.

5. Obstructed pens should be emptied and rinsed thoroughly. An ultrasonic pen cleaner may be used to loosen dried ink and rinse it away. Pen cleaning solvents are also available to facilitate cleaning obstructed pens.

6. Pens should be protected from severe variations in temperature (above 90°F or below 35°F).

7. Pens should not be dropped on a hard surface or severely jolted.

Specialized ink should be used for technical pens. Ink not specified for use in a technical pen does not have the same consistency and may obstruct the pen point or flow too quickly. Ink is available in a variety of colors including white, non-photo blue, and black. Black ink is used by a paste-up artist to create a dense black image. Grayness or transparency that allows the artboard to be seen results in poor reproduction on film.

Trim Marks

Trim marks are thin, dense black lines approximately $\frac{1}{2}''$ in length that indicate the trim size of a job. Trim marks are aligned with the trim line $\frac{1}{16}''$ outside the image area. See Figure 2-16. Accuracy of trim marks is important to ensure that the job is accurate. Inaccurate trim marks may cause an entire job to be inaccurate. A camera operator uses trim marks to align the mechanical in position on the camera. A stripper uses trim marks to align the film on the goldenrod. A stripper also uses trim marks to align the image on the flats. Trim marks are primarily used by the bindery operator to position the press sheet when removing waste. The trim marks are removed when the press sheet is trimmed. Since many processes depend upon the use of trim marks for alignment, it is mandatory that trim marks be accurate.

The trim size is commonly centered on the artboard. The artboard is cut at least 2″ larger on all sides than the final trim size. The artboard

is squared and taped into position on an art table. The trim size is then centered. See Figure 2-17.

1. Determine the center of the artboard. Measure the trim size of the comprehensive layout. Divide the horizontal and vertical measurements by 2.

2. Place a ruler along the upper edge of the T-square. Lay out the horizontal measurements from the center point toward the edges of the artboard. Draw vertical guidelines using a triangle.

3. Place the ruler along a triangle. Lay out the vertical measurements from the center point toward the top and bottom of the artboard. Draw horizontal guidelines using a T-square.

4. Compare the trim size dimensions on the artboard to the comprehensive layout.

A beveled triangle may be used to avoid ink bleeding when drawing trim marks. *Ink bleeding* is caused by capillary action, which pulls the ink beneath the triangle. Ink bleeding may also be avoided by placing two thicknesses of masking tape along the bottom of a triangle. A $\frac{1}{16}''$ margin should be allowed between the edge of the triangle and the tape.

Trim marks are drawn on the mechanical after the guidelines for the trim size are laid out. Trim marks are drawn in black ink with a technical pen so that they reproduce on film.

Trim marks do not extend into the image area. When inking trim marks on a mechanical, start at the top and proceed downward; then start at the left and proceed to the right. See Figure 2-18.

1. Align the T-square with the upper horizontal guideline. Draw the left horizontal trim mark starting approximately $\frac{9}{16}''$ away from the left vertical guideline and continuing to approximately $\frac{1}{16}''$ outside of the vertical guideline. Draw the right horizontal trim mark without moving the T-square. Start approximately $\frac{1}{16}''$ outside of the right vertical guideline, and continue to approximately $\frac{9}{16}''$ outside of the guideline.

2. Reposition the T-square to align with the lower horizontal guideline. Draw the left and right horizontal trim marks using the same procedure as for the upper trim marks.

3. Position the T-square near the bottom of the artboard, allowing space for the lower vertical trim marks to be drawn. Place a triangle along the left vertical guideline. Draw the upper vertical trim mark starting approximately $\frac{9}{16}''$ away from the upper horizontal guideline and continuing to approximately $\frac{1}{16}''$ outside of the guideline. Draw the lower vertical trim mark without moving the triangle. Start approximately $\frac{1}{16}''$ outside of the lower horizontal guideline, and continue to approximately $\frac{9}{16}''$

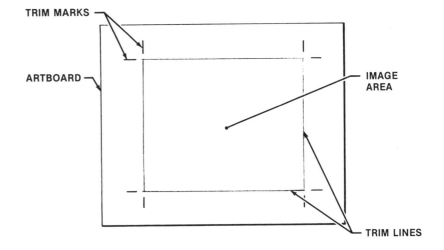

Figure 2-16. Trim marks indicate the trim size of a job.

Laying Out Trim Size

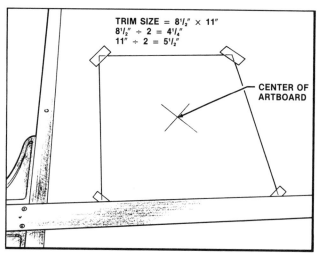

Step 1. Determine center of artboard. Measure trim size from comprehensive layout. Divide measurements by 2.

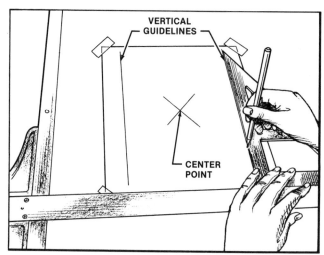

Step 2. Lay out divided horizontal measurement from center point. Draw vertical guidelines.

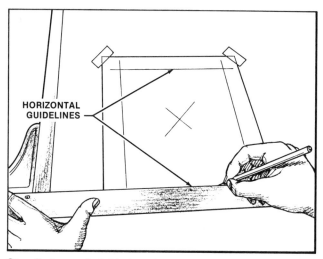

Step 3. Lay out divided vertical measurement from center point. Draw horizontal guidelines.

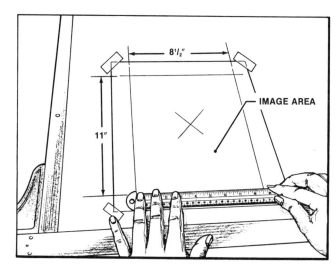

Step 4. Verify trim size dimensions.

Figure 2-17. The dimensions of the trim size are transferred from the comprehensive layout to the artboard.

outside of the guideline.

4. Carefully lift the triangle away from the artboard. Reposition the triangle along the right vertical guideline. Draw the upper and lower vertical trim marks using the same procedure as for the trim marks on the left side. Verify accuracy of the trim marks by measuring from the edge of the artboard to the trim marks.

Center Marks

Center marks indicate the center of the mechanical. Center marks are commonly drawn like a trim mark: approximately ½″ long and ¹⁄₁₆″ outside of the image area using dense black ink. Center marks are also indicated by placing an uppercase *C* through

the mark or placing a register mark over the center mark. See Figure 2-19.

Center marks are used by a camera operator to align camera copy on the copyboard to the film in the camera. Strippers use center marks to accurately align film on goldenrod. Bindery operators use center marks to align large press sheets in the bindery. Center marks are used in automated platemaking machines to align image areas on the plate.

Fold, Score, and Perforation Marks

Fold, score, and perforation marks are drawn on the mechanical for use in bindery processes. Fold, score, and perforation marks are similar in appearance. Each is a series of three short dashes drawn in dense black ink that are a total of ½″ in length. The marks are drawn ¹⁄₁₆″ away from the image area. Fold, score, and perforation marks are differentiated by writing *fold, score,* or *perf* in the margin with red or black ink. See Figure 2-20.

Fold marks indicate where a job is to be folded. The style of fold is not indicated on the mechanical, but is shown with the folding dummy which accompanies the press sheets to the bindery. *Score marks* indicate where stock is to be indented to facilitate folding or tearing by easing the tension of the stock. *Perforation marks* indicate where small, evenly spaced cuts are to be made in stock. Perforations are used to facilitate manual tearing of stock at a predetermined location.

Drawing Trim Marks

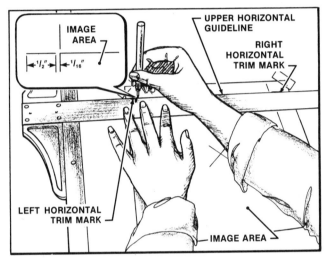

Step 1. Align T-square with upper horizontal guideline. Draw left and right horizontal trim marks.

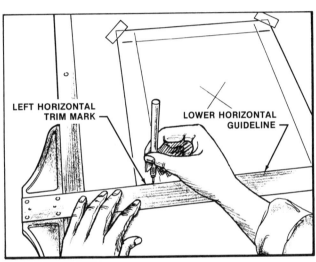

Step 2. Reposition T-square to align with lower horizontal guideline. Draw left and right horizontal trim marks.

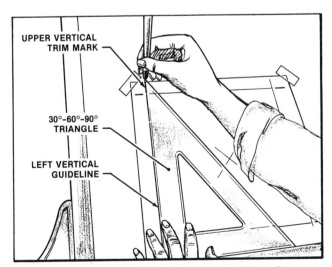

Step 3. Align triangle with left vertical guideline. Draw upper and lower vertical trim marks.

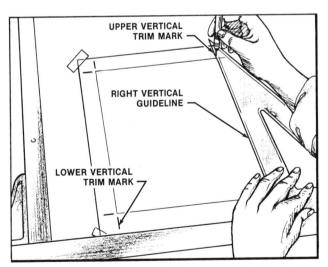

Step 4. Reposition triangle to align with right vertical guideline. Draw upper and lower vertical trim marks.

Figure 2-18. Trim marks are drawn with dense black ink. They should be approximately ¹⁄₁₆″ outside of the image area.

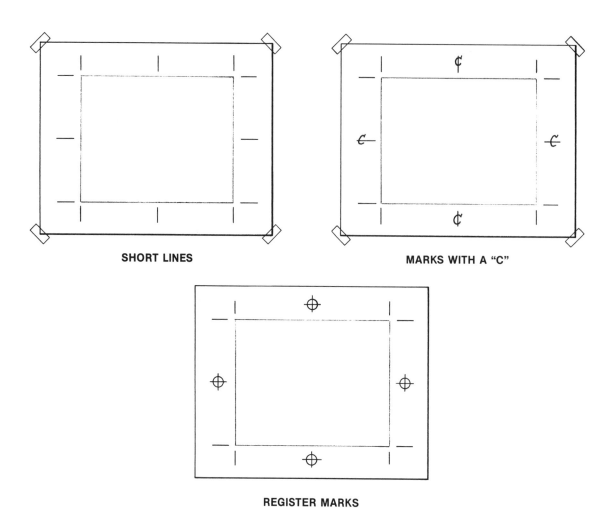

Figure 2-19. Center marks are indicated with a short line, a short line with an uppercase *C*, or a register mark.

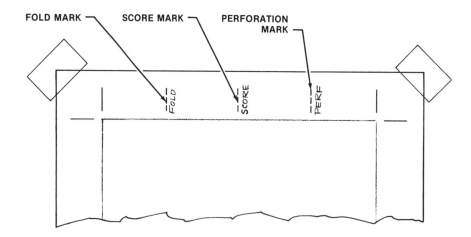

Figure 2-20. Fold, score, and perforation marks are drawn with three short dashes measuring a total of ½″ in length. Fold, score, or perf is written in the margin to distinguish the marks.

Comprehensive Layout

True-False

T   F   **1.** Keyline and paste-up or page assembly is the production process that takes a design and creates a reproducible image.

T   F   **2.** The comprehensive layout is used to reproduce the job.

T   F   **3.** A folding dummy is a sheet of stock that is folded and marked to indicate how the pages are arranged.

T   F   **4.** A job ticket gives instructions about production requirements.

T   F   **5.** A paste-up artist lays out the trim size according to the comprehensive layout.

T   F   **6.** Baselines on a comprehensive layout indicate where 30-point type and smaller is to be positioned.

T   F   **7.** A designer pastes the original photograph to the comprehensive layout.

T   F   **8.** The comprehensive layout is commonly drawn in colored pencil or marker.

T   F   **9.** Process color inks are transparent inks.

T   F   **10.** A paste-up artist may alter the position of elements of a job as required.

T   F   **11.** Display type is represented by baselines on a comprehensive layout.

T   F   **12.** Keying is a method of identifying photographs.

T   F   **13.** Tint screen percent refers to the density of a color value.

T   F   **14.** A moisture reservoir is located in the barrel of a technical pen.

T   F   **15.** Nibs are available in typographic point sizes ranging from 2 x 0 to 4 point.

Multiple Choice

_____   **1.** A _____ layout is a blueprint of the printed piece.
   A. thumbnail
   B. comprehensive
   C. rough
   D. mechanical

_____   **2.** _____ are a series of lines on a comprehensive layout that represent the height, width, and vertical spacing of copy.
   A. Keylines
   B. Guidelines
   C. Trim lines
   D. Baselines

_____ **3.** A designer uses a perforated square of an ink sample from a _____ color swatch book to ensure accuracy in matching color.
   A. flat
   B. process
   C. PMS
   D. MSP

_____ **4.** A _____ pattern is the most common tint screen pattern.
   A. triangle
   B. dot
   C. square
   D. texture

_____ **5.** The artboard for a mechanical should be _____.
   A. white
   B. dull
   C. stiff
   D. all of the above

_____ **6.** An ink cartridge should be filled approximately _____ full.
   A. one-fourth
   B. one-third
   C. one-half
   D. three-fourths

_____ **7.** A non-photo blue _____ transfers wax to an artboard.
   A. pen
   B. pencil
   C. marker
   D. all of the above

Completion

_____ **1.** The _____ size is the final size of a printed piece after waste has been removed.

_____ **2.** A job _____ is printed on the job ticket, artboards, film, flats, plates, and press sheets.

_____ **3.** A(n) _____ screen is a lighter value of a color created with a screen pattern.

_____ **4.** _____ refers to the coarseness of a tint screen.

_____ **5.** Right-angle and parallel _____ are used for 6-, 8-, 12-, and 16-page jobs.

_____ **6.** An artboard is cut at least _____″ larger on all sides than the final trim size.

_____ **7.** _____ are thin, non-photo blue lines drawn on an artboard for reference by a paste-up artist.

_____ **8.** A(n) _____ is the space between columns of copy.

_____ **9.** A(n) _____ fold is a combination of a parallel and right-angle fold created by folding the back side inward before making the parallel fold.

_____ **10.** Trim and fold marks are drawn with dense _____ ink.

Identification

_____ **1.** Trim mark

_____ **2.** Center mark

_____ **3.** Fold mark

_____ **4.** Letter fold

_____ **5.** Accordion fold

_____ **6.** French fold

_____ **7.** Gutter

_____ **8.** Margin

_____ **9.** Back margin

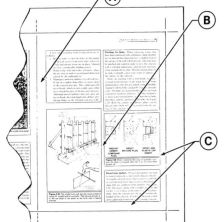

_____ **10.** Cap

_____ **11.** Ink cartridge

_____ **12.** Needle

_____ **13.** Barrel

_____ **14.** Nib

_____ **15.** Air-ink exchange unit

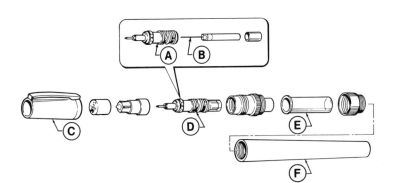

Matching

_____ **1.** Nib

_____ **2.** Needle

_____ **3.** Cartridge

_____ **4.** Barrel

_____ **5.** Air-ink exchange unit

_____ **6.** Cap

A. Used as a handle
B. Valve that allows air to enter the cartridge
C. Protects the nib from damage
D. Ink reservoir
E. Retains the writing tip
F. Plunger that allows ink to flow smoothly

3 RULING

A rule is a line that is reproduced on the printed piece. Ruling is the process of drawing rules on an artboard with ink or applying adhesive rules to an artboard. A technical pen is used to draw rules of weights up to 4 points. A technical pen and brush are used to create wide rules. A T-square and/or triangle is used to guide the technical pen when ruling with ink.

Adhesive material is used to create straight and curved rules on an artboard. Adhesive material is available in rolls and preprinted sheets. Non-photo blue guidelines are used when applying adhesive material to allow accurate placement of rules.

RULING WITH INK

Ruling with ink is an economical method of creating rules on an artboard. The weight of a rule is measured in points. The length of a rule is measured in inches or picas. See Figure 3-1.

Rules are drawn in dense black ink with crisp, clean edges. Dense black rules on an artboard produce crisp, rigid lines on the film negative and printed piece. Ink that is not dense black produces a mottled image on the film negative and reproduces as a broken image on the printed piece. See Figure 3-2.

Inking Tools and Techniques

A technical pen is used to create rules of weights up to 4 points. Technical pens with nib sizes between 4 and 7 points may allow ink to flow too quickly. A technical pen and fine-bristle brush are used to create wide rules. A T-square is used as a guide when drawing horizontal rules. A triangle is used as a guide when drawing vertical and inclined rules.

A technical pen is held vertically when inking to facilitate even ink flow. The pen is grasped firmly, but comfortably, with light pressure applied to the point. The pen is guided at a consistent rate along the artboard. Slow or staccato movements result in rough, irregular rules.

Point Size Ruling. *Point size ruling* is the creation of rules on an artboard that are specified by the designer on a comprehensive layout. If the rule size is not specified, the weight of the rule is measured with a rule scale. See Figure 3-3.

Guide marks are commonly used to lay out the position of an inked rule. *Guide marks* are non-photo blue marks on an artboard that indicate the end points and position of a rule. Several guide marks can be placed on an artboard without greatly marring the surface. Guidelines drawn with non-photo blue pencil may cause improper ink coverage on the artboard and should not be used when laying out multiple rules. Guidelines drawn with non-photo blue ballpoint pen indent the artboard causing ruling ink to accumulate in the corners of guidelines. Guidelines drawn with a non-photo blue marker may be inaccurate because the marker tip spreads with excessive pressure.

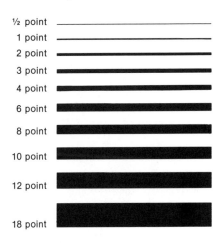

Figure 3-1. The weight of a rule is measured in points.

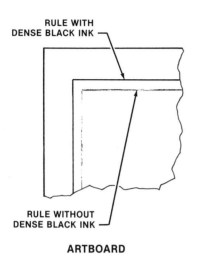

ARTBOARD

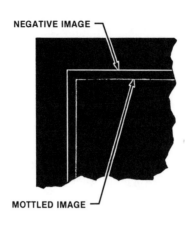

FILM NEGATIVE

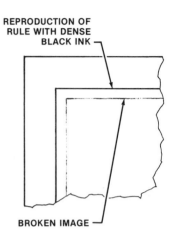

PRINTED PIECE

Figure 3-2. Dense black rules on an artboard produce a crisp, sharp image on the film negative and reproduce as solid rules on the printed piece.

Horizontal Rules. Horizontal rules are drawn on an artboard using a T-square as a guide. A piece of scrap stock is used to verify ink flow prior to inking the rule. Multiple horizontal rules are drawn starting at the top of an artboard and proceeding downward. See Figure 3-4.

1. Determine the point size of the rule from the comprehensive layout. Lay out a guide mark and end points for the rule on the artboard.

2. Position a T-square along the guide mark. Select a technical pen with the required nib. Verify ink flow of the pen by drawing a few short rules on a piece of scrap stock.

3. Begin at the left end point. Guide the technical pen along the T-square as the needle contacts the artboard and ink begins to flow.

4. Lift the technical pen cleanly from the artboard at the end of the rule. Move the T-square down the artboard, and inspect the quality of the rule.

Vertical Rules. Vertical rules are drawn on an artboard using a triangle as a guide. Vertical rules are either drawn from the bottom of the rule upward, or from the top of the rule downward. Light, even pressure is applied to the technical pen throughout the

pen stroke. Multiple vertical rules are drawn starting at the left side of the artboard and progressing to the right. See Figure 3-5.

1. Determine the point size of the rule from the comprehensive layout. Lay out a guide mark and end points for the rule on the artboard.

2. Position a triangle along the guide mark. Select a technical pen with the required nib. Verify ink flow of the pen by drawing a few short rules on a piece of scrap stock.

3. Begin at the lower end point. Guide the technical pen along the triangle as the needle contacts the artboard and ink begins to flow.

4. Lift the technical pen cleanly from the artboard at the end of the rule. Lift the triangle carefully from the artboard, and inspect the quality of the rule.

Inclined Rules. Inclined rules are drawn using a triangle as a guide. A 45°–90° triangle or 30°–60°–90° triangle is used to ink rules at 15° increments. An adjustable triangle is used to ink rules at all other angles. See Figure 3-6.

1. Determine the point size of the rule from the comprehensive layout. Lay out a guide mark and end points for the rule on the artboard.

2. Position a triangle along the guide mark. Select a technical pen with the required size nib. Verify ink flow of the pen by drawing a few short rules on a piece of scrap stock.

3. Begin at the lower end point. Guide the technical pen along the triangle as the needle contacts the artboard and ink begins to flow.

4. Lift technical pen cleanly from the artboard at the end of the rule.

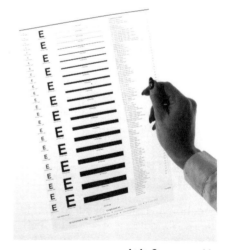

Agfa Compugraphic

Figure 3-3. A rule scale is used to determine the weight of a rule.

Lift the triangle carefully from the artboard, and inspect the quality of the rule.

Wide Rules. Wide rules are created using a technical pen and fine-bristle brush. An outline of the rule is drawn with 1-point rules, and the inner area is filled with india ink. See Figure 3-7.

1. Determine the point size of the rule from the comprehensive layout. Lay out the baseline guide mark on the artboard. Lay out the height guide mark on the artboard. Lay out end points for the rule on the artboard.

2. Position a T-square along the height guide mark. Select a technical pen with a 1-point nib. Verify ink flow of the pen by drawing a few short rules on a piece of scrap stock. Align the technical pen with the left end point along the height guide mark. Guide the pen along the T-square as the needle contacts the artboard and ink begins to flow. Lift the technical pen cleanly from the artboard at the end of the rule. Reposition the T-

square along the baseline guide mark. Select a technical pen with a 1-point nib. Align the technical pen with the left end point along the baseline guide mark. Guide the pen along the T-square as the needle contacts the artboard and ink begins to flow. Lift the technical pen cleanly from the artboard at the end of the rule.

3. Position a triangle along the left end point and join the height and baseline rules. Reposition the triangle along the right end point and join the height and baseline rules.

Drawing Horizontal Rules

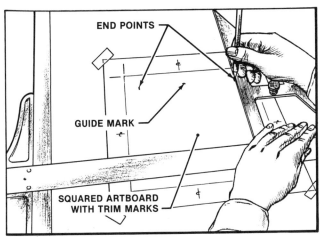

Step 1. Determine point size of rule. Lay out guide mark and end points for rule.

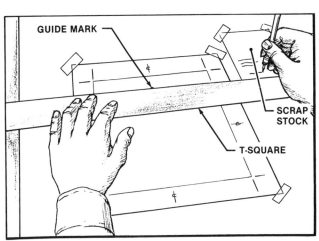

Step 2. Position T-square along guide mark. Select technical pen and test on scrap stock.

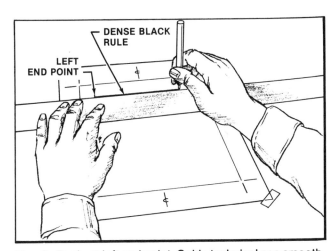

Step 3. Begin at left end point. Guide technical pen smoothly along T-square as needle contacts artboard.

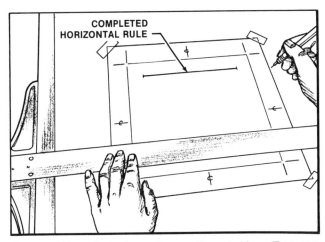

Step 4. Lift technical pen from artboard. Move T-square down artboard. Inspect quality of rule.

Figure 3-4. A T-square is used to guide a technical pen when inking horizontal rules. Guide marks indicate the end points and position of inked rules.

4. Fill the area between the rules with india ink using a fine-bristle brush, #0 or #00 wide.

Correction Techniques

Correction techniques are used to save time when preparing an artboard for reproduction. Corrections made on an artboard also reduce additional expenses incurred in photography and production. Film used to photograph an artboard is highly sensitive. Overlapped corners, rough lines, or smudges reproduce on the film. Imperfections on film are difficult and sometimes impossible to correct. Various correction techniques are used to improve the quality of reproduction including the use of liquid white opaque and white tape, and scribing or cutting the artboard.

Liquid White Opaque. *Liquid white opaque* is quick-drying material used to cover undesired images on an artboard. Only liquid white opaque designed for graphics reproduction should be used to make corrections. A single coat should be sufficient to cover images and allow for reapplication of ink without chipping or causing the technical pen to skip. Liquid white opaque is available as a paint or ink.

An extra-fine bristle brush is used to apply liquid white opaque paint. A #0 or #00 brush is used for general correction purposes, and a #000 or #0000 brush is used in tight locations. An opaquing brush is used

Drawing Vertical Rules

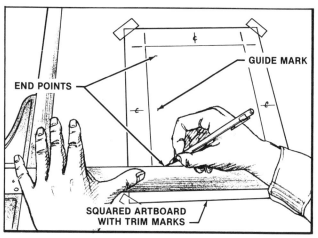

Step 1. Determine point size of rule. Lay out guide mark and end points for rule.

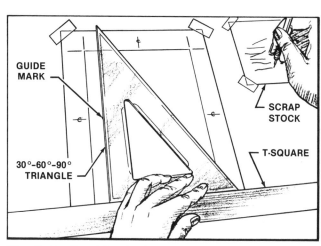

Step 2. Position triangle along guide mark. Select technical pen and test on scrap stock.

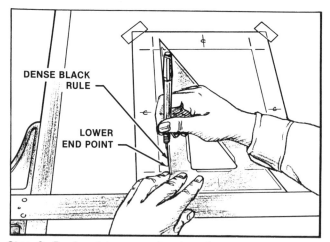

Step 3. Begin at lower end point. Guide technical pen smoothly along triangle as needle contacts artboard.

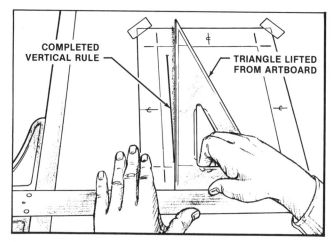

Step 4. Lift technical pen cleanly from artboard. Lift triangle carefully from artboard. Inspect quality of rule.

Figure 3-5. A triangle is used to guide a technical pen when inking vertical rules.

Drawing Inclined Rules

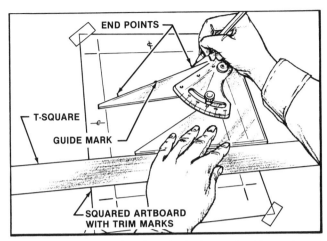

Step 1. Determine point size of rule. Lay out guide mark and end points for rule.

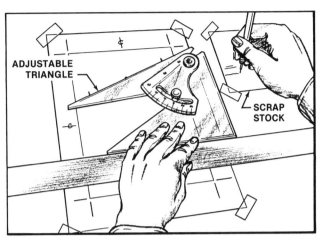

Step 2. Position triangle along guide mark. Select technical pen and test on scrap stock.

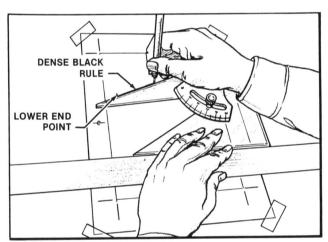

Step 3. Begin at lower end point. Guide technical pen smoothly along triangle as needle contacts artboard.

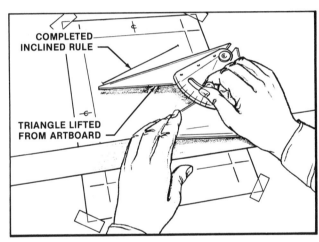

Step 4. Lift technical pen cleanly from artboard. Lift triangle carefully from artboard. Inspect quality of rule.

Figure 3-6. A 45°–90°, 30°–60°–90°, or adjustable triangle is used to guide a technical pen when inking inclined rules.

only for white opaque. An opaquing brush previously used with ink may contain ink particles which create an off-white or gray area on the artboard. A small amount of opaque paint is applied. The side of a brush is used to make corrections in large areas, and the tip of the brush is used to make corrections in tight locations. See Figure 3-8.

Liquid white opaque ink is specially formulated for use with a technical pen and is primarily used for fine, accurate corrections. Pens with a 1-point minimum size are recommended when using white opaque ink. White opaque ink should be labeled for use in a technical pen.

Liquid white opaque ink dries quickly and may cause the technical pen to become obstructed and skip. Thinning the ink with water increases the ink flow, but results in decreased opacity. A second application may be required when white opaque ink has been thinned. Technical pens should be thoroughly cleaned and filled with water after each use to avoid permanent damage to the nib. Ultrasonic pen cleaners are also available for cleaning technical pens. They are plug-in units that use a cleaning solution and clean by a vibrating wave motion.

White Tape. White tape or white pressure-sensitive paper is used for corrections in large areas or for quick corrections. The tape or paper must be thin, pure white, and opaque to provide quality reproduction. A smooth surface tape or paper provides a surface for reinking.

The type of correction material required for a job depends on the dimensions of the correction area. Pressure-sensitive paper is used to make corrections in larger areas. White tape is used to make corrections in a limited area. Correction material must be positioned carefully along rules or corners. Correction material should not be overlapped. Shadows resulting from improperly positioned correction material may reproduce on film. An L-shaped piece of tape or paper is commonly used to make corrections to 90° corners. See Figure 3-9. Correction material is aligned with the desired area with a metal T-square or triangle. Then correction material is cut with an *art knife*, a knife with a single-edge blade fastened to the end of a cylindrical body. The sharp, angular blade allows material to be cut in tight locations.

Scribing and Cutting. Scribing and cutting are techniques used to make corrections on coated artboard. *Coated artboard* is heavy white stock with a white clay coating that facilitates smooth ink coverage. *Scribing* is the process of removing an image

Drawing Wide Rules

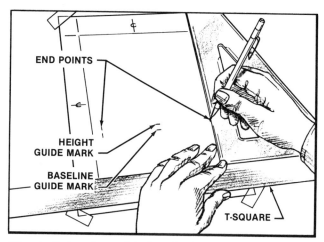

Step 1. Determine point size of rule. Lay out baseline and height guide marks and end points.

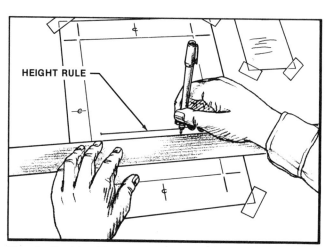

Step 2. Position T-square along height guide mark. Select 1-point technical pen and test on scrap stock. Draw 1-point rule. Reposition T-square along baseline guide mark. Draw 1-point rule.

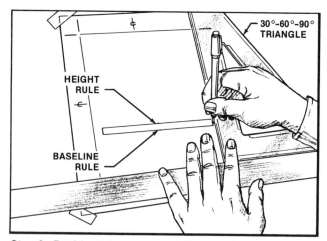

Step 3. Position triangle along left end point. Draw 1-point rule. Lift triangle carefully from artboard and reposition along right end point. Draw 1-point rule. Lift triangle carefully from artboard.

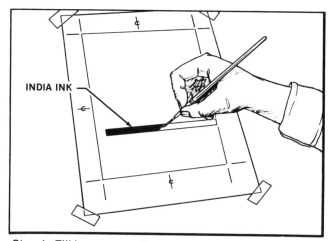

Step 4. Fill inner area using india ink and fine-bristle brush.

Figure 3-7. Wide rules are created by outlining the area with 1-point rules and filling the area with india ink.

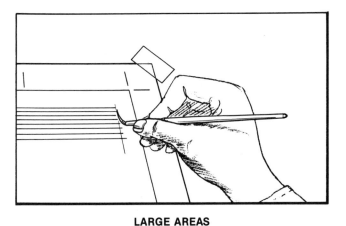

LARGE AREAS

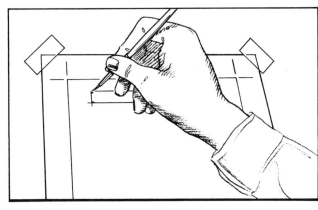

TIGHT LOCATIONS

Figure 3-8. An extra-fine bristle brush is used to apply liquid white opaque paint to an artboard. The side of the brush is used for general corrections, and the tip is used to make corrections in tight locations.

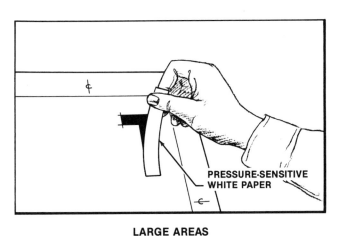

LARGE AREAS

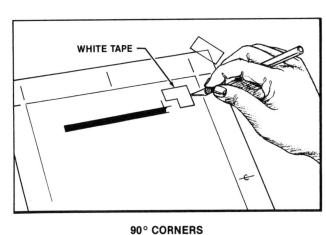

90° CORNERS

Figure 3-9. Pressure-sensitive white paper or white tape is used to cover undesired images on an artboard.

from an artboard by scratching the clay coating with the edge of an art knife. *Cutting* is the process of removing an image from an artboard by making shallow cuts around the perimeter of the image and removing the clay coating and upper layer of artboard. See Figure 3-10. A coated artboard remains white after removing an image using the scribing or cutting techniques, but the surface is not satisfactory for inking.

RULING WITH ADHESIVE MATERIAL

Adhesive material may also be used to create rules on an artboard. Adhe-

sive material is available in rolls of adhesive tape rules or sheets of preprinted adhesive rules in a variety of point sizes, patterns, and colors. See Figure 3-11. Matte-finish tape is commonly used for straight ruling. Flexible or crepe-finish tape is used for curves and irregular shapes. Sheets of preprinted rules are more expensive to use than rolls of adhesive tape rules, but preprinted rules are more accurate. Preprinted sheets of rules cause less shadowing than rolls because they are printed on thinner material.

Ruling Techniques

Rules from a roll or sheet are pasted

up on an artboard using different methods because the substrate on which the rules are printed is different. Adhesive tape rules are made of a heavy-gauge plastic or paper that is precut to various widths, creating assorted weights. Preprinted rules are printed on large sheets of acetate.

Adhesive tape rules must be removed from the roll carefully to avoid stretching or buckling the rules. A piece of tape slightly longer than required is cut from the roll. The tape should be held taut, but excessive tension should not be applied. The tape is held at both ends and carefully aligned with the guideline. The

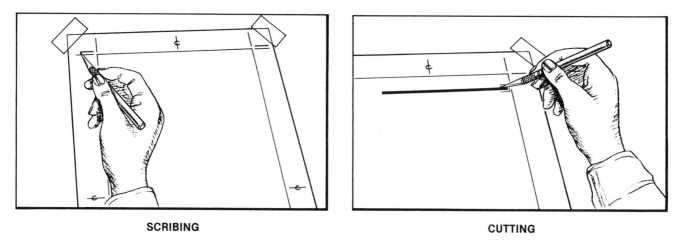

SCRIBING   **CUTTING**

Figure 3-10. Corrections to coated artboard are made by scribing or cutting away the undesired image.

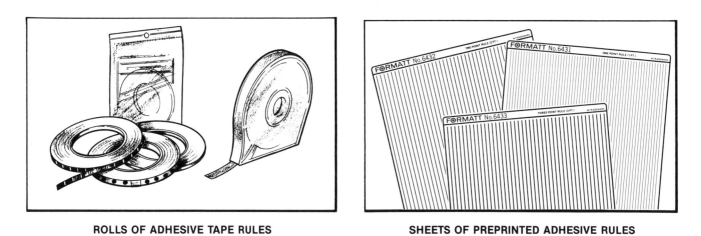

ROLLS OF ADHESIVE TAPE RULES   **SHEETS OF PREPRINTED ADHESIVE RULES**

Figure 3-11. Adhesive rules and patterns are available in rolls and preprinted sheets.

position of the rule is verified with a T-square or triangle. If the tape is inaccurately aligned, it is removed by pulling at a close angle to the artboard to avoid tearing the surface of the artboard. See Figure 3-12. When the tape is aligned properly, excess tape is removed from the ends of the rule with an art knife, and a sheet of tissue is placed over the rule. Then the rule is *burnished,* or applied to the artboard by rubbing the surface with a flat, dull, plastic instrument called a *burnisher* which is used to transfer pressure to copy on an artboard.

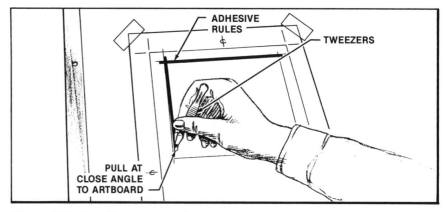

Figure 3-12. An adhesive tape rule is removed by pulling it at a close angle to the artboard.

Transparent or frosted acetate is used as a substrate for preprinted sheets of rules. A light adhesive coating is applied to the back of the acetate so that the rules will adhere to an artboard. When applying rules, the acetate is cut approximately 1/16″ larger than the rule to allow for a margin. The rule is carefully lifted from the paper backing. Contact between the adhesive coating and dust, dirt, and oil from fingers should be avoided. Tweezers or the edge of an art knife blade is commonly used to handle rules to avoid marring the surface.

Quality tweezers have a flat end and loose tension between the prongs. See Figure 3-13. The rule is carefully aligned with the guideline and lightly rubbed. If the rule is positioned inaccurately, it is carefully lifted and reapplied. The rule is then covered with a sheet of tissue and burnished thoroughly into position.

Adhesive rules are generally applied to guidelines on an artboard. The bottoms of horizontal rules are aligned with the horizontal guidelines. Vertical rules are applied to the insides of vertical guidelines. See Figure 3-14. Mitered or overlapped rules may be used to create various shapes. Mitered rules are used for 90° angles. Overlapped rules are used for intersections that are not 90° angles and column rules within tables or charts.

Mitered Corners. Mitered corners are used to give the artboard a professional appearance. Mitered rules are used to create 90° angles by cutting the intersecting rules at 45° angles. The triangle method is commonly used to create mitered corners. See Figure 3-15.

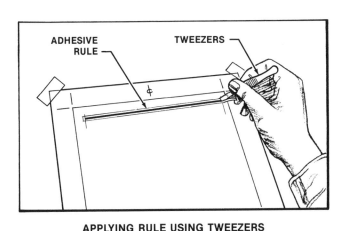

APPLYING RULE USING TWEEZERS

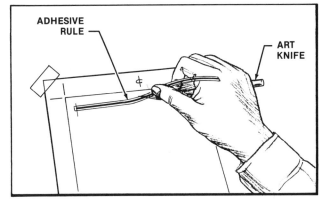

APPLYING RULE USING ART KNIFE

Figure 3-13. Tweezers or the edge of an art knife is used to position rules from preprinted sheets.

Figure 3-14. The bottom of a horizontal rule is applied to horizontal guidelines. Vertical rules are applied to the insides of vertical guidelines.

1. Lay out guidelines for the rule on an artboard. Apply adhesive rules to the inside of the guidelines, and burnish lightly to secure them in position.

2. Position a triangle across the corner intersecting the inside and outside corners.

3. Position an art knife blade along the edge of the triangle, and guide the blade from the inside corner to the outside corner.

4. Remove excess rules using tweezers or the point of an art knife. Burnish the rules thoroughly.

The blade pressure method may

Mitering Ruled Corners—Triangle Method

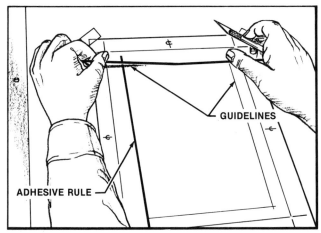

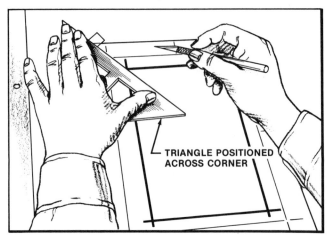

Step 1. Lay out guidelines on artboard. Apply rules and burnish lightly.

Step 2. Position triangle across corner.

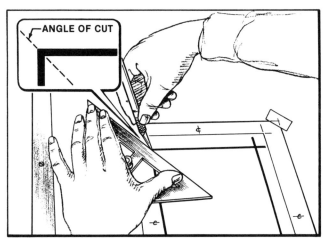

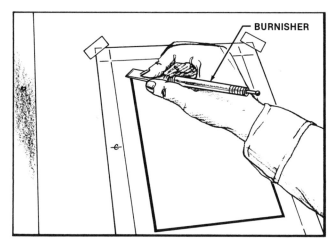

Step 3. Guide blade from inside to outside of corner.

Step 4. Remove excess rule and burnish thoroughly.

Figure 3-15. A triangle is used as a guide for an art knife when mitering corners.

also be used to miter corners. An art knife blade is placed across the corner and pressed firmly to the artboard to cut the rule. See Figure 3-16.

1. Lay out guidelines for the rule on an artboard. Apply adhesive rules to the inside of the guidelines and burnish lightly.

2. Position an art knife blade across the corner while intersecting the inside and outside corners. Apply firm pressure to the blade until the rules are completely cut.

3. Remove excess rules using tweezers or the point of an art knife.

4. Burnish the rules thoroughly.

Overlapped Corners. Overlapped corners are created by placing a rule over another rule and cutting it in the center. Multiple overlapped rules are commonly used to create columns for a table or chart. See Figure 3-17.

1. Lay out guidelines for the rules on an artboard. Apply border rules to

Mitering Ruled Corners—Blade Pressure Method

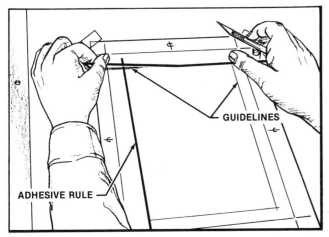

Step 1. Lay out guidelines on artboard. Apply rules and burnish lightly.

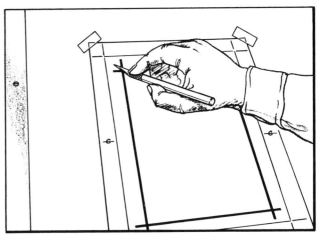

Step 2. Position art knife blade across corner. Apply pressure to blade to cut rules.

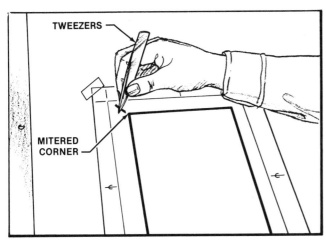

Step 3. Remove excess rule.

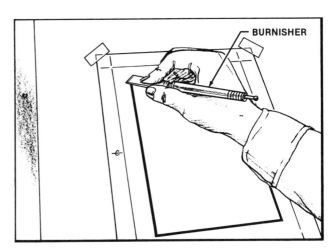

Step 4. Burnish thoroughly.

Figure 3-16. An art knife blade is positioned across a corner, and pressure is applied to cut through the rules.

the inside of the guidelines. Apply column rules, and burnish lightly to secure in position.

2. Cut column rules in the center of the border rules.

3. Remove excess rules using tweezers or the point of an art knife.

4. Burnish the rules thoroughly.

Flexible Tape. Flexible tape is used to create curved rules. The crinkled surface of the flexible tape allows it to be easily stretched and formed to create curves. See Figure 3-18. Flexible tape is available in different thicknesses and colors and is ideal for the preparation of graphs.

1. Lay out a guideline in the desired curved shape for the rule on an artboard. Remove the flexible tape from the roll as it is applied to the artboard.

2. Stretch and form the rule to the shape of the guideline. Burnish the rule thoroughly.

Applying Overlapping Rules

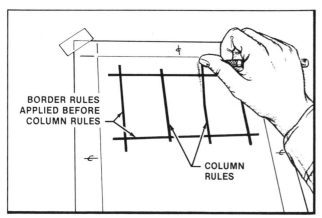

Step 1. Lay out guidelines on artboard. Apply rules and burnish lightly.

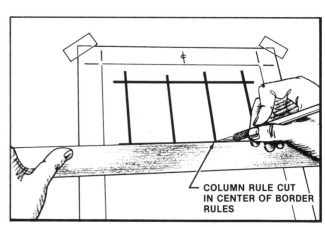

Step 2. Cut column rules in center of border rules.

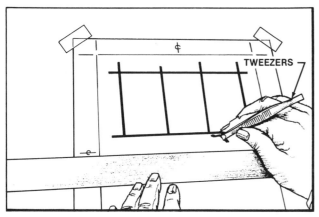

Step 3. Remove excess rules.

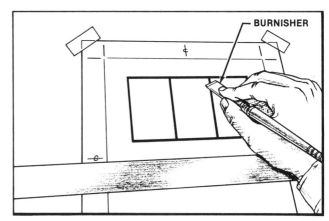

Step 4. Burnish thoroughly.

Figure 3-17. Border rules are positioned and burnished lightly before applying column rules. Column rules are cut in the center of the border rules, and the excess is removed.

Applying Flexible Tape

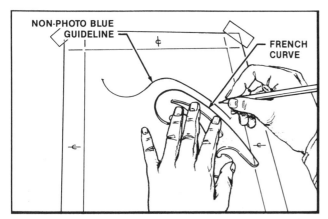

Step 1. Lay out guideline on artboard. Apply flexible tape.

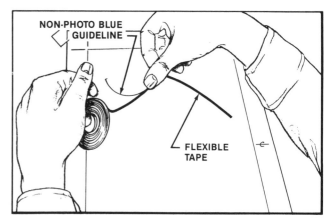

Step 2. Stretch and form rule to guideline. Burnish thoroughly.

Figure 3-18. Flexible tape is used to create curved rules.

3 Ruling

True-False

T　F　**1.** A rule is a line that is reproduced on a printed piece.

T　F　**2.** A rule on an artboard is drawn in non-photo blue ink.

T　F　**3.** A technical pen is used to draw 2 × 0 to 14-point rules.

T　F　**4.** A technical pen and fine-bristle brush are used to create wide rules.

T　F　**5.** Guidelines on an artboard for multiple rules may cause improper ink coverage.

T　F　**6.** A rule scale is used to measure the weight of a rule.

T　F　**7.** Undesired images on film may be impossible to correct.

T　F　**8.** India ink is used to create the inner area of a wide rule.

T　F　**9.** Scribing and cutting are techniques used to make corrections on coated and uncoated artboards.

T　F　**10.** A burnisher secures the artboard to the top of the table.

T　F　**11.** Adhesive material may be used to create rules on an artboard.

Multiple Choice

_____　**1.** The weight of a rule is measured in _____.
　　　　　A. picas
　　　　　B. points
　　　　　C. inches
　　　　　D. agates

_____　**2.** _____ is the process of removing an image from an artboard by scratching the clay coating.
　　　　　A. Cutting
　　　　　B. Ruling
　　　　　C. Scribing
　　　　　D. none of the above

_____　**3.** A _____ is used to guide a technical pen when drawing horizontal rules.
　　　　　A. T-square
　　　　　B. triangle
　　　　　C. ruler
　　　　　D. protractor

_____　**4.** A _____ is used to guide a technical pen when drawing vertical and inclined rules.
　　　　　A. T-square
　　　　　B. triangle
　　　　　C. ruler
　　　　　D. protractor

5. _____ is the process of applying copy to an artboard by rubbing the surface with a dull, plastic instrument.
   A. Mitering
   B. Burnishing
   C. Scribing
   D. Cutting

6. Rules on a transparent or frosted substrate should be cut approximately _____ ″ larger than the rule.
   A. ¹⁄₆₄
   B. ¹⁄₃₂
   C. ¹⁄₁₆
   D. ⅛

7. Mitered corners create _____° angles.
   A. 15
   B. 30
   C. 45
   D. 90

8. A #_____ extra-fine bristle brush is used to apply liquid white opaque in tight locations.
   A. 0
   B. 00
   C. 000
   D. 00000

9. White tape or white pressure-sensitive paper should be _____ to provide quality reproduction.
   A. pure white
   B. thin
   C. opaque
   D. all of the above

Completion

1. Only dense _____ ink reproduces clearly on the film.

2. The _____ of a brush is used to make corrections in large areas.

3. The _____ of a brush is used to make corrections in tight locations.

4. A(n) _____ is used to facilitate the placement of copy without fingerprints, dust, or dirt.

5. A(n) _____ is a flat, dull, plastic instrument used to secure copy in position.

6. Two intersecting rules are cut at _____° angles to create a mitered corner.

Matching

1. Matte-finish tape
2. Flexible tape
3. Adhesive tape rules
4. Preprinted rules

A. Made of heavy-gauge plastic
B. Used for straight line ruling
C. Used for curved ruling
D. Printed on large sheets of acetate

4 SPECIALIZED ART ELEMENTS

Specialized art elements are art elements that enhance the appearance of a printed piece. Specialized art elements are combined with copy, illustrations, photographs, and rules. Specialized art elements include circles, curves, borders, and tint screens. Circles are drawn or traced with a compass or circle template. Curves are drawn or traced with an irregular curve or flexible curve. Borders are mitered to produce 90° corners, or preprinted adhesive corners are used to produce curved borders. Ornate borders are commonly created with preprinted adhesive material. Adhesive tint screens are used to add depth to an illustration. Film tint screens create a lighter value of a solid color.

CIRCLES AND CURVES

Circles and curves are used on various types of printed pieces to increase the communicative ability or enhance the appearance of the piece. Charts, graphs, borders, and advertisements commonly use circles and curves to communicate more effectively.

Creating Circles

Diameter is the distance across a circle while intersecting the center point. Circles are created by drawing or tracing depending on their diameters. A compass is used to draw a circle with a 3″ minimum diameter. A circle template is used to trace circles smaller than 3″ in diameter.

All circles, drawn or traced, must be neatly and accurately created. Each *quadrant*, or one-fourth of a circle, must be identical. Line thickness should be uniform throughout the circumference.

Compass. A *compass* is an instrument used to draw circles of varying sizes. See Figure 4-1. A *bow compass* is commonly used to draw circles from 3″ to 10″ in diameter. A bow compass consists of two legs that are joined at a pivot point, a handle, and an adjustment mechanism. A removable leg enables accessories, such as a technical pen, ruling pen, or scribe, to be used with the compass. A *beam compass* is used to draw circles larger than 10″ in diameter. A beam compass consists of a horizontal beam with two adjustable legs that can be positioned at any point along the beam.

A compass is adjusted to the desired dimension by verifying the size against the comprehensive layout or determining the diameter and calculating the radius. The compass is then adjusted to the radius dimension. The *radius* is the distance from the center point to the circumference or the diameter divided by 2. The point of the compass is placed at the center point of the circle. The point

holds the compass securely in position as the other leg is rotated. The handle is grasped between the index finger and thumb, and the compass is rotated smoothly. See Figure 4-2.

1. Lay out the center point and radius of the circle on an artboard. Place the compass point on the artboard at the center point.

2. Hold the compass with the thumb and index finger, keeping the compass perpendicular to the artboard. Draw a circle using a smooth, rotational motion. Carefully remove the compass, and inspect the circle for quality.

Circle Template. A *circle template* is a thin piece of plastic or metal with circles of various sizes cut in it. The edges of the circles should be beveled to prevent ink from bleeding under the template. See Figure 4-3. Centering guides along the edge of a circle are aligned with non-photo blue crosshairs on the artboard. The circle is traced by guiding a technical pen smoothly along the circumference of

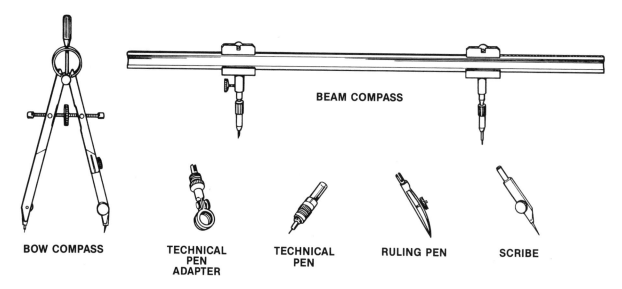

BEAM COMPASS

BOW COMPASS   TECHNICAL   TECHNICAL   RULING PEN   SCRIBE
              PEN   PEN
              ADAPTER

Figure 4-1. A compass is used to draw circles. Accessories allow the compass to be used for a variety of purposes.

Drawing a Circle

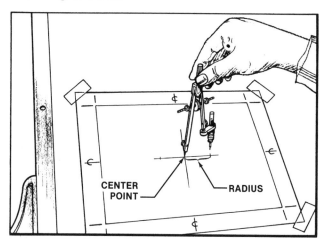

Step 1. Lay out center point and radius. Place compass point on center point.

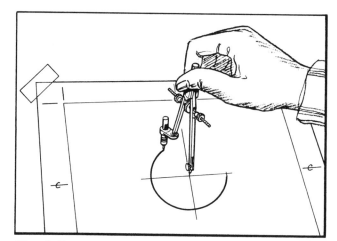

Step 2. Rotate compass smoothly. Carefully remove compass and inspect quality of circle.

Figure 4-2. The center point and radius of a circle are laid out on an artboard in non-photo blue. The compass is rotated smoothly to ensure a crisp, clean circle.

the circle. See Figure 4-4.

1. Lay out vertical and horizontal non-photo blue crosshairs on an artboard. Align the centering guides on the circle template with the crosshairs.

2. Guide a technical pen around the circumference of the circle, keeping the pen perpendicular to the artboard. Carefully lift the template from the artboard, and inspect the circle for quality.

Creating Curves

Curves are drawn or traced using an irregular curve, or flexible curve, as a guide. An *irregular curve*, or french curve, is a clear plastic instrument with a variety of curves along the edges. A *flexible curve* is a flexible ruler consisting of a lead bar encased in smooth plastic. See Figure 4-5. Drawing charts, graphs, or maps, and

aligning irregular type involves using an irregular curve or flexible curve.

Irregular Curve. An irregular curve is used to draw curves or irregular shapes. A set of irregular curves is commonly used to create complex curves. An irregular curve is adjusted frequently to align with guidelines or guide marks on an artboard. A minimum of three guide marks should be

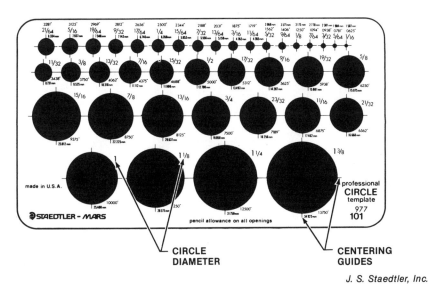

CIRCLE DIAMETER

CENTERING GUIDES

Figure 4-3. A circle template is used to trace a circle smaller than 3″ in diameter.

aligned with the irregular curve at all times. A line is drawn only between two of the guide marks, and the irregular curve is repositioned to align with three more guide marks. See Figure 4-6.

1. Lay out guide marks for the curve on an artboard.

2. Align an irregular curve with a minimum of three consecutive guide marks. Guide a technical pen along the edge of the irregular curve connecting the two guide marks.

3. Carefully lift the irregular curve from the artboard, and reposition it to align with a minimum of three consecutive guide marks. Guide a technical pen along the edge of the irregular curve connecting the two guide marks.

Tracing a Circle

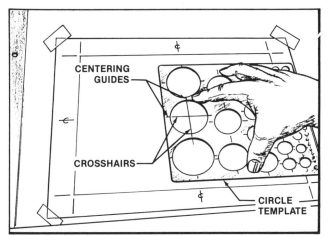

CENTERING GUIDES

CROSSHAIRS

CIRCLE TEMPLATE

Step 1. Lay out crosshairs. Align centering guides with crosshairs.

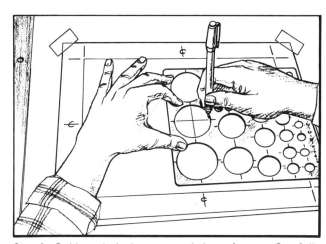

Step 2. Guide technical pen around circumference. Carefully lift template and inspect quality of circle.

Figure 4-4. The centering guides on a circle template are aligned with non-photo blue crosshairs on the artboard. The technical pen should be held perpendicular to the artboard.

IRREGULAR CURVES

FLEXIBLE CURVE

Figure 4-5. An irregular curve or flexible curve is used as a guide when drawing curves.

Drawing a Curve

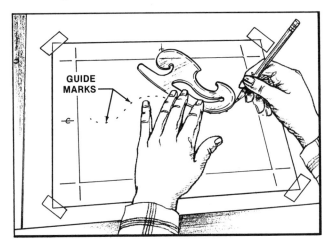

Step 1. Lay out guide marks.

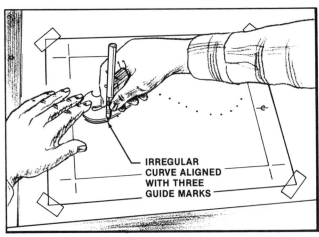

Step 2. Align irregular curve with three consecutive guide marks. Draw line connecting guide marks.

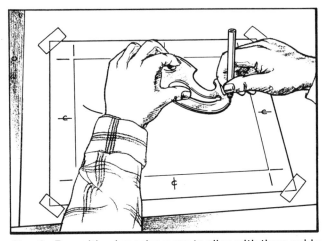

Step 3. Reposition irregular curve to align with three guide marks. Draw line connecting guide marks.

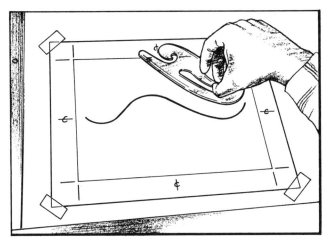

Step 4. Repeat process to complete curve. Inspect quality of curve.

Figure 4-6. An irregular curve is aligned with a minimum of three consecutive points, and a line is drawn between two end points.

4. Carefully lift the irregular curve, and repeat the process until the curve is complete. Inspect the quality of the curve.

Flexible Curve. A flexible curve is used as a guide to trace curves without the tedious task of repositioning an irregular curve. Most wide curves can be traced using a flexible curve, but curves less than 1″ diameter should be drawn with an irregular curve. See Figure 4-7.

1. Align a flexible curve with the desired curve on the comprehensive lay-

out. Position the flexible curve on an artboard without changing its shape.

2. Guide a technical pen along the beveled edge of the flexible curve. Carefully lift the flexible curve from the artboard, and inspect the quality of the curve.

BORDERS

Borders are art elements, such as lines or designs, that surround a printed piece or group similar elements. Borders are used to promote eye movement and provide continuity for a printed piece. See Figure 4-8.

Preprinted borders are commonly available from copy-free illustration catalogs. Although preprinted borders are easy to use, they are not always proportional to the shape of the printed piece. A paste-up artist may create a border when preprinted borders are not available in the correct size, shape, or style.

Creating Borders

Borders are created by altering a preprinted border to conform to job requirements. Preprinted borders can be cut and pieced together to fit the

Tracing a Curve

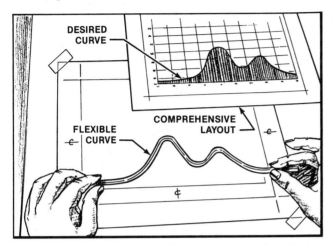

Step 1. Align flexible curve with curve on comprehensive layout. Position flexible curve on artboard.

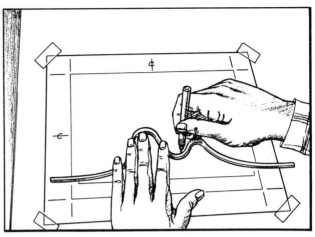

Step 2. Guide technical pen along flexible curve. Carefully lift flexible curve and inspect quality of curve.

Figure 4-7. A flexible curve is aligned with a curve on the comprehensive layout and repositioned on the artboard.

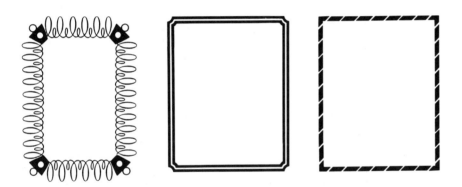

Figure 4-8. Borders promote eye movement and provide continuity for a printed piece.

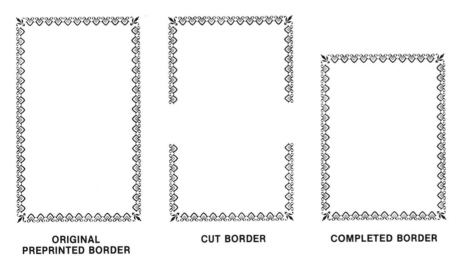

ORIGINAL PREPRINTED BORDER   CUT BORDER   COMPLETED BORDER

Figure 4-9. Preprinted borders can be cut and manipulated to fit a required area.

required area. See Figure 4-9. Altering a preprinted border may be more time-consuming than creating a border through other methods. Rules are used to create a dramatic border when mitered at the corners. Borders that are inked and curved around the text are simple, yet effective. Ornate borders, commonly used on certificates and bonds, are easily adapted to most square or rectangular shapes.

Mitered Border. A mitered border is cut at a 45° angle at each corner to form a 90° angle. Adhesive materials are commonly used to create mitered borders. Creating a mitered border is similar to creating a miter with rules. A triangle is positioned across the corner, and an art knife is used to cut the border; or an art knife is positioned across the corner, and pressure is applied to cut through the border. The excess border is removed, and the border is burnished thoroughly.

Curved Border. A curved border is created by using preprinted adhesive corners and rules or by drawing the border with ink. Preprinted adhesive corners, or *elbows,* are available in a variety of styles and sizes. Preprinted sheets of elbows are preferable to adhesive tapes because tape is inconsistent in weight. See Figure 4-10.

1. Lay out guidelines for the border on an artboard.

2. Apply elbows to the inside of the guidelines at each corner.

3. Apply adhesive rules to the inside of the guidelines along the top, bottom, and sides, overlapping the rules approximately ⅛″.

4. Cut the adhesive rules allowing an overlap of approximately 1/16″ at each corner. Remove excess rules, and burnish thoroughly.

Inked curved borders may be drawn to any size and shape. Corners and rule weight do not limit the size that a radius can be. The rules are drawn on the artboard, and corners are drawn on a separate sheet of coated stock then transferred onto the artboard. See Figure 4-11.

1. Lay out guide marks for the border on an artboard. Draw horizontal and vertical rules with a technical pen.

2. Lay out non-photo blue crosshairs on a separate sheet of coated stock. Trace a circle with a technical pen using a circle template.

3. Cut the circle along the nonphoto blue crosshairs, creating four quadrants.

4. Position the quadrants in the corners of the inked rules, aligning the circle rules to the border rules. Burnish the coated stock thoroughly, and remove adhesive residue.

Ornate Border. An ornate border is commonly created with preprinted adhesive material. Some ornate borders are easily adapted to various size jobs, although intricate borders

Creating Curved Borders Using Adhesive Material

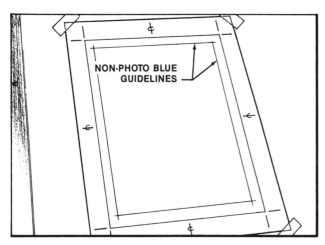

Step 1. Lay out guidelines.

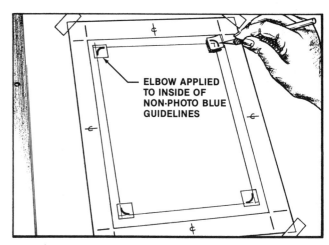

Step 2. Apply elbows to guidelines.

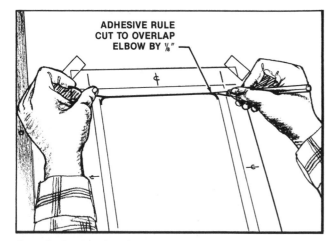

Step 3. Apply adhesive rules.

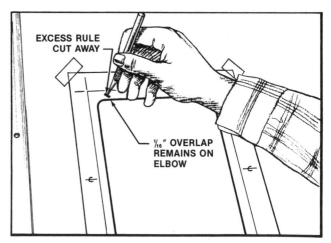

Step 4. Cut adhesive rules. Remove excess and burnish thoroughly.

Figure 4-10. Adhesive rules and elbows may be used to create curved borders.

Creating Curved Borders Using Ink

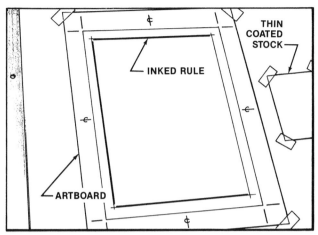

Step 1. Lay out guide marks. Draw horizontal and vertical rules with technical pen.

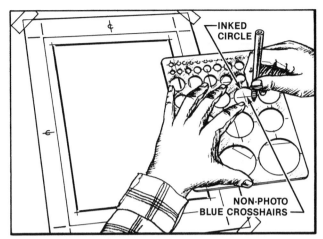

Step 2. Lay out crosshairs. Trace circle with technical pen.

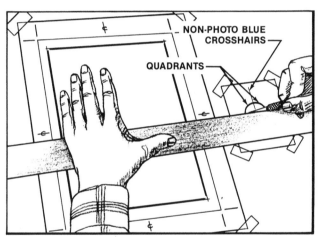

Step 3. Cut circle into quadrants.

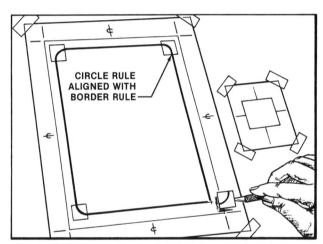

Step 4. Position quadrants. Burnish thoroughly. Remove adhesive residue.

Figure 4-11. The radius of inked curved borders is not limited by corners or rule weight.

may require using the cut-and-butt technique. The cut-and-butt technique is used to splice and align two images next to one another. See Figure 4-12.

1. Lay out guidelines for the border on an artboard. Align the upper right corner of the border with the upper right corner of the guidelines. Lightly burnish in position.

2. Cut the border in half using a sharp art knife.

3. Lift the left side of the border. Align the upper left corner of the border with the upper left corner of the guidelines. Lightly burnish in position.

4. Make sure the top and bottom pattern of the overlapping area match. Cut the border at the point where the top and bottom patterns overlap.

5. Remove excess border material.

6. Reposition the two sections of border, and burnish thoroughly. Repeat the process for the other sides of the border.

TINT SCREENS

Tint screens are values or shades of color created by a screened pattern.

Tint screens are an illusion created through the use of a dot pattern. The reflection of the stock surrounding the dots is perceived by the eye as values or shades of a color. Dark ink values are obtained with closely spaced dots, and lighter ink values are obtained with dots spaced farther apart. The value of a color created by a tint screen is designated by percentage and screen ruling. Percentages of tint screens range from 3% to 95%. Solid ink coverage is designated as 100%.

Screen ruling is the coarseness of

Creating Ornate Borders

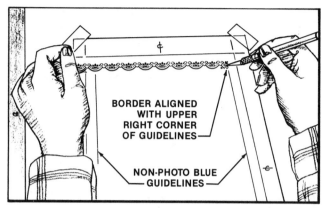

Step 1. Lay out guidelines. Align border with guidelines. Burnish lightly.

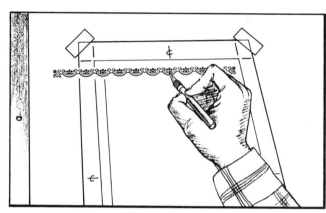

Step 2. Cut border with art knife.

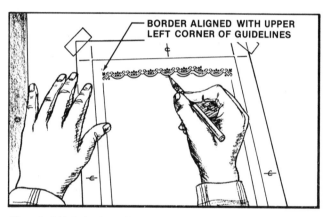

Step 3. Lift left side of border. Align left side of border with guideline. Burnish lightly.

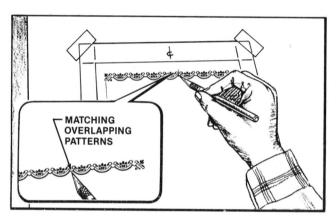

Step 4. After matching top and bottom patterns at area of overlap, cut the border at point of overlap.

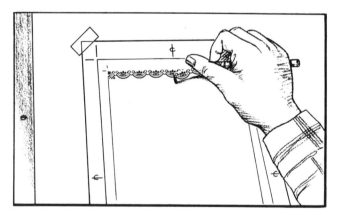

Step 5. Remove excess border.

Step 6. Reposition border and burnish thoroughly.

Figure 4-12. Preprinted adhesive material is used to create an ornate border.

a tint screen. Screen rulings are expressed as lines. A *line* is the number of dots per linear inch. Fine tint screens have many small dots, and coarse screens have fewer and larger dots. A high numerical value for a screen ruling indicates a fine tint screen. A low numerical value for a screen ruling indicates a coarse tint screen. Screen rulings commonly range from 25 line to 300 line. See Figure 4-13.

A tint screen is applied to a mechanical during paste-up or to film during stripping. An adhesive tint screen is used for paste-up, and a film tint screen is used for stripping. Reproduction quality and exactness of the job must be considered before selecting the type of tint screen to be used.

Adhesive Tint Screens

Adhesive tint screens are printed in black ink on thin sheets of acetate.

Adhesive tint screens in dot, rule, and circle patterns are used to add depth and definition to illustrations.

Dot pattern adhesive tint screens that are commonly used range from 27.5 line through 85 line screen rulings. Dot pattern screen rulings that are finer than 100 line are difficult to photograph without loss of dots. Adhesive tint screens are adhered directly to a mechanical and photographed with type and illustrations. See Figure 4-14.

1. Cut an adhesive tint screen approximately ½″ larger than dimensions of area to be screened. Carefully remove adhesive tint screen from protective backing.

2. Place the tint screen over the object to be screened and lightly burnish.

3. Cut the tint screen to the desired shape. Lift away excess adhesive tint screen.

4. Burnish tint screen thoroughly.

Most tint screens are not designed to overlap one another. Rules are used to cover the overlap when two or more tint screens are adjacent to one another. Overlapped adhesive tint screens may result in a moiré or a rosette. A *moiré* is an undesirable pattern produced by incorrect alignment and overlapping of dot pattern tint screens. A *rosette* is a desirable pattern produced by overlapped dot pattern tint screens. See Figure 4-15.

Texturing and Mapping. *Texturing* is the process of adding depth or texture to an illustration using an adhesive tint screen. The tint screen pattern selected is based on the depth or texture desired for an illustration. *Mapping*, or benday, is the process of defining areas of an illustration by using a variety of tint screen patterns. Screen patterns should differ from one another, yet maintain continuity

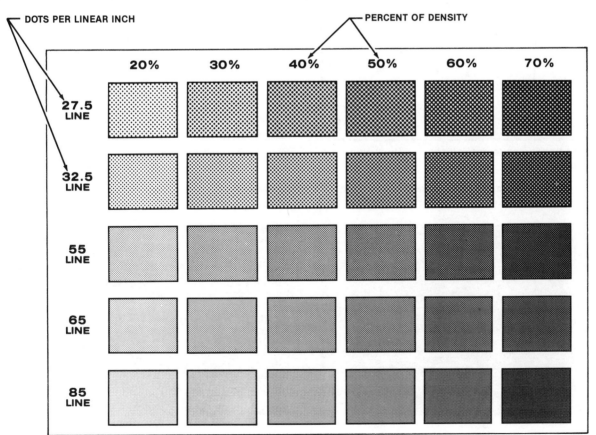

Graphic Products Corp.

Figure 4-13. Tint screens are an illusion created through the use of a dot pattern. A line is the number of dots per linear inch.

Applying Adhesive Tint Screens

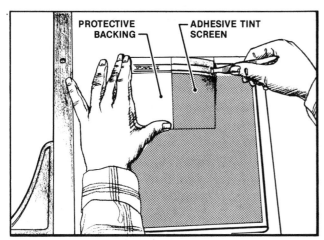

Step 1. Cut adhesive tint screen. Remove from backing.

Step 2. Place tint screen over object to be screened.

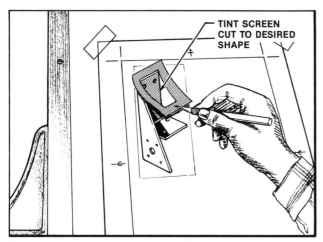

Step 3. Cut tint screen to desired shape. Lift away excess tint screen.

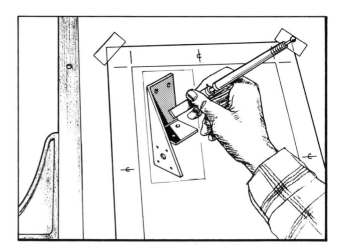

Step 4. Burnish thoroughly.

Figure 4-14. Adhesive tint screens are applied directly to a mechanical.

MOIRÉ

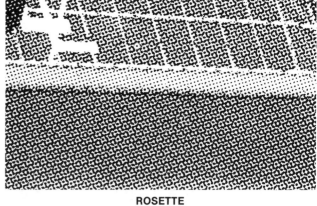

ROSETTE

Figure 4-15. A moiré is an undesirable tint screen pattern produced by incorrect alignment of overlapped dot pattern tint screens. A rosette is a desirable tint screen pattern produced by overlapped dot pattern tint screens.

in the illustration. The screen patterns are usually separated by rules. See Figure 4-16.

Film Tint Screens

Film tint screens create a better quality reproduction for fine line rulings than adhesive tint screens. A paste-up artist does not use film tint screens in the preparation of a mechanical because the tint screens are not photographically reproduced. Film tint screens are applied to film negatives during the stripping process. Film tint screens are taped to the flat before the plate is burned and allow only a portion of the light to reach the plate. Film tint screens are commonly dot patterns ranging from 3% to 95% with 65 line to 300 line screen rulings. A paste-up artist indicates a film tint screen by placing red keylines on the mechanical or writing instructions on a tissue overlay covering the mechanical.

Red Keylines. Red keylines on a mechanical indicate the position of an element not directly pasted on it. The area of a printed piece that is to be tinted is indicated by drawing the boundaries in red ink on the mechanical. Red ink reproduces as a clear line on the film negative. See Figure 4-17. A red keyline is for indication only and is not meant as copy for reproduction. The stripper tapes the tint screen on a separate piece of goldenrod in the position indicated by the keyline. The stripper does not allow the keyline to print on the printed piece.

Tissue Overlay. A tissue overlay indicates where a tint screen is to be printed. Type or illustrations are commonly printed in a lighter ink value and must be reproduced with a film tint screen. An adhesive tint screen cannot be used to make type or illustrations a lighter color value. Detailed instructions on a tissue overlay indicate the position, screen ruling, and percentage of the tinted element. See Figure 4-18.

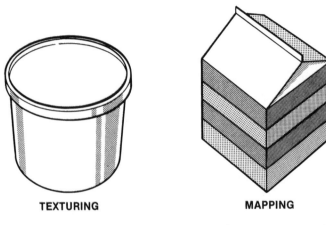

TEXTURING   **MAPPING**

Figure 4-16. Texturing is the process of adding depth or texture to an illustration. Mapping is the process of defining areas of an illustration using a variety of tint screens.

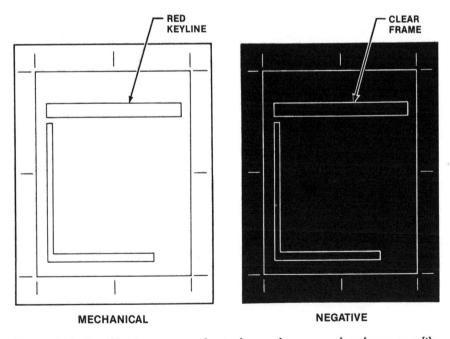

RED KEYLINE

CLEAR FRAME

MECHANICAL   **NEGATIVE**

Figure 4-17. A red keyline on a mechanical reproduces as a clear frame on a film negative.

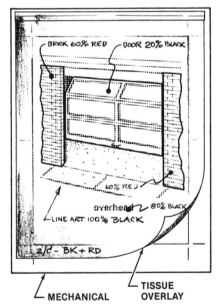

BRICK 60% RED — DOOR 20% BLACK

60% RED

overhead — 80% BLACK

LINE ART 100% BLACK

2/c - BK + RD

MECHANICAL   TISSUE OVERLAY

Figure 4-18. A film tint screen is used when type or illustrations are printed in a lighter value of ink. Detailed instructions on a tissue overlay indicate where type or an illustration is to be tinted.

4 Specialized Art Elements

True-False

T F **1.** A compass is used to draw circles with a 3″ minimum diameter.

T F **2.** The diameter is one-half the distance across a circle while intersecting the center point.

T F **3.** A removable arm on a compass enables accessories to be used with the compass.

T F **4.** A quadrant is one-half of a circle.

T F **5.** A border is the white space surrounding the image area of a printed piece.

T F **6.** A circle is traced with a compass.

T F **7.** A minimum of three guide marks should be aligned with the edge of an irregular curve when drawing a curve.

T F **8.** Curves less than 1″ in diameter are drawn with a flexible curve.

T F **9.** A mitered border is created by cutting the corners of the border at a 90° angle.

T F **10.** A film tint screen is applied to a mechanical.

T F **11.** Dark ink values are obtained with a closely spaced tint screen pattern.

T F **12.** Large screen rulings indicate a coarse tint screen.

T F **13.** A rosette is an undesirable pattern produced by overlapped dot pattern tint screens.

T F **14.** Mapping is the process of adding depth or texture to an illustration.

T F **15.** Red keylines are used to indicate the position of an element not directly pasted on the mechanical.

Multiple Choice

_____ **1.** A(n) _____ curve is a plastic instrument with a variety of curves cut along the edges.
  A. Swiss
  B. irregular
  C. flexible
  D. none of the above

_____ **2.** A(n) _____ curve is easily formed to align with wide curves.
  A. Swiss
  B. irregular
  C. flexible
  D. none of above

_____ 3. _____ are art elements used to promote eye movement and provide continuity for a printed piece.
   A. Borders
   B. Margins
   C. Circles
   D. Curves

_____ 4. _____ are preprinted adhesive corners.
   A. Curves
   B. Elbows
   C. Borders
   D. Quadrants

_____ 5. A(n) _____ is used to trace circles smaller than 3″ in diameter.
   A. compass
   B. irregular curve
   C. flexible curve
   D. circle template

_____ 6. The _____ of a circle is the distance from the center point to the circumference.
   A. diameter
   B. quadrant
   C. radius
   D. secant

_____ 7. A _____ is used to draw circles larger than 10″ in diameter.
   A. flexible curve
   B. circle template
   C. beam compass
   D. bow compass

_____ 8. A(n) _____ is a ruler consisting of a lead bar encased in a smooth plastic case.
   A. flexible curve
   B. irregular curve
   C. circle template
   D. french curve

_____ 9. Screen ruling is the _____ of a tint screen.
   A. percentage
   B. density
   C. coarseness
   D. all of the above

_____ 10. _____ are values or shades of color created by a screened pattern.
   A. Moirés
   B. Screen rulings
   C. Rosettes
   D. Tint screens

Matching

_____ 1. Template

_____ 2. Bow compass

_____ 3. Beam compass

_____ 4. Flexible curve

_____ 5. Tint screen

_____ 6. Adhesive tint screen

_____ 7. Film tint screen

_____ 8. 100%

_____ 9. 65 line

_____ 10. 300 line

_____ 11. Benday

A. Mapping
B. Coarse screen ruling
C. Applied in paste-up
D. Value of color
E. Tool for tracing circles
F. Tool for drawing circles 3″ to 10″ in diameter
G. Tool for drawing circles above 10″ in diameter
H. Fine screen ruling
I. Solid ink coverage
J. Applied in stripping
K. Tool for tracing curves

Completion

_____ 1. A(n) _____ keyline is for indication only and is not meant to reproduce.

_____ 2. _____ ink coverage is designated as 100%.

_____ 3. Screens with large screen ruling are _____ line screens.

_____ 4. Screens with low screen ruling are _____ line screens.

_____ 5. _____ screens are used for tint screens that are applied to the mechanical.

_____ 6. _____ screens are used for tint screens that are applied during stripping.

_____ 7. A(n) _____ is an undesirable tint screen pattern.

_____ 8. A(n) _____ is a desirable tint screen pattern.

_____ 9. Mapping is another term for _____.

_____ 10. _____ adds depth in an illustration.

Identification

_____ **1.** Ruling pen

_____ **2.** Scribe

_____ **3.** Technical pen

_____ **4.** Texturing

_____ **5.** Moiré

_____ **6.** Mapping

_____ **7.** Rosette

(A)

(B)

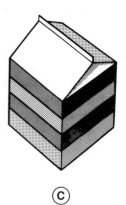

(C)

(D)

(E)

(F)

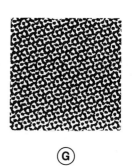

(G)

5 TYPOGRAPHY

The designer and paste-up artist use typography to communicate effectively and efficiently with the typesetter. A designer identifies the anatomy of a character and a word. Basic guidelines regarding legibility and readability help determine the appropriate typestyle and size. A type arrangement is selected to develop the desired appearance. Type arrangement affects the readability and aesthetics of a printed piece, while type classifications create the mood and appearance. Copyfitting, proofreading, and type specification allow a designer to effectively communicate with a typesetter.

TYPE LEGIBILITY AND READABILITY

Type legibility and readability affect how the reader perceives the layout of a printed piece. *Type legibility* is the visual distinction between individual letters or groups of letters. *Type readability* is the speed at which the words are perceived. The anatomy of a word, typographical layout, type specifications, and type classifications are of primary concern to a designer and typesetter. A paste-up artist also uses these elements to visualize the spatial relationship between type and layout.

Anatomy of a Word

The anatomy of a word refers to the structure of the characters. *Characters* are the letters of the alphabet, numerals, punctuation marks, and other symbols used in typesetting. Characters are categorized as uppercase characters and lowercase char-acters. *Uppercase characters,* or capital letters, rest on a baseline and extend upward. *Lowercase characters,* or small letters, rest on a baseline and may extend above or below the baseline. See Figure 5-1. Lowercase characters are composed of an x-height and may have an ascender or a descender. The *x-height,* or body, is the area between the baseline and approximately one-half the height of an uppercase character. An *ascender* is the portion of a lowercase character that extends above the x-height. A *descender* is the portion of a lower-case character that extends below the x-height.

The legibility and readability of a typestyle, or typeface, are determined by the shape and size of the x-height, ascender, and descender. A typestyle with a tall x-height and a wide open area is more legible than a typestyle with a short, thin x-height. Ascenders and descenders of moderate length are more legible than those that are shortened or elongated. The eye defines a word composed of lowercase characters more readily than a word composed of uppercase characters because the shape of the lowercase word is easier to identify than the boxed shape of the uppercase word. See Figure 5-2.

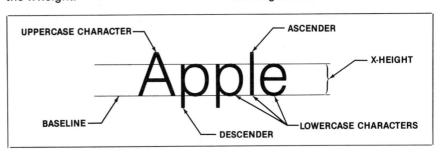

Figure 5-1. Uppercase characters rest on a baseline and extend upward. Lowercase characters rest on a baseline and may extend above or below the baseline.

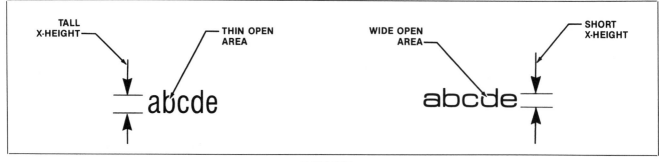

X-HEIGHT

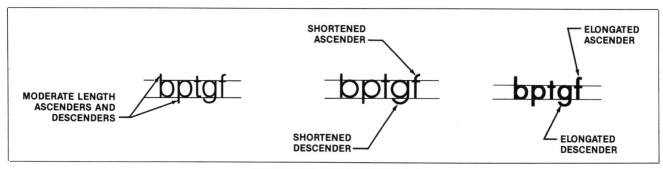

ASCENDERS AND DESCENDERS

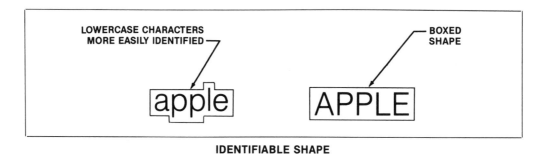

IDENTIFIABLE SHAPE

Figure 5-2. Legibility and readability of a typestyle are determined by the shape and size of the x-height, ascender, and descender. The shapes of lowercase words are easier to identify than those of uppercase words.

Type Measurement. Type measurement was founded when three-dimensional type was used to set words and lines of type. The type character was centered on a type block to facilitate placement. Space above and below the type character allowed the use of lines of type without ascenders and descenders overlapping. See Figure 5-3. The practice of allowing white space has been transferred to the present type measurement system. The given point size of a typestyle is larger than measured point size because white space is included in the given height of the typestyle. Therefore, a 36-point typestyle may be 32 or 34 points when measured with a type scale.

Type size is estimated by measuring from the top of an ascending character to the bottom of a descending character. The type size is expressed in points. See Figure 5-4.

Typographical Layout

Typographical layout is the manner in which type is placed on the printed piece. Typographical layout includes the type and the space surrounding characters, words, and sentences. Good typographical layout improves the readability of a printed piece, while poor typographical layout reduces the readability. A designer determines typographical layout, and the typesetter or desktop publisher fits the typographical layout to the comprehensive layout. Occasionally a paste-up artist is required to hand set or paste up type according to a specified typographical layout.

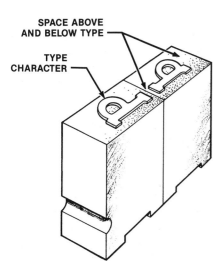

Figure 5-3. Space above and below the type character on three-dimensional type prevents ascenders and descenders from overlapping.

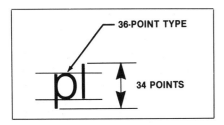

Figure 5-4. Type size is estimated by measuring from the top of an ascending character to the bottom of a descending character.

Letterspacing. *Letterspacing* is the space between type characters. Each typestyle has a specified amount of letterspacing for maximum readability. Letterspacing increases as the size of the type increases. Proper letterspacing facilitates eye movement and recognition of words when reading. A small amount of letterspacing results in congestion of type and eyestrain as words appear to run together. A large amount of letterspacing separates type and words, causing slower eye movement and reduced reader concentration. See Figure 5-5.

Kerning is another form of letterspacing. *Kerning* is the removal of space between certain character combinations. Common character combi-nations, or *kerning pairs,* include Yo, We, To, Tr, Ta, and Wo. Kerning pairs are kerned to improve the readability of a word. See Figure 5-6.

Wordspacing. Type size and read-ability are affected by the amount of *wordspacing,* the space between words. Each typestyle requires a dif-ferent amount of wordspacing. Large type requires more wordspacing than small type. *Optimum wordspacing,* the amount commonly used for even spacing of words, allows the reader's eyes to pause comfortably at each word and proceed to the next word. Optimum wordspacing is approxi-mately equal to the width of a lower-case "i" of the typestyle and type size being used. Words with tight word-spacing run together, making a sen-tence difficult to read. Words with loose wordspacing cause the sen-tence to appear fragmented, creating eye fatigue and loss of comprehen-sion. See Figure 5-7. Automated type-setting equipment commonly pro-duces uneven wordspacing causing confusion for the reader as the eye is forced to jump along the sentence.

Leading. *Leading* is the space between lines of type measured in points. Proper leading allows the reader's eyes to flow freely from line to line. Type with too little leading ap-pears as a solid mass that is difficult to read. Type with too much leading appears lost on the page, causing discontinuity in the flow of the mes-sage. See Figure 5-8. Although type has a predetermined amount of space above and below each character, ex-tra space is commonly added for readability. Type set without addi-tional space between lines relies on the predetermined space to separate ascenders and descenders. The aver-age amount of leading for 7-, 8-, 9-, or 10-point type is 2 points. Leading in-creases as the type size increases.

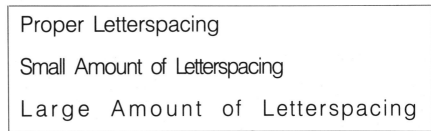

Figure 5-5. Proper letterspacing facilitates eye movement and recognition of words when reading.

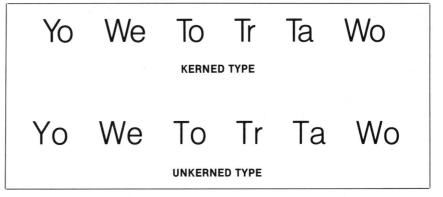

Figure 5-6. Removing white space between kerning pairs increases the readability of a word.

Optimum wordspacing allows the reader's eyes to

Tight wordspacing results in words running toget

Loose wordspacing results in a fragmented

Figure 5-7. Optimum wordspacing allows the reader's eyes to pause comfortably at each word then proceed to the next.

Proper leading allows the reader's eyes
to flow freely from line to line.

Too little leading appears as a solid mass
and results in difficulty in reading.

Too much leading causes discontinuity
in the flow of the message.

Figure 5-8. Proper leading allows the reader's eyes to flow freely from line to line.

Type Arrangement

Type arrangement is the form in which the type is set on the printed page. Six basic forms of type arrangement are justified, flush left, flush right, centered, run-around, and artistic. See Figure 5-9. The designer determines type arrangement by considering the readability of the typestyle, the amount of type to be set, and the mood to be created by the printed piece.

Justified Type. *Justified type* is type that has even right and left margins. Lines of type of the same length create a column. Justified type is the most common type arrangement. Justified type is easy to read because the lines of type begin and end evenly allowing the reader's eyes to flow along the sentences in a quick succession of jumps.

Lines of type of five words or fewer and headline type should not be jus-

tified. Short lines of type cause difficulty in typesetting because words are frequently hyphenated which slows the reader's comprehension. Rivers and pools of white space also appear throughout the copy creating an undesirable appearance.

Flush Left Type. *Flush left type,* or ragged right type, is type that begins evenly along the left margin and ends unevenly along the right margin. Flush left type is highly readable because as the reader's eyes finish a word on the right they automatically returns to the left margin for the start of the next line. Since flush left type does not create even-width columns, it is easier to typeset than justified type. Hyphenated words and uneven wordspacing are avoided by using flush left type.

Flush Right Type. *Flush right type,* or ragged left type, is type that be-

gins unevenly along the left margin and ends evenly along the right margin. Flush right is commonly used beside a photograph or illustration. Flush right has low readability because as the reader's eyes finish a word on the right they must search for the beginning of the next line. Flush right type should be avoided when a large amount of type is used.

Centered Type. *Centered type* is type that is mathematically centered on each line. Centered type is commonly used for headline type. Centered type should be avoided for text and when a large amount of type is used.

Run-around Type. *Run-around type* is type that follows the perimeter of an illustration or photograph. Run-around type is commonly used for gaining attention in an advertisement. Run-around is set in a flush left or flush right arrangement. Flush left run-around type is easier to read because the reader's eyes have a common starting point for each line. Run-around type is difficult to typeset because photographs and illustrations are not shown on the typesetter's screen. Sizes of illustrations and photographs must be determined, and placement within the text must be indicated. Run-around type, however, may easily be produced in desktop publishing because the illustrations are visible on screen. Run-around type should not be used for a large amount of text.

Artistic Type. *Artistic type* creates an image through the layout of the type. Artistic type has low readability and is time-consuming to produce. Artistic arrangements are avoided when informational material is to be included.

Type Specifications

Type is specified by font, family, series, and layout. A designer marks up copy with type specifications for the typesetter. See Figure 5-10. Type arrangement and specifications are commonly indicated as baselines on

Justified type is type that has even right and left margins. Lines of type of the same length create a column. Justified type is the most common type arrangement. Justified type is easy to read because the lines of type begin and end evenly allowing the reader's eyes to flow along the sentences in a quick succession of jumps. Lines of type of five words or fewer and headline type should not be justified.

JUSTIFIED

Flush left type, or ragged right type, is type that begins evenly along the left margin and ends unevenly along the right margin. Flush left type is highly readable because as the reader's eyes finish a word on the right they automatically returns to the left margin for the start of the next line. Since flush left type does not create even-width columns, it is easier to typeset than justified type.

FLUSH LEFT

Flush right type, or ragged left type, is type that begins unevenly along the left margin and ends evenly along the right margin. Flush right is commonly used beside a photograph or illustration.

FLUSH RIGHT

Centered type is type that is mathematically centered on each line. Centered type is commonly used for headline type. Centered type should be avoided for text and when a large amount of type is used.

CENTERED

Run-around type is type that fo llows the perimeter of an illust ration or photograph. Run-a round type is commonly u sed for gaining at tentio n in an advertisement. Run-around is set in a flush left or flush r ight arrangement. Flush left run-aroun d type is easier to rea d because the reader's e yes have a common start ing point for each line. Ru n-around type is difficult to t ypeset because photographs a nd illustrations are not shown

RUN-AROUND

Ar tistic typ e creates an im age through the layo ut of the type. Artistic t ype has low readability an d is time-consuming to types et. Artistic arrangements are av oided w hen info rmation al mater ial is to be inclu

ARTISTIC

Figure 5-9. The readability of the typestyle, amount of type to be set, and mood created by the printed piece are considered when determining type arrangement.

a comprehensive layout or written on the manuscript copy.

Font. A *font* is a complete assortment of one typestyle in one size. It is composed of all characters required for general composition. A designer specifies a font by writing the font name in the margin of the manuscript copy.

Family. A *family* is all styles and variations of a font. Characters vary in weight, width, and other treatments, such as bold or italic. A designer specifies a family by writing its name in the margin of the manuscript copy.

Series. A *series* is all sizes of a particular font. Type size is indicated next to the leading requirement and is marked in the margin of the manuscript copy. For example, type that is specified as 10/12 indicates 10-point type. The slash separates the type size from the leading requirement.

Type Layout. *Type layout* includes the leading of the type and type arrangement. Leading is determined by adding the point size of the type and the amount of desired space between the lines of type. The total, or leading, is the number after the slash and is given after the type size. For example, 10-point type with 2 points of leading

between lines is expressed as 10/12. See Figure 5-11.

Type Classifications

Type classifications are categories of typestyles with similar characteristics. Type classifications are serif, sans serif, script or cursive, textletter, and decorative. Legibility and readability of type are affected by point size, whether characters are upper- or lowercase, and the amount of *type matter,* which is copy set in a particular typestyle.

The designer selects a typestyle based on the aesthetic quality of the

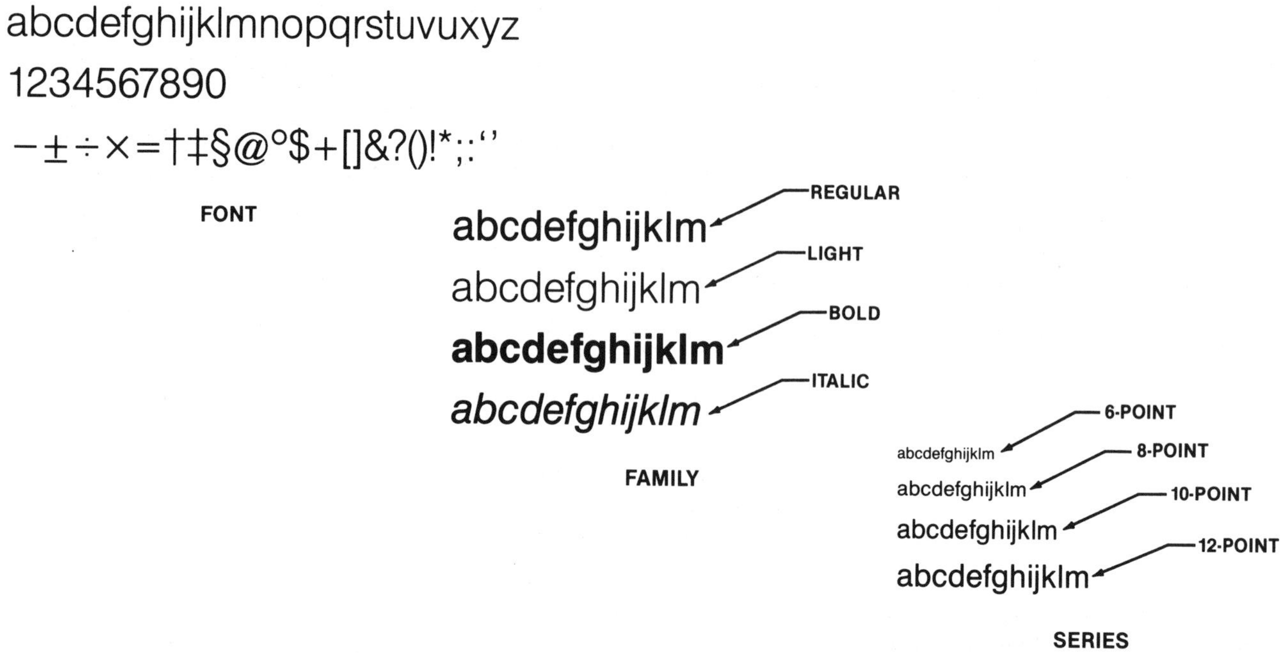

abcdefghijklmnopqrstuvuxyz
1234567890
−±÷×=†‡§@°$+[]&?()!*;:''

FONT

abcdefghijklm ← REGULAR

abcdefghijklm ← LIGHT

abcdefghijklm ← BOLD

abcdefghijklm ← ITALIC

FAMILY

abcdefghijklm ← 6-POINT

abcdefghijklm ← 8-POINT

abcdefghijklm ← 10-POINT

abcdefghijklm ← 12-POINT

SERIES

Figure 5-10. A font is a complete assortment of one typestyle in one size. A family is all styles and variations of a font. A series is all sizes of a particular font.

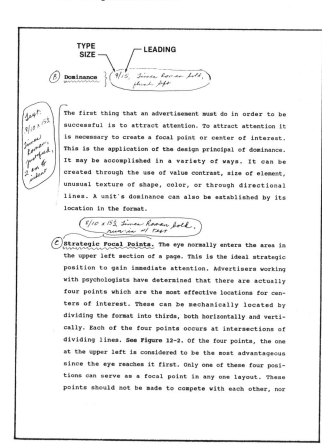

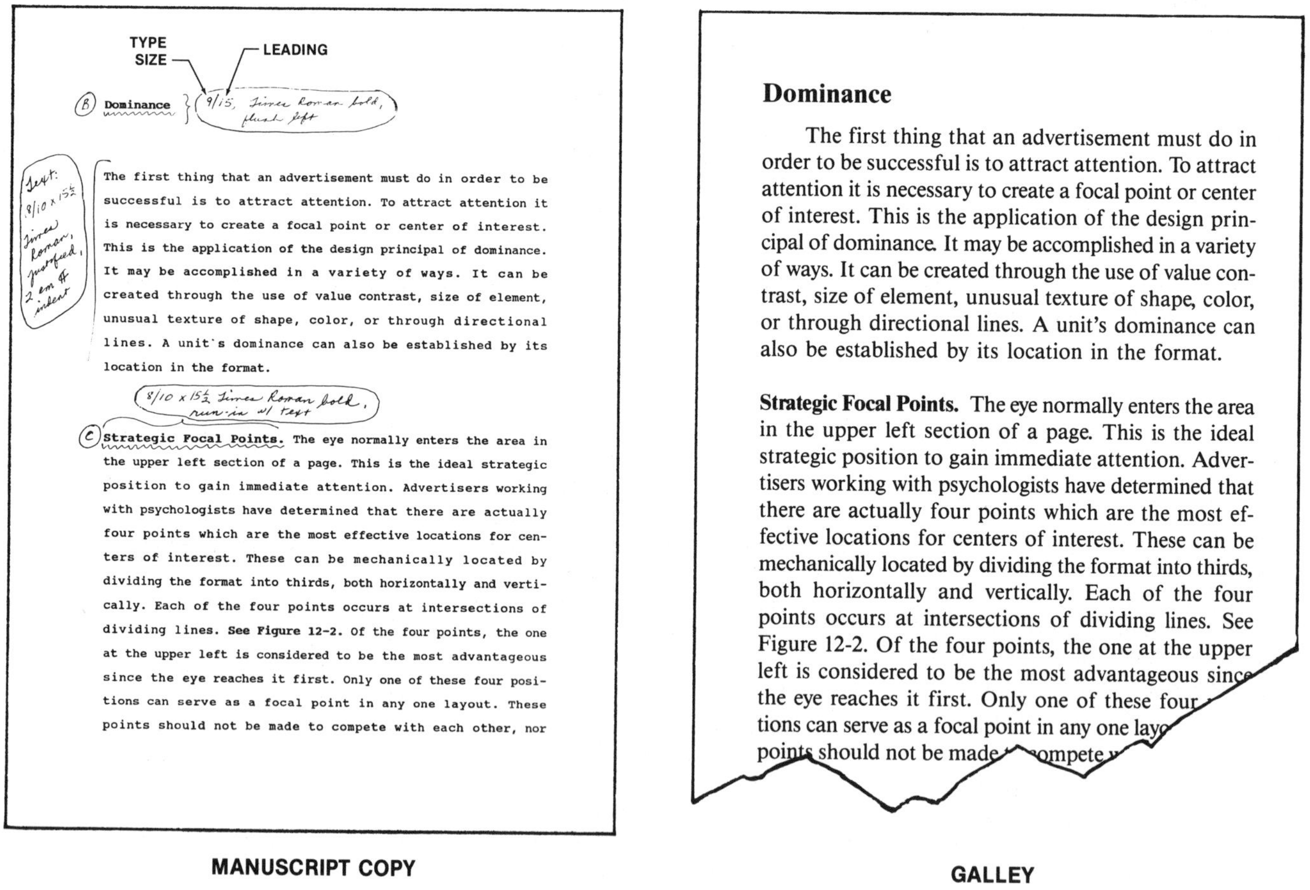

MANUSCRIPT COPY

GALLEY

Dominance

The first thing that an advertisement must do in order to be successful is to attract attention. To attract attention it is necessary to create a focal point or center of interest. This is the application of the design principal of dominance. It may be accomplished in a variety of ways. It can be created through the use of value contrast, size of element, unusual texture of shape, color, or through directional lines. A unit's dominance can also be established by its location in the format.

Strategic Focal Points. The eye normally enters the area in the upper left section of a page. This is the ideal strategic position to gain immediate attention. Advertisers working with psychologists have determined that there are actually four points which are the most effective locations for centers of interest. These can be mechanically located by dividing the format into thirds, both horizontally and vertically. Each of the four points occurs at intersections of dividing lines. See Figure 12-2. Of the four points, the one at the upper left is considered to be the most advantageous since the eye reaches it first. Only one of these four tions can serve as a focal point in any one layo points should not be made to compete

Figure 5-11. Type layout includes leading and type arrangement.

type. Basic rules accompanying the type classification enable a designer to select the amount of type used in one style and the size and location of that type. As a general rule, a designer selects a maximum of three typestyles per printed piece. Three typestyles create interest for the reader without interrupting the continuity of the printed piece. Headline and text type should be selected to complement one another.

Serif Type. Serif type has *serifs,* or small appendages, extending from the free strokes or ends of a character. See Figure 5-12. Smooth, pointed, or rounded serifs contribute to the identifiable shape of the type, causing greater legibility. Serif type is easily read in uppercase and lowercase characters. The legibility and readability of serif type give it a wide variety of applications. Serif type is available in a variety of sizes and is often used to give a structured feeling to a printed piece.

Square serif type has square serifs which are designed for their bold appearance. Square serif type is less readable than smooth, pointed, or rounded serif type. Combining different typestyles that have square serifs results in even less legibility. Square serif type is primarily used for headline type and should be avoided for large amounts of text. Square serif type is commonly used in advertisements to appear bold and eye-catching.

Sans Serif Type. *Sans serif type* contains letters without serifs. Sans serif type is designed for a clean, sleek appearance. It is used to give a modern appearance to a printed piece. See Figure 5-13. The readability and legibility of sans serif type are approximately equal to that of serif type. Although serif type is more prevalent, sans serif type is gaining in popularity.

Script and Cursive Type. *Script* and *cursive type* are similar in appearance to handwritten copy. The lowercase characters in script type con-

Figure 5-12. Serif type has serifs at the free strokes, or ends, of a character.

Figure 5-13. Sans serif type is designed for a clean, sleek appearance.

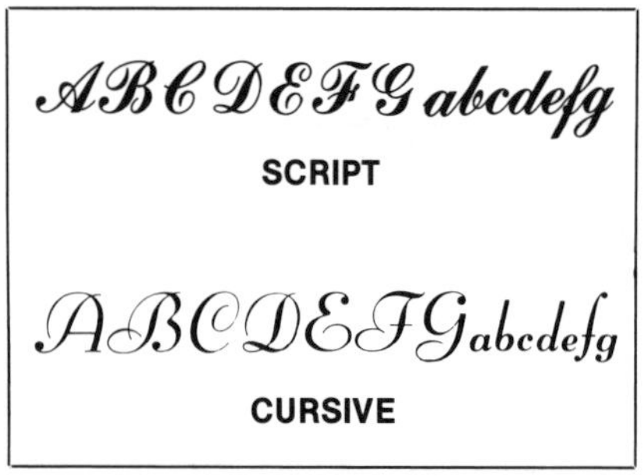

Figure 5-14. Script and cursive type simulate handwritten copy. The lower-case characters in script type connect to one another.

Figure 5-15. Textletter type is an ornate typestyle derived from hand-scribed characters used by fourteenth and fifteenth century monks.

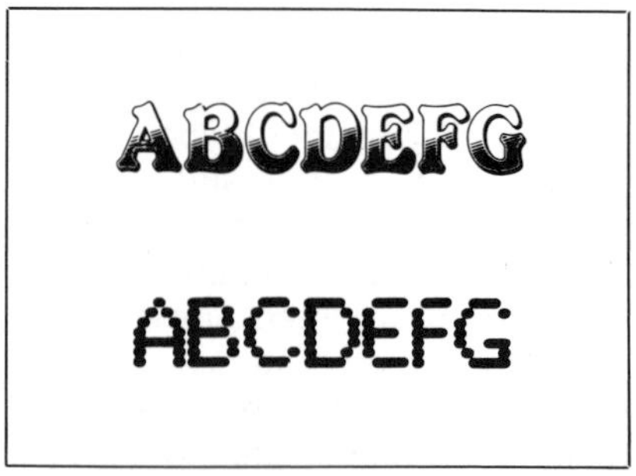

Figure 5-16. Decorative type is selected for its ability to complement the printed piece.

nect to one another. The characters in cursive type appear to flow together but do not actually connect. See Figure 5-14. The legibility and readability of script and cursive type are relatively low. Script and cursive type should not be used in all upper-case characters or for large amounts of text. Although script and cursive were originally designed to give the printed piece a formal appearance, a wide variety of script and cursive typestyles are now available, ranging from formal to informal type.

Textletter Type. *Textletter type* is an ornate typestyle derived from the hand-scribed characters used by four-teenth and fifteenth century monks. See Figure 5-15. The ornamentation of the characters results in low legi-bility and readability. Multiple vertical strokes combined with the *filigree,* or intricate design, make characters dif-ficult to recognize. Textletter type is commonly used for certificates, greet-ing cards, and titles containing single words or short phrases. Textletter type imparts an old and formalized feeling.

Decorative Type. *Decorative,* or novelty, type is a classification that includes a wide variety of typestyles. Generally, typestyles not included in other classifications are categorized as decorative type. See Figure 5-16. Decorative type is used to comple-ment the printed piece and help con-vey its message to the reader.

Readability and legibility of decor-ative type vary greatly. Decorative

type is primarily used for headlines or a small amount of copy. General-ly, only one style of decorative type is used per page. Decorative type draws attention to itself and may be distracting if more than one style is used.

COMMUNICATING WITH THE TYPESETTER

A designer must communicate with the typesetter to expedite production of a job. Communication eliminates time-consuming errors and ensures that type is set efficiently. The type-setter follows the designer's instruc-tions. Neat, accurate, and concise type specifications on the manu-script copy and a complete compre-hensive layout facilitate efficient typesetting.

Copyfitting

Copyfitting is the process of deter-mining the correct type size and lead-ing of copy required to fill a predeter-mined space. Most copyfitting meth-ods are based on a character count formula. The *character count formula* determines the number of characters in copy and converts the total to a character per pica (CPP) number. The *character per pica number,* or CPP number, is a decimal value indicating the number of characters that fit in-to a pica. The CPP number for a type-style and size is commonly specified by the typesetter. The CPP number is

used to determine copy specifica-tions for a predetermined space and the amount of space required on a rough layout for a specified typestyle and size.

The character count formula is used to determine the CPP number if it is not specified by the typesetter. A line of lowercase or uppercase alpha-betic (A–Z) type is measured in picas. The measurement is divided by the number of characters plus 2.5. The 2.5 is added to allow for punctuation marks and spaces. The decimal value obtained by division is the CPP num-ber. See Figure 5-17. A large CPP number indicates that a small num-ber of characters fit into a space, while a small CPP number indicates that a large number of characters fit into a space.

Copyfitting a Fixed Space. A *fixed space* is the estimated amount of space allowed for the copy on a rough layout. A fixed space is copyfit to de-termine the number of typeset lines that will fill the space. The number of typeset lines produced from a manu-script copy may also be estimated by copyfitting.

A designer outlines the fixed space for the copy on the rough layout. The designer then selects typestyles and sizes that can be used to convey the message of the job. Various type-styles and sizes are selected to en-sure optimum fit of the copy and read-ability of the job.

Several variables determine the number of typeset lines that fill the

---

Determining CPP Number

Determine the CPP number of the typeface using the character count formula.

Step 1. Measure the length of a line of alphabetic (A–Z) characters.

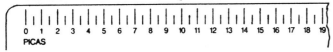

ABCDEFGHIJKLMNOPQRSTUVWXYZ

Line length = 15.6 picas

Step 2. Add 2.5 to the total number of characters in the line.
26 + 2.5 = 28.5

Step 3. Divide the line length by the sum.
15.6 ÷ 28.5 = .547

Answer. **CPP no. = .547**

Figure 5-17. The character count formula is used to determine the CPP number.

---

er must select a typestyle with a larger CPP number or enlarge the fixed space. When possible, the fixed space is altered to allow for greater readability of the type.

1. Determine the average number of typeset characters per line by multiplying the CPP number of the selected typestyle by the line length (in picas).

2. Determine the number of typeset lines required by the manuscript copy by dividing the total number of characters in the manuscript copy by the average number of typeset characters per line.

Determining Space for Manuscript Copy. Determining space for manuscript copy is another way to fixed space. Depth and line length of the fixed space, type size and leading, CPP of the selected type, and total number of characters in the manuscript copy must be considered when copyfitting. See Figure 5-18.

1. Measure the depth of the fixed space in picas using a combination ruler.

2. Convert the depth in picas to points by multiplying by 12.

3. Determine the line depth by adding the type size (in points) and the leading (in points).

4. Determine the number of typeset lines that will fit into the fixed space by dividing the depth of the fixed space by the line depth. If a decimal value is calculated, round off to the next higher whole number.

Determining Number of Typeset Lines in Manuscript Copy. When creating a rough layout, a designer designates the amount of space for various copy elements. The designer cannot determine the exact amount of space required for manuscript copy until a typestyle is selected. The designer sketches ruled blocks to indicate the space allotted for elements of a manuscript copy. See Figure 5-19. If the number of typeset lines required by the manuscript copy is greater than the number of typeset lines in the fixed space, the design-

---

Determining Number of Typeset Lines for a Fixed Space

Determine the number of typeset lines used to fill a fixed space measuring 27 picas in depth. Ten-point type is to be used with 2-point leading.

Step 1. Determine the depth.
Depth = 27 picas

Step 2. Convert the depth to points.
No. of picas × 12 = no. of points
27 × 12 = 324

Step 3. Determine the line depth.
Type size + leading = line depth
10 + 2 = 12

Step 4. Determine the number of typeset lines.
Depth ÷ line depth = no. of typeset lines
324 ÷ 12 = 27

Answer. **27 typeset lines**

Figure 5-18. A fixed space is copyfit to determine the number of typeset lines.

Determining Number of Typeset Lines Required by Manuscript Copy

Determine the number of typeset lines required by a manuscript copy containing 800 characters. Ten-point Helvetica Medium type (*CPP = 2.65*) is to be used with a 19-point line length.

Step 1. Determine the average number of typeset characters per line.
CCP no. × line length = average no. of typeset characters per line
2.65 × 19 = 50.35

Step 2. Determine the number of typeset lines required.
Total no. of characters ÷
average no. of typeset characters per line = no. of typeset lines
800 ÷ 50.35 = 15.89

Answer. **16 typeset lines**

Figure 5-19. The number of typeset lines required by manuscript copy is used to plan the rough layout.

copyfit type to a rough layout. This method is commonly used to plan a multipage layout. Copyfitting before developing the rough layout enables a designer to plan the piece efficiently. The trim size of the printed piece, photographs, and illustrations are sized for maximum readability. See Figure 5-20.

1. Determine the average number of typeset characters per line by multiplying the CPP number of the selected type by the line length.

2. Determine the total number of typeset lines by dividing the total number of characters in the manuscript copy by the number of typeset characters per line.

3. Determine line depth by adding type size (in points) and leading (in points).

4. Determine depth of the typeset copy (in points) by multiplying line depth by total number of typeset lines.

Convert depth of the typeset copy (in points) to picas by dividing the depth by 12. The depth of the typeset copy (in points) may be converted to inches by dividing the depth by 72.

Type Specification and Proofreading

Type specification and proofreading facilitate efficient communication between a typesetter and designer. *Type specification* is the process of indicating type requirements for typesetting. Type specifications may be written on the manuscript copy or a separate specification sheet may be developed. See Figure 5-21.

Proofreading is the process of reading manuscript copy to locate errors, such as grammatical errors or incorrect letterspacing. Proofreading is a basic responsibility of every production stage; however, it is most efficient when performed in the design, copywriting, and typesetting or desktop publishing stages. Errors found in early production stages are less costly to correct than those found in later stages. Errors are indicated on the manuscript copy with standardized proofreaders' marks.

Determining Space Required by Typeset Copy

Determine the space required by a manuscript copy containing 900 characters. Ten-point Times Roman type (*CPP* = 2.80) and 2-point leading is to be a 19-point line length.

Step 1. Determine the average number of typeset characters per line.
CCP no. × *line length* = *average no. of typeset characters per line*
2.80 × 19 = 53.2

Step 2. Determine the total number of typeset lines required.
Total no. of characters ÷
average no. of typeset characters per line = *no. of typeset lines*
900 ÷ 53.2 = 16.92

Step 3. Determine line depth.
Type size + *leading* = *line depth*
10 + 2 = 12

Step 4. Determine the depth of typeset copy.
Line depth × *no. of typeset lines* = *depth of typeset copy*
12 × 17 = 204 points

Answer. **204 points, or 17 picas**

Figure 5-20. Space for typeset copy is commonly determined when planning multipage layouts.

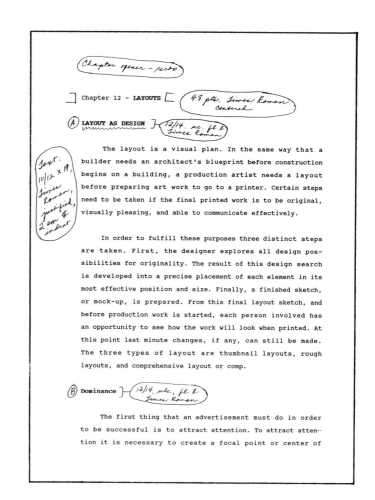

Figure 5-21. Type specification is indicating type requirements to the typesetter.

Type Specification. *Type specification,* or marking copy, is indicating type requirements to the typesetter or desktop publisher. A designer specifies the font, family, posture, characteristics, point size, leading, type arrangement, and line length. Type specifications are written in abbreviated form in red ink on the manuscript copy. If a separate specification sheet is developed, specifications for all variations of type, such as headlines, body copy, and captions, are included in a list.

The *font* is the name of the typestyle, such as Times Roman, Helvetica, or Bodoni. The *family* indicates the weight of the type, such as light or semibold, and the type width, such as condensed or extended. *Type posture* is the position of a character on the baseline, such as italic, oblique, or slanted. *Type characteristics* indicate letter classification, such as upper- or lowercase, outline characters, or reverse characters. *Type arrangement* is the layout of the type, such as flush left, flush right, or centered. Type size, leading, and line length are indicated in points.

Proofreaders' Marks. Proofreaders' marks are a standardized form of communication between a designer, copywriter, or an editor and the typesetter. Proofreaders' marks are symbols and written instructions indicating a specific typesetting task, such as set in boldface, or delete a word.

Proofreaders' marks are indicated on a photocopy of the galleys in red ink to contrast with the black type of the galleys. The original manuscript copy is stored for future reference. The proofreaders' mark is drawn directly on the character or word to be altered. The instruction is written in the left or right margin on the line in which the change is made. See Figure 5-22.

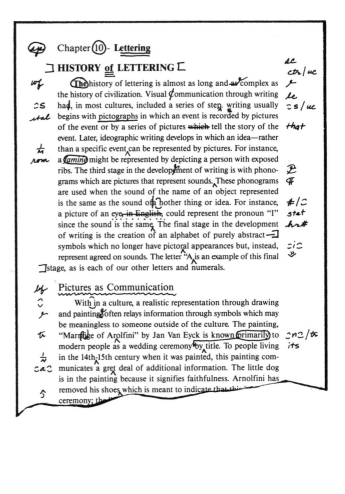

PROOFREADERS' MARKS

GALLEY

Figure 5-22. Proofreaders' marks indicate operations to be performed by the typesetter. They are indicated on a photocopy of the galley.

5 Typography

True-False

T F **1.** Type legibility and type readability have the same meaning.

T F **2.** Paste-up artists study typography to visualize spatial relationships between type and layout.

T F **3.** The legibility and readability of a word are generally not affected by the size and shape of the x-height, ascender, and descender.

T F **4.** An uppercase word is generally more readable than a lowercase word.

T F **5.** Type is measured from the top of the x-height to the bottom of the descender.

T F **6.** Type size is variable because white space is built into the type size to allow for ascenders and descenders.

T F **7.** Typographical layout is the manner in which type is placed on the page.

T F **8.** Letterspacing increases as type size decreases.

T F **9.** Kerning is a form of letterspacing.

T F **10.** There are six basic forms of type arrangement.

T F **11.** A typesetter or desktop publisher follows type specifications on the manuscript and the comprehensive layout when setting type.

T F **12.** The character per pica number is a decimal point equivalent of the number of characters in a linear inch.

T F **13.** The character per pica number is used by the designer in four formulas.

T F **14.** Computing the required space for type is one method of copyfitting.

T F **15.** The designer writes proofreaders' marks and type specifications on the comprehensive layout to communicate with the typesetter.

T F **16.** Standard proofreaders' marks are symbols and written communication.

T F **17.** Proofreaders' marks are indicated in red on the manuscript copy.

T F **18.** Correcting a mistake on manuscript copy is more cost-effective than correcting one at later stages of production.

T F **19.** Line length is indicated as a pica number on the manuscript copy.

Completion

_____ **1.** Type _____ are categories of typestyles.

_____ **2.** _____ type has small appendages that extend from the free strokes or ends of the characters.

_____ **3.** _____ serif typestyles do not have rounded or pointed serifs.

_____   **4.** _____ serif typestyles do not contain serifs.

_____   **5.** Cursive and _____ typestyles resemble handwriting.

_____   **6.** _____ is a very old typestyle carried over from hand-scribed typestyles of the monks.

_____   **7.** _____ type is sometimes referred to as novelty.

_____   **8.** A decorative typestyle is chosen for its ability to combine the _____ of the type with the message to be communicated.

_____   **9.** _____ and _____ typestyles should never be used in all uppercase characters.

_____   **10.** As a general rule a designer chooses up to _____ typestyles per printed piece.

_____   **11.** _____ a fixed space is a method used to determine the number of typeset lines.

_____   **12.** The depth of a fixed space is measured in _____.

_____   **13.** The depth of one line is multiplied by the total typeset lines to determine the total depth in _____.

_____   **14.** The comprehensive layout serves as a(n) _____ direction to the typesetter.

_____   **15.** Concise type specifications on the manuscript copy and a complete comprehensive layout facilitate efficient _____.

_____   **16.** Proofreaders' marks are written in _____ ink.

_____   **17.** Type specifications are abbreviated along the upper _____ corner of the manuscript.

Multiple Choice

_____   **1.** The white space between words is _____.
    A. letterspacing
    B. wordspacing
    C. kerning
    D. leading

_____   **2.** The white space between characters is _____.
    A. letterspacing
    B. wordspacing
    C. kerning
    D. leading

_____   **3.** The removal of white space between specialized character pairs is _____.
    A. letterspacing
    B. wordspacing
    C. kerning
    D. all of the above

_____   **4.** Type _____ refers to the individual identification of a single character.
    A. readability
    B. legibility
    C. kerning
    D. comprehension

_____ 5. Type _____ refers to the arrangement of letters or characters in a word and the speed at which words are perceived.
    A. readability
    B. legibility
    C. kerning
    D. comprehension

_____ 6. The designer communicates with the typesetter through _____.
    A. layout
    B. copyfitting
    C. specifications
    D. all of the above

_____ 7. The variable required to determine the number of typeset lines is _____.
    A. line length
    B. total characters
    C. characters per pica
    D. all of the above

_____ 8. The total number of _____ allows the designer to plan the size of the job.
    A. inches
    B. agates
    C. characters
    D. all of the above

_____ 9. Proofreaders' marks are a standard method of communicating with the _____.
    A. designer
    B. typesetter
    C. keyliner
    D. all of the above

_____ 10. The best method of assuring accurate communication with the typesetter is to _____ proofreaders' marks.
    A. write out
    B. spell
    C. abbreviate
    D. standardize

Matching

_____ **1.** x = leading

_____ **2.** Variations of a typestyle

_____ **3.** Type follows an illustration

_____ **4.** Type with even right and left margins

_____ **5.** Type is ragged right

_____ **6.** Space between type lines

_____ **7.** Type is ragged left

_____ **8.** Type set mathematically

_____ **9.** x = type size

_____ **10.** Type creates an image

A. Leading
B. Run-around
C. Artistic
D. Family
E. x/12
F. 12/x
G. Flush right
H. Flush left
I. Centered
J. Justified

_____ 11. One typestyle

_____ 12. Multiple sizes of type

_____ 13. Marks for type changes

_____ 14. Calculating type size

_____ 15. Characters per pica

_____ 16. Type size + leading

_____ 17. Oblique

_____ 18. Reverse

_____ 19. Condensed

_____ 20. Semibold

A. Copyfitting
B. Type characteristic
C. CPP
D. Font
E. Type family
F. Depth of line
G. Series
H. Type width
I. Proofreaders' marks
J. Type posture

Identification

_____ 1. Ascender

_____ 2. Descender

_____ 3. x-height

Apple

_____ 4. Serif

_____ 5. Sans serif

_____ 6. Square serif

_____ 7. Script

_____ 8. Textletter

_____ 9. Decorative

ABCDEFG (A)   ABCDEFG (B)

ABCDEFG (C)   ABCDEFG (D)

ABCDEFG (E)   ABCDEFG (F)

_____ 10. Stet

_____ 11. Delete

_____ 12. Insert space

_____ 13. Make new paragraph

_____ 14. Transpose

_____ 15. Italicize word

Writing usually begins with pictographs in which an event is recorded by pictures of the event or else by a series of pictures that tells the story of the event. Later, ideographic writing develops in which an idea—rather than a specific event can be represented by pictures. For instance, a *famine* might be represented by depicting a person with exposed ribs. The third stage in the development of writing is with phonograms which are pictures that represent sounds. These phonograms are used when the sound of the name of an object represented is the same as the sound of another thing or idea. For instance, a picture of an eye, in English, could represent the pronoun "I" since the sound is the same.

6 INKED AND HAND-SET TYPE

Inked type is drawn on an artboard, character by character. Hand-set type, such as adhesive or transfer type, is affixed to the artboard, character by character. Both inked and hand-set type are commonly used for headlines or other large type size applications. When applying inked and hand-set type, the paste-up artist uses visual letterspacing and wordspacing. A variety of methods and tools enable the paste-up artist to apply inked and hand-set type accurately.

CREATED TYPE

Created type is a broad category encompassing all forms of inked type, adhesive type, and transfer type. Inked type is applied to an artboard with a pen and dense black ink. Adhesive type adheres to the artboard with a low-tack adhesive. Transfer type is burnished to the artboard. The paste-up artist chooses the form of created type to best suit job requirements.

Inked Type

Inked type is created with a lettering pen, or with a template and lettering device. A *lettering pen* is a pen with a broad, flat tip, generally used for calligraphy. A *template and lettering device* is a precision tool used to create type with ink. To create type using a template and lettering device, the template is laid along the T-square on the art table. A pen is set in the socket of the scribe, and the tail pin of the scribe is set in the straight horizontal groove in the template. The tracer pin of the scribe is used to trace the grooved letters in the template, and the attached pen follows the same tracing movements, forming letters on the artboard. See Figure 6-1.

Calligraphy style and manuscript style characters are commonly inked. *Calligraphy style* characters are used on cards and certificates; *manuscript style* characters are used on charts, graphs, and architectural drawings. Inked type gives the printed piece a personalized or customized appearance but is not practical for a large amount of copy. Inked type often has flaws or imperfections that may reproduce on the printed piece. Inked type is reproduced at the same size it was inked or at a reduced size to prevent noticeable imperfections.

Hand-set Type

Hand-set type is preprinted type, the most common of which are adhesive type and transfer type. *Adhesive type* is pressure-sensitive type printed in dense black ink on transparent sheets of adhesive acetate. *Transfer type*, or dry-transfer type, is printed in dense black ink on frosted acetate. Adhesive type and transfer type produce quality reproductions and can be enlarged to 300% without visible imperfections.

To apply adhesive type, a cut is made around the desired character. The character is removed from the backing sheet and applied to an artboard. To apply transfer type, the character selected is positioned on an artboard and burnished in place. Errors can be corrected because transfer type is easily removed from the artboard with masking tape.

Adhesive and transfer type are available on sheets containing one or two fonts. Frequently used characters are repeated several times on a sheet. Many typestyles are available, and additional typestyles are introduced periodically. Type sizes range from 6 points to 214 points. Hand-set type in large point sizes is easier to letterspace than type in small point sizes.

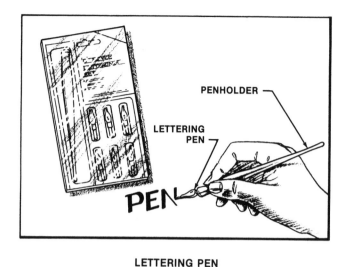

LETTERING PEN

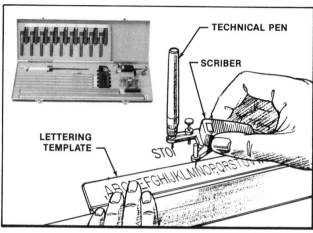

J. S. Staedtler, Inc.

TEMPLATE AND LETTERING DEVICE

Figure 6-1. A lettering pen and a template and lettering device are used to hand-set type.

LAYOUT OF HAND-SET TYPE

Hand-set type is visually laid out and positioned on a non-photo blue baseline drawn on the artboard. Some hand-set type has black baselines printed on the acetate for alignment with the non-photo blue baseline. The amount of letterspacing varies with each character of a font. The paste-up artist determines the necessary letterspacing and wordspacing by following established guidelines for letterspacing hand-set type. See Figure 6-2.

1. Letterspacing is determined by whether the character has a straight side, curved side, and/or an indented area.

2. One unit of letterspacing is used when curved sides of two characters are adjacent. These characters have minimum letterspacing.

3. Two units of letterspacing are used when the curved side of one character is adjacent to the straight side of another character. These characters have moderate letterspacing.

4. Three units of letterspacing are used when the straight sides of two characters are adjacent. These characters have maximum letterspacing.

5. Kerning is used with characters that have indented areas. These char-

acters have the smallest amount of letterspacing.

6. Different typestyles, such as reversed-out and outlined type, may require additional letterspacing.

Adhesive Type

Adhesive type is printed on pressure-sensitive acetate. Characters are printed on the adhesive side to prevent scratching, smearing, or chipping. A low-tack adhesive is applied over the printed character to facilitate application. The adhesive allows the type to be applied to almost all surfaces. However, the acetate on which the type is printed gives an unfinished appearance when applied to glass, cloth, or a comprehensive layout. A paper backing is applied to the acetate to stabilize it and facilitate storage. See Figure 6-3. Adhesive type has a *shelf life,* the amount of time it can be stored and remain usable, of approximately five years when stored flat and protected against excessive heat and humidity.

To apply adhesive type, a cut is made around an adhesive type character, penetrating only the acetate. The character is removed from the backing with the edge of an art knife or a pair of tweezers and positioned

on the artboard. The type is burnished thoroughly after all characters are positioned.

Creating a Headline with Adhesive Type. A headline is created with adhesive type using the guideline method or headline setter method. The *guideline method* is used to create headlines that have a straight, curved, or an irregular baseline. The *headline setter method* is commonly used to create headlines that have a straight baseline.

In the guideline method, a preprinted guideline below the type character is aligned with a non-photo blue guideline drawn on the artboard. The distance between the baseline of the type character and the preprinted guideline is measured. This measurement is used to draw an original baseline and a baseline guideline on the artboard being used. The distance between the type character and the preprinted guideline is equal for all characters of the same font. The guidelines are removed from the artboard when all characters are thoroughly burnished. See Figure 6-4.

1. Draw a non-photo blue baseline on the artboard.

2. Measure the distance between the baseline of the type character and preprinted guideline below the

Letterspacing Guidelines

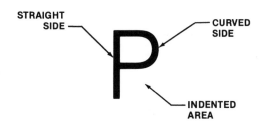

A type character has a straight side, curved side, and/or an indented area.

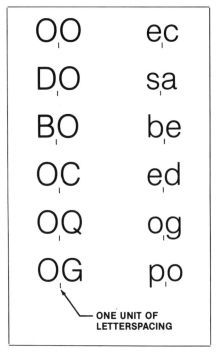

ONE UNIT OF LETTERSPACING

Use one unit of letterspacing for two characters with adjacent curved sides.

TWO UNITS OF LETTERSPACING

Use two units of letterspacing when the curved side of one character is adjacent to the straight side of another.

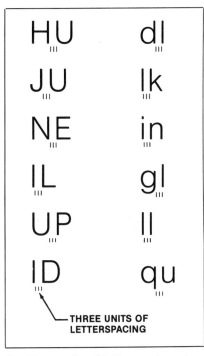

THREE UNITS OF LETTERSPACING

Use three units of letterspacing when the straight sides of two characters are adjacent.

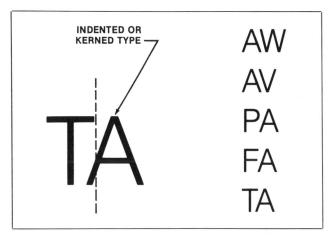

Kern characters that have indented spaces.

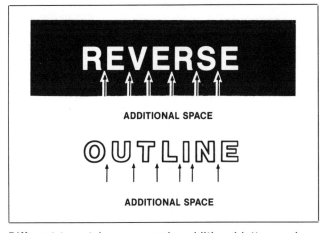

Different typestyles may require additional letterspacing.

Figure 6-2. A type character has a straight side, curved side, and/or an indented area. These characteristics determine letterspacing.

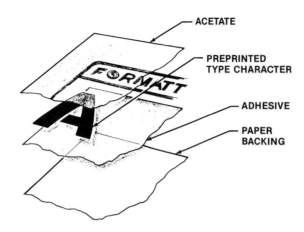

ACETATE

PREPRINTED
TYPE CHARACTER

ADHESIVE

PAPER
BACKING

Figure 6-3. Adhesive type is printed on the back of a thin acetate base. Adhesive is applied over the type characters, and the characters are protected by a paper backing sheet.

character. On the artboard, measure this distance down from the non-photo blue baseline and draw a non-photo blue guideline.

3. Penetrating only the acetate, cut around the adhesive type character and the preprinted guideline. Carefully remove the character from the backing using an art knife or a pair of tweezers.

4. Align the preprinted guideline with the non-photo blue guideline on the artboard. Gently burnish in position.

5. Cut and remove the preprinted guideline from the artboard.

6. Burnish the adhesive type headline thoroughly.

In the headline setter method, the preprinted guideline is aligned with a guideline on the headline setter. A *headline setter* is a thin plastic ruler with a series of guidelines used to align type characters. Using a headline setter also helps in letterspacing and wordspacing adhesive type before it is applied to the artboard. See Figure 6-5.

1. Draw a non-photo blue guideline on the artboard.

2. Penetrating only the acetate, cut around the type character and the preprinted guideline. Carefully remove the character from the backing using an art knife or a pair of tweezers.

3. Position type characters on the headline setter, aligning the preprinted guidelines with a headline setter guideline. Letterspace and wordspace as required.

4. Move the completed word or group of words to the artboard. Align the headline setter guideline with the non-photo blue guideline on the artboard. Gently burnish the adhesive type to the artboard.

5. Cut and remove the preprinted guideline from the artboard. Burnish the adhesive type thoroughly.

Artistically Aligning Type. Adhesive type is artistically aligned by using a headline template or flexible tape. A *headline template* is a headline setter with a curved or an irregular shape. French curves and protractors are often used as headline templates. Custom-made shapes can also be created using heavy-gauge clear acetate or mylar (.004″ to .007″ thick). The shape of the headline template is traced from the comprehensive layout onto the acetate or mylar. The acetate or mylar is cut $\frac{1}{16}$″ larger than the size of the desired shape. Adhesive tape is applied to the acetate or mylar along the traced line to create a guideline. The *flexible tape* used to artistically align type is crepe

tape. Crepe tape is very flexible and curves without distorting. See Figure 6-6.

In the *headline template method* of aligning adhesive type, a headline template is used to align adhesive type to the baseline of a curve on the artboard. See Figure 6-7.

1. Lay out a non-photo blue guideline on the artboard. Align a standard shape headline template to the guideline, or create a custom-made template to conform to the shape of the guideline.

2. Penetrating only the acetate, cut around the adhesive type character and the preprinted guideline. Remove the type character from the backing using an art knife.

3. Position the type character along the headline template, allowing for proper letterspacing and wordspacing. Gently burnish the type on the headline template.

4. Align the headline template with the non-photo blue guideline on the artboard. Press the type characters onto the artboard. Burnish thoroughly.

In the *curved rule method,* flexible tape is used to create an irregular shape, and adhesive type is aligned with the shape created. A non-photo blue guideline is laid out on the artboard in the desired curved shape. The flexible tape is applied to the artboard following the curved shape of the guideline. The preprinted guideline of the adhesive type character is aligned with the bottom edge of the flexible tape. The type characters are letterspaced then burnished lightly on the artboard. The preprinted guidelines are cut and removed, and the flexible tape is removed by pulling it away from the artboard at a 30° angle. The adhesive type is then burnished thoroughly on the artboard. The curved rule method is a quick method of laying out adhesive type in irregular shapes. However, it involves the additional cost of the flexible rule.

Altering Characters. Adhesive type has an advantage over other type methods because characters can be

Applying Adhesive Type—Guideline Method

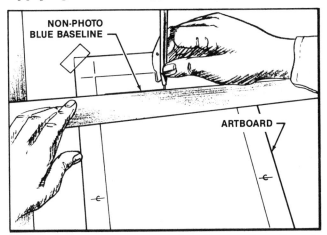

Step 1. Draw a non-photo blue baseline on the artboard.

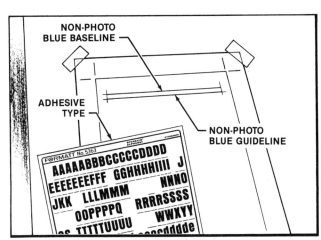

Step 2. Draw a non-photo blue guideline below the baseline, using the distance measured between the baseline and preprinted guideline on the sheet of adhesive type.

Step 3. Cut the type character and carefully remove the character using an art knife.

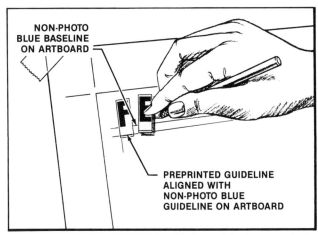

Step 4. Align the preprinted guideline with the non-photo blue guideline on the artboard.

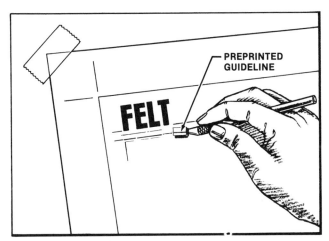

Step 5. Cut and remove the preprinted guideline.

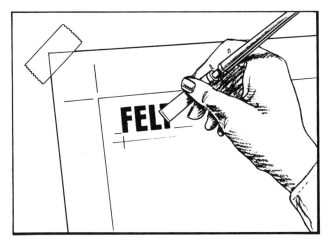

Step 6. Burnish the adhesive type thoroughly.

Figure 6-4. The guideline method of applying adhesive type is used for headlines with a straight, curved, or an irregular baseline.

Applying Adhesive Type—Headline Setter Method

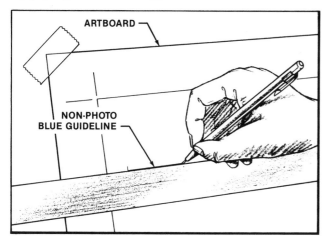

Step 1. Draw a non-photo blue guideline.

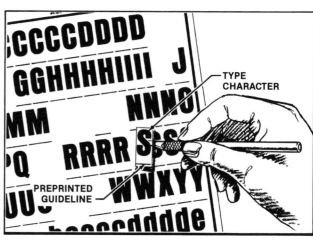

Step 2. Cut and remove the type character using an art knife.

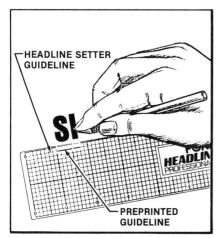

Step 3. Position type characters, aligning preprinted guideline with headline setter guideline.

Step 4. Align the completed word on the artboard, using the headline setter guideline and non-photo blue guideline. Gently burnish type onto artboard.

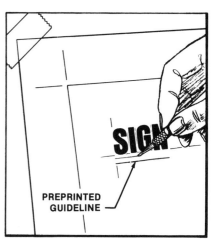

Step 5. Cut and remove the preprinted guideline.

Figure 6-5. The headline setter method of applying adhesive type is used for headlines with a straight baseline.

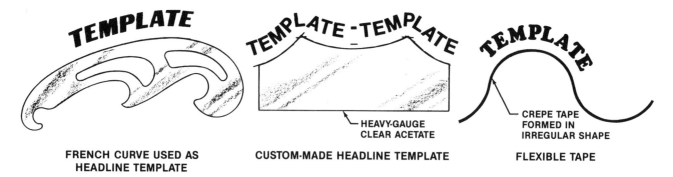

FRENCH CURVE USED AS HEADLINE TEMPLATE

CUSTOM-MADE HEADLINE TEMPLATE

FLEXIBLE TAPE

Figure 6-6. French curves, custom-made headline templates of heavy-gauge clear acetate or mylar, and flexible tape can be used to artistically align adhesive type.

Applying Adhesive Type—Headline Template Method

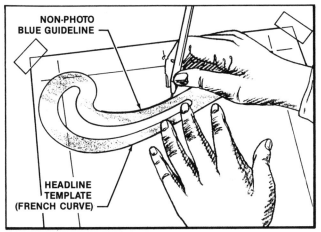

Step 1. Lay out non-photo blue guideline. Align headline template with non-photo blue guideline.

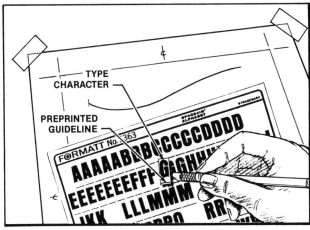

Step 2. Cut and remove type character, including preprinted guideline.

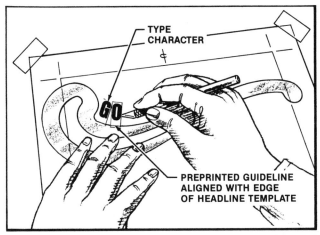

Step 3. Position type character along headline template and burnish lightly on headline template.

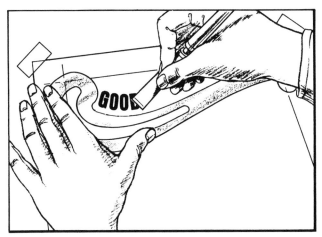

Step 4. Align headline template with non-photo blue guideline and press characters onto artboard. Burnish thoroughly.

Figure 6-7. A french curve is used to create a curved arrangement in the headline template method of applying adhesive type.

altered easily. Adhesive type is easily cut, extended, overlapped, and textured to create new appearances. See Figure 6-8. Adhesive type gives the designer or paste-up artist the ability to create new typestyles that may be used to emphasize an idea or create a logo. A *logo* is letters and/or artwork used as an advertising trademark for a company or product. See Figure 6-9.

Transfer Type

Transfer type is an alternative to adhesive type. Transfer type, rules, and symbols are printed with a flexible vinyl ink on the underside of a heavy acetate sheet. A waxed backing sheet protects the transfer material. See Figure 6-10. To transfer type, the selected character is positioned on an artboard and carefully rubbed in place with a burnisher.

Unlike other forms of hand-set type, transfer type has the advantage of transferring easily to the artboard, film, acetate, frosted glass, or tissue. Transfer type creates a smooth appearance and is commonly used to give a finished look to the comprehensive layout. White transfer type may be colored with marker to create colored type for a comprehensive layout.

Transfer type, however, is delicate. If stored flat in a cool, dry place, transfer type lasts three to five years at most without chipping or cracking when applied. In addition to having a shorter shelf life than adhesive type, some brands of transfer type are nearly twice as expensive as adhesive type.

Creating a Headline with Transfer Type. Creating a headline with transfer type is done by aligning a

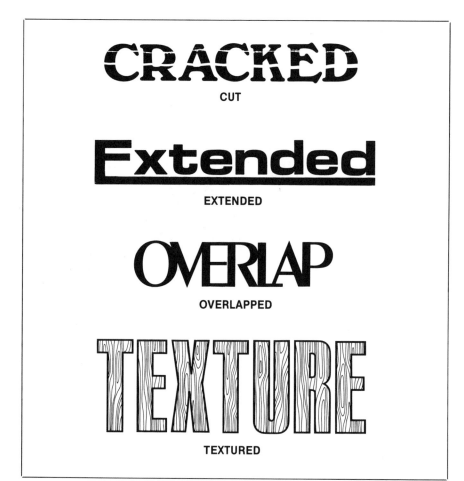

Figure 6-8. Adhesive type is easily altered to create new appearances.

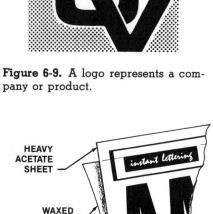

Figure 6-9. A logo represents a company or product.

Figure 6-10. Transfer type is printed on heavy acetate with a special vinyl ink that resists cracking and chipping. When the waxed backing sheet is burnished over the type, it puts a protective layer of wax on the transfer type.

character with the non-photo blue guideline drawn on an artboard. Each character is positioned and transferred onto the artboard by burnishing with a smooth-tipped instrument. After a word is created, the type is protected from chipping by placing the waxed backing sheet over the word and burnishing. See Figure 6-11.

1. Draw a non-photo blue baseline on the artboard and indicate a line length, or starting and ending point, for the type. Measure the distance between the baseline of the type character and preprinted guide marks below the character. On the artboard, measure this distance down from the non-photo blue baseline and draw a non-photo blue guideline.

2. Position the first type character of the word being created at the left margin on the guideline. To ensure squareness, align the preprinted guide marks on the transfer type with the non-photo blue guideline on the artboard.

3. Burnish the type character thoroughly, using a burnisher with a round tip or blunt edge. When the entire type character changes to a gray-black tone, it is transferred.

4. Transfer each character individually, paying close attention to visual letterspacing and the line length of the type.

5. Remove mistakes or improperly aligned type characters with a piece of masking tape.

6. Cover the completed line with the waxed backing sheet and burnish thoroughly to protect the type from chipping.

Applying Transfer Type

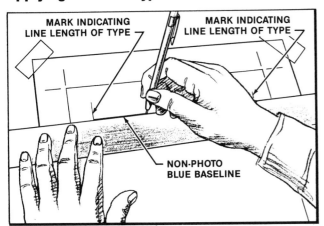

Step 1. Draw non-photo blue baseline on artboard. Indicate line length of the type. Draw a non-photo blue guideline below the baseline, using the distance measured between the baseline and preprinted guide mark on the sheet of transfer type.

Step 2. Position first type character at left margin and align with guideline.

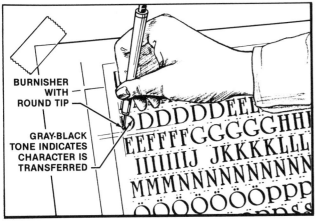

Step 3. Burnish type character thoroughly. A gray-black tone indicates character is transferred.

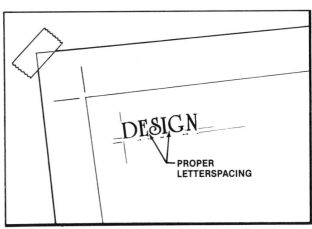

Step 4. Pay close attention to letterspacing and designated line length when transferring each letter.

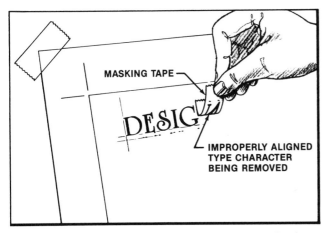

Step 5. Use a piece of masking tape to remove mistakes.

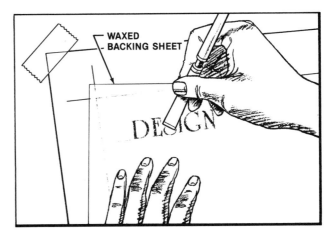

Step 6. Place waxed backing sheet over completed line of type and burnish thoroughly.

Figure 6-11. Type characters must be letterspaced carefully when applying transfer type.

6 Inked and Hand-set Type

REVIEW QUESTIONS

True-False

T   F   **1.** Inked copy is often enlarged or reduced to fit a designated space.

T   F   **2.** The two most common methods of hand setting type are the adhesive type and transfer type methods.

T   F   **3.** Adhesive type is printed on acetate sheets in black ink.

T   F   **4.** The layout of hand-set type is the comprehensive layout drawn by the designer.

T   F   **5.** Letterspacing of adhesive and transfer type is visually determined by the artist.

T   F   **6.** Most type smaller than 18-point in height is easily letterspaced by hand.

T   F   **7.** Adhesive type has a shelf life of approximately five years when stored flat and protected from heat and humidity.

T   F   **8.** Artistic alignment is easily created with adhesive type.

T   F   **9.** Adhesive type is difficult to cut, overlap, texture, or extend.

T   F   **10.** Transfer type, rules, and symbols are printed with flexible vinyl ink on the underside of an acetate sheet.

Multiple Choice

_____   **1.** Adhesive type and transfer type can be enlarged to _____% without visible flaws.
A. 100
B. 200
C. 300
D. 400

_____   **2.** The layout of hand-set type is the _____ of the type characters on the mechanical.
A. drawing
B. adhering
C. measuring
D. aligning

_____   **3.** _____ type is pressure-sensitive.
A. Transfer
B. Adhesive
C. Inked
D. all of the above

_____   **4.** The _____ setter is a tool used to align adhesive type on an artboard.
A. headline
B. adhesive
C. ruler
D. type

_____ 5. _____ type is rubbed onto the surface of an artboard.
    A. Adhesive
    B. Transfer
    C. Burnish
    D. Rub-on

Completion

_____ 1. A(n) _____ is made of letters and/or artwork and is used as an advertising trademark for a company or product.

_____ 2. Adhesive type and transfer type are popular for their _____ of application.

_____ 3. Adhesive type is _____ spaced on non-photo blue baselines.

_____ 4. Adhesive type is printed on the _____ of an acetate sheet to avoid damaging the image.

_____ 5. Both adhesive and transfer type are _____ to assure reproduction quality.

_____ 6. The acetate backing of adhesive type prevents it from appearing _____ when applied to fabric or glass.

_____ 7. The guideline and headline setter methods are two ways of creating a headline with _____ type.

_____ 8. _____ type can be applied to a comprehensive layout for a finished appearance.

_____ 9. The ability to easily manipulate characters is an advantage of _____ type.

_____ 10. White _____ type may be colored to create colored type for presentations.

Matching

_____ 1. Transfer type

_____ 2. Adhesive type

_____ 3. Inked type

_____ 4. 6-point to 214-point

_____ 5. Letterspacing

_____ 6. 18-point to 214-point

_____ 7. Headline template

_____ 8. Headline setter

_____ 9. Three to five years

_____ 10. At least five years

_____ 11. Conditions for storage of type

_____ 12. Transfer type protector

A. Cool and dry
B. Average life of transfer type
C. Easily positioned type
D. Hand-drawn
E. Rub-on
F. Pressure-sensitive
G. Visually estimated
H. Available type sizes
I. Wax-coated backing sheet
J. Tool for straight type alignment
K. Tool for curved type alignment
L. Average life of adhesive type

TYPE AND ILLUSTRATIONS

Pasting up type and illustrations is the most common form of copy adhesion required of the paste-up artist. Type and illustrations come in a variety of sizes and are produced on a variety of paper stocks. The technique and adhesive used to paste up the copy vary with the job requirements. The paste-up artist may be required to paste up type in a long column or in a circle. Choosing the correct technique and adhesive for the job allows quality reproduction.

BASIC PASTE-UP PROCEDURE

The basic paste-up procedure selected is based on job requirements. Job size, type and intricacy of copy to be pasted up, quality of job, and design of layout are considered before paste-up is begun. Each of these aspects requires the use of a specific adhesive or paste-up procedure.

Choosing Correct Adhesive

A variety of adhesives is available for paste-up, each with individual characteristics. Three commonly used adhesives are rubber cement, wax, and spray adhesive. Other adhesives are available, such as paste and liquid glue, but are undesirable for most paste-up applications because they do not provide high-quality mechanicals.

Rubber Cement. *Rubber cement,* the most commonly used adhesive,

has a thin, liquid consistency and is easily applied to the back of copy with a flat-end brush. Rubber cement, which dries quickly, is kept in an airtight container. Copy coated with rubber cement bonds quickly to the artboard. Excess rubber cement is easily removed from the artboard with a commercial rubber cement pickup or ball of dried rubber cement.

Rubber cement is widely used in paste-up because it is flexible enough for temporary or permanent adhesion. For temporary adhesion, rubber cement is applied only to the back of copy, and copy can be repositioned until the rubber cement has dried. For permanent adhesion, rubber cement is applied to the back of copy and the surface of the artboard. Rubber cement must dry on both surfaces before copy is pasted up on the artboard. Once pasted up and burnished, the copy can only be removed from the artboard through application of rubber cement thinner. See Figure 7-1.

Rubber cement has a wide range of applications in the paste-up pro-

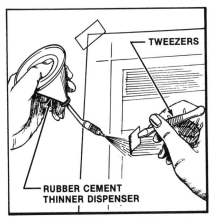

Figure 7-1. Rubber cement thinner does not damage copy when used to remove copy from an artboard.

cess. Artboards that will be kept for a long time, or those that are expensive or time-consuming to produce, are generally pasted up using rubber cement. Rubber cement is stable and will not shrink, flake, or melt under variable environmental conditions. Small pieces of copy are less likely to fall off the artboard if affixed with rubber cement rather than another form of adhesive. Although generally more time-consuming, using rubber cement is cleaner than using other forms of copy adhesive.

Wax. Wax is an alternate method of adhering copy to an artboard. A thin coat of melted wax is applied to the back of the copy with a waxer. Waxers are available as hand-held applicators for small copy or tabletop models for larger copy. See Figure 7-2.

Wax has an advantage over all other methods of adhesive because it does not bond to the artboard until it is burnished. This slightly tacky adhesive property allows for repositioning of copy. Once burnished, waxed copy can be removed from the artboard with rubber cement thinner. Rubber cement thinner dissolves wax and is, therefore, also used to clean up wax residue on artboards.

Wax is a quick adhesive generally used in paste-up jobs where speed and quantity are more important than quality. Wax is not a stable adhesive; it is affected by environmental conditions. Extreme heat causes wax to melt, penetrating the paper-based copy and dissolving the wax. Heat also causes copy elements to fall off the artboard. Under cold conditions, wax shrinks and cracks, again causing copy elements to fall off the artboard.

Wax residue is another disadvantage of wax adhesive. Although rubber cement thinner removes most wax residue, a thin layer often remains on the copy. This thin layer of wax may create difficulties during photographic reproduction. Fine lines may be obliterated on film because the wax residue does not allow proper reflection off white areas of copy. In addition, wax residue on the artboard may transfer to the glass of the copyboard during photography, creating extra, time-consuming steps for the camera operator who must continually clean wax from the copyboard glass.

Spray Adhesive. *Spray adhesive* is a quick-drying, rubber cement-based adhesive sold in aerosol cans. High-tack and low-tack spray adhesives are available. High-tack adhesive results in permanent adhesion. For copy 12″ × 12″ and smaller, only the copy is sprayed. For copy larger than 12″ × 12″, both the copy and artboard are sprayed. Copy must be carefully positioned when using high-tack adhesive because the bond is immediate, and the copy cannot be repositioned.

Low-tack adhesive provides temporary adhesion when applied only to the back of the copy. Copy may be repositioned easily using low-tack adhesive. A more permanent bond can be achieved by spraying both copy

and artboard, or by spraying a heavy coat on the copy. However, repositioning copy is difficult when these techniques are used.

Spray adhesive is best used for pasting up large copy elements. Copy elements 8½″ × 11″ and larger are easier to work with if spray adhesive is used because spray adhesive provides more even coverage than rubber cement or wax. Rubber cement dries too quickly, and coverage is uneven. Wax often spreads unevenly over a large size sheet of copy and may bleed through the copy. Although rubber cement thinner partially dissolves most brands of spray adhesive, spray adhesive is not easily removed from the artboard and should therefore be used with caution.

Miscellaneous Adhesives. Miscellaneous adhesives such as paste, liquid glue, glue stick, dry-mount tissue, and double-sided adhesive material have their own adhesive properties. Although these adhesives have many applications, they are generally considered undesirable for quality paste-up. Adhesives that respond to alcohol or benzine-based solvents are recommended for pasting up artboards. Only those adhesives that can be removed from the artboard without damage to the copy should be used.

HAND-HELD WAXER

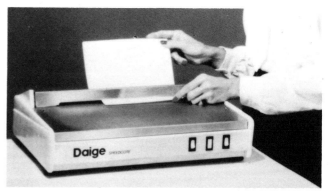

Daige Products, Inc.

TABLETOP WAXER

Figure 7-2. Wax is one of the adhesives most commonly used in paste-up.

Applying Adhesives

Applying adhesives during paste-up is a process that varies with each job. Long columns of type are usually affixed to the artboard with rubber cement because wet rubber cement allows for ease of positioning. Intricate paste-up, such as type set in a circle, is done with wax, which allows type to be repositioned without adhering to the artboard. Large size copy, such as typewritten pages, is affixed with spray adhesive because it creates an even coat of adhesive and will not discolor.

Column Type. Column type is the most common form of copy. The paste-up artist often has to cut a long galley of type and fit it to the column dimensions indicated on the comprehensive layout. See Figure 7-3.

1. Take width and depth measurements of copy from the comprehensive layout. Draw non-photo blue guidelines on the artboard according to these measurements, including column dimensions, gutter, and margins.

2. Position the copy (galley) in the space allotted for the first column. Mark the column depth in non-photo blue on the copy.

3. Align the copy with the T-square and carefully cut between lines of type at the non-photo blue mark.

4. Apply adhesive to the back of the first column of copy.

5. Using the T-square, align the copy horizontally in the allotted space.

6. Burnish the copy thoroughly and remove excess adhesive. Repeat steps 1–6 until all copy is pasted up.

The column type should completely fill the artboard according to the comprehensive layout. If the last column pasted on the artboard is too short or too long, adjustments are made by increasing or decreasing the space between paragraphs. If severe inaccuracies occur, the comprehensive layout may have to be altered, returned to the typesetter, and the copy reset.

Circular Type. Circular type requires intricate paste-up in which the paste-up artist cuts between type characters and bends the type around a circle. Although not often required of the paste-up artist, pasting type into a circle is a skill that will save many time-consuming steps when needed. See Figure 7-4.

1. Draw a non-photo blue circle on the artboard in the size indicated on the comprehensive layout. Divide the circle into quadrants.

2. Apply adhesive to the copy, and place the copy on a backing sheet of cardboard or acetate.

3. Determine line length of the copy, and mark the center of the copy in non-photo blue. Measure down from the descender of the copy, and cut away the white paper below this point.

4. Cut the copy between each character from the top down, leaving $\frac{1}{32}''$ uncut at the bottom.

5. After loosening the copy from the backing sheet with an art knife, line up the center of the copy with the vertical center of the circle. Align the center character with the circle and gently burnish.

6. Align the remainder of the copy with the circle. Burnish the copy thoroughly and remove excess adhesive.

To paste up copy that runs along the bottom of a circle, the height of the copy is measured. This height measurement is transferred to the bottom of the first circle, and a second non-photo blue circle is drawn below the first circle. Steps 2–6 are followed, except that when cutting between each character (step 4), the cutting is done from the bottom up rather than from the top down.

Printed and Typewritten Copy. Printed and typewritten copy require delicate handling by the paste-up artist. In both forms of copy, the type image is on the surface of the artboard, and type characters may be easily damaged. The stock on which the copy is printed or typewritten may also be thin. Therefore, printed and typewritten copy are often pasted up

on the artboard using spray adhesive. See Figure 7-5.

1. Draw non-photo blue guidelines on the artboard, indicating position of copy and its horizontal and vertical center. Also draw non-photo blue guidelines on the copy, indicating horizontal and vertical center.

2. Spray fixative on the face of printed or typewritten copy to protect the copy from smearing or smudging.

3. Place the copy face down on a large sheet of cardboard, or in a spray booth. Spray a fine layer of adhesive on the back of the copy.

4. Turn the copy over, handling it by the edges. Align the center marks on the artboard.

5. Cover the positioned copy with a sheet of tissue and burnish thoroughly from the center outward. Allow excess adhesive spray to dry, then remove.

PRODUCTION TECHNIQUES

Specific job requirements are more easily reproduced if pasted up on separate artboards, or in layers, rather than on a single artboard. By separating certain copy elements, the camera operator is able to photograph similar elements on one piece of film while other elements are photographed on another piece of film. The films are repositioned in the stripping process. This technique, the *overlay method*, improves reproduction quality in paste-up and facilitates camera work and stripping.

Overlay Method

The overlay method of pasting up a mechanical includes the artboard and an acetate sheet, which is the overlay. (Mylar may also be used.) The acetate sheet used as the overlay is cut slightly shorter than the depth of the artboard and taped to the top of the artboard. Specific copy elements, such as elements to appear in a second color, are pasted up on the overlay. Placing elements to appear in a second color on an overlay separates them from elements to appear in the first color. Register marks, or targets,

Pasting Up Column Type

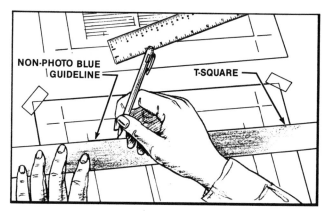

Step 1. Draw non-photo blue guidelines on artboard according to measurements from comprehensive layout.

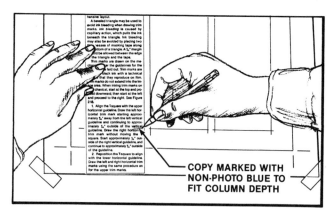

Step 2. Position copy (galley) in space allotted for first column and mark depth of column on copy in non-photo blue.

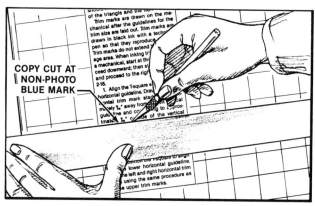

Step 3. Align copy with T-square and cut at non-photo blue mark between lines of type.

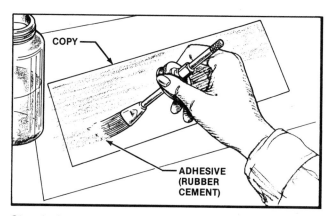

Step 4. Apply adhesive to back of copy.

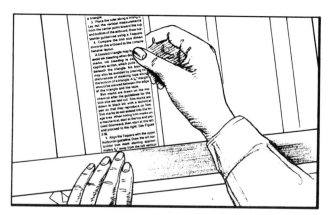

Step 5. Align copy in allotted space.

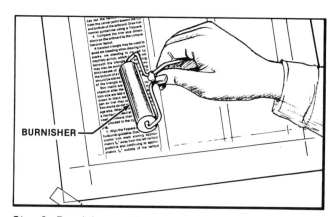

Step 6. Burnish copy thoroughly.

Figure 7-3. Column type is the most common form of copy arranged by paste-up artists.

Pasting Up Type in a Circle

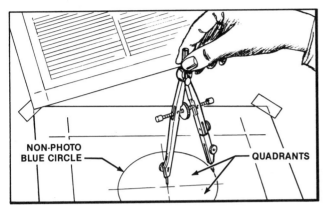

Step 1. Draw non-photo blue circle on artboard according to measurements from comprehensive layout.

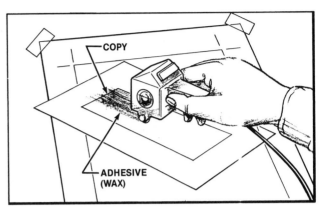

Step 2. Apply adhesive to back of copy and place on backing sheet.

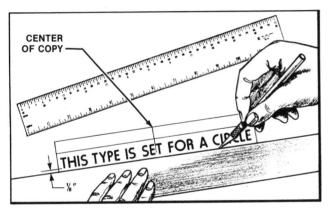

Step 3. Measure line length of copy and mark center in non-photo blue. Measure ⅛″ down from descender and cut white paper away below this point.

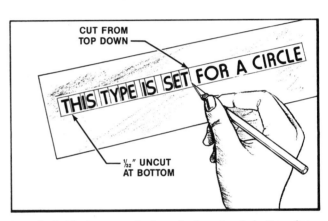

Step 4. Cut between each character from top to bottom, leaving ¹⁄₃₂″ uncut at bottom.

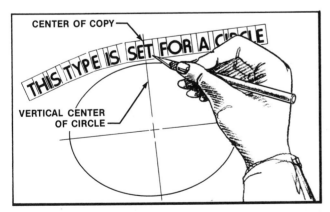

Step 5. Using art knife, line up center of copy with vertical center of circle.

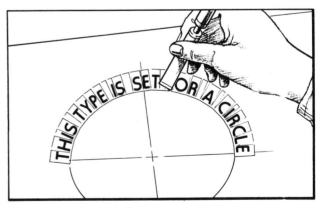

Step 6. Align remainder of copy with circle and burnish thoroughly.

Figure 7-4. Pasting up type in a circle requires cutting between type characters.

Pasting Up Printed and Typewritten (Delicate) Copy

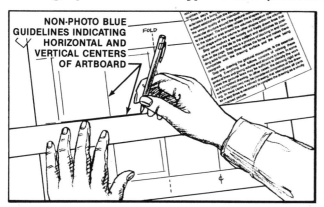

Step 1. Draw non-photo blue guidelines on artboard and copy, both indicating center of copy.

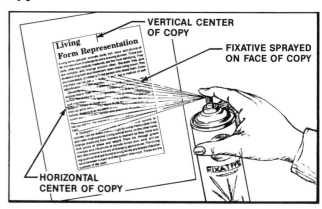

Step 2. Spray fixative on face of copy to protect copy from smearing or smudging.

Step 3. Place copy face down and spray fine layer of adhesive on back of copy.

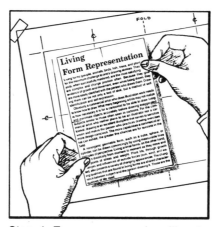

Step 4. Turn copy over, handling by edges, and align on artboard.

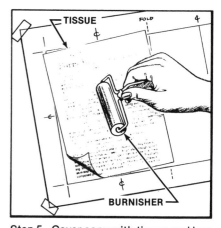

Step 5. Cover copy with tissue and burnish thoroughly from center outward.

Figure 7-5. Printed and typewritten copy are delicate and require careful handling when being pasted up.

are applied at the same place on the artboard and overlay to aid the stripper in aligning the films. See Figure 7-6.

The artboard and overlay are photographed as if the elements were affixed to separate artboards. The acetate sheet, however, allows the paste-up artist to intricately align type elements with elements on the artboard. Therefore, the overlay method is commonly used to paste up intricate type and line art, such as forms, surprinted copy, or reverses.

Pasting up a Form. Pasting up a form involves pasting it up on a single artboard or using the overlay method. If pasted up on a single artboard,

all rules and type are on the artboard. Cutting and pasting type adjacent to inked or taped rules is difficult, time-consuming, and sometimes inaccurate. Intricate forms pasted up using an overlay are more accurate and simpler to produce. See Figure 7-7.

1. Draw all non-photo blue guidelines for the form on the artboard, indicating position of rules and type. Apply register marks. Ink rules or apply adhesive rules.

2. Tape an acetate sheet over the artboard. Apply register marks on the acetate sheet.

3. Cut type elements and apply adhesive. Position the type elements on the artboard with tweezers and burnish thoroughly.

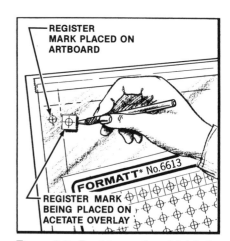

Figure 7-6. Register marks, which help the stripper align films, are positioned at the same place on the artboard and acetate overlay.

Pasting Up Forms

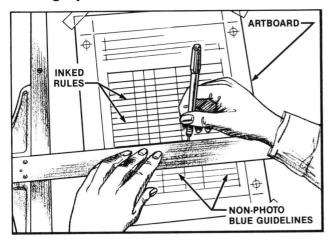

Step 1. Draw all non-photo blue guidelines for the form. Apply register marks on artboard. Ink rules or apply adhesive rules.

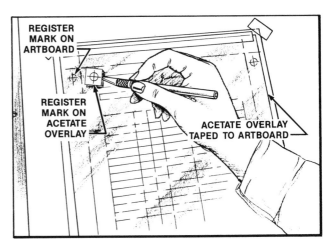

Step 2. Tape acetate sheet over artboard. Apply register marks on acetate sheet.

Step 3. Position type elements on acetate sheet using tweezers.

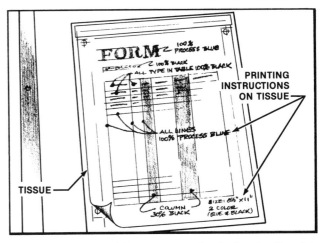

Step 4. Tape sheet of tissue over mechanical and write printing instructions on the tissue.

Figure 7-7. Pasting up a form using the overlay method saves time and ensures accurate alignment.

4. Remove excess adhesive. Tape a sheet of tissue over the mechanical, and write complete printing instructions on the tissue.

The artboard and overlay are photographed separately and repositioned during stripping.

Surprinting. *Surprinting* is the process of printing type over an alternate form of copy. The alternate form of copy may be a tint screen, photograph, or an illustration. Although an adhesive tint screen can be overlapped on type, the preferred method is to paste up the type and tint screen separately. To ensure accurate alignment and prevent loss of copy, all photographs and most illustrations should be surprinted.

To paste up for surprinting, the alternate copy is pasted in position on the artboard, and the type is pasted in position on the overlay. This overlay method allows the paste-up artist to better visualize the layout and position of the copy. See Figure 7-8.

1. Draw non-photo blue guidelines on the artboard according to the comprehensive layout.

2. Apply register marks. Paste up alternate copy on the artboard.

3. Tape an acetate sheet to the artboard and apply register marks. Position type elements on the acetate overlay.

4. Place a sheet of tissue over the mechanical, and burnish the alternate copy and type elements thoroughly. Remove excess adhesive. Tape a sheet of tissue over the mechanical, and write complete printing instructions on the tissue.

Surprinting Copy

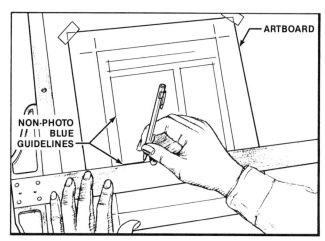

Step 1. Draw non-photo blue guidelines on artboard according to comprehensive layout.

Step 2. Apply register marks and paste up alternate copy on artboard.

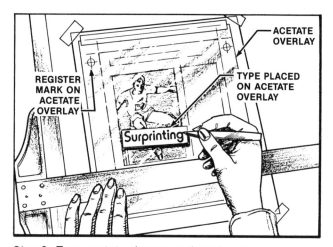

Step 3. Tape acetate sheet to artboard and apply register marks. Position type elements on acetate overlay.

Step 4. After alternate copy and type elements are pasted up, tape sheet of tissue to mechanical and burnish thoroughly. Write complete printing instructions on tissue.

Figure 7-8. All photographs and most illustrations should be surprinted.

The artboard and acetate overlay are photographed separately and repositioned during stripping. The reproduction appears as background copy with type printed over the background.

Reversing Type. *Reversing type* is the process of printing the background on which type is pasted a different color from the stock, while the type remains the color of the stock. Condensed or lightface type should not be used. Some typestyles are available in reverse, but most forms of reverse are created by the camera operator and stripper.

The camera operator photographs type to be reversed onto positive film, which is stripped over the alternate copy. The alternate copy may be a tint, photograph, illustration, or solid color. The positive film holds back all light in the type area, creating a reverse when it is burned onto the plate. Since the reverse copy is photographed onto positive film and the other copy is photographed onto negative film, the overlay method is used in paste-up. See Figure 7-9.

Reversing Type

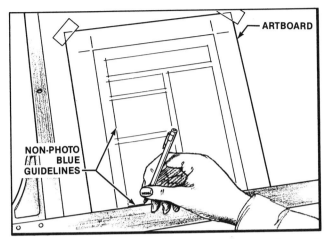

Step 1. Draw non-photo blue guidelines on artboard according to comprehensive layout.

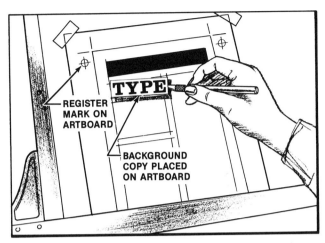

Step 2. Apply register marks and paste up background copy on artboard.

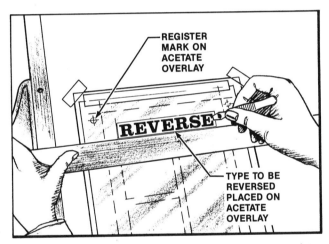

Step 3. Tape acetate overlay over artboard and apply register marks. Paste up type to be reversed on acetate overlay.

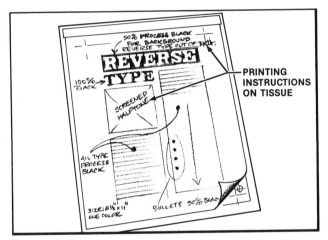

Step 4. After background copy and type elements are pasted up, tape sheet of tissue to mechanical and burnish thoroughly. Write complete printing instructions on tissue.

Figure 7-9. Type that is reversed remains the same color as the stock.

1. Draw non-photo blue guidelines indicating position of elements on the artboard, according to the comprehensive layout.

2. Apply register marks on the artboard. Paste up the background copy on the artboard, or indicate the background copy on the artboard with a red keyline.

3. Tape an acetate overlay over the artboard. Apply register marks on the acetate overlay. Paste up the type to be reversed in position on the acetate overlay.

4. Place a sheet of tissue over the artboard, and burnish the background copy and type elements thoroughly. Remove any excess adhesive. Tape a sheet of tissue over the mechanical, and write the complete printing instructions on the tissue.

The artboard and acetate overlay are photographed separately. The reverse is reproduced on positive film. The two films are repositioned during the stripping process. The final reproduction appears as different color background ink with reverse type the same color as the stock.

True-False

T   F   **1.** The best adhesive for paste-up is chosen by analyzing the needs of the job.

T   F   **2.** Each adhesive has its own characteristics and use.

T   F   **3.** Rubber cement is rarely used in paste-up.

T   F   **4.** Rubber cement is used for permanent adhesion only.

T   F   **5.** A waxed type block does not bond to the artboard until it is thoroughly burnished.

T   F   **6.** Rubber cement adhesion is used primarily when speed of application is more important than quality.

T   F   **7.** Wax is an unstable adhesive.

T   F   **8.** In general, rubber cement is a cleaner adhesive than wax.

T   F   **9.** Spray adhesive is best applied in paste-up for small copy elements.

T   F   **10.** Only adhesives that may be removed from the artboard without damage to the copy should be used in paste-up.

Completion

_____   **1.** _____ pieces of copy are less likely to fall off the artboard if adhered with rubber cement.

_____   **2.** For permanent adhesion, rubber cement is applied to the back of the element and the _____ of the artboard.

_____   **3.** Once affixed to the artboard with rubber cement, the copy can only be removed with rubber cement _____.

_____   **4.** A thin coat of wax is applied to the _____ of the copy.

_____   **5.** Heat causes the _____ to melt and penetrate the paper of the copy.

_____   **6.** Cold causes the _____ to shrink, causing the copy elements to fall off.

_____   **7.** Wax _____ is a disadvantage of wax adhesive.

_____   **8.** The application of _____ in the paste-up process varies with each job.

_____   **9.** The _____ method of paste-up improves reproduction quality in paste-up and facilitates camera work and stripping.

_____   **10.** _____ copy may print over a tint screen, a photograph, or an illustration.

Multiple Choice

_____ 1. _____ is an adhesive that can be easily removed from unwanted areas of the artboard.
A. Rubber cement
B. Wax adhesive
C. Spray adhesive
D. Glue stick

_____ 2. _____ is an adhesive that allows the paste-up artist to apply a very thin coat to large size copy.
A. Rubber cement
B. Wax adhesive
C. Spray adhesive
D. Glue stick

_____ 3. A rubber cement _____ is used to remove dried rubber cement from the artboard.
A. pickup
B. thinner
C. acetate
D. eraser

_____ 4. Rubber cement _____ is used to remove excess wax from the surface of the artboard.
A. pickup
B. thinner
C. acetate
D. eraser

_____ 5. _____ is an adhesive that allows the paste-up artist to easily reposition type.
A. Rubber cement
B. Wax adhesive
C. High-tack spray adhesive
D. Glue stick

Matching

_____ 1. Rubber cement

_____ 2. Wax

_____ 3. Spray adhesive

_____ 4. Glue stick

_____ 5. Type in a circle

_____ 6. Type in a column

_____ 7. Typewritten copy

_____ 8. Overlay method

_____ 9. Reverse type

_____ 10. Surprinting copy

_____ 11. Acetate sheet

_____ 12. Adhesive remover

A. Printing type over a photo
B. Delicate copy
C. Intricate form of paste-up
D. Stable, clean adhesive
E. Unstable, messy adhesive
F. Adhesive unsuitable for paste-up
G. Adhesive for large copy
H. Most common form of copy
I. Rubber cement thinner
J. Surface for overlay method
K. Background is ink, type is stock
L. Separating specific copy elements

8 CAMERA COPY

Camera copy is the original artwork or mechanical used to create negatives for printing production. Camera copy is divided into two categories: line copy and continuous tone copy. The paste-up artist must be familiar with quality control methods used to prepare and reproduce line copy and continuous tone copy. Instructions given on mechanicals by the paste-up artist define methods of production used by the camera operator and stripper.

LINE AND CONTINUOUS TONE COPY

Line copy and continuous tone copy are the two types of photographic reproduction that make up graphic arts photography. *Line copy* is copy that has a single color and tone, for example, type, line illustrations, and rules. *Continuous tone copy* is copy that has shades or tones, *tonal gradation,* of a color or black. Continuous tone copy includes photographs, paintings, and pencil renderings.

Line photography is the reproduction of line copy on high-contrast film using a process camera. A *process camera* is a camera designed to photograph flat copy for printing. A single calculated exposure of a bright light through the process camera lens produces good-quality line copy. See Figure 8-1.

Black-and-white continuous tone copy is reproduced onto high-contrast film through a series of exposures. Because no major printing process can lay down ink of varying densities,

continuous tone copy cannot be reproduced as continuous tones. The range of tones from black through white, which includes all grays, is broken into a series of dots. These dots create the illusion of continuous

tone. The process of using dots to give an illusion of continuous tone is the *halftone process.*

In a *halftone,* which is a screened continuous tone image, small dots appear light to the eye because of

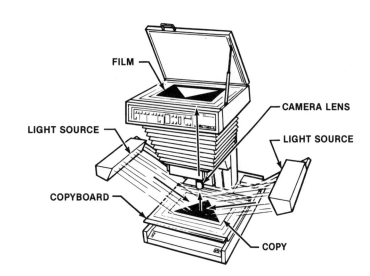

Figure 8-1. Light reflecting off white areas of the copy travels through the process camera lens and exposes the film. Black areas of the copy absorb light and do not expose the film.

FILM

CAMERA LENS

LIGHT SOURCE

LIGHT SOURCE

COPYBOARD

COPY

the white background surrounding each dot. As dot size increases, the surrounding background decreases, absorbing a portion of the light reflected to the eye. The larger the dots are, the darker the image appears. Most printed halftone dots range from 5% in the lightest area, which are *highlight dots,* to 95% in the darkest area, which are *shadow dots.* Halftone dots between highlight and shadow dots, in the 30% to 70% range, are *middletone dots,* or midtone dots. See Figure 8-2.

Halftone dots are created through a contact screen. A *contact screen* is a film screen approximately .007″ thick used in direct contact with light-sensitive film. Contact screens have a pattern of *vignette dots,* which are

a series of equally spaced dots of varying densities. Vignette dots are clear in the center and become gradually darker toward the edges. See Figure 8-3. In the halftone reproduction process, the contact screen is placed over the film, and a series of exposures is made. The halftone process uses more than one type of exposure to record the range of tones from copy onto film. The exposures include the main, flash, and bump exposures.

The *main exposure* is an exposure of white light reflecting off the copy, through the lens, penetrating the contact screen, and exposing the film. It is a *screened image exposure* because the light reflects off the image, and the image is screened before it reaches the film. The main exposure is sometimes called the *detailed exposure* because it exposes the broadest range of tones, the midtones.

The *flash exposure* is an exposure of dim yellow light through the contact screen. The flash is a *nonimage screened exposure* because the yellow light is exposed directly through the screen without reflecting off a copy. The flash adds density to shadow areas of the halftone negative. The light reflecting off shadow areas of the copy is often too weak to create a dot on the film. The flash exposure enables the shadow areas to print a 95% dot.

The *bump exposure* is an exposure of white light reflecting off the copy, through the lens, and directly onto the film. The bump exposure is a *nonscreened image exposure* because the contact screen is removed from the film before the exposure is made. The bump exposure adds detail in the highlight areas of the halftone.

Since line copy and halftone copy differ in their makeup and photographic reproduction process, they are treated differently in paste-up. Line copy and halftone copy are prepared separately for photographic reproduction.

Continuous tone copy containing color, such as photographs, illustrations, and paintings, is reproduced through the color separation process. In the *color separation process,* the original continuous tone color is exposed through filters to produce negatives used to make plates for 4-color reproduction. Four-color reproduction produces a full range of colors with the four process ink colors: yellow, magenta, cyan, and black.

Line Copy

Good camera-ready line copy consists of dense lines, dots, type, or solid areas of a single color. This color, ideally black, is mounted on a contrasting background, which is usually

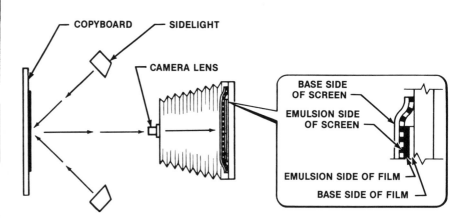

5% HIGHLIGHT DOTS 50% MIDTONE DOTS 95% SHADOW DOTS

Armstrong World Industries, Inc.

Figure 8-2. In halftones, small dots are highlight dots, mid-size dots are midtone dots, and large dots are shadow dots.

COPYBOARD SIDELIGHT CAMERA LENS BASE SIDE OF SCREEN EMULSION SIDE OF SCREEN EMULSION SIDE OF FILM BASE SIDE OF FILM

Figure 8-3. A contact screen is placed in direct contact over the film for photographic reproduction of a halftone. During exposure, vignette dots on the contact screen cause light reflecting off the copy to create dots of varying size on the film.

white. The camera operator computes the exposure that will reproduce the line image on film in the size required for reproduction. To produce high-quality negatives or positives, the camera operator must start with good-quality copy. Poor-quality line copy often results in poor-quality reproduction.

The paste-up artist follows quality control standards in the photographic reproduction of copy. To ensure high-quality reproductions, the paste-up artist should pretest for copy density, copy size, fine line copy, shadowing, and color. Although most quality control standards are universal throughout the industry, the paste-up artist should discuss special requirements with the camera operator.

Copy Density. *Copy density* is the darkness, or light-absorbing ability of copy. Although all line copy is to reproduce equally on film, the density of the copy often varies greatly on the mechanical. Copy with varying densities reproduces poorly on film. Type and rules may appear in different thicknesses, as broken characters, or not appear at all because of variations in light reflection from copy to film.

To assure high-quality reproduction of type and line art, all copy density must be equal. If copy elements are not equally dense, type should be reset on the typesetter, or type and art elements should be reproduced on high-contrast photographic paper. The most common method of obtaining equal density on high-contrast paper is through a diffusion transfer process, such as the photomechanical transfer (PMT) process by Kodak. When all copy is of equal density, it is pasted up to create a mechanical. Although densities may be equal, type and illustrations could vary in thickness when reproduced on PMT paper. Equal density and copy thickness enable the camera operator to make high-quality film reproductions of mechanicals. See Figure 8-4.

Copy Size. *Copy size* is the reproduction size of copy after it has been

MECHANICAL   PRINTED PIECE

Figure 8-4. For optimum reproduction quality, the density of all line copy on a mechanical must be equalized.

photographed. If a mechanical is pasted up at a size different from its final reproduction size, the paste-up artist must be aware of sizing limitations. Most process cameras have a size range from 20% to 300%. *Same size reproduction* is 100%. Any percentage below 100% is a *reduction,* and any percentage above 100% is an *enlargement.* See Figure 8-5.

If original line copy is to be enlarged or reduced at a percentage beyond camera limitations, extra photographic steps are required. The camera operator photographs the line copy at the smallest or largest size possible, depending on job requirements. The camera operator then reproduces, or contact prints, the image onto photographic paper and rephotographs the image onto film at another reduction or enlargement size. This copy-to-copy reproduction process often lowers the quality of the image. To ensure good reproduction quality and eliminate extra steps, size limitations of the camera should be known before the paste-up process.

Fine Line Copy. *Fine line copy* is type, line illustrations, and rules of 1-point line thickness or below. Most fine line reproductions are photographed without difficulty when reproduced at 100%. It is common practice, however, for an illustrator or a keyliner to create an image two times larger than required and reduce it to fill a designated space. The reduction process reduces imperfections in illustrations and produces a crisp image. Reducing the image, however, can cause poor-quality reproduction. The difficulty of reproducing oversize original line art becomes apparent when the rule sizes in the original art are not drawn to compensate for the size of reduction.

A fine line test board is made to test for line thickness reproduction. Rules of commonly used thicknesses are drawn on an artboard using a technical pen with black ink. Rule thicknesses are labeled on the fine line test board, and the board is reduced to a variety of percentages. See Figure 8-6. Reproductions of the

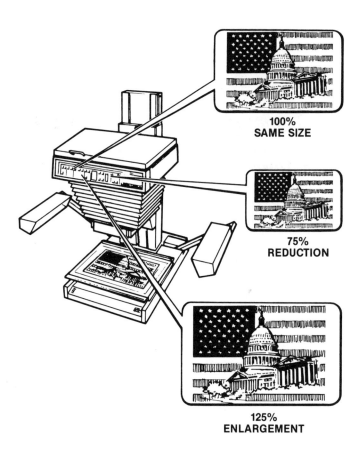

Figure 8-5. Percentage selection at 100% is same size reproduction, below 100% is a reduction, and above 100% is an enlargement.

fine line test board are contact printed onto paper or, if feasible, printed on a press.

Test boards serve as a reference for line thicknesses needed for oversize art. Intricate line art with many rules adjacent to one another should be drawn 100% for reproduction. If intricate line art were drawn oversize, reducing the art would cause fine lines to run together.

Shadowing. *Shadowing* on film is caused by cutlines on copy. When copy is photographed, it is illuminated by lights on either side of the copyboard. The sidelighting throws shadow lines wherever cuts are made. Shadow lines appear on negatives as thin, clear lines along the copy. Shadow lines, if not corrected, reproduce on the final printed piece. To eliminate shadow lines, the negative is painted during stripping with *opaque,* a thick black liquid used to hide shadow lines. The process of opaquing shadow lines is time-consuming and adds labor cost to the job.

Various methods can be used to reduce shadow lines. The best method is to have typeset copy reset. Small changes in copy, such as a

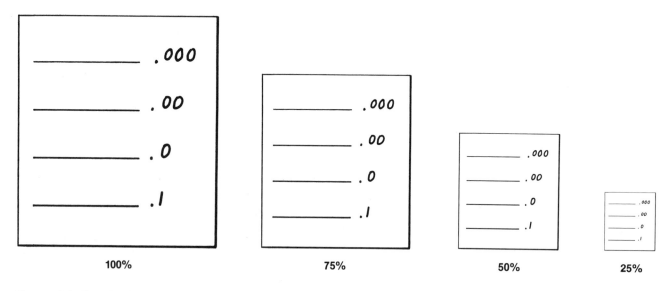

Figure 8-6. Fine line test boards serve as a quality control guide for reducing lines of 1-point thickness and finer.

missing character, are especially difficult to cut out and replace without shadow lines appearing. Resetting copy eliminates shadows and the chance of small pieces falling off the artboard. Also, resetting copy saves paste-up and stripping time.

If time or budget does not permit resetting copy, cutlines on the artboard can be carefully covered with white opaque and the copy reproduced with the PMT process. This method reduces stripping time and cost. Cleaning up shadow lines in paste-up also ensures high-quality reproductions before the copy goes to film.

Shadow lines can also be eliminated through backlighting. *Backlighting* is using the camera lights that illuminate copy from behind the copyboard. See Figure 8-7. Backlighting used with a sidelighting exposure is successful only when lightweight (about 80 lb. to 100 lb.) cover stock is used as the artboard. Lightweight cover stock allows light from the backlights to pass through the artboard, illuminating shadows caused by the sidelighting. When shadows are illuminated, shadow lines disappear. The paste-up artist should check with the camera operator before requesting that a job be backlighted.

Colors. Colors that appear on mechanicals commonly include non-photo blue, red, and black ink. These colors are drawn or written on mechanicals using pencils, pens, and markers. Poor-quality reproductions may result if ink colors are not tested. To test for quality of ink reproduction, a color test board is made showing all inks used by the paste-up artist. See Figure 8-8.

The color test board is reproduced onto film with various exposures. The film reproduction indicates potential problems with an ink color or density. Problems may include non-photo blue ink reproducing or black ink reproducing too lightly. Testing the reproduction of the ink used in paste-up eliminates time-consuming corrections in the stripping process.

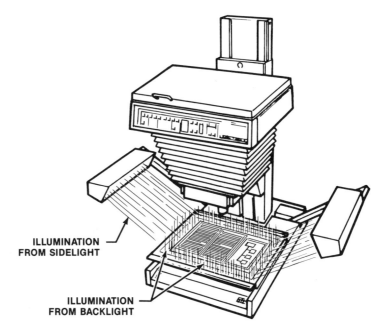

ILLUMINATION FROM SIDELIGHT

ILLUMINATION FROM BACKLIGHT

Figure 8-7. Shadow lines may be eliminated by backlighting if the artboard used is lightweight.

This is non-photo blue pencil.
This is non-photo blue marker.
This is non-photo blue pen.
This is blue ink pen.
This is black ink pen.
This is red ink pen.
This is red ink marker.
This is red pencil.
This is black india ink.

COLOR TEST BOARD

This is blue ink pen.
This is black ink pen.
This is red ink pen.
This is red ink marker.
This is red pencil.
This is black india ink.

REPRODUCTION OF COLOR TEST BOARD

Figure 8-8. Color test boards are used as a quality control guide for reproducing various ink colors.

Halftone Copy

Quality control of halftone copy is virtually in the hands of the camera operator. The paste-up artist, however, may take various steps in pasting up the mechanical to ensure the best possible reproduction of halftone copy. Because halftone copy is photographed separately from line copy, continuous tone photographs are not pasted directly on the mechanical. Two methods of handling continuous tone photographs are to indicate halftone position on mechanicals, or to paste up prescreened halftones directly on mechanicals.

Halftone Position. The paste-up artist indicates halftone position on the mechanicals to specify the location of continuous tone images. Halftone position is indicated on the mechanicals for use in the stripping process. When halftone position is indicated on mechanicals, separate photographic reproductions of line copy and continuous tone copy are made. See Figure 8-9.

The mechanical, marked with the halftone position, is photographed as line copy. The resulting film is the base, or key, negative. A *base negative* is the line image reproduction. It contains the halftone position. The stripper positions the base negative and halftone negative on separate flats.

The paste-up artist is responsible for accurately indicating halftone position so the stripper can easily position the negatives without taking additional measurements from the mechanical. Halftone position may be indicated on a mechanical with a position stat, black or red keyline, or black or ruby film box. See Figure 8-10.

The *position stat* is a line image of the original continuous tone copy.

The line image is produced on high-contrast paper, such as PMT, in the size needed for reproduction. Since the position stat is a line image, not a halftone reproduction of a continuous tone image, it is of unsuitable quality for reproduction. The position stat is used to indicate the *position* of the halftone only. On the mechanical the position stat is clearly marked "FOR POSITION ONLY" in red ink so it is not inadvertently used for reproduction on the printed piece.

The position stat not only shows the halftone position on the printed piece, but it also makes clear to the stripper which portion of the photograph to use. Another advantage of the position stat is that it shows the direction in which a halftone will print. If the halftone is of an image not commonly recognized, such as a machine part, the halftone could inadvertently be stripped upside down. A position stat on the mechanical eliminates this problem.

A keyline is an alternate method of indicating halftone position on a mechanical. A black or red ink keyline is used to show halftone position.

Both the black and red keyline reproduce as a clear frame on the base negative. On mechanicals, a black keyline indicates halftone position and also prints as a black frame around the halftone. A red keyline indicates halftone position. It also indicates to the stripper that it is not to print. Therefore, the stripper uses the red keyline for halftone position, but opaques it once the halftone is in place. Non-photo blue must not be used because it does not reproduce on film. Therefore, it will not show halftone position to the stripper.

The black box and ruby film box are other methods of indicating halftone position on a mechanical. They reproduce as windows on negatives. *Windows* are clear areas on negatives that are used by the stripper to position halftones. Black boxes are more economical to create but more time-consuming than ruby film boxes. Black boxes are created with only black ink, but time is taken to completely ink in the boxes. Ruby film boxes incur the cost of using ruby film, a two-layer acetate film of red on clear acetate. Regardless of the

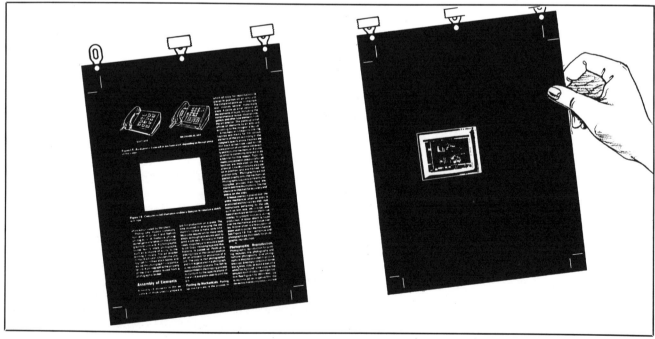

BASE NEGATIVE   HALFTONE NEGATIVE

Figure 8-9. Separate negatives are made for the mechanical and halftone when the halftone position is indicated on the mechanical.

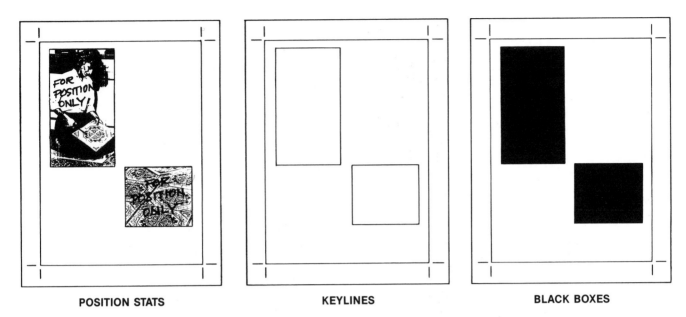

| POSITION STATS | KEYLINES | BLACK BOXES |

Figure 8-10. Halftones can be indicated on mechanicals by using position stats, keylines, or boxes.

method used, the paste-up artist should consult the stripper. The stripper can recommend time-saving steps and the preferred method for indicating halftone position on mechanicals.

Prescreened Halftones. *Prescreened halftones* are continuous tone copies broken into dots through the halftone process and reproduced on paper rather than film. Prescreened halftones have no continuous tones and may be reproduced on film as line copy. The most common uses of prescreened halftones are in desktop publishing, newspapers, newsletters, food advertisements, or any publication where speed is essential. Prescreened halftones are pasted up directly on the mechanical and reproduced along with line copy on a single sheet of film.

Although the cost of additional film and labor for stripping are avoided, reproduction quality of printed prescreened halftones is often sacrificed. Reproduction quality of the dots in halftones determines the overall quality of halftones. Each time an image is reproduced on film or paper, plate or stock, the reproductions become successive generations.

Image to film is the first generation of reproduction. Film to plate is the second generation. Plate to stock is the third generation. With each successive generation, especially in halftone reproduction, some details may be lost. With prescreened halftones, at least four generations are required: 1. image to paper, 2. paper to film, 3. film to plate, and 4. plate to stock. As a result of this additional generation, loss of dots in highlight areas and enlargement of dots in shadow areas are common. Enlargement of dots, or *dot gain,* results in loss of detail in shadow areas. See Figure 8-11.

Photographically reproducing prescreened dots with accuracy is difficult. To compensate for detail loss, prescreened halftones are often produced with a coarse line screen. As with tint screens, the line value of halftone screens refers to the number of dots per linear inch. The finer the screen is, the more dots there are per linear inch. Most film halftones reproduced for offset lithography are made with a 133 line to 200 line screen, as opposed to a 65 line to 100 line screen generally used for prescreened halftones. See Figure 8-12.

In addition to using a coarse line screen to compensate for detail loss,

| 0% HIGHLIGHT DOTS | 50% MIDTONE DOTS | 100% SHADOW DOTS |

Bruce Hardwood Floors

Figure 8-11. Reproducing halftones as prescreened halftones can result in a loss in quality.

dot percentages are often manipulated to provide better reproduction of highlight and shadow areas. Highlight dots for a prescreened halftone may be 10% to 15%, instead of 5% for standard halftone reproduction. Shadow dots may be 85% to 90%, instead of 95% for standard halftone reproduction. This change in dot percentage for highlight and shadow dots gives prescreened halftones a flat appearance, resulting in little contrast, yet allowing for dot gain on press. See Figure 8-13.

If finer line screens are desired for prescreened halftones, for example, 120 line or 133 line, high-quality reproductions can be achieved by copy dotting. *Copy dotting* is a photographic method of reproducing prescreened halftones by photographing dot for dot to match the prescreened halftone exactly. Copy dotting requires extremely careful photography to ensure high-quality results.

FINE LINE SCREEN   **COARSE LINE SCREEN**

Figure 8-12. Most film halftones reproduced for offset lithography are 133 line to 200 line screen halftones. Sixty-five line to 100 line screens are generally used for prescreened halftones.

PRESCREENED HALFTONE WITH   **REPRODUCTION OF MANIPULATED**
20% TO 80% DOT MANIPULATION   **PRESCREENED HALFTONE**

Figure 8-13. Dot size manipulation of prescreened halftones allows for dot loss and dot gain.

8 Camera Copy

Name _____

Date _____

REVIEW QUESTIONS

True-False

T   F   **1.** Line copy and continuous tone copy are the two forms of photographic reproduction that comprise graphic arts photography.

T   F   **2.** Halftone dots are created with a tint screen.

T   F   **3.** Continuous tone copy containing color is reproduced through the color separation process.

T   F   **4.** The most common method of equalizing density is through the diffusion transfer process.

T   F   **5.** It is common practice for an illustrator to create an original image at one-half the required size and enlarge it to 200%.

T   F   **6.** Reduction of intricate line copy causes fine lines to run together.

T   F   **7.** Backlighting copy to reduce shadows from cutlines is only effective if the copy is pasted onto heavyweight stock.

T   F   **8.** Testing reproduction quality of various inks used in paste-up helps eliminate time-consuming steps in the stripping process.

T   F   **9.** Indicating halftone position on mechanicals is a method the paste-up artist uses to specify the location of line art.

T   F   **10.** Using non-photo blue to indicate halftone position on mechanicals is the most accurate method.

Matching

_____   **1.** Photograph

_____   **2.** Type

_____   **3.** Continuous tone

_____   **4.** 95% dot

_____   **5.** 50% dot

_____   **6.** 5% dot

_____   **7.** Contact screen

_____   **8.** 4-color reproduction

_____   **9.** PMT

_____   **10.** Base negative

_____   **11.** Above 100%

_____   **12.** Below 100%

A. Tonal gradation
B. Highlight
C. Midtone
D. Halftone copy
E. Reduction
F. Enlargement
G. Diffusion transfer process
H. Key negative
I. Color separation
J. Vignette dot pattern
K. Shadow
L. Line copy

Multiple Choice

_____   1. Line copy consists of _____.
- A. type
- B. clip art
- C. rules
- D. all of the above

_____   2. Continuous tone copy is a _____.
- A. photograph
- B. painting
- C. pencil drawing
- D. all of the above

_____   3. Line copy is produced with a _____ exposure(s).
- A. single
- B. series of
- C. halftone
- D. all of the above

_____   4. The dots of a contact screen are _____ dots because they are diffused.
- A. variette
- B. rosette
- C. densette
- D. vignette

_____   5. _____ copy is produced with multiple exposures.
- A. Continuous tone
- B. Series
- C. Halftone
- D. Line

Completion

_____   1. _____ copy is copy containing one color and tone.

_____   2. _____ tone copy has tonal gradation.

_____   3. The halftone process uses _____ to give an illusion of tonal gradation.

_____   4. As dot size _____, the surrounding background _____, absorbing light reflected to the eye.

_____   5. The larger the printed dot is, the _____ the image will be.

_____   6. Copy _____ is the dark- or light-stopping ability of the image.

_____   7. To assure reproduction quality of all line copy, the density must be _____.

_____   8. _____ is the reproduction size of copy after it has been photographed.

_____   9. Intricate line copy includes line thicknesses of _____-point and below.

_____   10. There are two methods of handling _____ on a mechanical.

9 COLOR AND IMPOSITION

Color and imposition are two of the most important specifications in the layout of the printed piece. Color and imposition requirements may be laid out by the paste-up artist or indicated and completed in successive production steps. The paste-up artist must be aware of steps necessary to accurately assemble the mechanical for reproduction. In general, the more colors or pages there are, the more complicated the production requirements will be. The paste-up artist makes an educated decision whether to create a detailed mechanical or indicate the job requirements to be completed in the stripping process.

COLOR AND REGISTER

Color and register of a job are considered in determining paste-up procedure. The *color* of a job is the type and color of ink used to print the job. The two types of ink colors are flat and process colors. The *register* of a job is the placement of ink on the printed piece. The three types of register are hairline register, commercial register, and nonregister.

Color

Colors are chosen for a job by the designer based on stock to be used, budget, time allowed for the job, and specific color requirements of the printed piece. The stock chosen greatly affects ink selection. The designer chooses the stock and ink to work with one another. For example, opaque ink may be chosen for colored stock to allow only the ink color to show. Transparent ink shows the color of the stock through the ink.

Color requirements also vary depending on specific job requirements.

Specialized color matching is best accomplished with flat colors. Full color originals are reproduced with process colors. Flat color work is generally less expensive and less time-consuming than process color work.

Flat Colors. Flat colors are premixed at the ink factory. For short runs they are often mixed in the pressroom. Flat colors are chosen from a color selection book. Ink color is mixed according to the formula written in the color selection book. The most common ink color selection book is the *PANTONE® Matching System* book, also known as the PMS book.

The designer requests flat color ink to be made either transparent or opaque. Transparent inks can be used to create a third color by overlapping two ink colors. The third color, however, is not always predictable with flat color inks. To achieve predictable results with flat color inks, transparent ink colors are usually used singly. Opaque flat colors may be overlapped and still maintain predictable results. Flat color ink may be used as a solid

color, tint screen, or a combination of solid with a tint screen of a second color (usually black). A *PANTONE® Color and Black Selector* book shows the results of PMS flat colors combined with black tint screens.

Flat color inks can be used to print halftones, duotones, and tritones. Halftones reproduce better when dark flat color inks are chosen. Different color stocks can be used and still produce high-quality halftones. See Figure 9-1.

Duotones are halftones printed using two colors. Duotones are commonly reproduced in black and another color. The black plate, or *black printer,* usually prints from the midtone (50% dot areas), to the shadow (95% dot areas). The second color, usually a lighter color, prints in the shadow, midtone, and highlight (5% dot areas). The combination of two colors adds interest and detail to halftones. See Figure 9-2. When the two colors selected to print a duotone are two blacks, the reproduction is a *double-dot* reproduction. *Tritones* are halftones printed using three colors.

Process Colors. Process colors are used to print a full range of colors. The process colors are yellow, magenta (red), cyan (blue), and black. All process colors are transparent inks. The process color inks are printed one over the other to create additional colors. By varying values of process colors with tint screens and overlapping the colors at specific angles, a predictable range of colors can be created. See Figure 9-3.

The most common use of process colors is in the 4-color reproduction of color originals. *Color originals* may be a transparency, photograph, or painting. To reproduce color originals with the process colors, four negatives and four plates are made. To print each of the process colors, one negative and one plate are used for each color.

In *color separation* the reflected or transmitted light from the color original is separated using filters. The yellow, magenta, cyan, and black plates each represents areas of color on the original image. The four colors are printed one on top of another at the correct screen angle to achieve full color reproduction. Color separation is a time-consuming process requiring highly skilled camera or scanner operators. Some desktop publishing software programs allow color separation to be done on a computer.

Register

Register of printed pieces is the alignment of images on stock. Register is controlled in paste-up, stripping, and presswork. The paste-up artist may use overlays to separate colors for registering one color in relation to another. The stripper is responsible for registering the elements on flats to ensure properly made plates for each color. The press operator is responsible for aligning the inked image on stock.

Three categories of register are hairline register, commercial register, and nonregister. The type of register used depends on accuracy requirements for the printed piece.

Hairline Register. *Hairline register* is critical alignment of elements. Hairline register allows no room for movement or adjustment of one element in relation to another. For example, hairline register may be printing one color adjacent to another, touching but not overlapping. Elements must be in the exact place on the printed piece or they will be off-register. *Off-register* is improper alignment of elements. See Figure 9-4. Most registration of process color work is hairline register.

Commercial Register. *Commercial register* is the alignment of elements, allowing some movement of elements on the printed piece. The amount of movement allowed varies. A common acceptable amount of movement is $\frac{1}{64}''$. In commercial register of process color work, an acceptable amount of movement is one dot overlap or underlap. See Figure 9-5. Commercial register is sometimes called *lap* or *close register* because the images are often overlapped or aligned closely. The amount of movement allowed in any commercial register job should be discussed with the stripper and press operator before paste-up is started.

Nonregister. *Nonregister* is the alignment of elements, allowing more than $\frac{1}{64}''$ movement of elements on the printed piece. Although all elements on the printed piece are in register, the alignment of color is not critical. See Figure 9-6. Nonregister is the simplest form of color alignment.

PASTE-UP FOR COLOR AND REGISTER

Paste-up for color and register may be done using the indicated color method or preseparated color method. The *indicated color method* involves alignment of all elements on one artboard. A tissue overlay is taped over the artboard and the paste-up artist writes complete color requirements on the tissue overlay.

The *preseparated color method* involves pasting up different color ele-

ments on overlays in alignment with each other. Generally, all hairline register is done using the indicated color method. Some commercial register and nonregister are done using the preseparated color method. Before the paste-up artist begins a paste-up, register requirements of the job should be discussed with the stripper.

Process Color and Hairline Register Paste-up

Paste-up for process color and hairline register requires critical alignment. All elements are generally aligned on the artboard. The paste-up artist uses a red keyline to indicate placement of color and a detailed tissue overlay for instructions to the stripper. See Figure 9-7.

In 4-color work, the camera operator creates four negatives of the artwork. Each of the four process color inks is used to produce one negative, or printer, of each color. See Figure 9-8.

Flat Color and Commercial Register Paste-up

Flat color and commercial register paste-up involves alignment of flat colors that have some freedom of movement. Most flat color work does not have the register requirements that process color work has. Although flat colors may require hairline register, commercial register is more common. The amount of commercial register movement allowed for a job determines the paste-up method used. Commercial register allowing $\frac{1}{64}''$ can be preseparated. See Figure 9-9.

1. Paste up copy that will print in the base color (usually black) on the artboard. This is the base art. Apply register marks. Label the artboard with desired color.

2. Tape a sheet of amber film (or ruby or masking film) to the artboard. The sheet of amber film will become the second color overlay. Using an art knife, lightly cut into the emulsion of the amber film, outlining the image to be in second color.

WHITE STOCK

GRAY STOCK

BLUE STOCK

W.W. Grainger, Inc.

Figure 9-1. Dark inks are chosen to print halftones because they create a better illusion of tonal gradation. Dark inks on light stock give the best halftone reproduction.

Figure 9-2. Duotones have greater density and detail than halftones and do not incur the high cost of 4-color reproduction.

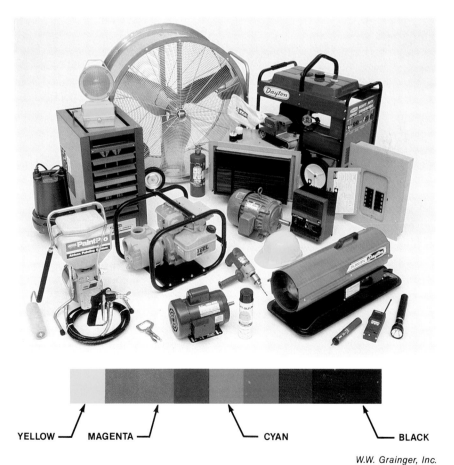

YELLOW — MAGENTA — CYAN — BLACK

W.W. Grainger, Inc.

Figure 9-3. The four process colors used in 4-color reproduction are yellow, magenta, cyan, and black.

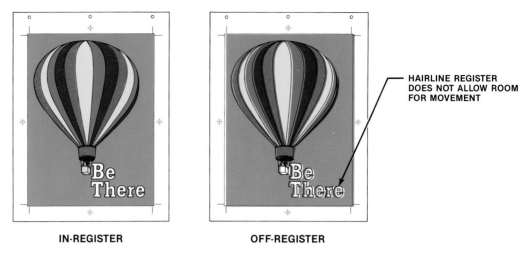

IN-REGISTER   OFF-REGISTER

HAIRLINE REGISTER DOES NOT ALLOW ROOM FOR MOVEMENT

Figure 9-4. Hairline register does not allow for movement of color images. Placement of color must be exact or the image is off-register.

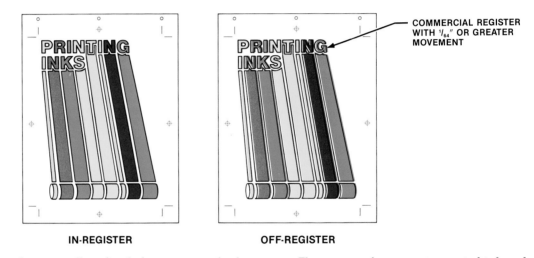

IN-REGISTER   OFF-REGISTER

COMMERCIAL REGISTER WITH $\frac{1}{64}$" OR GREATER MOVEMENT

Figure 9-5. Commercial register allows for slight movement of color images. The amount of movement accepted is based on job requirements.

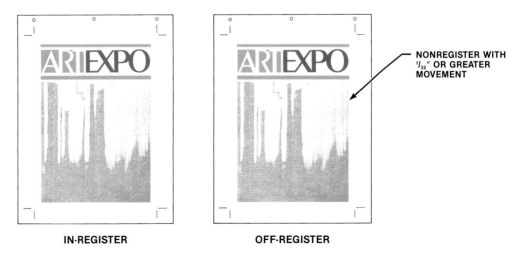

IN-REGISTER   OFF-REGISTER

NONREGISTER WITH $\frac{1}{32}$" OR GREATER MOVEMENT

Figure 9-6. Nonregister allows for the greatest amount of movement of color images, generally greater than $\frac{1}{64}$".

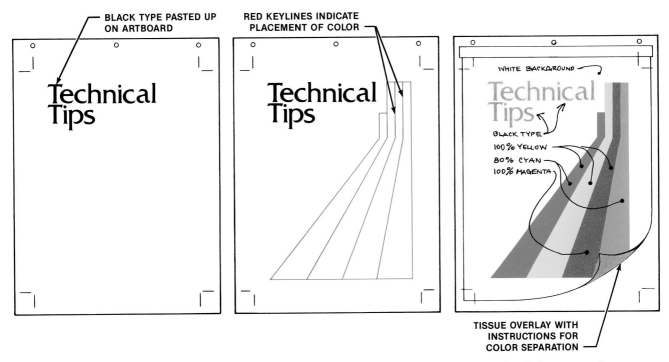

Figure 9-7. Red keylines are used to show the position of color breaks in hairline register. A detailed tissue overlay gives instructions for the color separation of elements.

Figure 9-8. Yellow, magenta, cyan, and black printers are used in the production of a 4-color job.

Pasting Up for Flat Color and Commercial Register

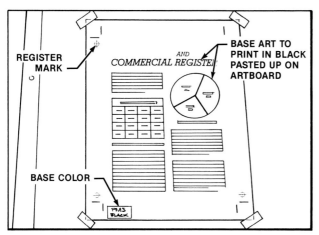

Step 1. Paste up base art. Apply register marks and label artboard with color.

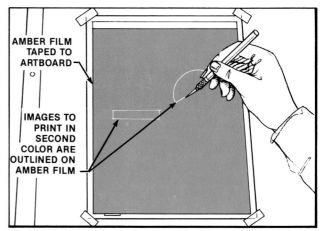

Step 2. Tape a sheet of amber film, which becomes the second color overlay, to the artboard. Cut lightly into the amber film, outlining the image to be in second color.

Step 3. Peel away amber film where color is not required.

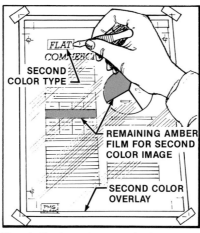

Step 4. Paste up type to print in second color on the overlay.

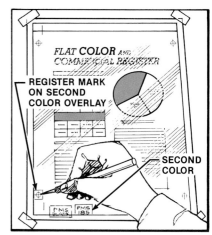

Step 5. Apply register marks on the overlay and label with color.

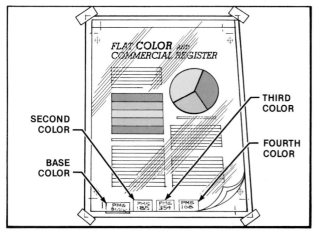

Step 6. Repeat steps 2 through 4 for third and fourth colors.

Figure 9-9. Commercial register allowing $1/64''$ movement of color images can be pasted up using the preseparated method of paste-up.

3. Peel away the amber film in areas where color is not required.

4. Paste up type to print in second color on the second color overlay.

5. Apply register marks. Label the second color overlay with the desired second color.

6. Repeat steps 2 through 4 for the third and fourth colors.

Commercial register allowing less than $\frac{1}{64}$″ alignment is not easily separated in paste-up. Elements should be indicated on a tissue overlay.

Nonregister Paste-up

Nonregister paste-up is the register of elements without critical alignment. Nonregister alignment is easily pasted up using the overlay method to preseparate color. Although the overlay method saves time in stripping, it requires additional films. Before a nonregister job is preseparated, the job should be discussed with the stripper. The high cost of film may prove the job more cost-efficient if color separated in the stripping process.

IMPOSITION

Imposition is the alignment of images for press and binding. An imposition layout is generally prepared by the stripping or binding department to show how images should be positioned to meet press and binding requirements. Imposition layouts may be prepared for a one-sided job or for a multipage document. A paste-up artist aware of imposition requirements can create more accurate mechanicals. This accuracy saves time and cost in stripping and binding.

One-sided, One-up Imposition

One-sided, one-up imposition is the simplest imposition layout. The page is printed *one-sided,* or on one side of the page, and *one-up,* that is, only one piece is printed on a press sheet. A *press sheet* is the full-size sheet of paper on which the job will be printed. Although the imposition is basic,

variables such as nonprinting margins, bleeds, and folds must be observed in paste-up.

Nonprinting and Gripper Margins. As a quality control measure, all printed jobs should be printed on an oversized press sheet and the waste trimmed. However, the most common image produced is 8½″ × 11″ and often one-sided. Because of this standard size, it may be more cost-efficient to produce a same-size press sheet. A *same-size press sheet* is a press sheet on which a job prints without allowing for trim. Reproducing an image without a trim allowance poses certain difficulties in reproduction.

The mechanical must allow for nonprinting margins on same-size press sheets. These nonprinting margins commonly run along the short end of an 8½″ × 11″ press sheet. A *gripper margin* is a ³⁄₈″ space on the press sheet that allows for the gripper. The *gripper* is a bar of mechanical fingers on a press that grab the press sheet and pull it through the press. See Figure 9-10.

The gripper holds the paper throughout printing and releases it at the delivery end of the press. The gripper margin is a nonprinting area because the mechanical fingers hold the press

sheet and the plate is unable to make contact with the stock. Copying machines and laser printers also require nonprinting margins. Some nonprinting margins are required on all edges of stock. The paste-up artist should investigate the amount of nonprinting area required on jobs to be reproduced on same-size press sheets.

Bleeds. *Bleeds* are printed images that extend all the way to at least one edge of a printed sheet. A *full bleed* is an image that extends to all four edges of a printed sheet. To ensure that an image prints at the edge of a printed sheet, the bleed is extended beyond the trim size. This extended margin, or *bleed margin,* allows for inaccuracies in printing and trimming. The standard bleed margin is $\frac{1}{8}$″.

A paste-up artist indicates a bleed with a red keyline drawn $\frac{1}{8}$″ beyond the image area of the mechanical. If a rule for an illustration is to bleed, the rule also is extended $\frac{1}{8}$″ beyond the trim. See Figure 9-11.

Bleeds are not recommended for jobs that will print on same-size press sheets. Without oversized stock, the extended image will cause ink buildup on a press. Even a 1-point rule extended $\frac{1}{64}$″ beyond the press sheet size will cause ink buildup on the plate and offset blanket. This ink

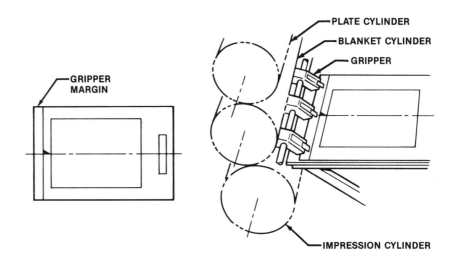

Figure 9-10. The gripper margin is a nonprinting margin allotted for the mechanical fingers of the gripper. The fingers pull the paper through the press.

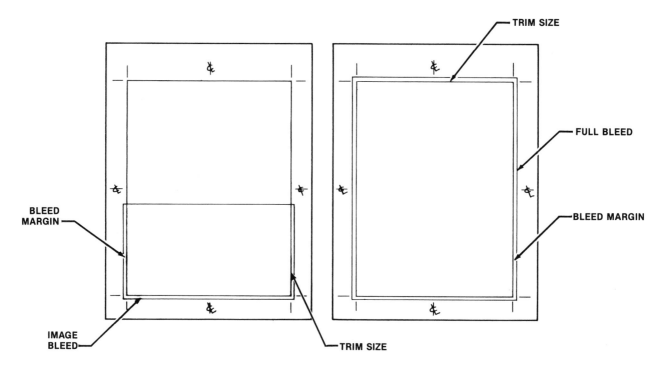

Figure 9-11. Standard bleed and full bleed allowance is ⅛″ beyond the image area of the trim size.

buildup spreads, causing ink sneak. *Ink sneak* is the spreading of ink onto the back of the press sheet.

Bleeds cannot be reproduced on a copying machine or laser printer unless an oversized stock is used. When a bleed is indicated for a job to be printed on same-size stock, the layout should be altered to allow for nonprinting margins. Otherwise, an oversized stock should be used.

Folds. Jobs to be folded should be accompanied by a folding dummy. If the comprehensive layout does not include a folding dummy, the paste-up artist makes a folding dummy before beginning the mechanical. The stock on which the job is to be printed is used. Fold marks are placed in the nonimage area of the mechanical, regardless of stock size used to print the job.

Folds should not be made across lines of type. The paste-up artist should alter the position of type to fall before or after a fold. Type printed across a fold lowers readability of type. Type or illustrations printed across a fold on coated stock may

chip and crack, causing additional loss in readability.

The stripper and bindery operator use fold marks for alignment. The stripper aligns the flats to ensure accurate folding position. The bindery operator uses fold marks and the folding dummy to set fold positions on the folding machine.

Two-sided, One-up Imposition

Two-sided, one-up imposition has printing on both sides of the page and produces one printed piece per press sheet. Since the job is to print on both sides, imposition requirements increase and back-to-back alignment is necessary. *Back-to-back alignment* requires elements on each side of the page to mirror one another, including margins, folds, scores, perforations, and die cuts.

Margins. Nonprinting margins on two-sided jobs must align for printing accuracy, readability, and aesthetics.

Nonprinting margins must align at the top, bottom, and on all four edges when required. These margins must be equal on both sides of the printed piece. For example, a nonprinting margin on the top of the sheet must align at the top of the sheet on both sides of the printed piece. See Figure 9-12.

Column alignment margins, or gutters, must also align on both sides at the top, bottom, and in the width of the page. *Column alignment margins* are margins that surround type blocks.

Folds, Scores, and Perforations. Folds, scores, and perforations are created in bindery operations. They are commonly specified on two-sided jobs. When these bindery operations are required, a designer and paste-up artist must plan the layout of both sides of the printed piece. The paste-up artist measures the designer's comprehensive layout and indicates the position of folds, perforations, and scores to match exactly on both sides of the printed piece.

Die Cuts. *Die cuts* are special shaped cuts made in printed pieces using a sharp rule. Die cuts are indicated on mechanicals with dashed red keylines. Die cuts must align exactly on the front and back of the printed piece. See Figure 9-13.

Back-to-back Alignment

Back-to-back alignment done in paste-up increases accuracy throughout production. The paste-up artist may create back-to-back alignment boards by planning the artboards side-by-side, back-to-front, or by using the master grid method.

Side-by-side. In the side-by-side paste-up method of two-sided imposition, the paste-up artist uses an artboard twice the width of one page. The double width allows the paste-up artist to align the back and front of the job side-by-side. At least 2″ on all edges and 1″ in the center of the artboard are allotted as nonimage areas. Measurements are taken from the comprehensive layout and folding dummy and transferred to the artboard. Paste-up continues until all elements are affixed. The side-by-side paste-up method allows the paste-up artist to align margins and columns of two-sided pages horizontally next to each other. See Figure 9-14.

1. Select an artboard twice the width of the trim size, plus at least 5″. The artboard should also measure at least 4″ more than the depth measurement of the trim size. Locate the center of the artboard. Mark the center point with non-photo blue.

2. Measure ½″ away from each side of the vertical center of the artboard, leaving 1″ in the middle of the artboard. Using the vertical center of the artboard, measure and mark the trim size height in non-photo blue. From the inside vertical trim, measure and mark the trim size width with non-photo blue. Mark each side of the artboard in red ink as "FRONT" and "BACK" in the lower right-hand corner outside the trim area.

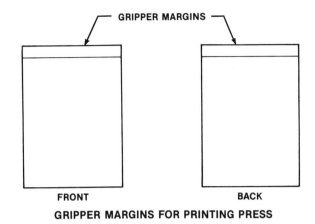

GRIPPER MARGINS FOR PRINTING PRESS

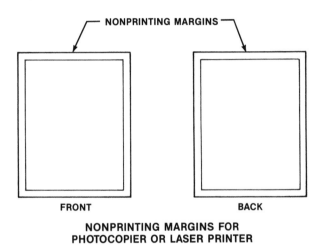

NONPRINTING MARGINS FOR
PHOTOCOPIER OR LASER PRINTER

Figure 9-12. Nonprinting margins must align with each other on both sides of a two-sided press sheet.

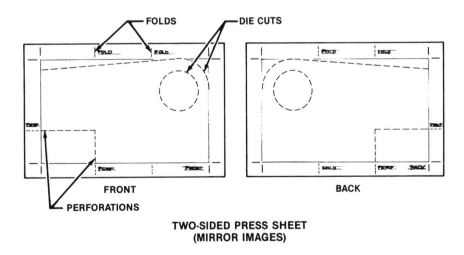

TWO-SIDED PRESS SHEET
(MIRROR IMAGES)

Figure 9-13. Die cuts must align on both sides of a two-sided press sheet.

Pasting Up for Back-to-back Alignment—Side-by-side Method

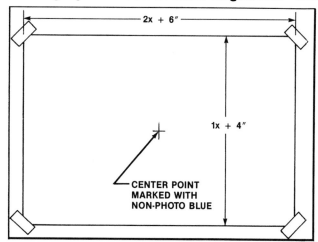

Step 1. Locate center of artboard and mark center point with non-photo blue.

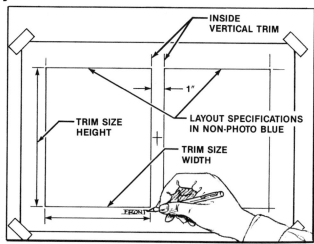

Step 2. Measure 1″ space in middle. Mark trim size of each page with non-photo blue. Mark each side of artboard in red ink as "FRONT" and "BACK" in lower right-hand corner outside trim area.

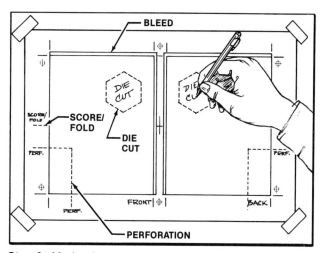

Step 3. Mark mirror images of scores, folds, perforations, and die cuts on each side of artboard.

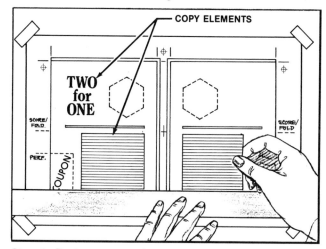

Step 4. Paste up copy elements.

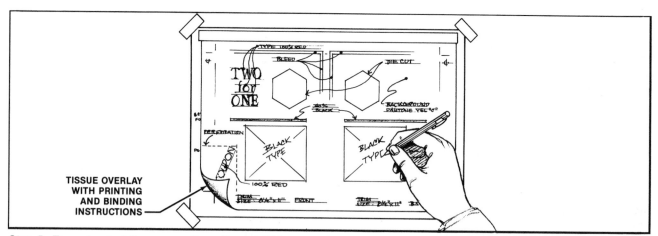

Step 5. Tape sheet of tissue over the artboard. Write complete printing and binding instructions on tissue.

Figure 9-14. The side-by-side paste-up method allows for margin and column alignment of two-sided pages next to each other.

3. Mark all scores, folds, perforations, and die cuts on each side of the artboard. These specifications must mirror each other to ensure back-to-back alignment.

4. Paste up copy elements.

5. Tape a sheet of tissue over the artboard. Write complete printing and binding instructions on the tissue.

Back-to-front. The back-to-front paste-up method involves using a two-sided artboard. The front of the page is on one side of the artboard and the back of the page is on the other side. The artboard used must be white and coated on both sides. Light should transmit through the artboard when viewed on a light table. The two-sided artboard allows the paste-up artist to view the marks from one side of the artboard while marking the other side. This method allows exact positioning of specification marks. See Figure 9-15.

1. Select a translucent artboard with width and depth measurements 4" larger than the trim size of the printed piece. Draw all layout specifications on the front of the artboard.

2. Paste up all copy for the front. Mark "FRONT" in red ink in the lower right-hand corner outside the trim area.

3. Turn the artboard front down on the light table. Square the artboard by aligning the T-square with top trim marks showing through the artboard from the front.

4. Draw all layout specifications on the back of the artboard by aligning with layout specifications drawn on the front.

5. Paste up all copy for the back. Mark "BACK" in red ink in the lower right-hand corner outside the trim area.

6. Tape a sheet of tissue over both sides of the artboard. Write complete printing and binding instructions on both sheets of tissue.

Master Grid. The master grid paste-up method involves using a grid to align marks and elements on translucent artboards. This method is especially useful when many jobs, such as books, require the same layout. A master grid is created on positive film and used under the translucent artboards to align marks and elements. The master grid is used right side up to align the front of the page and flopped to align the back of the page. Since the master grid is used to align both the front and back of the page, the marks are accurate because they are mirrored. See Figure 9-16.

1. Select an artboard with width and depth measurements 4" larger than the trim size of the printed piece. Draw all layout specifications in black ink using a 1-point technical pen. Make a positive film reproduction of the artboard, which will serve as the master grid.

2. Square the master grid and tape it to the light table. Square a translucent artboard over the master grid and tape the artboard to the light table.

3. Paste up all copy, aligning the copy with layout specification marks showing through the artboard from the master grid. Mark "FRONT" in red ink in the lower right-hand corner outside the trim area.

4. Remove the artboard. Flop the master grid so it is face down. Square the master grid and tape it to the light table. Square a new artboard over the master grid and tape it to the light table.

5. Paste up all copy, aligning the copy with layout specification marks showing through the artboard from the master grid. Mark "BACK" in red ink in the lower right-hand corner outside the trim area.

6. Check all positioning by aligning the master grid over the marks on each artboard.

Stepped Image Imposition

A *stepped image,* or step-and-repeat job, is a job printed more than once on the same press sheet. A stepped image may be printed on one- or two-sided pages. Stepped images may require layout specifications for their trim, retrim, folds, scores, and perforations.

Trim and Retrim. The trim of a stepped image requires the image to be laid out on the page so it may be trimmed by standard trimming procedures. In *standard trimming procedures* one blade is used to cut images in a straight line. A job laid out without consideration of standard trimming procedures may require a special die to cut the job. *Retrim* is the process of double-trimming a job. A retrim on a book is usually done after a book has been folded and gathered. A retrim is also done to align pages in a book. The standard allowance for retrim is $\frac{1}{16}$".

Folds, Scores, and Perforations. Folds, scores, and perforations on a stepped image should be laid out according to binding requirements. Stepped images are commonly manipulated in binding. The imposition layout must meet the physical requirements of the binding equipment.

The grain of the stock is important in printability and folding of the job. The *grain* of the stock is the direction of fibers created by the papermaking process. On the press, grain is usually aligned *grain long,* or parallel to the gripper. However, a fold may require the grain to be *grain short,* or perpendicular to the gripper. See Figure 9-17.

In folding, the grain may create a smooth or coarse fold. A fold created along the grain is smooth. A fold created against the grain is rough, although generally stronger because the fibers hold together. A score is used to indent the stock to create a smooth fold, especially when folding against the grain. A perforation should run with the grain for best results. A paste-up artist should investigate grain requirements of the press and binding before creating the layout for a stepped image.

Signature Imposition

Signature imposition is a layout commonly of 4-, 8-, 16-, 24-, 32-, and 64-page groups. These page groups are *signatures* and are folded as units. These units are bound together to create a

Pasting Up for Back-to-back Alignment—Back-to-front Method

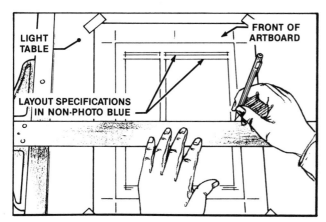

Step 1. Draw layout specifications on front of artboard.

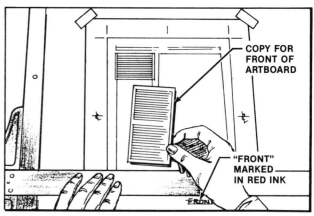

Step 2. Paste up copy for front. Mark "FRONT" in red ink in lower right-hand corner outside trim area.

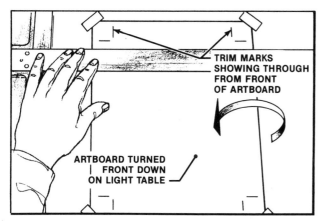

Step 3. Turn artboard front down on light table. Square artboard by aligning T-square with top trim marks, which show through artboard from front.

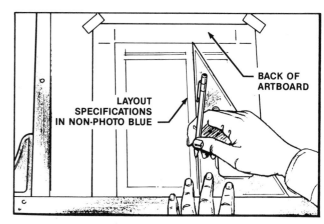

Step 4. Draw layout specifications on back of artboard by aligning with layout specifications showing through from front.

Step 5. Paste up copy for back. Mark "BACK" in red ink in lower right-hand corner outside trim area.

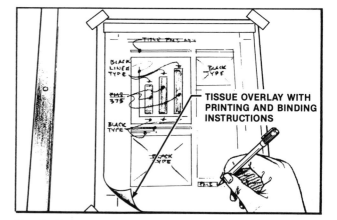

Step 6. Tape tissue over both sides of artboard. Write complete printing and binding instructions on both tissues.

Figure 9-15. The back-to-front paste-up method involves using a translucent artboard. A translucent artboard allows specification marks on one side to be seen through the other side when viewed through a light table.

Pasting Up for Back-to-back Alignment—Master Grid Method

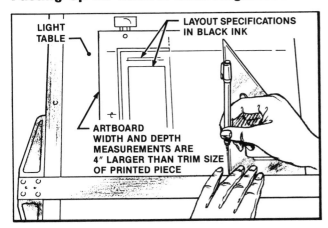

Step 1. Draw all layout specifications in black ink using a 1-point technical pen. Make positive film reproduction of artboard to serve as master grid.

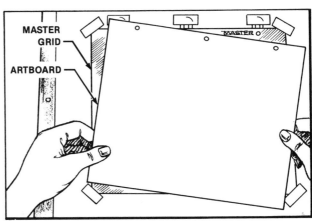

Step 2. Square and tape master grid on light table. Square and tape artboard over master grid.

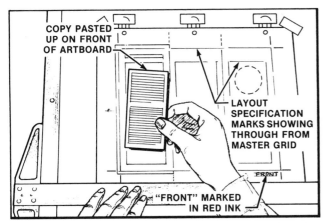

Step 3. Paste up all copy, aligning copy with specification marks showing through from master grid. Mark "FRONT" in red ink in lower right-hand corner outside trim area.

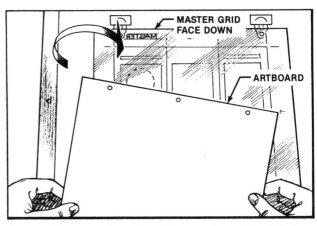

Step 4. Remove artboard and flop master grid so it is face down. Square and tape master grid back on light table. Square and tape new artboard over master grid.

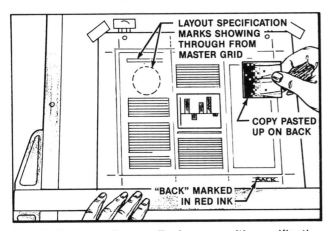

Step 5. Paste up all copy, aligning copy with specification marks showing through from master grid. Mark "BACK" in red ink in lower right-hand corner outside trim area.

Step 6. Check position of copy on front and back boards by aligning master grid over them.

Figure 9-16. The master grid method of paste-up is useful for jobs, such as books, that require the same layout specifications.

book. Layout of pages into signatures is done by the stripper.

Book pages that make up a signature often have running heads. *Running heads,* or headers, are lines of type containing the book or chapter title. Running heads are displayed, or run, at the top of pages. When displayed at the bottom of pages, they are *running feet,* or footers. A *folio,* or page number, may be placed next to the running head or foot. See Figure 9-18.

Facing Pages. When laying out *facing pages,* which are pages adjacent to one another, a paste-up artist creates margins so the pages are vertically and horizontally centered. These facing pages compose a two-page spread. The size of margins on two-page spreads varies with page size. The paste-up artist uses visual units of measure to center the facing pages.

One unit is used for gutter, or back, margins. One-and-one-half units are used for head margins. Two units are used for trim, or outside, margins. Three units are used for tail, or foot, margins. See Figure 9-19. Once a *page style,* or standard page layout, is determined, the paste-up artist assembles the pages in reader's spread or printer's spread.

Reader's Spread. *Reader's spread* is a spread of two facing pages as they would appear in an assembled book. The pages are aligned in the way a reader would view them. The page numbers of a reader's spread are consecutive. Reader's spread is the most common form of page assembly done by the paste-up artist. Reader's spread allows more accurate alignment of facing images and breakacross images. *Facing images* are elements on facing pages that must mirror each other in position. *Breakacross images* are elements of facing pages that align across the gutter. See Figure 9-20. The stripper must align breakacross images very carefully when stripping the flats to ensure alignment.

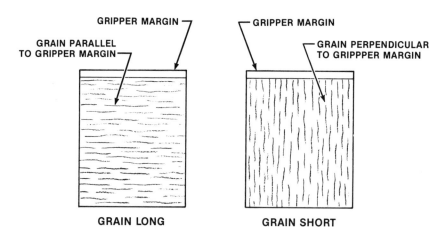

Figure 9-17. The grain of stock is usually aligned grain long, or parallel to the gripper. Fold specifications may require the grain to be aligned grain short, or perpendicular to the gripper.

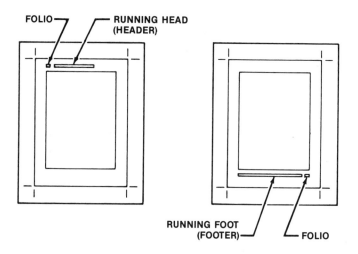

Figure 9-18. Book pages include a running head or foot and folio.

Printer's Spread. *Printer's spread* is a spread of two pages based on signature imposition. Occasionally, a paste-up artist may align pages in printer's spread if pages do not have facing or breakacross images. However, it is usually the stripper's job to assemble pages on the flats in printer's spread. The folios of a printer's spread are not consecutive. Their sequence depends on the number of pages in the book and type of press used to print the job.

To verify consecutive page numbering, the folios of the two pages on the spread are added. Their sum should be one more than the total number of pages in the book. For example, in a 64-page book, page 12 and page 53 are laid out as a two-page spread (12 + 53 = 65). See Figure 9-21. If this does not result, a page is out of position. A paste-up artist discusses the assembly of pages with the stripper or press operator before preparing a job in printer's spread.

Binding Imposition

Requirements for binding imposition are based on the binding method used. Four major binding methods are saddle stitching, side stitching, adhesive binding, and mechanical binding.

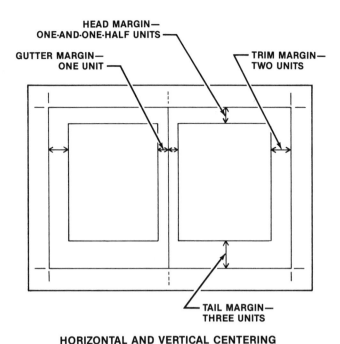

HORIZONTAL AND VERTICAL CENTERING
OF FACING PAGES

Figure 9-19. Book pages are visually spaced so they are vertically and horizontally centered.

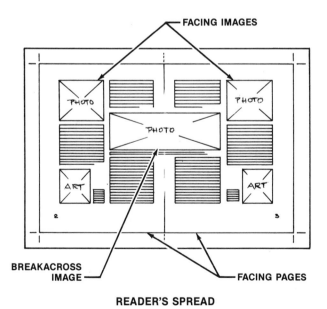

READER'S SPREAD

Figure 9-20. Facing images align as mirror images on adjacent pages. Breakacross images align across the gutter of adjacent pages.

Saddle Stitching.

A *saddle stitched* book is bound through the center of the fold with wire. The wire of a saddle stitch is similar to an office staple. A book bound through the center of the fold with thread is *saddle sewn*. Saddle stitched and saddle sewn books allow the book to be opened nearly flat.

Because of binder's creep, or push-out, the cover and front and back pages of saddle stitched books should be made wider than center pages. *Binder's creep* is the pushing out of centermost pages when the pages are folded down the middle. This is caused by the thickness of the book. The thicker the book is, the greater the amount of creep will be. Once the book is trimmed, the inside pages have a progressively smaller trim size. If all pages are laid out with equal trim and gutter margins, the center pages will have smaller trim margins than the outer pages. The fold of the pages will make the gutter margins of outer pages appear smaller than those of inner pages.

To compensate for binder's creep, the paste-up artist creates a folding dummy using the stock chosen for the job. A hole is drilled through all pages at the edge of the trim margin of the first page. When opened the hole shows the distance required for movement of the outside and inside margins. The paste-up artist leaves the center pages with the greatest amount of trim margin and the least amount of gutter margin. Outer pages have less trim margin and greater gutter margin. See Figure 9-22.

Side Stitching.

A *side stitched* book is bound with wire through the entire book at the bind, or gutter, margin. A *side sewn* book is bound with thread at the bind margin. Both methods of side binding allow the pages to open only to the bind margin. The fold is not visible.

Pages in a side stitched book must have a greater gutter margin for the bind margin and bend of the book. See Figure 9-23. An inadequate bind margin could cause the type to bend

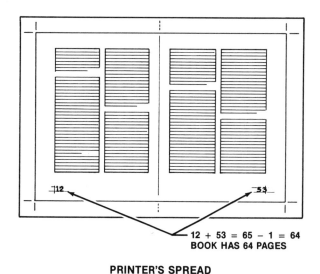

PRINTER'S SPREAD

12 + 53 = 65 – 1 = 64
BOOK HAS 64 PAGES

Figure 9-21. Folios on printer's spreads are not consecutive. Folios on facing pages must add up to one more page than the total number of pages in the book.

too severely into the margin, causing poor readability. Side stitching allows groups of signatures to be bound together. Therefore, compensation for binder's creep is unnecessary.

Adhesive Binding. *Adhesive binding,* or perfect binding, uses glue to hold the pages of a book together. The signatures are rough-trimmed at the bind margin to improve adhesion. Rough-trimming creates frayed edges, which allow better glue absorption into the paper. Glue is applied to the spine of the cover as it is attached to the pages. The cover and pages are retrimmed at the head, tail, and trim margins. A $\frac{1}{8}''$ margin is allotted for retrim while a $\frac{1}{16}''$ margin is allotted for the rough-trim at the bind margin.

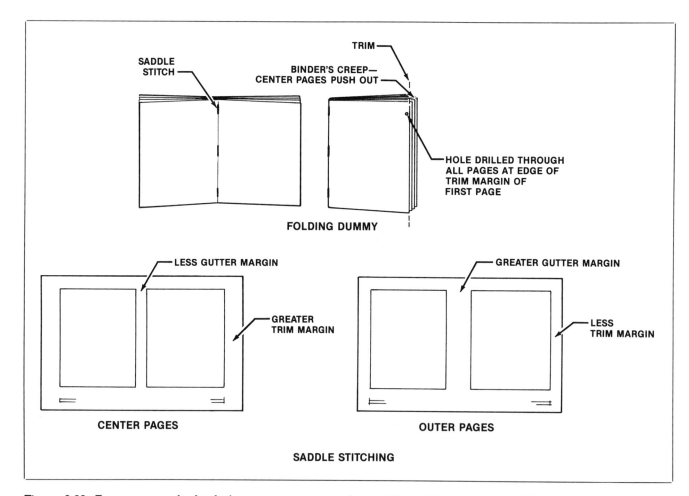

SADDLE STITCH

TRIM

BINDER'S CREEP—
CENTER PAGES PUSH OUT

HOLE DRILLED THROUGH ALL PAGES AT EDGE OF TRIM MARGIN OF FIRST PAGE

FOLDING DUMMY

LESS GUTTER MARGIN

GREATER TRIM MARGIN

CENTER PAGES

GREATER GUTTER MARGIN

LESS TRIM MARGIN

OUTER PAGES

SADDLE STITCHING

Figure 9-22. To compensate for binder's creep, center pages have additional front margin and less gutter margin. Outside pages have additional gutter margin and less front margin.

Adhesive binding allows pages to be opened to the bind and does not require additional margin for gutter. See Figure 9-24.

Mechanical Binding. Mechanical binding uses a mechanical device to hold pages together. Three common types of mechanical binding are spiral, plastic comb, and loose-leaf binding. See Figure 9-25.

Spiral bound books have a metal or plastic wire looped through holes at the binding edge of the pages, forming a spiral shape. The margin required for the wire depends on the hole size. Generally, a margin of ⅜″ to ½″ is sufficient to accommodate the spiral. The paste-up artist marks the margin and indicates the size of the holes in red ink.

Spiral bound books are generally bound by binding trade shops or very large printing companies with spiral binding capabilities. Spiral binding equipment is costly. Spiral binding is efficient for books with more than 50 pages and for press runs of more than 100 books.

Plastic comb bound books are bound with a circular comb. The circular comb has teeth that slide through rectangular holes in the stock. The teeth lock into a sleeve to secure enclosure. The margin required for the plastic comb depends on book thickness and comb diameter. The larger the comb is, the wider the margin for binding is. The paste-up artist indicates the margin required for the comb in red ink.

An advantage of plastic comb binding is that it is available at most small print shops. The hand-operated binding machine is more cost-efficient than large spiral binding machines. Plastic comb binding is efficient for books with fewer than 200 pages and for orders of 100 books or fewer.

Both spiral and plastic comb binding are permanent forms of binding. Pages may be removed without damaging other pages, but the pages cannot be reinserted. The most flexible method of binding is loose-leaf binding.

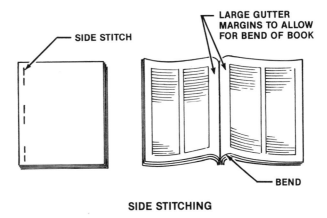

SIDE STITCHING

Figure 9-23. A side stitched book requires a greater gutter margin to allow for the bend in the page at the bind than a saddle stitched book.

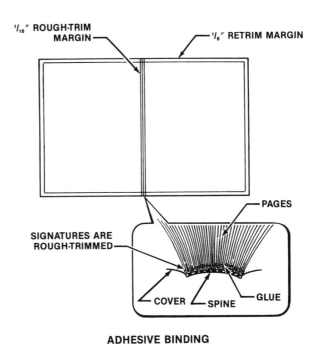

ADHESIVE BINDING

Figure 9-24. Adhesive binding requires a ⅛″ retrim allowance at the head, trim, and tail margins and a 1/16″ rough-trim allowance at the bind margin.

Loose-leaf bound books are held together by metal rings. The metal rings open easily for inserting pages. The metal rings clamp closed to allow smooth turning of pages. The most common loose-leaf binder is the three-ring binder. Three-ring binders use pages that have standard ¼″ holes. A hole is measured down the vertical center of the page and 4¼″ out from center in both directions. Loose-leaf binders are available in many styles. The designer and paste-up artist should investigate the best style of loose-leaf binder for a job. Once chosen, the paste-up artist indicates margin and hole size and position in red ink.

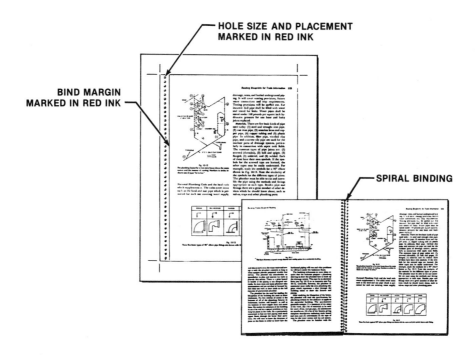

HOLE SIZE AND PLACEMENT
MARKED IN RED INK

BIND MARGIN
MARKED IN RED INK

SPIRAL BINDING

SPIRAL BINDING

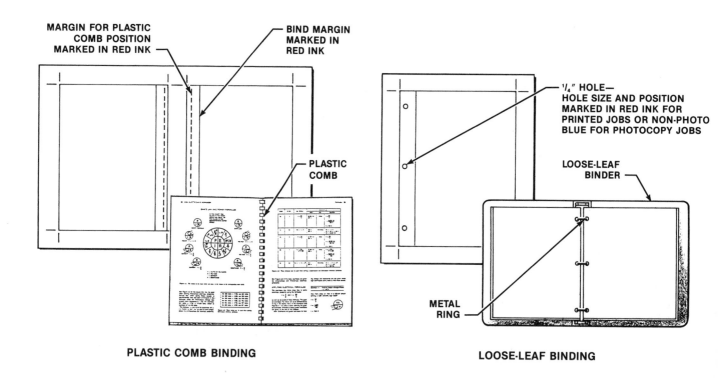

MARGIN FOR PLASTIC
COMB POSITION
MARKED IN RED INK

BIND MARGIN
MARKED IN
RED INK

PLASTIC
COMB

PLASTIC COMB BINDING

¹/₄″ HOLE—
HOLE SIZE AND POSITION
MARKED IN RED INK FOR
PRINTED JOBS OR NON-PHOTO
BLUE FOR PHOTOCOPY JOBS

LOOSE-LEAF
BINDER

METAL
RING

LOOSE-LEAF BINDING

Figure 9-25. In mechanical binding, a mechanical device is used to hold pages together. Three types of mechanical binding are spiral, plastic comb, and loose-leaf binding.

9 Color and Imposition

True-False

T   F   **1.** Color and register of a job are two factors used to determine paste-up procedure.

T   F   **2.** Color separation is the ink color chosen by the designer to print a job.

T   F   **3.** The stock on which a job will print affects the designer's choice of inks.

T   F   **4.** In general, process color jobs are easier and more cost-efficient to produce than flat color jobs.

T   F   **5.** Transparent inks can be overlapped to create additional colors.

T   F   **6.** Flat color inks may be used as a solid color, tint, or combination of solids and tints.

T   F   **7.** Halftones produce better when light color inks are used.

T   F   **8.** Color separation is a highly skilled operation produced by the camera or scanner operator.

T   F   **9.** The stripper is responsible for register of elements on flats to ensure properly made plates for each color.

T   F   **10.** Commercial register allowing $1/64''$ or less movement should be preseparated in paste-up.

T   F   **11.** Imposition is the alignment of images for press and binding.

T   F   **12.** One-sided, one-up imposition is the most common and most difficult imposition layout.

T   F   **13.** A gripper margin is a nonprinting margin.

T   F   **14.** A gripper is a part of a press.

T   F   **15.** Full bleeds extend to at least two edges of the printed piece.

T   F   **16.** A paste-up artist may alter the placement of type so it does not fall on a fold line.

T   F   **17.** Nonprinting margins do not align on both sides of a two-sided job.

T   F   **18.** Die cuts are indicated on a mechanical with a dashed non-photo blue guideline.

T   F   **19.** Two-sided artboards have the front of the job on one side of the artboard and the back of the job on the other side.

T   F   **20.** Stepped images are trimmed as a die cut.

Multiple Choice

_____   **1.** The designer chooses ink to meet the requirements of _____.
     A. stock
     B. budget
     C. colors
     D. all of the above

2. A halftone printed in two colors is a _____.
   A. two-tone
   B. color separation
   C. duotone
   D. all of the above

3. Register is controlled in _____ production processes.
   A. two
   B. three
   C. four
   D. five

4. The register of a printed piece may have requirements for _____.
   A. hairline register
   B. commercial register
   C. nonregister
   D. all of the above

5. Process color and hairline register require _____ alignment.
   A. critical
   B. loose
   C. variable
   D. lap

6. Standard bleed allowance is _____ ".
   A. ⅟₁₆
   B. ⅛
   C. ⅜
   D. all of the above

7. Nonprinting margins align on the _____ edges.
   A. top
   B. bottom
   C. four
   D. all of the above

8. The paste-up artist may create back-to-back alignment boards by planning the artboards _____.
   A. back-to-front
   B. side-by-side
   C. with a master grid
   D. all of the above

9. A _____ book is bound through the center with wire.
   A. side stitched
   B. saddle stitched
   C. spiral bound
   D. all of the above

10. _____ binding is an example of mechanical binding.
    A. Loose-leaf
    B. Spiral
    C. Plastic comb
    D. all of the above

Matching

_____ **1.** Covers stock color

_____ **2.** Shows stock color

_____ **3.** 4-color reproduction

_____ **4.** Premixed colors

_____ **5.** Process red

_____ **6.** Process blue

_____ **7.** 2-color halftone

_____ **8.** 3-color halftone

_____ **9.** Overlap alignment

_____ **10.** Critical alignment

_____ **11.** Simple alignment

_____ **12.** Printed image alignment

A. Magenta
B. Cyan
C. Process color
D. Flat color
E. Opaque ink
F. Transparent ink
G. Duotone
H. Tritone
I. Register
J. Commercial register
K. Hairline register
L. Nonregister

_____ **13.** Page alignment after binding

_____ **14.** Page alignment before binding

_____ **15.** Two-page artboard

_____ **16.** Two-sided artboard

_____ **17.** Positive film

_____ **18.** Images mirror each other

_____ **19.** Image over gutter

_____ **20.** Job printed more than once on same press run

A. Facing images
B. Breakacross image
C. Reader's spread
D. Printer's spread
E. Side-by-side
F. Back-to-front
G. Master grid
H. Stepped image

Completion

_____ **1.** The color of a job refers to the type of _____ used to print the job.

_____ **2.** The _____ of a job refers to placement of the ink on the printed piece.

_____ **3.** _____ color ink is mixed according to a formula.

_____ **4.** When two colors of black ink are used to print a(n) _____, the reproduction is a double-dot.

_____ **5.** _____ color inks are used to print a full range of colors.

_____ **6.** _____ register allows for the greatest amount of color movement.

_____   7. _____ register allows for ¹⁄₆₄″ movement.

_____   8. _____ register involves critical alignment of color elements.

_____   9. To reproduce color photographs on a printing press, _____ plates are required.

_____   10. Tritones are _____ flat color inks used to print a halftone.

_____   11. A press sheet with only one page has _____ imposition.

_____   12. The _____ is a bar of mechanical fingers on a press.

_____   13. Ink _____ is the spreading of ink onto the back of the press sheet.

_____   14. The master grid method of paste-up involves using a(n) _____ grid to align images on the front and back of pages.

_____   15. A line of type displayed at the top of all pages of a book is a(n) _____.

_____   16. A line of type displayed at the bottom of all pages of a book is a(n) _____.

_____   17. A page number is a(n) _____.

_____   18. The position of all type on facing pages should be _____ and _____ centered.

_____

_____   19. Facing images are elements that align on facing pages in _____ image.

_____   20. A(n) _____ is an image that prints across the gutter of two facing pages.

Identification

_____   1. Saddle stitch binding

_____   2. Side stitch binding

_____   3. Loose-leaf binding

_____   4. Spiral binding

_____   5. Plastic comb binding

(A)

(B)

(C)

(D)

(E)

DESIGN SPECIFICATIONS

Design specifications are elements of a printed piece that a designer chooses to communicate a message to its best advantage. These specifications include all elements of a job, such as layout, typography, color, and stock.

The designer uses design principles to plan the job. A series of drawings is created to allow the designer to visualize the printed piece. The final drawing, or comprehensive layout, serves as a blueprint for the production of the printed piece.

Stock is one of the most important and most costly design elements. The designer chooses the stock for the job carefully. The best stock is one that enhances all other elements of design on the printed piece. A poor choice of stock could result in loss in the communication of the message stemming from low readability and poor printability.

IDEA DEVELOPMENT

Idea development is a cumulative effort of the client, copywriter, and designer. The client's need to communicate is developed into an idea that will convey the message to the best of its ability.

The designer works with the client and copywriter to tailor the message to a specified audience. Once the message is defined, the designer begins the constructive form: the idea. The designer develops the idea by considering the message, reader, purpose, time frame, budget, and any elements specific to the job, such as corporation identification. The designer's idea for conveying the message may be a brochure, newsletter, book jacket, or an advertisement. Before the idea for a job can be developed into a layout, the designer further defines the idea by using design principles.

Design Principles

Design principles are conceptual tools the designer uses to envision the layout of elements. Design principles help the designer define size and shape of a piece, eye appeal of the copy, and the look or mood portrayed by the piece. The seven design principles are proportion, balance, contrast, rhythm, white space, unity, and harmony.

Proportion. *Proportion* refers to the shape of a printed piece and size of elements on the piece. Generally, the shape of a piece is a rectangle, either upright or oblong. Although squares, triangles, and curvilinear shapes are sometimes used, better eye movement is achieved with a rectangular job. *Eye movement* is the action of the eye as it follows the written message. Optimum eye movement brings the reader from the top of the page to the bottom. The goal of all written communication is to entice the reader to read and absorb the written message. Proportion also refers to the size of elements as they relate in importance to the message.

When determining proportion of a printed piece, the designer considers not only the importance of each element but also the size of each element in relation to others. Elements should flow easily from one size to another and be proportional to the size of the printed piece. See Figure 10-1.

Balance. *Balance* involves placement of elements on a printed piece. Two forms of balance are formal and informal balance.

Formal balance is symmetrical positioning of elements. The job is divided horizontally or vertically. Elements of equal size or importance are positioned so they are in balance with each other. Formal balance gives a strong feeling of structure and eye movement is difficult. Formal balance should be used with caution.

Informal balance is asymmetrical positioning of elements. The job is not equally divided horizontally or vertically. The elements may appear out of balance. Informal balance gives freedom of eye movement and is used in many forms of advertisement. Informal balance is avoided when a

Figure 10-1. A printed piece should be proportional in relation to elements on the printed piece and elements in relation to each other.

structured appearance is desired. See Figure 10-2.

Contrast. *Contrast* involves using an element to create interest in a printed piece. A job designed with column after column of one size of type in one color ink can cause eye fatigue and reader boredom. Contrast is added by using various type sizes, typestyles, borders, ornaments, tint screens, illustrations, and halftones.

Using color as contrast adds interest and draws attention on a printed piece. When multiple colors are used, similar values of color are chosen. *Value of color* is the lightness or darkness of a color. The chroma or brightness of a color is also considered. Bright colors gain attention but could be distracting if not used carefully. Dull colors are often insignificant and should not be used when an element is important.

When using contrast a designer must exercise caution. Too much contrast or improper use of color can cause elements to clash. Clash of elements results when elements fight for attention on a piece. Clash is disruptive to the communication of the message. Where too little contrast causes reader boredom, too much contrast causes a break in communication. See Figure 10-3.

Rhythm. *Rhythm* involves using an element repeatedly throughout a printed piece to encourage eye movement. As the eye scans a page it

Figure 10-3. Contrast adds interest in a printed piece. Varying type sizes and typestyles and using borders and illustrations are ways to add contrast.

seeks out similar elements. Rhythm used selectively draws the eye from the top of a page to the bottom. Some elements used to create rhythm are symbols, selected typestyles, ruling, and color. See Figure 10-4.

White Space. *White space* is the area of a printed piece that does not contain information. White space is breathing space for elements. It gives the reader a chance to absorb information before continuing. See Figure 10-5. White space is not always white; it may be any color.

White space is the most commonly misused design principle. The belief often is that the more information given the better a job will be, or if space is available, use it. This view of white space will only clutter a printed piece or cause type to be too crowded. Either will result in reader eye fatigue, thereby stopping the flow of communication.

Unity. *Unity* is the relation of the printed piece to the whole. The *whole* is the element to which the printed piece must relate in size or overall design. For example, if a business card is the piece, then the whole is

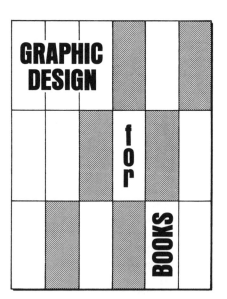

FORMAL BALANCE

INFORMAL BALANCE

Figure 10-2. Formal balance is very structured and eye movement is difficult. Informal balance allows freedom of eye movement.

Figure 10-4. Rhythm used selectively helps draw the eye along the piece as the eye seeks out like elements.

both the company it represents and the physical element in which it will be placed, such as a wallet or cardholder. See Figure 10-6.

If a business card is designed larger than cardholders and wallets, it will not fit and may not be retained. If the logo on the card is not recognizable as a symbol of the company

Enhance Your Productivity

Figure 10-5. White space does not contain information. It allows the reader to absorb information before continuing on to another part of the page.

it represents, the communication ability of the logo is lost. The result is a loss of unity and communication. Any printed piece that relates directly to another printed piece requires unity.

Harmony. *Harmony* is the result of design principles working with one another. Elements working together to enhance the communicative ability of a printed piece create harmony in the printed piece. A layout that is pleasing to the eye and communicates the message has harmony. See Figure 10-7.

Layout Development

Layout development is the process the designer uses to visualize a job in its final printed form. The designer uses information obtained from the client and applies design principles to the basic idea for the job to develop the layout.

Three stages in layout development are creating thumbnail sketches, a rough layout, and a comprehensive layout. The thumbnail sketches and rough and comprehensive layouts are used to develop a layout for a well-planned printed piece. The comprehensive layout is used as a blueprint

for the production process. Therefore, all stages of production can be planned.

Thumbnail Sketches. *Thumbnail sketches* are small but proportional drawings of the layout for a job. The designer renders many quick thumbnail sketches to visualize the printed piece. Thumbnail sketches help the designer plan the proportion of elements in the piece. The approximate space for all elements and copy is positioned quickly, without detail. See Figure 10-8. Once the initial proportion and positioning of elements are planned on a thumbnail sketch, the designer develops the layout further in a rough layout.

Rough Layouts. *Rough layouts* are full-size pencil drawings of the printed piece. The designer uses a thumbnail sketch as a guide to develop the rough layout. The designer draws all type and art elements and positions them by following the thumbnail sketch. Little attention is given to detail. The designer uses the rough layout to visualize size of elements. Changes are made as needed to alter the proportion and position of elements. The completed rough layout is used to finalize size and position of elements before the comprehensive layout is begun. See Figure 10-9.

Figure 10-6. Unity is the relation of the printed piece to the whole.

Vacation Homes

IT'S ONE OF THE BEST TIMES TO BUY.

Figure 10-7. Harmony results from design principles working together to enhance the communicative ability of a printed piece.

Comprehensive Layouts. *Comprehensive layouts* are final renditions of the printed piece in full size and full color. The comprehensive layout is made to look as close to the final printed piece as possible. Art and headline type elements are drawn in position. Photographs and body copy are usually indicated with lines showing size and position of elements.

Comprehensive layouts contain all information needed for the production of the printed piece. Type sizes and typestyles are indicated. Photographs, illustrations, stock, ink, and other elements specific to the job are

indicated on the comprehensive layout or tissue overlay. See Figure 10-10. Jobs with special binding requirements include a folding dummy with the comprehensive layout. The completed comprehensive layout serves as the detailed plan for the printed piece.

STOCK

Stock, also known as *substrate* and *paper,* is the material on which a job is printed. A designer chooses the best stock for a job by analyzing the appearance, texture, strength, printing brilliance, and printability of the stock. Stock is generally made from natural wood or cotton fibers but may also be produced synthetically. To choose the best stock for a job, the designer must be familiar with paper manufacturing techniques.

Paper Manufacturing

Paper manufacturing is the process by which paper is made. The method used to manufacture paper and ingredients added during processing affect paper quality. Natural papers are made from hardwood and softwood pulp, raw cotton fibers, linen, and cotton rags. Hardwood pulp comes from hardwood, or deciduous, trees, including birch, gum, maple, and oak. The fibers of hardwood trees are shorter than those of softwood trees and give the paper smoothness.

Softwood pulp comes from softwood, or coniferous, trees, including

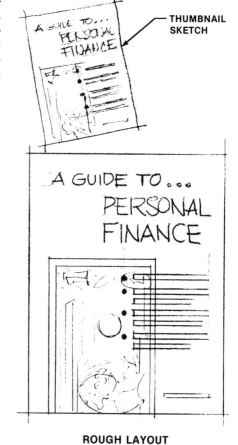

THUMBNAIL SKETCH

.A GUIDE TO...

PERSONAL FINANCE

ROUGH LAYOUT

Figure 10-9. The rough layout allows the designer to visualize the job in full size. The proportion and position of elements are often altered on the rough layout.

balsa, fir, spruce, and pine. The fibers of softwood trees are longer than those of hardwood trees. Long fibers create better bonding. Therefore, paper manufactured with softwood pulp is stronger than paper manufactured with hardwood pulp.

Since printing on paper requires both a smooth surface and strength, two parts of hardwood pulp are blended with one part of softwood pulp. This blending of fibers creates a quality printing paper.

Pulp Processing. Pulp processing methods are used to separate fibers or pulp of wood. *Cellulose* or *natural fibers* of wood make up approximately one-half the composition of wood. *Lignin* is the natural adhesive that

Figure 10-8. Thumbnail sketches allow the designer to plan proportion and position of elements and work through many ideas.

holds pulp together and makes up one-fourth the composition of wood. *Hemicellulose* is a by-product of cellulose and makes up one-fourth the composition of wood.

Paper is made of pulp, lignin, and water. Lignin is the natural adhesive of paper. In pulp processing the pulp is broken down into loose fibers of lignin and water. Hemicellulose is lost in processing. Pulp can be either mechanically or chemically processed.

Mechanical processing of pulp produces pulp through grinding stripped logs or steaming wood chips. Both methods produce groundwood pulp. Groundwood pulp is slightly weakened because the fibers are often damaged in processing. The pure lignin in groundwood pulp is not washed away through processing. This residual lignin causes groundwood paper to become sensitive to light. The lignin in groundwood paper turns yellow or amber with time and exposure to light.

The grinding process of groundwood paper creates a smooth surface and high opacity. However, groundwood paper is not recommended for jobs designed to last years or those that will be archived. Groundwood paper is commonly used for newsprint papers. When coated, groundwood paper may be used for magazines.

Chemical processing of pulp produces pulp through the use of strong chemicals that break down the lignin in wood. One of the greatest problems arising from chemical processing is the adverse conditions it causes in the environment. Acidic and odorous chemicals contaminate the air and water surrounding paper mills. Regulations have been passed to control this contamination. The process of controlling the waste contamination is costly. This cost raises the price of paper manufactured with chemically processed pulp. The strength and quality of the paper depend on the type of chemical used in processing.

Paper may also be made from cotton and rag fibers, which produce the finest quality papers. Cotton fibers come from cotton plants and require additives to bond the fibers. Rag fibers come from cotton and linen

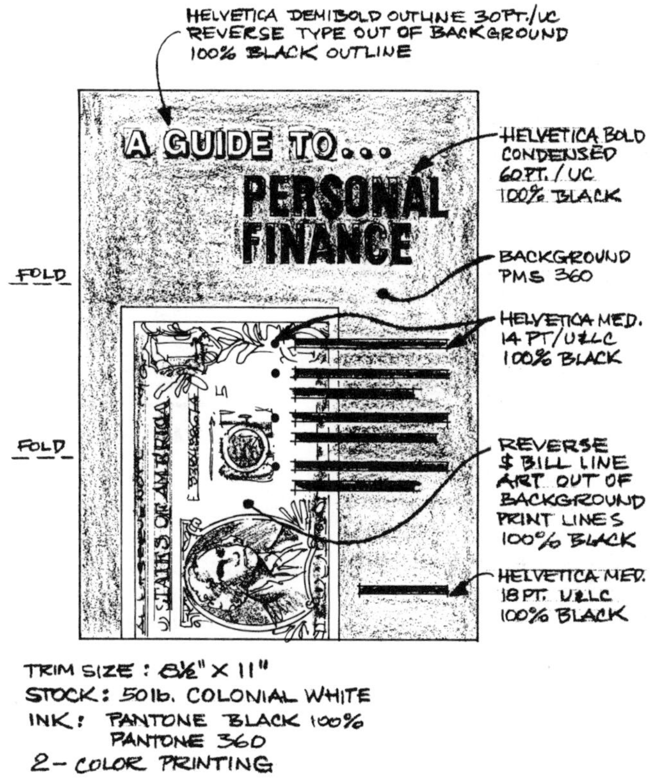

Figure 10-10. The comprehensive layout and folding dummy allow the designer and client to visualize the job in full size and color. A tissue overlay with detailed instructions gives production requirements.

rags. New uncolored rags make the strongest papers.

Papermaking. The papermaking process is a combination of science and machine. Each type of paper grade, color, weight, and surface requires its own formula. The formula includes ingredients added to the pulp and the procedure used to make the paper.

Most printing papers begin as a mixture of pulp and water. The mixture is blended and beaten to a smooth flowing consistency. Beating the pulp causes fibers to fray, creating improved bonding. Additives are mixed with the pulp in the blending process. Bleaches, pigments, starches, fillers, and synthetic modifiers are some common additives.

The prepared pulp is called *stuff,* or *stock.* When liquid stock is fed into the papermaking machine, or *four-*

drinier, the ratio of fiber to water is 1 to 99. This liquid consistency allows the fibers to be controlled as they enter the headbox. The *headbox* regulates the flow onto a screen called a *wire.*

The faster the flow of liquid stock is on the screen, the thicker the layer of stock will be. The screen is a constantly moving belt of wire or plastic mesh. The speed at which the screen moves also controls the bulk and grain of the paper. In general, the faster the belt moves, the more consistent the grain is.

Text papers, or textured papers, for example, have crisscross grain because the liquid stock quickly flows from the headbox and the screen moves at a slower rate. This allows the fibers to layer and does not allow them to flow out to straighten quickly, creating an inconsistent grain. Liquid stock released slowly out of the headbox onto a quickly moving belt allows the fibers to straighten and flow in the same direction, creating a consistent grain. See Figure 10-11.

As liquid stock flows along the screen, water drains off, leaving a very moist paper. Moisture is pressed out of the paper with blankets or felts covered with synthetic material. Paper generally has two surfaces: the wire side and felt side. The wire side is created by the screen. The felt side is created by the felts or blankets.

For papers designed to be printed only on one side, the felt side is the superior printing surface. Although much of the moisture is pressed out between the felts, the stock is at least one-third stock and two-thirds water after it has been pressed. To remove most of the remaining moisture, the stock is passed through heated metal drums. After the paper dries, it may be finished by passing it through a series of rollers.

Paper Finishing. The process of *paper finishing* creates a smooth surface. Paper is fed through a *calender stack,* which is a series of rollers. As the paper is pressed between the rollers, the surface is ironed smooth. The farther the paper feeds through the calender stack, the smoother the surface becomes. See Figure 10-12. However, as the amount of calendering increases, the stock becomes weaker and less opaque. Various uncoated stock surfaces include vellum, antique, English, wove, and smooth or luster.

Paper Coatings

Paper is coated with fine white clay, which gives the paper better ink holdout. *Ink holdout* is the paper's ability to resist ink absorption. The amount of clay and calendering applied to paper affects the appearance and light-reflecting ability of the stock. Four types of coated stock are matte, dull, gloss, and cast.

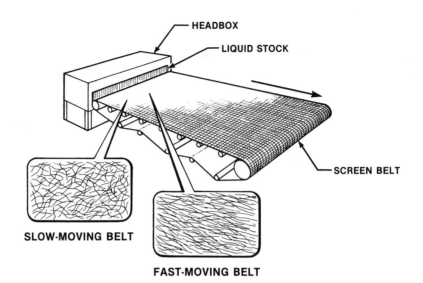

Figure 10-11. A slow-moving screen belt on the papermaking machine results in an inconsistent grain on the paper. A fast-moving screen belt on the papermaking machine results in a consistent grain on the paper.

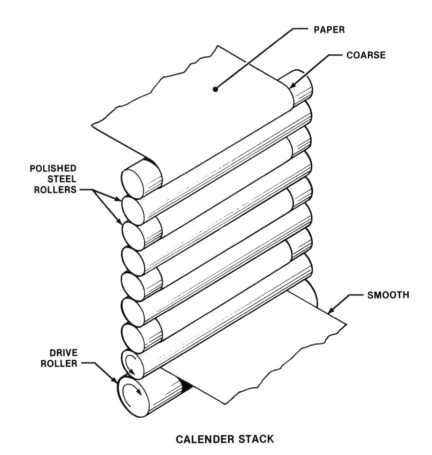

Figure 10-12. The calender stack is a series of rollers that iron the surface of the paper, creating a finished surface.

Matte Coated. *Matte coated stock* is the least coated and least calendered of the coated stocks. Matte coated stock is calendered once and coated once. This allows some of the fibers of the pulp to rise above the surface of the coating. See Figure 10-13. Matte coated stock may create a mottled image where a heavy ink layer is applied. The mottled image appears because ink is absorbed in areas where fibers have not been coated. Matte coated stock is best for jobs with a great amount of text and some halftones. Matte coated stock is not recommended for jobs that have large solid areas to be covered with ink.

Dull Coated. *Dull coated stock* is coated twice and calendered once. This double layer of clay covers most of the pulp fibers. See Figure 10-14. Dull coated stock has a smooth surface with consistent ink holdout. Dull coated stock does not allow ink to be absorbed and does not reflect a glaring light to the eye. Dull coated stock is a good choice for jobs with large amounts of text and halftones.

Gloss Coated. *Gloss coated stock* is calendered twice and coated twice. See Figure 10-15. *Gloss* refers to the glossy appearance of the surface. The gloss surface allows for the greatest ink holdout of all coated stocks. This surface is excellent for halftones because it creates high contrast between light and dark areas of photographs. However, gloss coated stocks are a poor choice for jobs with a large amount of text. The reflectance of light from the surface of the stock can create glare and cause eye fatigue for the reader.

Cast Coated. *Cast coated stock* has the greatest amount of clay coating that may be applied to a stock. The stock is dipped in a thick layer of clay and dried on a heated polished drum. See Figure 10-16. The surface

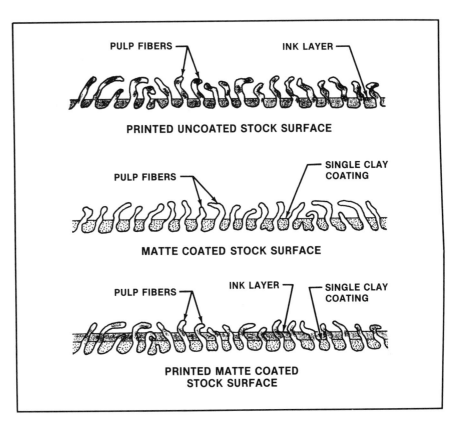

Figure 10-13. Matte coated stock has a single coat of clay that holds out most of the ink on the paper's surface. Some ink is absorbed by the fibers extending above the clay layer.

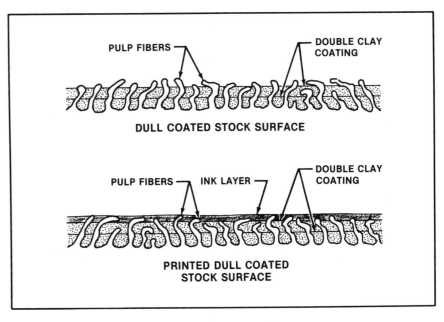

Figure 10-14. Dull coated stock has two layers of clay coating that create high ink holdout, producing good-quality reproductions.

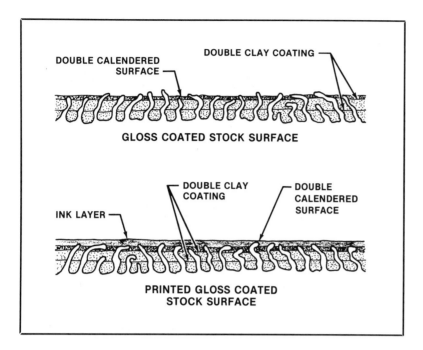

Figure 10-15. Gloss coated stock has the highest ink holdout of the coated stocks. It is coated twice and calendered twice, which creates a hard surface.

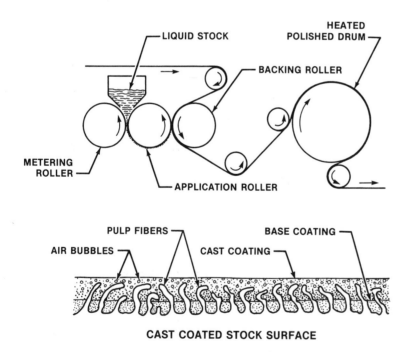

Figure 10-16. Cast coated stock is the most reflective of all coated stocks. However, tiny air bubbles from the thick layer of clay decrease ink holdout because the clay absorbs some ink.

of the dried clay mirrors the surface of the drum and creates a highly reflective surface. Cast coated stock is generally a heavyweight stock and is used for very high-quality, expensive jobs. The disadvantage of cast coated stock is that the clay absorbs some ink, lowering the ink holdout. In addition, surface cracks and chips appear when the stock is folded, making the image in the fold difficult to read.

Paper Specifications. Paper specifications are standards set by paper mills for specifying paper. A designer chooses a paper and specifies the manufacturer, weight, color, surface, and grade. The paper manufacturer may be the mill or the merchant. Generally, the mill carries the same name as the paper merchant. Occasionally the mill is independently owned and produces a variety of papers. The designer specifies the name of the paper merchant when specifying paper.

Weight. *Weight* of stock refers to basis weight. *Basis weight* is the weight in pounds of 500 sheets, or a ream, of the stock at the basic size. *Basic size* is a standard size sheet designated for each paper category or grade. Basic sizes resulted from the most common use of each of the paper grades.

Color. Color of stock is designated by the paper merchant. Peacock blue purchased from one merchant may differ greatly from peacock blue from another merchant. The color of a stock may differ from one dye lot to another in the same mill. A designer should purchase enough of a particular color paper to satisfy requirements of a job.

Surface. *Surface* of stock is the texture or finish of the stock. Texture is applied to stock when it is wet. A *dandy roller,* which is a large roller, presses the texture into the stock. A texture will penetrate the stock and may appear as a lighter density if the paper is held up to the light. A *watermark* is a unique texture that is applied with a wire or rubber embossing form attached to the dandy roller. See Figure 10-17.

A *finish* is a surface that is applied to stock after it is dried. Finishing is applied similarly to calendering and appears only on the surface on which it is applied. Finishing is similar to ironing or embossing. A stock that is finished has a compressed surface. This compressed surface is a better printing surface than a textured surface. However, it is a weaker paper and the compressed fibers crack when folded.

Grade. *Grade* of paper is the paper category. Each paper category is designed for a specific use. A designer must be aware of variations and printing qualities of paper grades. Many paper grades are available. The most common paper grades are bond, book, text, and cover. A variety of specialty stocks are also available.

Bond papers are considered fine writing papers. Bond papers are often high in cotton and rag pulp content. Most bond papers are designed to be printed on only one side. Watermark papers are usually bond papers. Bond papers are available in a variety of surfaces, colors, and grade qualities. Bond papers are uncoated because they are usually used for writing and typing. Basis size for bond is 17″ × 22″. The most common weights range from 16-pound to 28-pound.

Book papers are sometimes called offset papers because the printing process used for book papers is commonly offset lithography. Book papers are fine printing papers. Book papers are strong and opaque, designed to be printed on both sides. Book papers may be coated or uncoated. They are available in a variety of finishes and a few colors. Book papers are the most common papers used in the printing industry because of the high-quality reproduction of text and halftones. Basis size for book paper is 25″ × 38″. The most commonly used weights are 50-, 60-, and 70-pound.

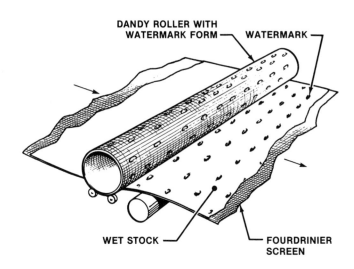

Figure 10-17. The watermark is a special texture applied to stock. A wire attached to the dandy roller on the papermaking machine presses the texture into the stock.

Text papers are available in a variety of textured surfaces and brilliant colors. Text papers are very strong and can be used to create unusual effects through different printing methods. Text papers may be combined with matching cover stocks of the same color and texture. Basis size of text paper is 25″ × 38″. The most commonly specified weight for text paper is 80-pound.

Cover papers are designed to work well with both book and text papers. They are generally available in the same colors and textures as book and text papers. Cover papers may also be manufactured to match the color and quality of some bond papers. Cover papers are sometimes called card stock because they are often used for business cards. Basis size for cover paper is 20″ × 26″. The most common weight is 65-pound to 80-pound.

Specialty papers are made for a variety of purposes. Some specialty papers are manufactured at the mill. Others are manufactured at aftermarket companies, which are companies that buy paper from mills and alter the paper to create specialty papers. Some common specialty stocks include noncarbon papers, pressure-sensitive papers, combined text papers (duplex), rough-edged text papers (deckled edge), and a variety of synthetic papers. Basis size and basis weight of specialty papers depend on the original grade of the paper. A designer should consult a paper representative for printing characteristics of the specialty paper.

True-False

T   F   **1.** The client's need to communicate is developed into an idea by the designer.

T   F   **2.** The goal of all written communication is to attract the reader's attention so the reader absorbs the information.

T   F   **3.** A printed piece designed for optimum eye movement brings the reader's eye from the bottom to the top of the page.

T   F   **4.** Informal balance is a restricting design format.

T   F   **5.** When multiple colors are used on a printed piece, similar values are used to avoid clashing of colors.

T   F   **6.** Rhythm used in a printed piece draws the eye from the right to the left side of the page.

T   F   **7.** White space is the most commonly used design element.

T   F   **8.** A printed piece has harmony when its elements work together to increase its communicative ability.

T   F   **9.** Comprehensive layouts contain all information necessary to produce the printed piece.

T   F   **10.** The completed rough layout serves as a detailed plan of the printed piece.

T   F   **11.** To choose the best stock for the job, the designer must become familiar with the paper manufacturing process.

T   F   **12.** The fibers of softwood trees are shorter than those of hardwood trees.

T   F   **13.** The longer the pulp fibers are, the stronger the paper is.

T   F   **14.** Two parts of softwood pulp are blended with one part of hardwood pulp to produce a smooth and strong paper.

T   F   **15.** Paper is made of pulp, lignin, and water.

T   F   **16.** Groundwood processing creates adverse conditions on the environment.

T   F   **17.** The beating of pulp causes the fibers to fray, which improves bonding.

T   F   **18.** The speed at which the screen moves on a papermaking machine controls the bulk and grain of the paper.

Matching

_____ **1.** The designer develops an idea for a job by keeping in mind the _____.
    A. message
    B. reader
    C. budget
    D. all of the above

_____   **2.** There are _____ design principles.
   A. five
   B. six
   C. seven
   D. eight

_____   **3.** _____ relates to the shape of the piece.
   A. Proportion
   B. Unity
   C. Harmony
   D. Balance

_____   **4.** _____ is the placement of elements on a page.
   A. Proportion
   B. Unity
   C. Harmony
   D. Balance

_____   **5.** _____ is the use of an element to create interest.
   A. Proportion
   B. Contrast
   C. Harmony
   D. Rhythm

_____   **6.** _____ is the use of an element repetitively throughout the piece.
   A. Proportion
   B. Contrast
   C. Harmony
   D. Rhythm

_____   **7.** _____ is the cumulative result of design principles working with one another.
   A. Proportion
   B. Contrast
   C. Harmony
   D. Rhythm

_____   **8.** A _____ is a small but proportionate drawing of the final job.
   A. comprehensive layout
   B. thumbnail sketch
   C. folding dummy
   D. rough layout

_____   **9.** A _____ is a full-color, full-size drawing of the final job.
   A. comprehensive layout
   B. thumbnail sketch
   C. folding dummy
   D. rough layout

_____   **10.** A _____ is a full-size pencil drawing of the final job.
   A. comprehensive layout
   B. thumbnail sketch
   C. folding dummy
   D. rough layout

Completion

_____   **1.** Using _____ as contrast on a printed piece adds interest and draws attention.

_____   **2.** A(n) _____ is the lightness or darkness of a color.

_____ 3. _____ colors tend to attract the reader's attention.

_____ 4. Too much contrast or improper use of color can cause _____ to clash.

_____ 5. _____ is the area of an image that does not give information.

_____ 6. _____ is the printed piece as it relates to the whole.

_____ 7. _____ is the natural fibers of wood.

_____ 8. _____ is the natural adhesive of wood.

_____ 9. _____ is the by-product of cellulose.

_____ 10. _____ processing produces pulp by grinding stripped logs.

_____ 11. _____ processing produces pulp through the use of strong chemicals.

_____ 12. _____ and _____ fibers are used to create the finest papers.

_____ 13. The _____ for papermaking includes the ingredients and the process.

_____ 14. The prepared pulp is known as _____ or stock.

_____ 15. The faster the screen belt moves on the papermaking machine, the more consistent the _____ is.

_____ 16. The two surfaces that paper has are the _____ and _____ sides.

_____ 17. Paper finishing creates a _____ surface.

_____ 18. Paper becomes more _____ with a greater degree of calendering.

_____ 19. The weight of stock refers to the _____ weight.

_____ 20. A(n) _____ is a unique texture applied with a wire attached to the dandy roller.

Matching

_____ 1. Matte coated stock

_____ 2. Dull coated stock

_____ 3. Gloss coated stock

_____ 4. Cast coated stock

_____ 5. Ream

_____ 6. Textured surface

_____ 7. Finished surface

_____ 8. Paper grade

_____ 9. Bond paper

_____ 10. Book paper

_____ 11. Text paper

_____ 12. Specialty paper

A. Coated twice, calendered once
B. Fine printing paper
C. Coated once, calendered once
D. Heaviest clay coating of all coated stocks
E. Applied when paper is wet
F. Paper category
G. Coated twice, calendered twice
H. Fine writing paper
I. 500 sheets of paper
J. Available as synthetic paper
K. Available in variety of textured surfaces
L. Applied when paper is dry

Identification

_____ **1.** Thumbnail sketch

_____ **2.** Rough layout

_____ **3.** Comprehensive layout

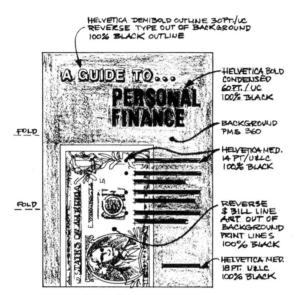

HELVETICA DEMIBOLD OUTLINE 30PT./UC
REVERSE TYPE OUT OF BACKGROUND
100% BLACK OUTLINE

HELVETICA BOLD
CONDENSED
60PT./UC
100% BLACK

BACKGROUND
PMS 360

HELVETICA MED.
14 PT/U&LC
100% BLACK

REVERSE
$ BILL LINE
ART OUT OF
BACKGROUND
PRINT LINES
100% BLACK

HELVETICA MED.
18 PT. U&LC
100% BLACK

FOLD

FOLD

TRIM SIZE : 8½" X 11"
STOCK: 50 lb. COLONIAL WHITE
INK: PANTONE BLACK 100%
PANTONE 360
2- COLOR PRINTING

# 11 PHOTOGRAPHIC DESIGN

Photographic design is the process of applying design concepts to photographic images. The designer uses a variety of methods to edit and prepare photographs for reproduction. Photographic design involves editing to create montages, manipulated images, extended images, textured photographs, posterizations, anamorphic images, silhouette images, and ghost images. Other quality control techniques can also be used. The preparation of photographic images for reproduction is done through cropping and scaling.

PHOTOGRAPHIC EDITING

A photograph on a printed piece adds labor and material costs. The increased cost is justified by the visual impact created by the photograph. No other element of design can give a printed piece a greater impact of reality. Photographic editing involves altering photographs to better convey the message of a printed piece.

The editing and proofing of a photograph is as important as editing and proofreading type. Yet photographic editing is often sacrificed because of time or layout limitations. Photographic editing is commonly a combination of decisions made by the photographer, and later by the designer. Photographs with the greatest communicative ability and highest visual impact are those that are edited from conception through the printed piece.

Visual Impact of Photographs

Creating a visual impact is the objective of any photographic image. A visual impact is achieved when a photograph is well-planned through the camera lens and on the art table. When a designer communicates the concept of the visual image to the photographer *before* the photograph is taken, the photographic editing process is enhanced. A planned photograph is easily altered to increase its communicative ability. Photographic editing left solely to the photographer limits the designer's ability to create a visual impact.

To enhance the visual impact of a photograph, a designer may request that the photographer take a specific point of view (perspective) or use a specific angle in taking the photograph. The designer may request a series or sequence of photographs. Action photographs may be used to create a feeling of movement on a piece. See Figure 11-1. These are specific settings, or *sets,* that the designer cannot create by altering the photographs.

Photographs can be altered in other ways by the designer. Cropping is the most common method of alter-ing an original photograph. *Cropping* is the cutting, masking, trimming, or opaquing of a photograph to fit it in a specified space. See Figure 11-2. A designer crops a photograph to increase eye movement, call attention to a specific area of the photograph, or remove distracting or unwanted images.

Photographic enhancement is created by the designer, camera/scanner operator, or stripper. *Photographic enhancement* is a drastic alteration of the original photograph. Photographic enhancement cannot be created through a commercial photographer's camera lens. Drastic alterations include montages, manipulated images, extended images, screened or textured photographs, posterizations, anamorphic images, silhouette images, and ghost images.

Montages. *Montages* are various photographs combined to form one image. See Figure 11-3. Although original photographs can be cut and combined either by the designer or in the stripping process, the best method

155

PERSPECTIVE

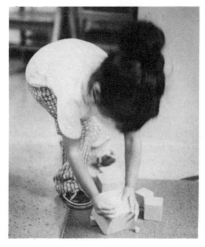

SERIES

ACTION

Figure 11-1. A designer may request that a photograph be taken in a specific perspective, or as a series or action photograph.

of creating a montage is using a pagination system. A *pagination system* uses electronic imaging to alter and combine images.

If the designer does not cut and combine the photographs, the designer may illustrate the position of the combined images on a layout. Another method is to create a mock-up using copies of the original photographs.

Manipulated Images. *Manipulated images* are photographs that are altered through cutting and repositioning. See Figure 11-4. Manipulated images may be created by the designer or stripper or on a pagination system. Manipulated images created by the designer may show cutlines on the printed piece. The reproduction of manipulated images is of higher quality when created on a pagination system.

Extended Images. *Extended images* are photographs enhanced with illustrations. Extended images are created by the designer, process camera operator, and stripper. Each image requires a separate photographic process, which are halftone and line photography. The designer creates the extended image. The camera operator photographs it twice: once as a line reproduction and once as a halftone reproduction. The stripper aligns the two photographic images to create an extended image. See Figure 11-5.

Textured Photographs. *Textured photographs* are photographs that contain a special effect screen in the image. A special effect contact screen is used to produce the halftone image for reproduction. The texture patterned contact screen is often comprised of lines rather than a dot pattern. See Figure 11-6.

Textured photographs can be an effective form of photographic design. However, special effect contact screens are costly and may add to the final cost of the job. Some scanners and most pagination systems can reproduce a variety of screen patterns. The cost and reproduction quality of textured photographs should be investigated by the designer before a textured photograph is specified.

Posterizations. *Posterizations* are continuous tone photographs reproduced without using a halftone contact screen. Images are reproduced by line photography using a single exposure. The high-contrast film used does not reproduce gray tones. Light areas reproduce as white on the final copy. Dark areas reproduce as black. See Figure 11-7.

Posterization is commonly used for special effects and in screen printing. The paste-up artist indicates a posterization by making a PMT of the original photograph and pasting it in position on the mechanical. The PMT may be used as final copy or as a position stat. Color posterizations are very effective as photographic designs. Color posterizations should be discussed with the camera operator and printer to ensure quality reproductions and predictable results.

Anamorphic Images. *Anamorphic images* are photographs that are enlarged or reduced disproportionately horizontally or vertically. See Figure 11-8. Anamorphic images can be produced through a camera with special lenses, on a computer with special software, on a scanner, or through a pagination system. The most common use of anamorphic imaging is stretching or shrinking a photograph to fit in a space that cannot accommodate the proportions of the photograph's original size.

A slight amount of anamorphic properties in a photograph often is not detected by the eye. Extreme amounts of anamorphic properties are considered special effects. A paste-up artist indicates an anamorphic image by marking the image reproduction size and indicating the dimension to be stretched or shrunk.

ORIGINAL PHOTOGRAPH   **CROPPED PHOTOGRAPH**

Figure 11-2. Cropping is the designer's most common method of photographic editing.

Silicon Beach Software, Inc.
MONTAGE

Figure 11-3. A montage is one photographic image created by combining several photographs.

ORIGINAL PHOTOGRAPH

MANIPULATED IMAGE

Figure 11-4. Manipulated images are created by cutting and repositioning an original photograph.

EXTENDED IMAGE

Figure 11-5. Extended images are created by the designer, reproduced on two films through halftone and line photography, and repositioned by the stripper.

Silhouette Images. *Silhouette images,* or outlined halftones, are photographic images that have their backgrounds removed. See Figure 11-9. A silhouette image is most commonly created in paste-up, stripping, or on a pagination system.

The paste-up artist may create a silhouette image by painting out the background of the photograph with white paint. This is the simplest and least expensive method. The retouched photograph is then reproduced on a process camera. However, painting out the background to silhouette an image has disadvantages. Mistakes are easily created and difficult to correct. Intricate images are difficult to outline with paint. Also, the background of a black-and-white photograph often blends into the image to be outlined. If painted, a loss of detail or an awkward final appearance could result.

Black-and-white halftone images are commonly reproduced on a flat-bed black-and-white scanner. See Figure 11-10. As a scanner scans the photographic image to record density, it also scans surface marks. If a silhouette image created by painting out the background is scanned, brush strokes from the paintbrush would appear as undesired images on the halftone film. Therefore, images to be photographically reproduced on a scanner cannot be silhouetted by painting.

The designer or paste-up artist may also indicate a silhouette image by drawing a detailed illustration of the desired image. The designer or paste-up artist can also create a silhouette mock-up of the image.

Images that are processed into halftones through a process camera may be silhouetted in stripping. The stripper separates the desired image from the background by the opaque or ruby film method.

In the opaque method, the stripper blocks out with opaque all areas of the halftone negative that are not to be reproduced. In the ruby film method, the stripper masks all unwanted areas of the background with ruby film. Only the desired image is left unmasked.

A pagination system electronically scans the original photograph and reproduces it on a viewing screen. The operator uses an electronic pencil to trace the image on the screen. The system is then programmed to electronically remove the background of the photographic image.

A pagination system is the best method for silhouetting detailed, 4-color originals. However, it is the most costly method. The pagination system is highly accurate, and multiple changes can be made without using excess film. The reproduction information can be stored in computer memory for later use.

Ghost Images. *Ghost images,* or dropped images, are reproductions of a continuous tone at a lighter percentage of ink coverage. Ghost images are used effectively behind type. A partial ghost image can be used to highlight specific areas of an original. See Figure 11-11.

Ghost images are created in stripping or by using a process camera. Partial ghost images are created in stripping. The designer requests a ghost image by indicating the percentage of ink for printing the ghost image. Indicating the percentage of ink for a ghost image is the same as that for a tint screen. For example, the designer would mark "10% ghost image," or "30% ghost image." A partial ghost image is requested on a sheet of tissue taped over the photograph. The specific area to be printed as a ghost image and the percentage of ink coverage is indicated.

Quality Control

Quality-control measures in photographic editing must be taken to ensure high-quality reproductions of original photographic images. The designer checks original photographs for undesired images such as wires, lights, people, dust, and smudges. These images may be removed by a retoucher or on a pagination system. The method used to improve the

American Plywood Association

TEXTURED PHOTOGRAPH

Figure 11-6. Textured photographs are created by using a special effect contact screen.

POSTERIZATION

Figure 11-7. Posterizations are continuous tone photographs that are photographed through line photography. No halftone contact screen is used.

ORIGINAL PHOTOGRAPH

DS America Incorporated

ANAMORPHIC IMAGE

Figure 11-8. Anamorphic images are created by enlarging or reducing photographs disproportionately horizontally or vertically.

ORIGINAL PHOTOGRAPH

SILHOUETTE IMAGE

Figure 11-9. Silhouette images are photographic images that have their backgrounds removed.

quality of an image should be discussed with the commercial photographer and the printer's photographer.

A designer tapes a sheet of tissue over the original photograph or a reproduction of the original photograph and marks corrections on the tissue. A red grease pencil is used to indicate changes. Not all undesired images warrant the expense of a retoucher or pagination system. Final costs should be reviewed because it may be more cost efficient to rephotograph the original.

REPRODUCTION SIZE AND DIMENSIONS

Reproduction size and dimensions are the final size and shape at which an image is to reproduce on the printed piece. Most camera-ready line copy is prepared to reproduce at the same size on the printed piece. Most continuous tone copy is reproduced at a smaller or larger size than the original by scaling. Also, the shape or proportion of the original is often altered by cropping.

Scaling is reducing or enlarging an image at a proportionate ratio to the original photograph. *Cropping* is altering the photograph by cutting away areas in order to fit it in a shape that does not match the proportions of the photograph. The designer determines the amount of scaling or cropping required and writes instructions to the camera operator and stripper.

Scaling

Scaling is reducing or enlarging an image proportionately. An image is photographically scaled on a process camera or scanner. All scaling is indicated by a percentage of the original size. The percentage of reproduction represents a ratio of the original to the reproduction. The designer marks the image to be reduced, enlarged, or reproduced at the same size as the original. See Figure 11-12.

Percentage of reproduction is calculated by various methods. Two common methods are the mathematical method of cross multiplying and dividing and using a calculator to calculate percentage. The diagonal line method can also be used to scale images. Regardless of the method used, two variables, the size of the original and the size of the reproduction, are required.

Mathematical Methods. Mathematical methods of scaling are used to calculate the percentage of an enlargement or reduction. The original size and reproduction size must be known. Any measurement system, such as inches or picas, may be used to find the original size and reproduction size. Inches are most commonly used. Inches, however, are awkward to work with if there are fractions. To work accurately with inches, fractions are often converted to decimal equivalents.

Hewlett-Packard Company

FLATBED BLACK-AND-WHITE SCANNER

Figure 11-10. Flatbed black-and-white scanners are often used to reproduce photographs.

PARTIAL GHOST IMAGE

Figure 11-11. A partial ghost image highlights certain areas of a photograph.

ENLARGEMENT

REDUCTION

Taney Supply & Lumber Corp.

SAME-SIZE REPRODUCTION

Figure 11-12. Photographs may be scaled for an enlargement, a reduction, or a same-size reproduction.

The following equation is used for the cross multiplying and dividing method of calculating reproduction size:

$$\frac{original\ width}{reproduction\ width} = \frac{original\ height}{reproduction\ height}$$

The original height and original width are known. Often only one factor of the reproduction size is known. An *x* represents the unknown factor:

$$\frac{2}{x} = \frac{5}{10}$$

In this example, the reproduction width is unknown. Cross multiply and divide to find the factor.

$$5x = 20$$

$$x = \frac{20}{5}$$

$$x = 4$$

The reproduction width is 4″.

Use the following equation to find the percentage of enlargement or reduction:

$$\frac{reproduction\ size}{original\ size} = \%\ of\ reproduction$$

Because the reproduction height and width are proportional to the original height and width, *either* the height *or* the width may be used for the equation.

$$\frac{reproduction\ height}{original\ height} = \%\ of\ reproduction$$

$$\frac{10}{5} = 2.\ (or\ 200\%)$$

$$\frac{reproduction\ width}{original\ width} = \%\ of\ reproduction$$

$$\frac{4}{2} = 2.\ (or\ 200\%)$$

Note: The equation results in a decimal point equivalent. All numbers to the left of the decimal point are enlargements. All numbers to the right of the decimal point are reductions below 100%.

Measurements that are not whole numbers or that include a fraction are easier to figure with a calculator. The measurements must first be converted to decimal point equivalents, and the following equation is used:

$$\frac{reproduction\ height}{original\ height} = \%\ of\ reproduction$$

OR

$$\frac{reproduction\ width}{original\ width} = \%\ of\ reproduction$$

$$\frac{2^{1}\!/_{64}}{5^{1}\!/_{8}} = x$$

$$\frac{2.016}{5.125} = .393\ (or\ 39.3\%)$$

Scanners and computerized cameras accept decimal point percentages. Noncomputerized cameras are adjustable only to whole numbers. When noncomputerized cameras are used, the percentage of reproduction is rounded to the nearest whole number above or below .5; for example,

.393 = 39.3 = 39% (rounded down)
.395 = 39.5 = 40% (rounded up)

Diagonal Line Method. The diagonal line method of scaling enables the designer to calculate an unknown reproduction factor and visualize proportional sizes. The diagonal line method is a graph of the original size with a diagonal line extending from the lower left corner through the upper right corner. See Figure 11-13. The diagonal line method does not calculate the percentage of enlarge-

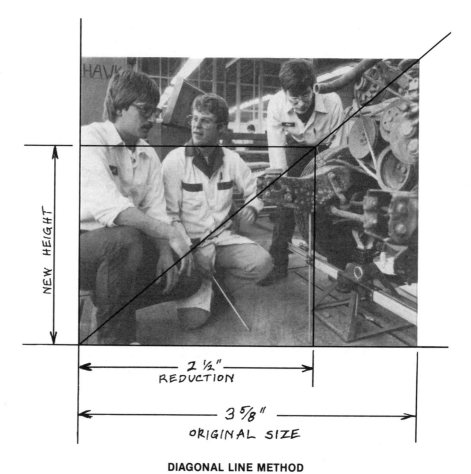

DIAGONAL LINE METHOD

Figure 11-13. The diagonal line method enables the designer to determine an unknown reproduction factor and visualize proportions.

ment or reduction. Therefore, the mathematical method of calculating percentage is used to mark the copy for reproduction.

Cropping and Scaling

Cropping and scaling is a process the designer uses to edit photographs. The designer indicates the cropped dimensions of the original with crop marks. *Crop marks* are dense, short black lines that are drawn in the margin of the photograph or outside of the desired image area. They are similar in appearance to trim marks. See Figure 11-14. Crop marks reproduce on the halftone negative and show the stripper where to crop the photograph.

The percentage of enlargement is marked either in the margin of the photograph or on a tissue overlay covering the photograph. Photographs or continuous tone art are never marked or cut. They are protected because much time and expense have been invested to create them.

A variety of methods is available for calculating cropping and scaling. The most common method of cropping and scaling is using a proportional scale. A *proportional scale* is a circular instrument with an inner and outer disk. It is used to calculate reproduction sizes and dimensions by aligning the size of the original with the desired size of reproduction on the outer disk. The reproduction size is then shown in the window on the inner disk. See Figure 11-15.

W.W. Grainger, Inc.

Figure 11-14. Crop marks are dense black lines drawn in the margins of the original photographs. They reproduce as clear lines on the halftone reproduction.

Chartpak

Figure 11-15. A proportional scale is used to determine percentages of desired reproduction sizes.

 **Photographic Design**

True-False

T   F   **1.** Photographic editing is the process in which the designer alters the photograph to better convey the message.

T   F   **2.** Photographs give the printed piece an impact of reality.

T   F   **3.** Photographic editing and proofing is less important than the proofreading of text.

T   F   **4.** A planned photograph cannot be easily altered.

T   F   **5.** A designer can enhance the communicative ability of the photograph by communicating with the photographer.

T   F   **6.** Photographic enhancement cannot be created through a commercial photographer's camera lens.

T   F   **7.** A designer cannot easily create a setting by altering an original photograph.

T   F   **8.** Manipulated images created by the designer may show cutlines on a printed piece.

T   F   **9.** Manipulated images reproduce at a lower quality when created on a pagination system than if they were created by other methods.

T   F   **10.** The designer creates the extended image.

T   F   **11.** Another term for an outline halftone is a backdrop halftone.

T   F   **12.** The simplest method of creating a silhouette image is to paint out the background.

T   F   **13.** Brush marks on a silhouette photograph reproduce when scanned.

T   F   **14.** Pagination systems create the highest quality and lowest cost outline halftone.

T   F   **15.** The designer requests the same percentage of ink for a ghost image as that for tint screens.

T   F   **16.** Any measurement system may be used to find the original size and reproduction size when mathematically scaling a photograph.

T   F   **17.** To work concisely with inches when scaling a photograph, fractions of an inch are converted into decimal point equivalents.

T   F   **18.** Original photographs are never marked or cut.

T   F   **19.** Retouching a photograph is always more cost-efficient than reshooting the photograph.

Completion

_____   **1.** _____ is the most common method of altering a photograph.

_____   **2.** A(n) _____ is one image created by combining photographs.

_____   **3.** A(n) _____ image is an alteration of the original photograph created by cutting and repositioning the image.

_____ **4.** A silhouette image is also called a(n) _____ halftone.

_____ **5.** _____ out the background is the most economic method of creating a silhouette halftone.

_____ **6.** As a scanner reads the photographic image, it also reads _____.

_____ **7.** A(n) _____ image is a reproduction of a continuous tone image at a lighter percentage of ink.

_____ **8.** A(n) _____ grease pencil is used to mark photographs for manipulated image changes.

_____ **9.** _____ is the process of enlarging or reducing an original photograph proportionately.

_____ **10.** The designer indicates the cropped image area with _____.

_____ **11.** A proportional scale is an instrument used to calculate size and _____ requirements.

Identification

_____ **1.** Montage

_____ **2.** Manipulated image

_____ **3.** Extended image

_____ **4.** Silhouette image

_____ **5.** Ghost image

_____ **6.** Anamorphic image

_____ **7.** Posterization

_____ **8.** Textured image

(A)

(B)

(C)

(D)

(E)

(F)

(G)

(H)

DESKTOP PUBLISHING SYSTEMS

Desktop publishing systems are page layout systems used to create pages on a personal computer (PC). Desktop publishing systems are composed of hardware (machinery) and software (computer programs) to produce pages of text and graphics.

HARDWARE

The *hardware* of a desktop publishing system consists of all physical units of a computer, including the keyboard, monitor, and disk drive. Although hardware varies in different computer environments, basic components of the hardware are the same. The two most common computer environments in desktop publishing are IBM and Macintosh. These differ in the ways the operating systems process information. All computer systems consist of input devices, a central processing unit (CPU), and output devices.

Input Devices

Input devices allow the operator to enter information, or data, into the computer. Input devices include the keyboard, mouse, stylus, light pen, and scanner. Storage devices can also act as input devices. Input devices can be direct input or indirect input. An operator may choose one input device or a combination of

direct and indirect input devices to *import,* or bring in, data into the desktop publishing system.

Direct input involves inputting data manually into a computer. Direct input of data may be done through the use of a keyboard, mouse, stylus, or light pen. *Indirect input* involves inputting data electronically into a computer. The most commonly used indirect input device in desktop publishing is the scanner.

Keyboard. The *keyboard* is the most common direct input device. See Figure 12-1. The inputting of data using a keyboard is also called *keyboarding.* In keyboarding, the operator strikes keys on an electronic keyboard similar to a typewriter keyboard. The alphanumeric characters and symbols on the keys are translated into corresponding codes to which the computer responds.

Mouse. A *mouse* is an electromechanical or optical device used for direct input. See Figure 12-2. It is a small hand-held device that allows

the user to enter coordinate-based data (horizontal and vertical locations on the screen) into the computer and to input programmed commands. The optical mouse has one to three buttons that are *clicked,* or pressed, to input commands.

The underside of the mouse contains either wheels, a ball, or a laser eye. A mouse with wheels or a ball is a *roller mouse.* It is maneuvered along a hard surface of a desk or table. A mouse with a laser eye is an *optical mouse.* The optical mouse reads coordinates as it is moved along a metal pad.

Using a mouse makes it easy for the operator to control manually created graphics. In addition, some wordprocessing (text) programs use a mouse to more easily activate screen commands. A disadvantage of the mouse is that it is cumbersome for freehand drawing.

Stylus and Light Pen. The *stylus* and *light pen* are hand-held devices shaped like a writing instrument. They are similar to a mouse in that they are used to input information

Apple Computer, Inc.

Figure 12-1. The keyboard is the most common direct input device and may be programmed to input specified codes into the computer.

Apple Computer, Inc.

Figure 12-2. A mouse used to input coordinates and commands may be a roller mouse or an optical mouse.

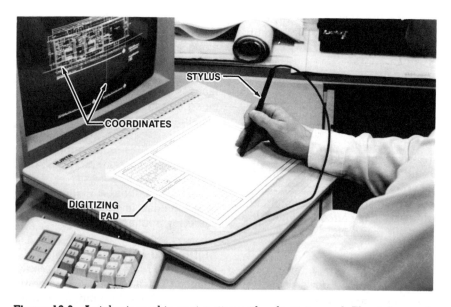

Figure 12-3. A stylus is used in conjunction with a digitizing pad. The stylus reads coordinates from the pad and the coordinates are displayed on the screen.

manually through coordinates and programmed commands. As the stylus is drawn along an electronically sensitive pad called a *digitizing pad,* or *tablet,* it reads coordinates from the pad and displays them on the screen. See Figure 12-3. Light pens work interactively with the screen, allowing the operator to use programmed commands.

The advantage of a stylus and light pen is that they are easier to hold than a mouse for drawing and graphics functions because of the similarity to holding a pencil or pen. The most common use of the stylus and light pen is in design applications.

Scanners. *Scanners* are devices that read an image and electronically digitize the image. *Digitizing* an image is dividing the image into dark and light points by creating codes that a computer can use. The digitized image looks much like a halftone. Scanners commonly read information at 300 dots per inch (dpi). Four types of scanners are flatbed, hand-held, sheetfed, and overhead. A combination flatbed/sheetfed scanner is also available. See Figure 12-4.

Flatbed scanners are similar in appearance and function to a photocopier. Copy to be scanned is placed on the flat surface (platen) of the scanner as the digitizing head scans the image horizontally line per line. Flatbed scanners are commonly used for copy that is adhered to a hard surface or an artboard.

Hand-held scanners read images in a similar manner as flatbed scanners. Hand-held scanners are moved across the image by hand. The digitized image is then saved for use with the desktop publishing program.

Sheetfed scanners transport the original image through the unit. As the copy travels through the scanner, the digitizing head reads the image. Sheetfed scanners are commonly used for scanning multipage documents and graphics because of the ease of page input.

Overhead scanners use a charged coupled device (CCD), which is similar to a video camera, to capture the

FLATBED/SHEETFED
Hewlett-Packard Company

HAND-HELD
DFI Diamond Flower International Co. (USA), Inc.

OVERHEAD
Mirror Technologies, Inc.

Figure 12-4. Scanners are available as flatbed, hand-held, sheetfed, and overhead scanners.

copy as a full-screen image. The captured image is then digitized into computer codes. Overhead scanners are commonly used for digitizing three-dimensional images and copy in books.

Copy digitized by a scanner is divided into two categories: text and graphics. Scanners that read text only are optical character reader (OCR) scanners. Scanners that read line art or continuous tone images are graphics scanners. Software programs are available that allow scanners to read both text and graphics.

OCR Scanners. *OCR scanners* scan text only. Early OCR scanners could only read specifically designed OCR typefaces. This was a problem because the user had to create the original typed manuscript on a specified OCR typewriter. The OCR scanner could not read other typefaces. As scanners were further developed, more and more typefaces were readable. Some new scanners have programmable intelligence, which allows the user to program the scanner to read previously unrecognizable characters and symbols. OCR scanners require

1. copy to be typed with crisp characters (no broken characters or dot matrix copy),
2. that the minimum size of characters is 6 point,
3. that the copy is not marked in pen or pencil, and
4. that the copy is black type on white stock for optimum reflectance and readability.

These requirements vary, depending on the scanner and software used. Once text is scanned, it is interfaced with the computer. The scanned information is then used with a text formatting program and/or wordprocessing program.

OCR scanners offer speed and accuracy. Scanning speeds are 25 times faster than a typist who can type 60 words-per-minute. Clean, sharp copy can be digitized as fast as 50,000 characters per hour. Therefore, OCR scanners are especially popular in book and magazine publishing where manuscript copy is produced through a variety of methods. Although the speed is greater than a typist typing, the scanner may not read the pages perfectly. Some characters may be misread because of typeface, quality of copy, or both.

Graphics Scanners. *Graphics scanners* read line and continuous tone images and digitize the images into computer codes. As the scanner reads an illustration, a digitized signal tells the computer to turn pixels ON or OFF. A *pixel* is the smallest element of a digitized image. ON refers to density. OFF refers to the white background. Each time the computer receives an ON signal, the computer records it as a single amount of density. An OFF signal tells the computer not to record density. Through the turning ON and OFF of pixels, an image is created.

Scanned line images match originals more accurately than scanned continuous tone images. Scanned continuous tone images are often not of high-quality. Reproduction quality of continuous tone images is determined by memory capacity and resolution of the scanner. Resolution is measured in dpi. Scanned continuous tone images occupy an extremely large amount of memory. Although a scanner can reproduce a 300 line image or 300 dpi image, the continuous tone image will reproduce as 60 line or 60 dpi. See Figure 12-5.

HALFTONE

SCANNED CONTINUOUS TONE IMAGE

Figure 12-5. Scanned continuous tone images often do not result in high-resolution reproductions.

Central Processing Unit

The *central processing unit* (*CPU*) is the control center of the computer. The CPU receives information through the input devices and outputs images. A CPU is classified by its memory capacity and the speed at which it carries out commands. The CPU stores information on disk drives and internal memory. The two types of drives are the floppy disk drive and hard disk drive. The two types of internal memory are random access memory (RAM) and read only memory (ROM).

Floppy Disk. A *floppy disk* stores data that can be transported from one computer to another. Floppy disks are available as 5¼″ and 3½″ disks. See Figure 12-6. Floppy disks are inserted in the floppy disk drive. Information stored on the floppy disk may be accessed and manipulated by the CPU. After the CPU manipulates the data, the data must be returned to the floppy disk for storage or it will be lost. A limitation of the floppy disk is the amount of data that can be stored on the disk.

Hard Disk. The *hard disk* has a much larger memory capacity than

the floppy disk. The hard disk is like an electronic file cabinet where software programs and text and graphics files may be stored for future use.

Random Access Memory. *Random access memory* (*RAM*) is the working memory of the computer. RAM is used to temporarily store information from software programs and data while a job is being worked on.

Read Only Memory. *Read only memory* (*ROM*) is permanent memory stored in the computer by the manufacturer. All computers contain ROM.

ROM is accessed when the computer is turned ON. ROM contains instructions for the computer on how software programs and data are to be used.

Output Devices

Output devices allow input material (text and graphics) to be output in printed form (hard copy) or video or electronic form (soft copy). Four major output devices are dot matrix and laser printers, imagesetters, and pen plotters. See Figure 12-7. The primary soft copy output form is the monitor, which displays the text and graphics.

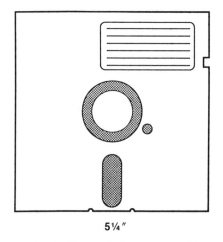

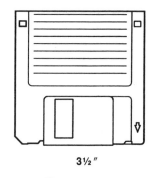

5¼″   3½″

Figure 12-6. Floppy disks are a portable mode of storage. They are available as 5¼″ and 3½″ disks.

Monitors are available in many sizes, shapes, and resolutions (sharpness). Most desktop publishing systems require a high-resolution monitor with text and graphics capabilities.

Dot Matrix Printers. Dot matrix printers are often used to print a quick hard copy of copy generated using desktop publishing, wordprocessing, or graphics programs. Although not quite letter quality, dot matrix printers are popular and relatively inexpensive.

Dot matrix printers use a row of tiny pins (usually 9- or 24-pin) that create a pattern of dots within a matrix. A *matrix* is an invisible mold that programs the dots to create character definition. Any pattern of dots can be made inside the matrix, and the matrix can be defined in numerous sizes. Therefore, any type size is possible as long as it can be defined by the matrix. Type can also be manipulated to create a variety of styles. Most printers have a double-dot option, which creates near letter quality type. A disadvantage of dot matrix printers is that because characters are defined in matrices, it is difficult to proportionately space type. Although possible, proportionately spaced type is time-consuming to obtain on dot matrix printers.

Dot matrix printers can also print graphics. Although the resolution of most dot matrix printers is generally poor, good dot matrix printers can produce various tint shades plus solids.

Laser Printers. Laser printers are designed much like the photocopier. Laser printers produce copy that simulates typeset copy. Hundreds of font styles and sizes are available for most laser printers.

Laser printers differ from photocopiers in that they have memory for programmable intelligence. This programmable intelligence is instructed

DOT MATRIX PRINTER
Hewlett-Packard Company

LASER PRINTER
Hewlett-Packard Company

IMAGESETTER
Linotype-Hell Company

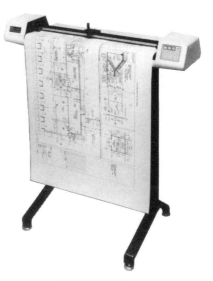

PEN PLOTTER
Ametek, Houston Instrument Division

Figure 12-7. Four major hard copy output devices are dot matrix and laser printers, imagesetters, and pen plotters.

by the computer on how to print a page. Two methods are used by which the computer may describe a page to the printer: bit-mapped imaging and page description language (PDL).

Laser printers that use bit-mapped imaging work on the same principle as a dot matrix printer in that the image is described and printed dot by dot. Bit-mapped images use a great amount of memory. When printing text, a bit-mapped laser printer must create each character dot by dot. Wordprocessing or page layout programs contain information for bit-mapping specific sizes and styles of fonts. Font information is sent with the file from the PC to the laser printer.

Font information can also be created using a font cartridge that is inserted in the laser printer, or by using a special font program to send (download) font information to the laser printer from the PC. Font cartridges contain the additional memory required for generating several font sizes and styles. Additional font cartridges can be purchased as required. Downloadable fonts are saved in RAM of the laser printer. If the laser printer is turned OFF, the font information must be downloaded again.

Describing graphics dot by dot requires a great deal of memory. Laser printer output based on the amount of memory is limited to the size of graphics memory available. The resolution of most laser printer output is from 300–600 dpi. The higher the dpi is, the better the resolution of the image will be.

A *page description language* is a computer language that describes the layout of the page. PostScript® is the most common page description language supported by software programs, laser printers, and imagesetters. PostScript® interprets information sent by the PC to the laser printer or imagesetter, describing the pages in graph-like points called *vectors* instead of dot by dot. A character is described by its outline shape from point to point. Once the outline is described it can be altered to any size. PostScript® also allows characters to be altered; for example, italic,

reverse, and bold can be obtained from the same character outline.

Imagesetters. *Imagesetters* are similar to phototypesetters in that they output high-resolution type. However, unlike phototypesetters, imagesetters also output images (line art and halftones). Imagesetters create the highest quality reproduction of all the output devices used in desktop publishing. Of all output devices, true typeset quality can only be obtained from an imagesetter because of the resolution it can obtain, which ranges from 900 dpi to 2540 dpi.

This higher resolution is possible because images are not reproduced as ink or tones on paper, but as light on film. An imagesetter uses a laser beam that focuses on light-sensitive material, usually paper. This photo process exposes small areas of a character, creating high-quality, high-resolution images.

At one time phototypesetters were dedicated machines that understood only limited codes. The advent of the PostScript® page description language into phototypesetting, and now imagesetting, has created flexibility in the typesetting environment. Input does not have to be directly into the imagesetter or phototypesetter. The PC is used as a front-end inputting station, transferring PostScript® codes into the imagesetter or phototypesetter. This method has many advantages:

1. The user has more control over the copy because the copy is produced in-house using a PC.
2. The imagesetter or phototypesetter may not require additional coding, which would reduce labor cost.
3. Proofs of copy and page layouts can be done on a PostScript® laser printer before the final copy is sent to the imagesetter or phototypesetter. This reduces mistakes, typesetting material costs, and time.
4. The copy and page layouts can be saved to disk or sent to a remote location by modem. A *modem* is a device that sends and receives data over telephone lines.
5. The services of typesetting houses, or service bureaus, can be used to obtain output on imagesetting or

phototypesetting equipment as necessary. The high cost of maintaining imagesetting or phototypesetting equipment would be eliminated for the occasional user.

Although graphics capabilities are available on many imagesetters, some imagesetters may not produce complicated bit-mapped images well. The programming output time can take hours for a full-page graphic image. In some cases, it is still more efficient to prepare text and graphics separately.

Pen Plotters. *Pen plotters* are automated mechanical drawing machines. A pen plotter uses a writing instrument (usually roller ball, fiber tip, or technical pen) to output drawings.

Pen plotters are most efficient for producing line art. Computer-aided design (CAD) programs are often used with a pen plotter. The CAD software allows the user to make precise and mathematically correct drawings in the computer and accurately output the image on a plotter.

Pen plotters are often used for architectural and engineering drawings. Pen plotters are used in desktop publishing when high-quality and accurate line is required.

Pen plotters are not efficient as sole output devices for full-page reproduction. Text reproduction on a plotter is adequate and readable. However, typestyles are limited and the reproduction is not considered letter quality. A large amount of text could not be reproduced efficiently on a pen plotter.

SOFTWARE

Software is the program that runs the PC system. The software distributes information to all areas of the PC system and directs each area to complete various functions.

Software is available in various programs, from simple text programs to detailed graphics and page layout programs. The computer code or "language" that the software uses varies depending on the type of software. When choosing software, the type of hardware that will support the software and whether the software is compatible with the output device must be known. For example, if output to a PostScript® laser printer or imagesetter is desired, then the software must be able to use the Post-Script® language.

Wordprocessing Software

Wordprocessing software is used to *process* (produce) *words* (text). Word-processing software is the most efficient software program for inputting a large amount of text.

In addition to the input of text, most wordprocessing software offer optional commands for simple text manipulation, such as bold, italic, flush left, and flush right. Simple graphics, such as rules and corners, are available on some wordprocessing software.

A common output device used with wordprocessing software is a dot matrix printer, which can offer near letter quality copy. Laser printers are also commonly used; however, not all wordprocessing software can drive a laser printer.

The main use of wordprocessing software in desktop publishing is for raw input of text. *Raw input* of text refers to pure copy, or copy without additional coding, such as bold or italic. This raw text is often imported into a variety of page layout software programs to create detailed page layouts. The *American Standard Code for Information Interchange* (*ASCII*) is a standard code for raw text to be input or imported into additional programs. A file of raw text is an *ASCII file.*

Graphics Software

Graphics software is used to produce illustrations and line art. Graphics software is available in a variety of programs, from very simple to very complex. Two basic forms of graphics software programs are draw programs and paint programs.

Draw programs use a vector system. The program is used to create geometric shapes and a few tint screens. See Figure 12-8. The draw program allows easy manipulation of geometric images. These geometric images can easily be drawn, copied, tinted, and overlaid. However, detailed manipulation (pixel by pixel) is not possible. Since drawn images are vector images, the computer creates each as a graph outline, not as a bit-mapped image. A draw program can be interfaced with most page layout programs to create page layouts with images.

A *paint program* is a bit-mapped graphics program. The computer creates the graphics images pixel by pixel. A paint program is very flexible in its ability to create images. The user can create a variety of free-form images, textures, and type. See Figure 12-9. A paint program is used with scanned graphics in order to manipulate digitized images. Since a paint program operates on a bit-mapped system, detailed images use a large amount of memory and can be time-consuming to output.

Page Layout Software

Page layout software for desktop publishing is used to create the style of the page and manipulate text and graphics. Page layout software is available in many programs from a variety of manufacturers. Each page layout program has its own characteristics and strengths.

Page layout software is available in interactive programs or batch programs. *Interactive programs* provide What You See Is What You Get (WYSIWYG) viewing on the monitor. This allows the user to see the layout (*ASCII*) on screen exactly as it will be output as the page is designed. WYSIWYG viewing is very helpful in design work with many details. See Figure 12-10. Interactive programs, because of the memory required for WYSIWYG viewing, are generally slower than other page layout programs.

Batch programs use coding in the text to define page layout commands. The codes used are similar to those used in traditional typesetting. Batch programs do not allow viewing of the page layout before final output, but they are more efficient for long documents than interactive programs. Batch programs are commonly used for books, magazines, and other long documents.

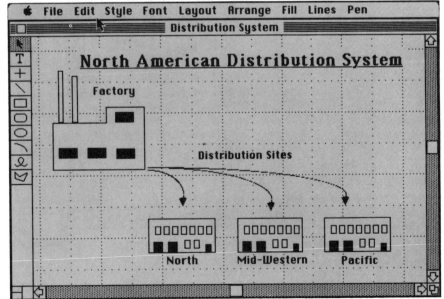

Apple Computer, Inc.

Figure 12-8. Draw graphics software programs are used to create geometric shapes and can create tint screens.

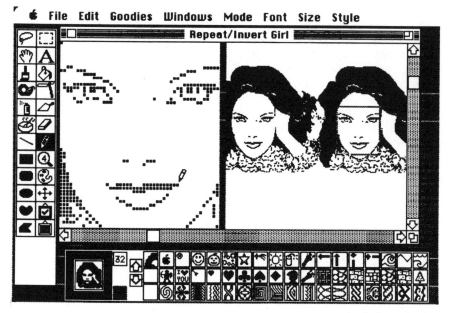

Figure 12-9. Paint programs create images pixel by pixel.

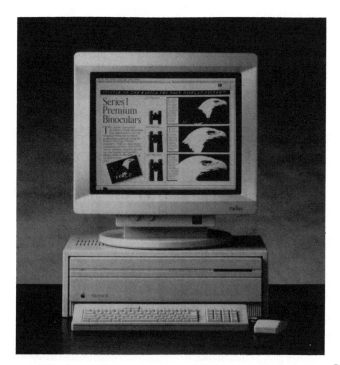

Figure 12-10. Page layout software allows the user to see the layout of a page before the page is output.

Desktop Publishing Systems

True-False

T   F   **1.** Desktop publishing systems are page layout systems that are used with a computer.

T   F   **2.** Desktop publishing systems are composed of both hardware and software.

T   F   **3.** A user may choose one input device or use a combination of direct and indirect input.

T   F   **4.** The keyboard is the most common form of indirect input.

T   F   **5.** A mouse with a wheel uses a metal pad that tracks coordinates as the mouse is drawn along the pad.

T   F   **6.** The most common method of direct input is the flatbed scanner.

T   F   **7.** A flatbed scanner is similar in appearance to a photocopier.

T   F   **8.** Graphics scanners read only line images.

T   F   **9.** An OCR scanner is 25 times faster than a typist who can type 60 words-per-minute.

T   F   **10.** Although a scanner can reproduce a 300 dpi image, a continuous tone image may reproduce as only 60 dpi.

T   F   **11.** The central processing unit is called the CPU.

T   F   **12.** Random access memory (RAM) is the control center of the computer.

T   F   **13.** Read only memory (ROM) is programmed by the manufacturer into the computer.

T   F   **14.** Bit-mapped fonts are purchased in font cartridges.

T   F   **15.** The introduction of PostScript® allowed typesetting equipment to be used with desktop publishing.

T   F   **16.** It is always more efficient to input text and graphics into a desktop publishing system than it is to prepare them separately.

Multiple Choice

_____ **1.** Data may be directly input into a computer with a _____.
    A. mouse
    B. keyboard
    C. stylus
    D. all of the above

_____ **2.** A(n) _____ scanner allows copy to travel through the scanner.
    A. overhead
    B. flatbed
    C. sheetfed
    D. OCR

_____ 3. A(n) _____ scanner uses a device similar to a video camera to capture the image.
    A. overhead
    B. flatbed
    C. sheetfed
    D. OCR

_____ 4. A(n) _____ scanner is commonly used to digitize copy that is mounted onto a hard surface.
    A. overhead
    B. flatbed
    C. sheetfed
    D. OCR

_____ 5. A(n) _____ scanner only reads text.
    A. overhead
    B. flatbed
    C. sheetfed
    D. OCR

_____ 6. Clean, sharp copy can be digitized as fast as _____ characters an hour.
    A. 25,000
    B. 35,000
    C. 50,000
    D. 60,000

_____ 7. _____ is a form of computer memory that is built into the computer and may not be altered.
    A. Random access memory
    B. Read only memory
    C. Rapid access memory
    D. all of the above

_____ 8. _____ is a form of computer memory that temporarily stores information from software programs and data.
    A. Random access memory
    B. Read only memory
    C. Rapid access memory
    D. all of the above

_____ 9. The disk that enables usable memory to be stored in the computer is the _____ disk.
    A. floppy
    B. hard
    C. 3½"
    D. 5¼"

_____ 10. The _____ disk drive uses portable memory.
    A. floppy
    B. hard
    C. soft
    D. internal

Matching

_____ **1.** ROM

_____ **2.** RAM

_____ **3.** ASCII

_____ **4.** Pixel

_____ **5.** PostScript®

_____ **6.** Draw program

_____ **7.** Paint program

_____ **8.** Page layout program

A. Standard code for raw text
B. Page description language
C. Working memory of computer
D. Bit-mapped imaging
E. Smallest element of a digitized image
F. Permanent memory of computer
G. Interactive software
H. Vector imaging

Completion

_____ **1.** _____ input is the process of manually creating data that is entered into the computer.

_____ **2.** The _____ is the most common form of direct input.

_____ **3.** The _____ is a hand-held device that uses an electromechanical or optical device to input commands.

_____ **4.** A(n) _____ or _____ is drawn along a digitizing pad to input data.

_____

_____ **5.** _____ input is the entry of data that is electronically input.

_____ **6.** As copy is read by the scanner it is _____ into codes.

_____ **7.** Overhead scanners are commonly used to digitize _____ images.

_____ **8.** Each time the computer receives a(n) _____ signal, the computer records it as a single amount of density.

_____ **9.** A(n) _____ disk drive is sufficient for use with software programs not requiring large amounts of storage.

_____ **10.** The characters of a(n) _____ printer are created in a pattern within a matrix.

_____ **11.** Downloadable fonts are saved in RAM in _____ printers.

_____ **12.** PostScript® is a page description language that describes the elements of the page as _____ instead of dot-by-dot.

_____ **13.** A higher resolution image is possible out of an imagesetter because the image is not reproduced as ink or toner on paper, but as _____ on film.

_____ **14.** _____ are automated mechanical drawing machines.

13. DESKTOP PUBLISHING APPLICATIONS

Desktop publishing allows the user to produce page layouts without the use of traditional paste-up and production methods. Page layouts are created using a PC. Users of desktop publishing systems must be aware of advantages and limitations of the desktop publishing system before choosing the method of production. Final output quality depends on hardware and software capabilities and job specifications, such as stock, color, quantity, and size of the printed piece.

DESKTOP PUBLISHING PRODUCTION

Desktop publishing production is a term often used to describe the layout and production of mechanicals or printed pieces through the use of a PC and desktop publishing program. Newsletters, brochures, and advertisements are common forms of jobs created on a desktop publishing system. Many software programs written for desktop publishing allow the user to lay out the job directly on the PC screen.

The user manipulates type size and typestyle and displays various page layouts. Graphic images such as line art and photographs can be digitized, inserted, and manipulated in the page layout. Laser printers and dot matrix printers supply quick proofs of the job before the page layout is finalized. Once complete, the document may be printed on a laser printer or output on an imagesetter and taken through traditional printing methods.

Users of desktop publishing systems may be designers, typesetters, paste-up artists, camera operators, strippers, printers, or bindery operators. See Figure 13-1. A comparative analysis of printing production through desktop publishing and traditional methods is necessary to determine advantages of each process. Although desktop publishing offers new and fast methods of production, basic production concepts remain unchanged. A desktop publishing system is a production tool and may not always be the most efficient method to use.

Specifications

Job planning in traditional production as well as in desktop publishing begins with basic specifications of a job. Once basic specifications are defined, the user has an idea for the layout of the job. Specifications include size, stock, color, quantity, budget, and quality of the printed piece. These specifications are used to determine whether desktop publishing is an efficient method of production for the job. Often, thumbnail sketches are created to help the user visualize the job before beginning work on the PC.

Size. Size limitations are greater in desktop publishing than in traditional printing. Just as size is limited in traditional printing by the capabilities of the press, size is limited in desktop publishing by the capabilities of the software program and output device.

Output on laser printers is most commonly on 8½″ × 11″ and sometimes on 8½″ × 14″ paper. If 8½″ × 11″ paper is used, the maximum image area is generally 8″ × 10½″. Any image larger than 8″ × 10½″ must be reproduced on a laser printer with capabilities greater than 8″ × 10½″. Either an 11″ × 17″ printer may be used, or the image may be prepared in sections and assembled through traditional methods. Final copy can be output on a laser printer or imagesetter. Specific output device requirements vary among desktop publishing programs and are listed in the program's documentation.

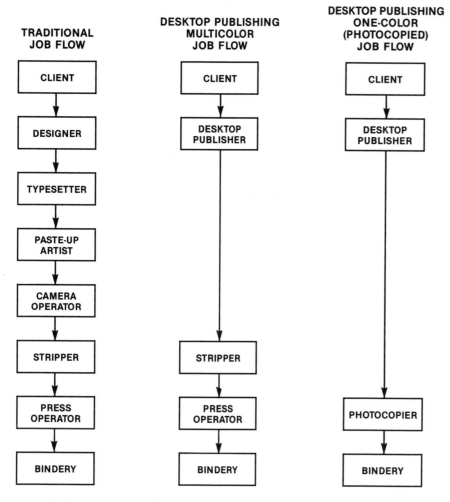

Figure 13-1. Desktop publishing production involves fewer production steps than traditional production methods.

are used as master copies and are printed in color through traditional methods. Generally, jobs output in color are for very short runs, usually 25 copies or less.

The output device used to reproduce color images varies according to the quality and color requirements of the job. Most output devices have a limited color option. Some dot matrix printers have changeable color ribbons. Colors can be reproduced on laser printers by changing toner cartridges and by using multiple cartridges. Pen plotters reproduce colors through different ink colors in the technical pens. The color capabilities of these output devices are generally for flat color reproduction. The ribbons, toners, and inks are not transparent and cannot be used to produce process color work.

Process color work, however, can be output on an ink jet printer. An ink jet printer forces liquid ink through tiny nozzles. Ink jet printing can produce process color reproductions because the ink is transparent. The tiny dots of ink create the appearance of a pallet of colors by printing over one another. The ink jet printer uses a similar method of color reproduction as that used in process color printing. Reproduction quality is determined by the capabilities of the software and ink jet printer.

Paper and Stock. The paper commonly used in laser printers is similar to the paper used in photocopiers. Both laser printers and photocopiers require a paper that can hold toner (powdered ink) without the copy cracking or chipping. Some papers are specifically manufactured for use in laser printers. These papers give a higher quality reproduction than photocopier papers because of a special coating. Laser printer paper that offers wax holdout is also available. When the paper is waxed, the wax does not bleed through, which would affect the image to be reproduced. This paper also provides a cleaner reproduction than those printed on standard photocopier paper.

Specialty stock is also available for laser printers. Specialty stock includes acetates and pressure-sensitive (adhesive) materials. Acetates and pressure-sensitive materials that are used must be specified for laser printers. Although generic materials may be used, heat generated by the laser printer may melt the acetate or adhesive, damaging the printer.

Color. Color used in a job may be produced in desktop publishing through a variety of methods. Many software programs have a color option, which allows the user to lay out the job in color on screen. The job may be output in color or black-and-white. Jobs output in black-and-white

Quantity. The quantity of reproductions desired must be considered when selecting a printing method. Most dot matrix, laser, or ink jet printers are designed for high-quality reproductions of a single image. Except for very low quantities, it is more efficient to produce a master image on the printer and reproduce it through traditional printing methods.

Budget. The budget of a job is affected by many variables. Generally, a job produced using a desktop publishing system is more cost-effective than one produced using traditional production methods. This lower cost results from lower labor costs and less materials required (especially silver-based paper and film).

Quality. Quality of the printed piece is determined by the capabilities of the hardware and software used in the desktop publishing system. Most laser printers can output at 300 dpi resolution while imagesetters commonly output at up to 2540 dpi. In cases where high quality is required, combining desktop publishing and traditional production methods may be needed.

Tint Screens and Textures

Tint screens and textures can be created on most desktop publishing systems. The reproduction quality of tint screens and textures depends on the resolution capabilities of the desktop publishing system, output device, and paper on which the image is output. The user should be aware of these variables before a tint screen or texture is used.

Tint Screens. Tint screens in traditional printing processes are created as film negatives or positives that are placed between the flat and the plate, or adhesive screen material is used. Tint screens created on a desktop publishing system are generally vector images. A dot arrangement in a specific size and density is programmed into the printer by the PC. PostScript®, for example, supports eight tint screen rulings, or *values*. The screen rulings range from one, which is about a 20%– 30% density, to eight, which is solid black. The screen rulings that can be achieved depend on the dpi capabilities of the system.

Tint screens in desktop publishing are generally used as background tints. If the desktop publishing system has a draw option, tint screens can be used to fill boxes, circles, and other geometric shapes. Rules may also be created as tint screens. Few vector software programs enable the user to print the text in graduated tints.

A higher quality tint screen reproduction is obtained by outputting on coated paper in the laser printer than on uncoated paper. Tint screen quality can be greatly diminished as the master copy is reproduced. Some photo-copiers, for instance, cause the tint screen to appear darker than the master because the spaces between the dots fill in. Reproducing the master copy through traditional printing methods requires that the master copy be photographed onto high-contrast film. This photographic process often results in loss of detail and a lighter tint screen than originally designated. Pretesting the quality of the reproduction method used ensures the desired results. See Figure 13-2.

Textures. Textures in traditional printing are generally created in paste-up with adhesive screen material. Textures are used to give depth, contrast, or variety to a piece. Textures created through a desktop publishing system are bit-mapped. That is, the texture is created pixel by pixel in the PC and printer. Many textures are available through paint programs. In addition to preprogrammed textures, the user may create textures that can be stored in the PC memory and reused. See Figure 13-3.

Paint programs allow versatility with textures. Textures can be used to fill in backgrounds, or a small area can be filled in with texture. Paint programs allow the user to "paint" with textures using tools such as a wide roller, a narrow paintbrush, or an airbrush for soft fill.

Paint programs can be used to create textured type. Type can be tinted, textured, or reversed out of a texture. Type created with paint programs should be treated the same way as adhesive or transfer type. It should be used in small amounts and in 14 points or larger.

Since textures are bit-mapped images, they require more memory and are more time-consuming than tint screens for initial output. Each pixel of the texture must be created by the PC and printer. The more varied the image is, the longer it will take to print. Once the first image is printed, multiple copies can be printed much quicker.

The reproduction quality of a textured image, like tint screens, depends upon the dpi of the system, output device, and stock on which it is printed. If a textured image is enlarged, the lines of the image will become more ragged as the pixels are enlarged. Improved resolution can be obtained and raggedness of the image can be minimized by creating the image at a larger size then reducing it.

Ruling

Ruling on a desktop publishing system is much more efficient than ruling through traditional methods. A rule is created by either indicating end points or by drawing a rule on the screen. A standard input device is used to create rules. Rule thickness is commonly specified by picas, points, inches, or centimeters, depending on the software used.

Reproduction quality of rules is determined by the software program and output device. A rule output on a dot matrix printer is not crisp along the edges and may not reproduce as a solid image. A rule output on a laser printer appears crisp and clean. A rule output on an imagesetter is of the highest quality.

High-quality angled lines are not easily accomplished with most output devices because angled lines are pixels connected on an angle. Angled rules output on a pen plotter are of higher quality because pen plotters do not depend upon resolution for output. The rule thickness of a plotted image is determined by the point thickness of the pen. Boxes ruled to any size and dimension are easily created on most desktop publishing programs. Some programs can draw curved corner boxes. These curved corners appear more ragged as dpi decreases. See Figure 13-4.

Type

Type is often the most important element of any printed piece. Type conveys the message to the reader. In desktop publishing the user is the typographic designer and typesetter. Type selection and quality depend on the desktop publishing system

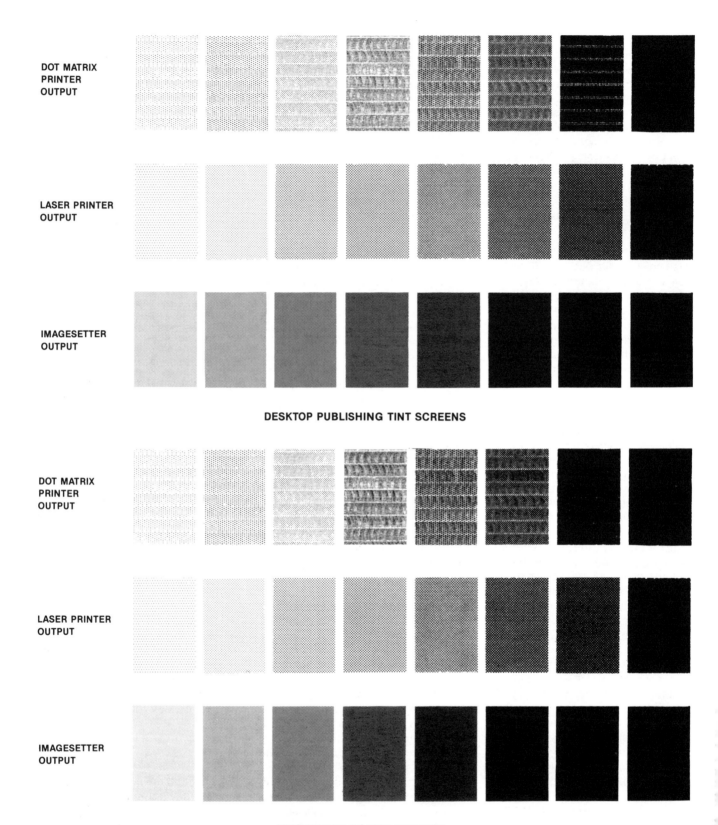

**DOT MATRIX
PRINTER
OUTPUT**

**LASER PRINTER
OUTPUT**

**IMAGESETTER
OUTPUT**

DESKTOP PUBLISHING TINT SCREENS

**DOT MATRIX
PRINTER
OUTPUT**

**LASER PRINTER
OUTPUT**

**IMAGESETTER
OUTPUT**

TEST PROOF OF TINT SCREENS

Figure 13-2. The reproduction quality of tint screens produced using a desktop publishing program varies, depending on the output device. Test prints should be made for quality control.

used and output device. See Figure 13-5. The user must choose the best typestyle and type size for optimum communication of the message. Typographical spacing and type arrangement also affect the overall readability of the piece and must be considered.

Typestyle. Typestyle variations are one of the greatest advantages in desktop publishing. The user has a vast library of typestyles available in all type classifications, including serif, sans serif, square serif, script, textletter, and decorative. However, typestyle choices for desktop publishing are limited by the software and output device of the system.

The user chooses the best typestyle to fit the job by reviewing availability, communicative ability, readability of the typestyle, and output device limitations. The software for desktop publishing varies greatly in sophistication from program to program. High-end programs generally offer selected styles in serif, sans serif, square serif, and script. Few programs offer textletter and decorative as options because these styles are designed to be used for headlines only. Textletter and decorative typestyles are available in most paint programs and can be imported into a desktop publishing system.

Although a desktop publishing program may offer a specific typestyle, the output device must also have that typestyle or it cannot be output. For example, some laser printers use cartridge fonts to program typestyles and can hold a limited number of typestyles. The user must know the limitations of the output device before choosing a typestyle in the desktop publishing program.

Some typestyles carry a message through the personality of the type. Script, decorative, and textletter typestyles project strong personalities that can enhance or impair communication of the message. Most serif, sans serif, and square serif typestyles have neutral personalities, which allow the written word to communicate. However, if improper size, leading, wordspacing, or letterspacing is used,

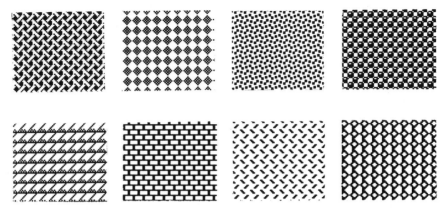

Figure 13-3. Paint programs produce a variety of textures and patterns. Some paint programs allow the user to alter existing textures and patterns or create new ones.

the communication may also be impaired. In addition, if variations of a typestyle are chosen, such as bold, extended, condensed, italic, and shaded, they must be used with caution. Typestyles should be chosen to create an overall tone to the piece. For example, headlines are to gain attention, not shout at the reader. Text must be of comfortable size and weight for optimum readability.

The reproduction quality of type is also considered when choosing a typestyle. Before a typestyle is chosen, the stock on which the job will be printed should be known. The best stock for optimum readability is a white, dull coated book paper. However, many colors and textures of stock are often used. Potential readability difficulties must be considered when the typestyle is not chosen to work with the stock. Typestyles with fine strokes should be avoided on textured stock. Larger point sizes should be used when stock has a low light reflectance quality, such as gray, blue-gray, brown, and olive green. To be sure of proper typestyle choice, proofs are made of various typestyles on different stocks. Laser printers accept many kinds of stocks and can be used to preview type choices.

Type Size. Various factors are considered when selecting type sizes for a job, including the following:
1. amount of space allotted for type;
2. each element's importance to the message;
3. amount of text the reader will be required to absorb;
4. type size options (some output devices have an unlimited type size capacity, while others have limited sizes);
5. reproduction quality of the output device;
6. stock and ink that will be used to print the job (texture and reflectance qualities); and
7. needs of the reader. For example, where will the reader be reading the type and at what distance? What are the lighting conditions? What is the age of the reader?

Once job requirements for type are determined, general guidelines for legibility and readability of type sizes are reviewed. These guidelines pertain to serif and sans serif typefaces.
1. Headlines, subheads, and text sizes should work together.
2. Text sizes for optimum readability range from 8 to 12 points.
3. Eight- to 9-point type can be used for jobs that will be printed on a laser printer or imagesetter, on good-quality paper with dark ink, and that are to be read under good lighting conditions.
4. Ten- to 11-point type is the optimum point size for general lighting conditions, large amounts of text, and when colored stock or light-colored inks are used.
5. Eleven- to 12-point type is recommended for use in poor lighting conditions, when textured or dark colored stock is used, when a dot

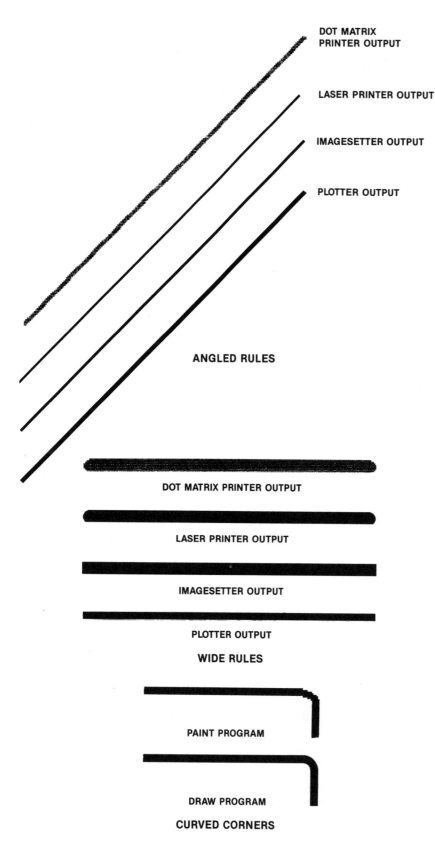

DOT MATRIX
PRINTER OUTPUT

LASER PRINTER OUTPUT

IMAGESETTER OUTPUT

PLOTTER OUTPUT

ANGLED RULES

DOT MATRIX PRINTER OUTPUT

LASER PRINTER OUTPUT

IMAGESETTER OUTPUT

PLOTTER OUTPUT

WIDE RULES

PAINT PROGRAM

DRAW PROGRAM

CURVED CORNERS

Figure 13-4. The quality of rules and curves depends on the software program and output device used.

matrix printer is used, and for very young or elderly readers.

6. Type above 8 points should be used when a tint screen behind the type is electronically produced on an imagesetter.

7. Type above 14 points should be used when a tint screen behind the type is electronically produced on a laser printer.

8. Type above 18 points should be used when a tint screen behind the type is electronically produced on a dot matrix printer.

9. Type reversed on a solid black background should be 14 points or larger.

10. Type reversed out of tint screens should be large enough to be distinguished easily and used for headlines only. Tint screens for reverse type should be at least 70% density for good contrast.

After the type has been output, the job is proofed for overall tone and contrast of the piece, communicative ability of the piece, and readability of the type under varied lighting conditions. The type size used on the piece should allow the reader ease of eye movement and convey the message effectively.

Typographical Spacing. *Typographical spacing* is the white space surrounding each letter, word, line, and paragraph. White space is variable and improves the readability of type. The highest quality typographical spacing is achieved on an imagesetter or phototypesetter. Some near-typeset quality spacing, however, can be achieved with a high-end desktop publishing program and a laser printer. Many programs allow linespacing (leading) and paragraph spacing manipulation. Some programs have a *kerning* option, which allows fine spacing manipulation between letters. Wordspacing can be manipulated through type arrangement and hyphenation.

Leading, the space between lines of type, allows the eye to read from line to line without eye fatigue. Leading is measured in points. Type can be set without leading (set solid) but this should be avoided because the type is difficult to read. A leading chart is used to find average amounts of leading recommended for specified type sizes. These leading averages are a starting point from which adjustments can be made. Some type variations such as bold need extra leading. The user begins with an average leading and adds points as necessary. Too much leading, however, causes the eye to drag from line to line, resulting in loss of comprehension.

Line length is the length of a line of type. Line length is measured in picas and points. Line length affects the readability, reader comprehension, and aesthetics of the piece. In general, line lengths that are too short or too long decrease readability. A line length chart gives the user average recommended lengths. The user sets the type to the recommended line length, then makes adjustments as necessary. Often when a line length is too short, the desktop publishing program has difficulty spacing the words. Uneven wordspacing causes undesirable vertical white space called *rivers*. Too long a line length causes loss in comprehension and eye fatigue.

A B C D E F G

BIT-MAPPED (PAINT) FONT

A B C D E F G

VECTOR (DRAW) FONT

A   DOT MATRIX PRINTER OUTPUT

A   LASER PRINTER OUTPUT

A   TYPESET OUTPUT

Figure 13-5. Type produced using a vector program is of higher quality than type produced using a bit-mapped program. Type quality also depends on the output device.

Type Arrangement. The most common type arrangements are ragged right (flush left) and justified. Studies show that either arrangement is easy to read. However, ragged right should be used for optimum flow of copy. See Figure 13-6. The even line endings of justified type are created through the manipulation of wordspacing and hyphenation. To justify line endings, wordspacing is sometimes spread out. This justified wordspacing can cause large open white space. To obtain type that allows proper eye movement, space between words should never exceed the vertical space between lines of type. Excessive vertical white space is distracting to the reader.

Hyphenation is the dividing of multiple syllable words at the end of lines of type. Many software programs are equipped with a hyphenation option. This option includes a hyphenation dictionary programmed to make decisions of where to hyphenate words. The more sophisticated the software is, the more extensive the hyphenation dictionary is.

Other forms of type arrangement are available on most desktop publishing programs. However, type that is centered or flush right (ragged left) is not as readable and should be used with caution.

Graphics

Graphics in desktop publishing include a broad range of line art, such as illustrations, charts and graphs, and photographs. Desktop publishing programs allow the merging of graphics and text to create full-page layouts.

Line Art. Line art used in desktop publishing may be created on screen, digitized with a scanner, or preprogrammed onto floppy disks. Illustrations can be created using draw, paint, or CAD software programs. See Figure 13-7. Draw illustrations are vector-type illustrations and consist of geometric forms. Draw illustrations are easily overlapped and tinted but cannot be manipulated pixel by pixel. This is because the PC stores each shape as a whole element in an x-y-z coordinate, not as a group of pixels. Draw illustrations are of higher quality and are output faster than paint illustrations because vector programs do not require as much memory.

Paint illustrations are bit-mapped illustrations that appear more artistic than draw illustrations. Paint illustrations are created pixel by pixel and are easily manipulated. Most paint programs have an option that shows an enlarged view of the pixel arrangement on screen. This option allows

This is a paragraph of type that shows proper wordspacing. Proper wordspacing should never exceed the amount of space between lines (linespacing). Proper wordspacing does not create rivers and allows ease of eye movement. Type that is ragged right or justified is easy to read and is most commonly used for large amounts of text.

Figure 13-6. Proper wordspacing does not exceed the amount of white space between lines, otherwise rivers may appear.

DRAW ILLUSTRATION

PAINT ILLUSTRATION

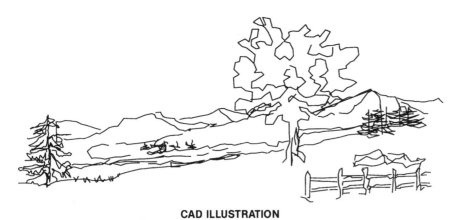

CAD ILLUSTRATION

Figure 13-7. Line art created using draw and CAD programs is vector-based. Line art created using a paint program is bit-mapped.

for very fine editing of illustrations. Paint illustrations may be enlarged, reduced, or stretched to fit a particular layout. Because paint illustrations are bit-mapped and require more memory, the output time is longer than that for draw illustrations. Some paint and draw programs are compatible, allowing the user to create clean, sharp draw illustrations and enhance them with screens and textures from a paint program.

Detailed illustrations that require a high degree of accuracy can be created on a CAD program and output on a laser printer or pen plotter. A CAD program can be used to create detailed two- and three-dimensional line drawings. Drawings can be rotated and viewed from any perspective. They can be accurately scaled to any size but are limited by the size of the output device. CAD drawing files may also be imported into a desktop publishing program.

Illustrations can be digitized into computer codes using a graphics scanner. The scanner reads line drawings and converts the drawings into electronic signals. These signals are translated in the PC into codes that specify the density of each pixel. The drawings become bit-mapped images made up of a pattern of pixels.

Bit-mapped images can be manipulated pixel by pixel. They can be screened or textured. Portions of the images can be electronically cut and pasted or copied and repeated. The images can be inverted or reversed. Some programs allow bit-mapped images to be stretched anamorphically. All of these alterations can be made without affecting the original illustration. Scanning allows many variations of the same image without time-consuming redrawing.

Another time-saving method of producing graphics is using electronic clip art, which is stored on disk. Electronic clip art are bit-mapped images that may be altered as necessary, again without affecting the original image.

Charts and Graphs. Charts and graphs are a very important element in many business publications and are often called *business graphics.* While business graphics may be drawn by hand using a draw or paint program, business graphics programs are available. The advantage of a program designed to create business graphics is that the user does not have to create the chart or graph. A good business graphics program allows the user to choose a chart or graph style, such as a pie chart. The user enters into the PC the numeric data, and the PC generates the graphics. This process is very fast and accurate. See Figure 13-8.

Photographs. Photographs are continuous tone images that must be converted into halftones to be reproduced either traditionally or on a desktop publishing system. Photographs can be indicated, prescreened, or scanned for desktop publishing use.

Indicated photographs do not appear on the master copy or mechanical. The photograph's size, shape, and position are indicated with a ruled frame or a black box drawn using the desktop publishing program. Master copies using the indicated method must be reproduced through traditional printing methods. The master copy is photographed onto film and the frame or box indicating position of the photograph shows the stripper where to position the halftone negatives. Since the photograph is converted into a film halftone, the reproduction quality is high. However, traditional printing methods are more time-consuming and costly than other methods of handling photographs for reproduction.

If prescreened halftones are used, the desktop publishing user creates the layout and leaves a frame where the halftones are to be positioned. The prescreened halftones are pasted

in position on the master copy. The prescreened halftone method saves the cost of stripping and can be reproduced on a photocopier or printing press. Prescreened halftone quality depends on the line value of the screen and reproduction method used.

Photographs that are scanned using a graphics scanner are broken up in a dot pattern in a bit-mapped paint file format. The dot pattern represents the grays of the photograph. The dots of a digitized halftone, or *gray-scale image,* differ from the dots of a traditional halftone. A traditional halftone contains dots of varying size while a digitized halftone contains equal-size dots. Dark areas of a photograph are represented by digitized dots spaced closely together and light areas are represented by dots spaced farther apart. See Figure 13-9.

The quality of a gray-scale image depends on the line value used and sophistication of the scanner and out-

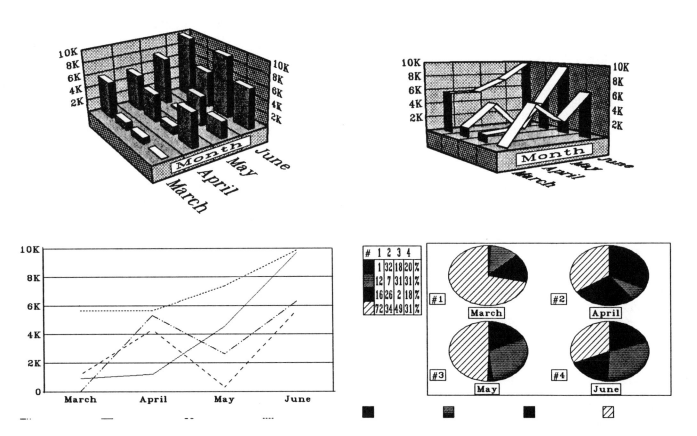

Figure 13-8. Chart and graph programs allow the user to input data and output a variety of charts and graphs.

GRAY-SCALE IMAGE

TRADITIONAL HALFTONE

Figure 13-9. A scanned photograph, or gray-scale image, usually has a lower range of gray values than a traditionally created halftone.

put device. Scanners have gray scales that range from 16 levels of gray to 256 levels of gray. The gray level and line value chosen also determine the quality of a gray-scale image.

A gray-scale image reproduces at a higher quality if output on a 2540 dpi imagesetter than a 300 dpi laser printer. See Figure 13-10. Also, gray-scale images reproduce at a lower resolution than the resolution of the output device. This low resolution appears similar to a 65- to 85-line halftone. In addition to a lower quality than a traditional halftone, gray-scale images use a great amount of computer memory and are time-consuming to output.

Master Copy Preparation

Master copy preparation is the process of creating high-quality master copies to be reproduced on a photocopier or through traditional printing methods. Master copies are prepared as a single page for one-color jobs or multicolor jobs with hairline registration. Master copies are prepared as multiple pages for multicolor jobs with commercial registration or nonregistration. Master copies may be output on a laser printer or an imagesetter.

If master copies are output on a laser printer, a white, dull coated paper should be used. White, dull coated paper gives good contrast between the background and the density of the toner. Gloss coated papers should not be used because toner cannot adhere to the surface and will chip and flake. Uncoated paper should not be used because it does not produce a crisp image.

If the master copy is to be reproduced through traditional printing methods, it should be pasted up on an artboard. Rubber cement applied to the back of the master copy at the corners is the best method of adhering copy to the artboard. If laser printer paper with wax holdout is used, the master copy can be waxed. Fixative is sprayed on the front of the master copy to protect the toner image from smearing.

Master copies may include trim marks. Many desktop publishing software programs include a trim mark option. However, if the master copy is output on a standard laser printer, maximum image area is 8″ × 10½″. Since most papers used in laser printers are 8½″ × 11″, trim marks cannot be applied if the entire image area is used, nor can there be bleeds. If trim marks or bleeds are required, the master copy must be output on

an 11″ × 17″ laser printer or an imagesetter. Both output devices allow for oversize images.

One-color or Hairline Registration Output. One-color jobs are output as a one-page master copy. Jobs that require hairline registration should be color separated by indicating colors on a tissue overlay taped over a one-page master copy. The master copy is output, pasted up on an artboard, and covered with a tissue overlay. The tissue overlay is marked with detailed instructions, including colors, tint screens, bleeds, trim size, and stock.

Multicolor Output. Multicolor jobs requiring commercial register or nonregister can be output using a color separation option offered on many desktop publishing programs. Color separation options commonly allow up to six colors, plus black and white, to be defined. The chosen colors on the page layout are displayed on screen. Colors may be proofed on a color PostScript® printer.

When the master copies are output, a separate sheet, printed in black, for each color is output. Each master copy is pasted up on an artboard and covered with a sheet of

IMAGESETTER—2540 DPI

tissue. A comprehensive layout or a color proof of the job is sent to the printer along with the master copies. Before multicolor master copies are created, the printer should be consulted for production requirements specific to the job.

LASER PRINTER—300 DPI

GRAY-SCALE IMAGES

Figure 13-10. A gray-scale image output on a 2540 dpi imagesetter is of higher quality than one output on a 300 dpi laser printer because of higher resolution.

Desktop Publishing Applications

REVIEW QUESTIONS

Name _____

Date _____

True-False

T   F   **1.** Process color work is the most common form of a printed job created on a desktop publishing system.

T   F   **2.** Graphic images such as photographs and line art may be digitized and imported into a desktop publishing system.

T   F   **3.** A desktop publishing system is a production tool.

T   F   **4.** Size limitations are less common in desktop publishing production than in traditional paste-up production.

T   F   **5.** The paper used in most laser printers is similar to the paper used in photocopiers.

T   F   **6.** Specialty stocks for desktop publishing include watermark and duplex.

T   F   **7.** Generally, jobs output in color on a desktop publishing system are for very short runs of 250 copies and less.

T   F   **8.** Ink jet printing is capable of printing 4-color reproductions because the ink is transparent.

T   F   **9.** A job produced through desktop publishing is more cost-effective than one produced through traditional printing methods.

T   F   **10.** A texture on a desktop publishing system is created pixel by pixel.

T   F   **11.** Ruling on a desktop publishing system may be more time-consuming than ruling by hand.

T   F   **12.** Type is the most important element of any printed piece.

T   F   **13.** Text sizes for optimum readability range from 8 to 12 points.

T   F   **14.** Draw images are vector images and consist of geometric forms.

T   F   **15.** Electronic clip art are vector images.

T   F   **16.** Photographs can be treated in a desktop publishing system by the indicated method, pre-screened method, or by using a scanner.

T   F   **17.** Prescreened halftones can be used in conjunction with master copies produced on a desktop publishing system.

T   F   **18.** Photographs can be converted into gray-scale images on a desktop publishing system.

T   F   **19.** Master copy preparation is used to reproduce a job through traditional printing methods.

Multiple Choice

_____ 1. In desktop publishing production, the user of the desktop publishing system is the _____.
  A. designer
  B. paste-up artist
  C. typesetter
  D. all of the above

_____ 2. A _____ helps the desktop publishing user to visualize the idea before entering the data into the computer.
  A. thumbnail sketch
  B. rough layout
  C. comprehensive layout
  D. all of the above

_____ 3. Job specifications include _____.
  A. size
  B. stock
  C. color
  D. all of the above

_____ 4. Laser printers can produce _____ dpi copy.
  A. 300
  B. 2540
  C. both A and B
  D. neither A nor B

_____ 5. Few vector software programs are able to print _____ in graduated tints.
  A. rules
  B. textures
  C. photographs
  D. text

_____ 6. Reproducing tint screens with photocopiers from a master copy image created on a desktop publishing system often results in a _____ tint screen than the original.
  A. darker
  B. lighter
  C. coarser
  D. all of the above

_____ 7. Rules may be produced using a _____ software program.
  A. desktop publishing
  B. vector
  C. bit-mapped
  D. all of the above

_____ 8. The _____ may be used to input a rule.
  A. keyboard
  B. mouse
  C. stylus
  D. all of the above

_____ 9. Rule output on a(n) _____ is of the highest quality.
  A. dot matrix printer
  B. laser printer
  C. imagesetter
  D. all of the above

_____ **10.** In general most serif and sans serif typestyles have a _____ personality.
- A. bold
- B. modern
- C. neutral
- D. all of the above

Matching

_____ **1.** Job specifications

_____ **2.** Laser printer paper

_____ **3.** Specialty stock

_____ **4.** Laser printer toner

_____ **5.** Ink jet printer ink

_____ **6.** High-quality copy for reproduction

_____ **7.** Output copy before final

_____ **8.** Laser resolution

_____ **9.** Imagesetter resolution

_____ **10.** Tint screen

_____ **11.** Textures

- A. Transparent
- B. Acetate
- C. Usually vector
- D. Master copy
- E. Dull coat
- F. 300 dpi
- G. Size, stock, color, quantity
- H. 2540 dpi
- I. Opaque
- J. Usually bit-mapped
- K. Proof

Completion

_____ **1.** Laser printers and dot matrix printers can be used to supply a quick _____ of a job before it is finalized.

_____ **2.** Most 8½″ × 11″ laser printers have a maximum image area of _____.

_____ **3.** An alternative to using a 11″ × 17″ laser printer is to prepare the image in _____.

_____ **4.** Both photocopiers and laser printers require a paper that holds _____ without chipping.

_____ **5.** Master images printed on _____ coated paper are a cleaner reproduction of the image than those printed on photocopier paper.

_____ **6.** A(n) _____ is an arrangement of dots of varying sizes.

_____ **7.** A(n) _____ is an arrangement of equal-size dots spaced varying distances apart.

_____ **8.** PostScript® supports eight tint screens called _____.

_____ **9.** The reproduction quality of a textured image depends on the _____ of the system.

_____ **10.** A texture is a(n) _____ image in desktop publishing software programs.

Identification

_____	**1.** Plotter output
_____	**2.** Laser printer output
_____	**3.** Dot matrix output
_____	**4.** Imagesetter output
_____	**5.** Bit-mapped font
_____	**6.** Vector font

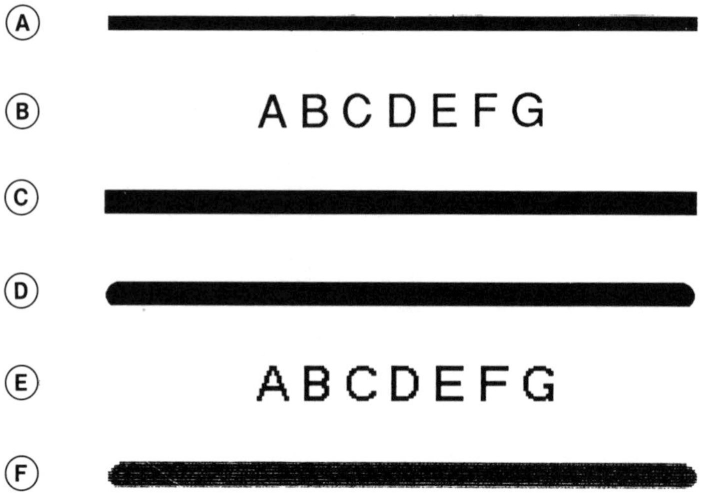

Ⓐ ▬▬▬▬▬▬▬▬▬▬▬▬▬▬▬▬

Ⓑ A B C D E F G

Ⓒ ▬▬▬▬▬▬▬▬▬▬▬▬▬▬

Ⓓ ▬▬▬▬▬▬▬▬▬▬▬▬▬▬

Ⓔ A B C D E F G

Ⓕ ▬▬▬▬▬▬▬▬▬▬▬▬▬▬

14 POSTAL REGULATIONS

Jobs delivered by the United States Postal Service are subject to restrictions and regulations. The production of mailed items must follow specifications throughout the design, layout, and printing of the job. Specifications for element alignment, typography, stock, and ink enable mail to move through the system efficiently. Improperly prepared mail may incur an additional postal fee, may be delayed, or may become dead mail. To avoid additional expenses, all pieces to be mailed must follow regulations issued by the United States Postal Service. Printed copies of regulations and their specifications are available through the United States Postal Service. To ensure accurate layout and production of the job, printed samples may be sent to the postal chief. These samples will be reviewed by any postal chief at no charge. All first-class mail falls into two basic categories: general mail and automated mail. General mail includes items that are sorted partially or fully by hand, while automated mail includes items that are sorted mechanically.

GENERAL MAIL REQUIREMENTS

General mail requirements are specified by the United States Postal Service and apply to correspondence mail. Although regulations for general mail are less stringent than those for automated mail, proper compliance with general mail regulations ensures accurate and timely delivery.

General Mail Specifications

General mail specifications refer to the address style, size, and stock and ink for correspondence mail. Although it is often taken for granted, the method of addressing a mail piece is important. The size of the piece and the stock on which the piece is printed or enclosed also require close attention. Improperly addressed, incorrectly sized, and low-reflectance stock will delay general mail or cause it to be undeliverable.

Addresses. Required addresses for general mail are the return address and the destination address. Each address is stacked flush left, usually in three or four lines. The horizontal positioning of the destination address must include at least a 1″ margin on the right and left. The vertical positioning requires a $5/_8$″ margin on the bottom. The last line of the address must begin within $2^1/_4$″ of the bottom of the envelope. The return address is positioned comfortably in the upper left corner of the mail piece. See Figure 14-1.

In addition to the positioning of addresses, the United States Postal Service recommends the following address format:
- Capitalize all characters.
- Eliminate all punctuation.
- Use the standard address and state abbreviations.
- Single-space lines of the address.
- Place one to two character spaces between words and two to five character spaces between the state and zip code.

- Type or print addresses; handwritten addresses are less efficient. Avoid script and italic typestyles.
- When sending mail to a foreign country, place only the name of the country on the last line of the address block; for example,

   KRISTEN BLAINE
   VIA ROCCA 17
   BERGAMO 11134
   ITALY

- When both the post office box number and street address are given, place the address that the mail is to be delivered to directly above the bottom line; for example,

1. PATRICIA SULLIVAN
   1923 BROWN ST
   P O BOX 512
   ALBANY NY 12123

2. PATRICIA SULLIVAN
   P O BOX 512
   1923 BROWN ST
   ALBANY NY 12123

In example 1, the mail will be delivered to P O BOX 512. In example 2,

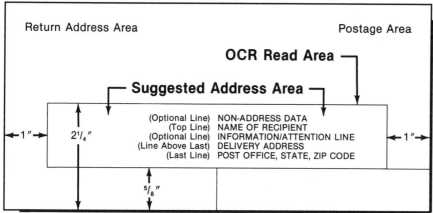

Last Line of Address Must be Completely Within Suggested Address Area
(Not Drawn to Scale)

Exhibit 122.33

Figure 14-1. Specifications for general mail addressing enable automated sorting machines to perform more efficiently.

the mail will be delivered to 1923 BROWN ST.
- Include the zip code on all mail.
- Alternate forms of addressing are accepted by the United States Postal Service. Direct requests to any local post office for information regarding alternate addressing formats.

Sizes. The size of general mail refers to the height and width of the piece. The piece is to be no smaller than $3\frac{1}{2}'' \times 5''$. Mail smaller than the minimum size is not deliverable. The piece should be no larger than $6\frac{1}{8}'' \times 11''$. Mail larger than the maximum size will be delivered, but at a higher postal rate.

Stocks and Inks. The stock for general mail is required to have good reflectance properties. The *reflectance property* of the stock is the amount of light that reflects off the stock. White stock has optimum reflectance.

The ink for general mail should have good light-absorbing properties, which make the address easily read. Black ink is the optimum ink color for addressing mail. Colored inks should be used with caution. The color and reflectance of the stock must be considered when colored ink is used for addressing.

Forms of General Mail

The form of general mail is the form or shape of the mail piece. The most common form of mail is the envelope, although a piece may be sent without an envelope if it is a postcard or a self-mailer.

Envelopes. General mail envelopes have no additional restrictions other than the size limitations and stock reflectance properties listed previously. All standard envelopes of minimum size are acceptable. See Figure 14-2. Special order envelopes may also be used for general mail. The following recommendations are suggested for choosing an envelope to be mailed:
- Standard envelopes are readily available at paper supply houses, printers, and stationery stores. Standard envelopes are recommended over custom envelopes because the stock used for the manufacture of standard envelopes is sufficient for most general mail needs.
- If custom envelopes are used, a mock or dummy envelope should be made. The contents are then inserted in the envelope and mailed to the originator's address to test the strength and quality of the custom envelope.
- Envelopes with a metal clasp, string and button, or staple or wax adhesive are not recommended for use in general mail. These envelopes are not stable unless they are reinforced with packaging tape.
- For easy insertion, the contents of an envelope should measure at least $\frac{1}{8}''$ less than the height of the envelope and $\frac{1}{4}''$ less than the width of the envelope. As the contents increase in depth (bulk), the size of the contents must decrease to allow for the displacement of the bulk in the envelope.
- When window envelopes are used, care must be taken so that the address is not obscured should the contents shift in mailing. Allowing for a margin of white space surrounding the address is recommended. The dimensions of the margin should be equal to or greater than the difference between the size of the envelope and the size of the contents. See Figure 14-3.

Postcards. Postcards, or general mail cards, are the simplest form of general mail. *Postcards* are single pieces of stock. The common postcard is the picture postcard, which has an image or a photograph on one side and space for the transcript and destination address on the other side. A postcard may also be blank on one side for transcript, while the other side is used for addressing information. Postcards are rectangular. The minimum size of a postcard is $3\frac{1}{2}'' \times 5''$ and the maximum size is $4\frac{1}{4}'' \times 6''$. The regulation size is $3\frac{1}{2}'' \times 5\frac{1}{2}''$. The stock thickness for postcards may vary from a minimum thickness of .007'' to a maximum thickness of .0095''. The main advantage of using postcards is a reduced postal fee. Cards not meeting the requirements for general mail will either be mailed for a higher fee or, in extreme cases, disposed of.

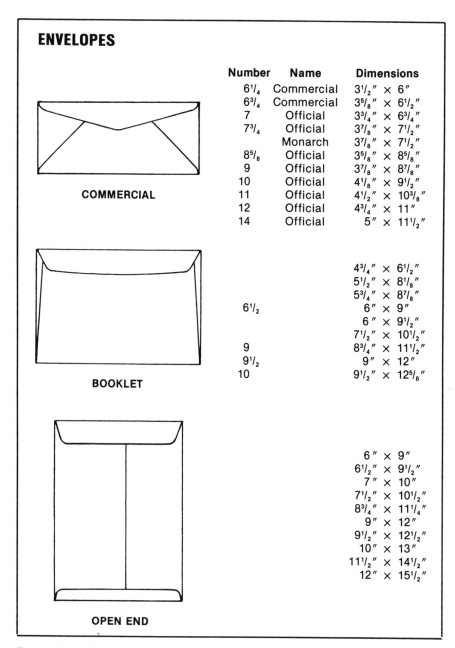

ENVELOPES

Number	Name	Dimensions
6¼	Commercial	3½″ × 6″
6¾	Commercial	3⅝″ × 6½″
7	Official	3¾″ × 6¾″
7¾	Official	3⅞″ × 7½″
	Monarch	3⅞″ × 7½″
8⅝	Official	3⅝″ × 8⅝″
9	Official	3⅞″ × 8⅞″
10	Official	4⅛″ × 9½″
11	Official	4½″ × 10⅜″
12	Official	4¾″ × 11″
14	Official	5″ × 11½″

COMMERCIAL

		4¾″ × 6½″
		5½″ × 8⅛″
		5¾″ × 8⅞″
6½		6″ × 9″
		6″ × 9½″
		7½″ × 10½″
9		8¾″ × 11½″
9½		9″ × 12″
10		9½″ × 12⅝″

BOOKLET

6″ × 9″
6½″ × 9½″
7″ × 10″
7½″ × 10½″
8¾″ × 11¼″
9″ × 12″
9½″ × 12½″
10″ × 13″
11½″ × 14½″
12″ × 15½″

OPEN END

Figure 14-2. General mail envelopes are available in a variety of sizes at stationery stores.

Self-mailers.
A *self-mailer,* or general mail self-mailer, is one or more pages of folded and bound stock. A self-mailer does not need an envelope. The stock, size, and bulk requirements for self-mailers are the same as those for general mail envelopes. A self-mailer may be bound by a staple, an adhesive, or a label tab. See Figure 14-4.

AUTOMATED MAIL REQUIREMENTS

Automated mail requirements have been established for mail that passes through automated machinery used by the United States Postal Service. Machinery that recognizes, or reads, the address through the use of char-acters and barcodes is commonly used to sort business mail.

Automated Systems

Automated systems are used by the United States Postal Service to increase the speed and accuracy of sorting mail. Two pieces of equipment included in the automated systems are the optical character reader (OCR) and the barcode sorter (BCS). *Optical character readers* read individual characters. Barcode sorters expedite the sorting of the mail. Each system requires specific layout and typography of jobs designed to be automated mail pieces.

Optical Character Readers.
Optical character readers used by the United States Postal Service consist of automated machinery that reads characters on a page and translates the information to sort mail. OCRs are programmed to sort outgoing mail at high speed. Mail may be sorted according to specific streets, specific buildings, or even a specific floor of a building.

OCRs read the characters of the address to find the address information. OCRs read the zip code and speed the sorting of mail. The *Zip + 4 system,* which is the original zip code plus a hyphen and four numbers, is used with OCRs. See Figure 14-5. Some OCRs print a barcode directly on the mail piece to expedite sorting.

Barcode Sorters.
Barcode sorters sort mail by reading a barcode printed on the mail piece. *Barcodes* are vertical rules printed on the face of the mail piece that facilitate automated sorting. A BCS will incorrectly read a disfigured barcode.

If barcodes are not printed by OCRs on-line, preprinted barcodes may be placed on the mail piece when it is prepared. When barcodes are printed on-line, the area on which the barcode is to print must be kept clear. Preprinted line copy for barcodes is available through the United States

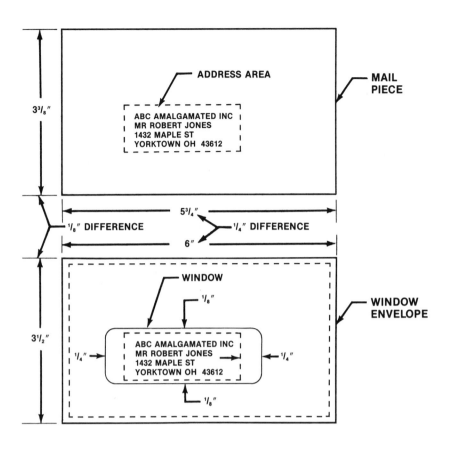

Figure 14-3. The difference between the size of the window envelope and the mail piece determines the amount of margin needed to position the address in the window.

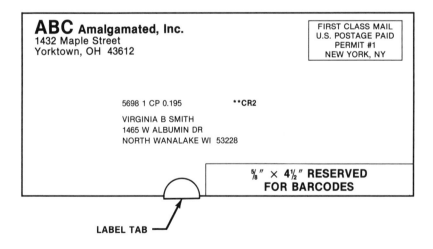

Figure 14-4. General mail self-mailers may be bound by a label tab.

Postal Service. The preprinted barcode copy is pasted on the mechanical of the mail piece. Preprinted barcodes must be accurately placed in the areas specified by the United States Postal Service. See Figure 14-6.

Automated Mail Specifications

Specifications for automated mail are designated by the United States Postal Service. These specifications provide the requirements of the OCR and BCS. Design specifications in layout and typography of automated mail are critical to ensure accuracy of sorting by the OCR and BCS. Specifications include stock and ink used to print the piece, and the bindery method used or the enclosure of an envelope or self-mailer. Failure to follow the designated specifications will cause a delay in delivery or a possible increase in postal fees.

Addresses. Addresses on automated mail pieces must follow typography specifications. Type specifications include standards for type size, typestyle, type spacing, and type alignment.

- The type size of automated mail ranges from 8 to 18 points. The height to width ratio of type ranges from 1.1 to 1 through 1.7 to 1. Letters should be all uppercase and punctuation marks should be omitted.
- Typestyles acceptable for OCRs include any typewritten or typeset style except script, italic, decorative, or styles made up of unconnected dots.
- Type spacing for automated mail includes letterspacing, wordspacing, leading, and type arrangement. Letterspacing of characters must not allow the characters to touch, overlap, or be closer than specified. Ten to 12 characters per inch letterspacing is preferred, while 7 to 12 characters per inch letterspacing is required for OCRs. Wordspacing of elements must provide

for one to two spaces between words. Preferred leading of type-written or typeset lines is 3 points. Two points of leading is minimal. Type arrangement for automated mail is flush left.

- Alignment of the address for automated mail is always horizontal. Vertical or slanted addresses cannot be read by OCRs.

The United States Postal Service publishes a list of common addressing problems. See Figure 14-7.

Sizes and Thicknesses.

The size and thickness of automated mail is critical for accurate reading and sorting. OCRs are designed to read the specific areas of a mail piece. The size of the piece and the placement of elements on the piece will help or hinder the accuracy of the OCR. The thickness of the automated mail piece is standardized for smooth automation through the OCR and BCS. Pieces that are too thin may be misguided through the machinery. Pieces that are too thick may get lodged. The size and thickness of mail forms such as cards, self-mailers, and envelopes differ. Cards are categorized separately from self-mailers and envelopes. Automated mail pieces that are larger or thicker than the specified size and thickness will be rejected as automated mail. These pieces will be processed by less efficient methods and may incur a surcharge.

Stocks and Inks.

The stocks and inks used for automated mail must meet specifications to be mechanically readable. Stock and ink specifications regulate the reflectance quality of the piece, whether the mail piece is a card, self-mailer, or an envelope.

Although size specifications vary for automated mail forms, the reflectance quality is standard. The *reflectance quality* is the difference between the light reflecting off the stock and the ink absorbing a portion of the reflected light. There must be at least a 40% contrast in reflectance quality between the stock and ink to provide

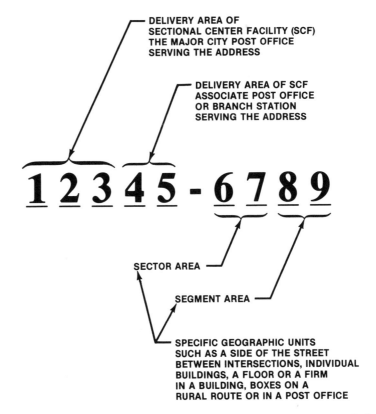

Figure 14-5. The Zip + 4 system is standard in the business industry to help speed automated mail sorting.

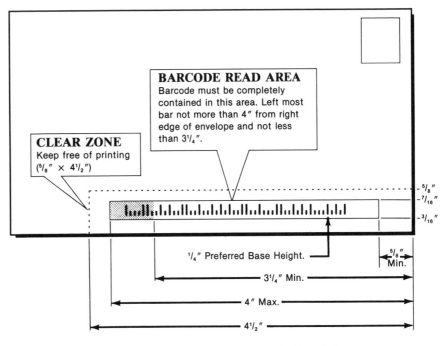

Exhibit 324.73, Barcode Read Area

Figure 14-6. Barcodes are printed on the mail piece to facilitate automated mail sorting.

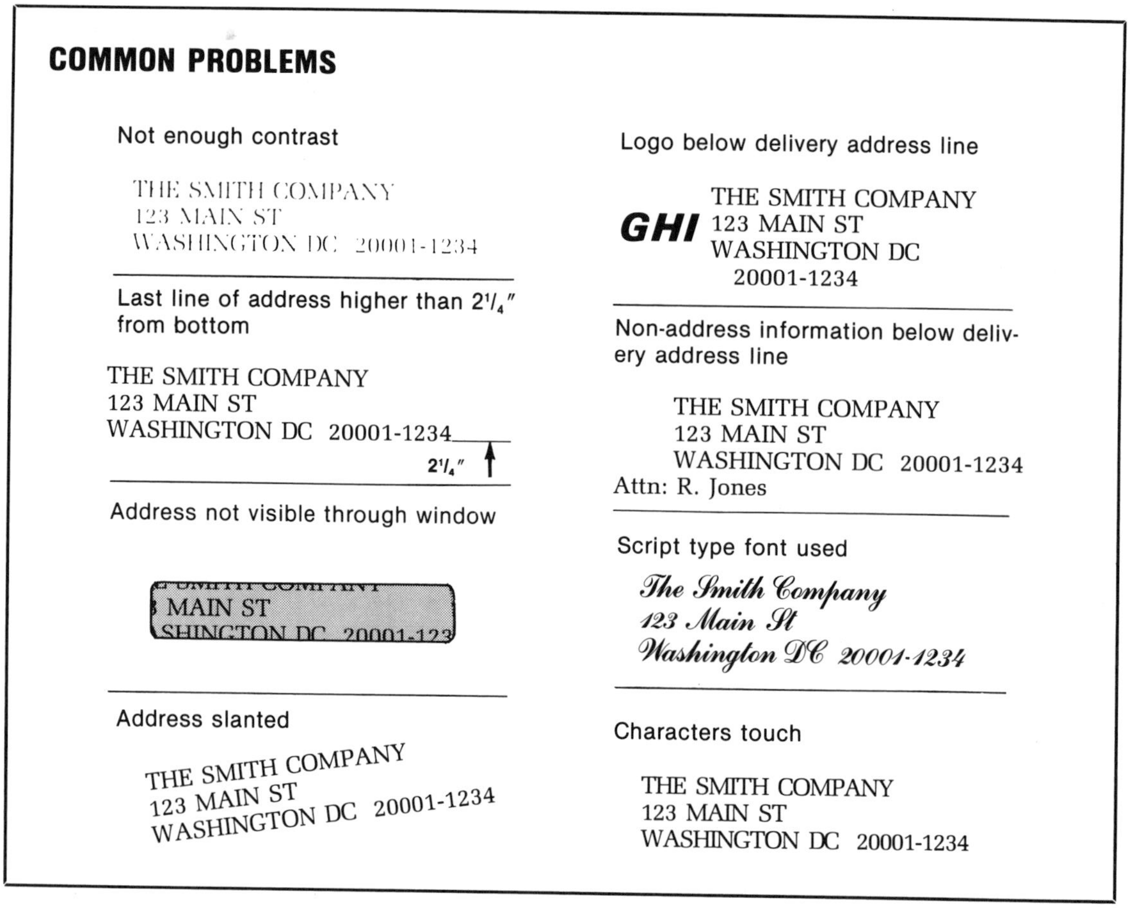

COMMON PROBLEMS

Not enough contrast

THE SMITH COMPANY
123 MAIN ST
WASHINGTON DC 20001-1234

Last line of address higher than 2¹/₄″ from bottom

THE SMITH COMPANY
123 MAIN ST
WASHINGTON DC 20001-1234

2¹/₄″ ↑

Address not visible through window

SMITH COMPANY
MAIN ST
SHINGTON DC 20001-123

Address slanted

THE SMITH COMPANY
123 MAIN ST
WASHINGTON DC 20001-1234

Logo below delivery address line

GHI THE SMITH COMPANY
123 MAIN ST
WASHINGTON DC
20001-1234

Non-address information below delivery address line

THE SMITH COMPANY
123 MAIN ST
WASHINGTON DC 20001-1234
Attn: R. Jones

Script type font used

The Smith Company
123 Main St
Washington DC 20001-1234

Characters touch

THE SMITH COMPANY
123 MAIN ST
WASHINGTON DC 20001-1234

Figure 14-7. Common addressing problems slow the flow of automated mail.

the reflectance quality required by the OCR and BCS. Black ink on white stock provides the best contrast. See Figure 14-8.

To ensure that the ink and stock combination produces the necessary 40% contrast, all potential automated mail pieces should be reviewed by the United States Postal Service. Local post offices will review automated mail pieces free of charge to ensure that they meet specifications. When in doubt, the designer or paste-up artist should contact the local post office customer service department.

Forms of Automated Mail

Forms of automated mail include automated business mail (ABM) and business reply mail (BRM). Both forms of automated mail require detailed, exact address and layout specifications. The address specifications for all automated mail are standard. The layout specifications for ABM and BRM differ slightly.

Automated Business Mail. The layout for automated business mail is specified for OCRs. OCRs are programmed to read information in a specific area of the mail piece. Only the information specified is to be in the optical reading area. See Figure 14-9.

Business Reply Mail. The layout for business reply mail is specified for both the OCR and BCS. Using BRM is an option offered by the United States Postal Service. The BRM option enables clients to receive first-class mail from their customers by paying only for those pieces that are returned from the original distribution of the mail pieces.

The BRM system uses a series of codes to identify the mail. Requirements of BRM include the permit number, the facing identification mark (FIM), horizontal identification bars, the NO POSTAGE NECESSARY endorsement (also called the indicia), the BUSINESS REPLY legend, the POSTAGE WILL BE PAID endorsement, and the address. See Figure 14-10. These requirements must be placed in accordance with the restrictions specified by the United States Postal Service. Detailed layouts are updated periodically and are available at local post offices.

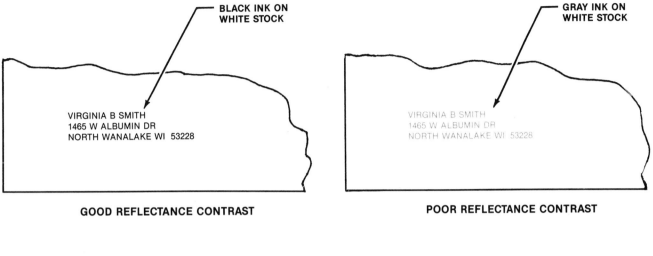

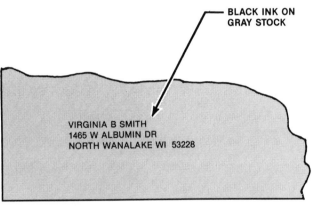

Figure 14-8. Automated mail requires at least a 40% contrast in reflectance quality between the stock and ink.

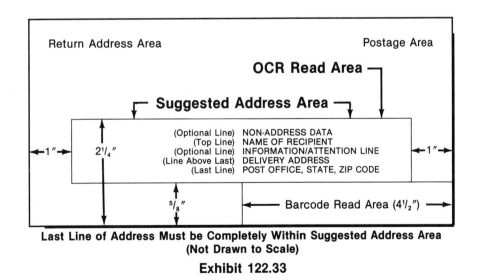

Last Line of Address Must be Completely Within Suggested Address Area
(Not Drawn to Scale)
Exhibit 122.33

Figure 14-9. For automated mail, only the address is required to be placed in the optical reading area.

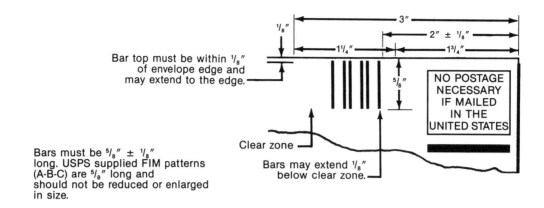

Bar top must be within ⅛″ of envelope edge and may extend to the edge.

Bars must be ⅝″ ± ⅛″ long. USPS supplied FIM patterns (A-B-C) are ⅝″ long and should not be reduced or enlarged in size.

Clear zone

Bars may extend ⅛″ below clear zone.

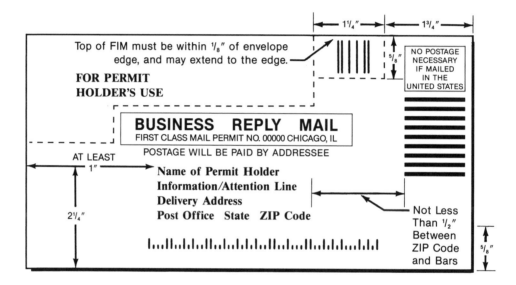

Horizontal identification bars must be at least 1″ in length, and must not extend vertically below the delivery address line.

Exhibit 917.52c, Business Reply Mail Format Requirements
Note: Both FIM and Barcode must have at least 30 percent print reflectance difference and the combined effects of positional and rotational skew must be limited to ± 5 degrees from the FIM or Barcode to the top or bottom edge of the mailpiece. Exhibit NOT drawn to scale.

Figure 14-10. Business reply mail requires strict addressing formats using the horizontal identification bars and permit number specified by the postal chief.

14 Postal Regulations

Name _____

Date _____

True-False

T   F   **1.** Improperly prepared mail may incur an additional postal fee.

T   F   **2.** To avoid added expenditure, all mail pieces should comply with the regulations issued by the U.S. Forms Service.

T   F   **3.** To ensure accuracy of the layout of a mail piece, samples may be reviewed by the postal chief for a nominal charge.

T   F   **4.** General mail is correspondence mail.

T   F   **5.** Addressing general mail requires two addresses.

T   F   **6.** General mail with a typed or printed address is more efficient than handwritten mail.

T   F   **7.** A zip code should be included on all mail.

T   F   **8.** Alternate forms of addressing automated mail are accepted by the United States Postal Service.

T   F   **9.** Mail smaller than the minimum size specified by the United States Postal Service cannot be delivered.

T   F   **10.** Mail larger than the minimum size specified by the United States Postal Service is charged a higher rate for delivery.

T   F   **11.** General mail envelopes must comply with strict postal codes.

T   F   **12.** The Zip + 4 system is designed for OCRs.

Multiple Choice

_____   **1.** Specified element alignment along with correct _____ enables all mail to move smoothly.
   A. typography
   B. stock
   C. ink
   D. all of the above

_____   **2.** All address typography is _____.
   A. flush left
   B. flush right
   C. centered
   D. justified

_____   **3.** All address typography is _____.
   A. uppercase
   B. upper- and lowercase
   C. bold
   D. sans serif

_____ 4. The minimum size specified by the United States Postal Service for general mail is $3\frac{1}{2}$″ × _____″.
A. $3\frac{1}{2}$
B. 4
C. 5
D. 6

_____ 5. The color of ink used for optimum light absorbency on general mail is _____.
A. black
B. blue
C. red
D. yellow

_____ 6. Envelopes with a _____ closure are not recommended for general mail.
A. metal clasp
B. string and button
C. staple
D. all of the above

Matching

_____ 1. Horizontal address margin

_____ 2. Vertical address margin

_____ 3. Minimum size general mail

_____ 4. Maximum size general mail

_____ 5. Maximum size postcard

_____ 6. Optical character reader

_____ 7. Barcode sorter

_____ 8. Automated business mail

_____ 9. Business reply mail

_____ 10. Facing identification marks

_____ 11. No postage necessary

A. $6\frac{1}{8}$″ × 11″
B. $\frac{5}{8}$″ on bottom
C. Indicia
D. ABM
E. $4\frac{1}{4}$″ × 6″
F. BRM
G. FIM
H. $3\frac{1}{2}$″ × 5″
I. OCR
J. BCS
K. 1″ or greater

Completion

_____ 1. Mail delivered to a foreign country requires only the _____ of the country on the last line of the address block.

_____ 2. The _____ of general mail refers to the height and width requirements.

_____ 3. The color and _____ of the stock must be considered before choosing a colored ink for addressing.

_____ 4. Testing a custom envelope by mailing it to the originator's address ensures the _____ and _____ of the envelope.

_____

_____ 5. The dimension of the address margin on a window envelope should be equal to or _____ than the difference between the size of the envelope and the size of the contents.

_____ 6. A general mail _____ is one or more folded and bound pages.

_____ 7. Some _____ machines print a barcode directly on the mail piece, which facilitates sorting.

_____ 8. When barcodes are printed _____, the area for printing must be kept clear of copy.

_____ 9. Stocks and inks selected for automated mail must be mechanically _____.

_____ 10. There must be at least a(n) _____ % contrast between the stock and ink on automated mail.

_____ 11. Typestyles comprised of unconnected _____ are unsatisfactory for automated mail.

_____ 12. The minimum recommended leading for typeset lines is specified as _____ points.

_____ 13. _____ mail enables postal clients to pay only for mail pieces that are returned from the original distribution.

Identification

_____ 1. Indicia

_____ 2. Barcode

_____ 3. Optical character reading area

_____ 4. Facing identification marks

_____ 5. Permit number

Return Address Area   Postage Area

(A)

NON-ADDRESS DATA
NAME OF RECIPIENT
INFORMATION/ATTENTION LINE
DELIVERY ADDRESS
POST OFFICE, STATE, ZIP CODE

(B)

(C)

NO POSTAGE
NECESSARY
IF MAILED
IN THE
UNITED STATES

BUSINESS REPLY MAIL
FIRST CLASS MAIL PERMIT NO. 00000
POSTAGE WILL BE PAID BY ADDRESSEE

Name of Permit Holder
Information/Attention Line
Delivery Address
Post Office State ZIP Code

(D)

(E)

15 FORMS DESIGN AND LAYOUT

Forms design is the process of creating a form that will increase understanding between the user and the reader. Understanding between form users and readers decreases if forms are improperly designed. Poorly organized forms result in lost work hours caused by unnecessary forms, repetition of forms, and forms that are poorly spaced and hard to complete. Before beginning any forms design, a designer should complete a forms analysis. The designer must analyze the need for the form to determine the correct form style and layout.

FORMS DESIGN

Forms design involves a forms analysis, or a written or verbal survey. Forms designers must ask the following questions:

1. Is a form needed?
2. Is there an existing form that could be altered or replaced?
3. What is the purpose of the form?
4. Where is the form to be used?
5. What are the form specifications?
6. Is the form to be used independently or in conjunction with another form?
7. What is the budget for producing the form?

With the answers to these questions, the forms designer is able to determine the form style needed.

Form style refers to the type of form. Each form style serves a different purpose. The five basic form styles are flat forms, pegboard forms, unit sets, salesbooks, and continuous forms. The designer must analyze the advantages and disadvantages of each form style before choosing one.

Flat Forms

A *flat form* is a one-sheet form. See Figure 15-1. It is the most common form. A flat form is the most economical form because it is

1. usually printed in one color of ink on white stock;
2. a simple form that usually does not require perforating, punching, or stapling;
3. designed to any size to reduce waste; and
4. reproduced using various presses or a photocopier.

Although common and economical, a flat form is appropriate if only one copy of the form is required. If carbon or duplicate copies of the form are needed, other form styles may be more efficient.

Pegboard Forms

Pegboard forms are individual forms held together by pegs or pins. The pegs are usually made of metal or plastic fastened to a bar. Holes are drilled or punched in the form to match the configuration of the pegboard or pin bar. See Figure 15-2. The pegs hold the forms in register with one another. Carbonized pegboard forms are available that have carbon sheets, carbonless paper, or carbonized strips inserted between forms. Carbonized pegboard forms are economical and efficient because they allow each form to be viewed (stacked longest to shortest or shingled to view title areas). Also, all forms are in register with one another, preventing errors in transferring information from line to line.

Pegboard forms are usually used for recording ledger information. Pegboard forms are available through most forms and stationery dealers. These forms can be used as purchased or customized by a printer. For example, the company name, logo, address, or numbering system may be added.

Unit Sets

A *unit set* is a multipage form that is duplicated throughout the set. A unit set is connected at one end to hold

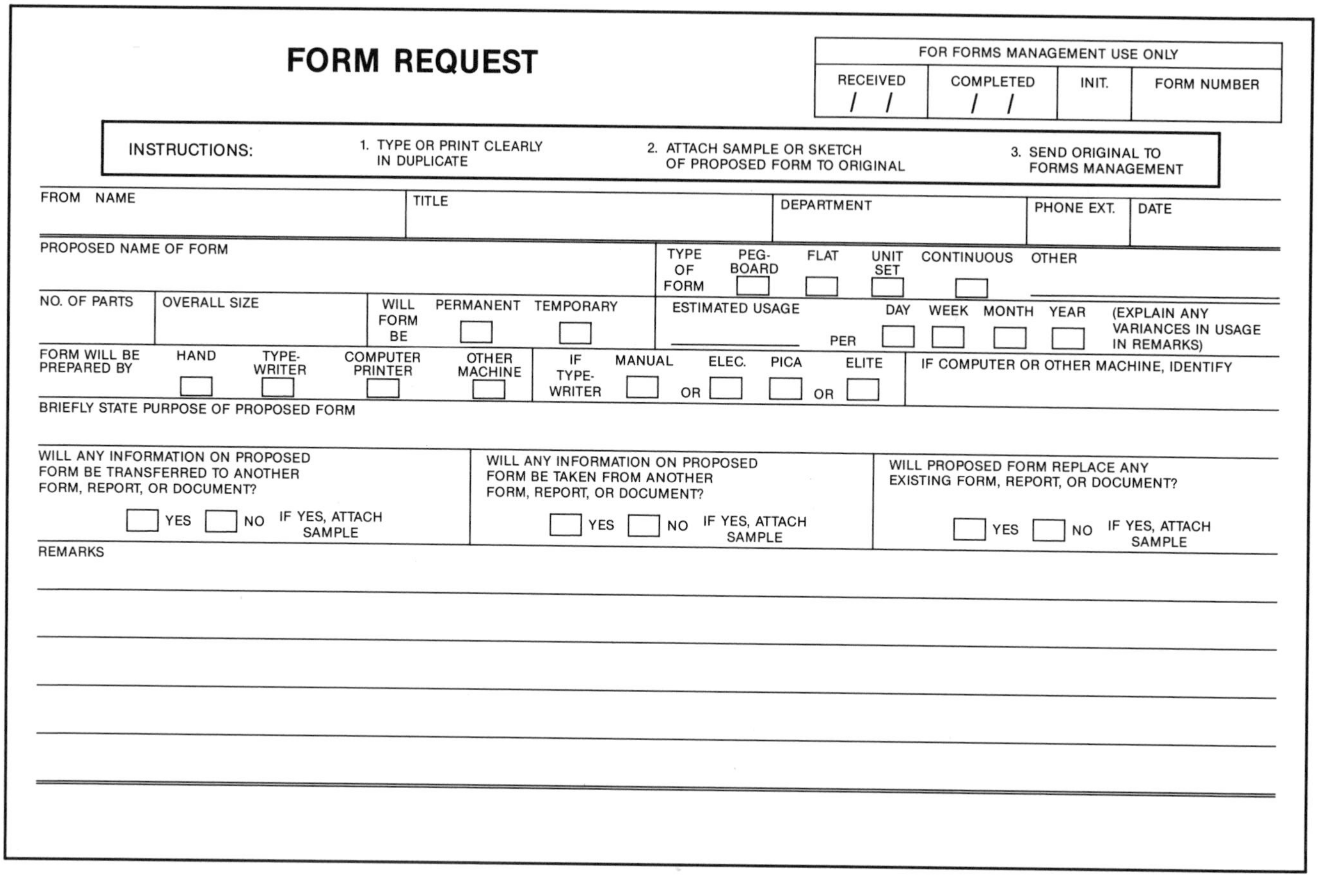

Figure 15-1. A flat form is a one-sheet form easily reproduced through photocopying.

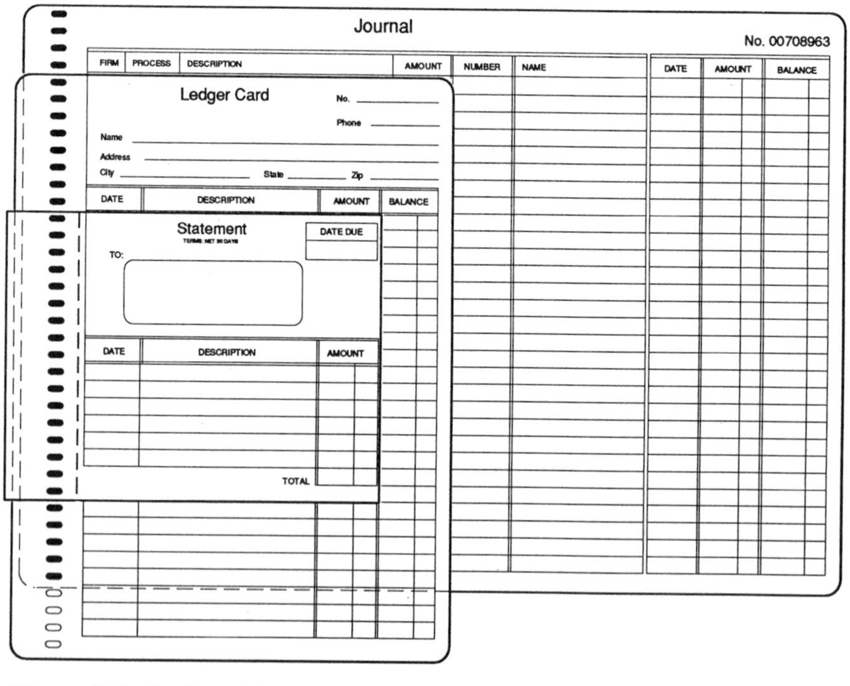

Figure 15-2. Pegboard forms, which are individual forms held together by pegs or pins, are in register with one another.

all the forms in register. As the user completes the top form, the duplicate forms are completed. Two types of unit sets are carbon and carbonless.

A carbon unit set has interleaved paper and carbon sheets and is glued at the *stub,* or margin. The carbon unit set, or *snap-out* or *snap-set* form, is perforated to allow individual sheets to be removed. The carbon sheets are usually ¼″ to ½″ shorter at the open end of the form. The open end is the side opposite the stub. See Figure 15-3. This short sheeting method allows the user to remove only the forms, not the carbon sheets, which remain connected to the stub because they are not perforated.

A carbonless unit set uses a chemically coated paper to create a duplicate copy of the form. Two chemicals, used to create the carbonless image, are encapsulated and coated on the paper. When pressure is applied to the paper, the capsules are broken.

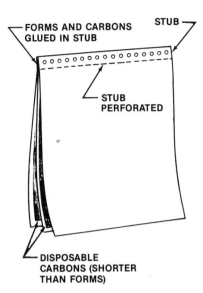

— FORMS AND CARBONS GLUED IN STUB

STUB

STUB PERFORATED

DISPOSABLE CARBONS (SHORTER THAN FORMS)

Figure 15-3. A unit-set form is a multi-page form that is glued at the stub, or margin.

The two chemicals intermix, triggering a reaction, which creates an image on the paper. The most common type of carbonless paper is chemically mated paper. *Chemically mated paper* is paper coated on both sides. The back of the paper is the *coated back* (*CB*) and contains the chemical with the dye. The front of the paper is coated with the chemical mating agent and is the *coated front* (*CF*). When pressure from a ballpoint pen or printer is applied to the form, a chemical reaction takes place, creating an image on the front of the paper only. Pages within a multiunit carbonless set are coated on the front with the mating agent and on the back with the chemical dye. *Coated front and back* (*CFB*) is carbonless paper coated on two sides. The last page of a carbonless unit set may be an index stock that has greater pressure resistance and is only coated on the front. See Figure 15-4.

Carbonless unit sets are either collated before printing in a sheetfed operation or printed, cut, and collated in a web-printing operation. Carbonless unit sets are bound after printing with a special fan-apart padding liquid, which is applied to the top or one edge of a stack of forms. The

liquid permeates the paper, reacting with the chemical coatings, forming an adhesive. When the adhesive dries, groups of the forms are fanned to separate them into individual sets. This occurs because the adhesive bond is weak between the uncoated sheets of each set. The last sheet is specially treated on the back so that it repels the padding liquid. As the pages are padded, individual forms are bound together. When dry, the stock is fanned and the back sheet of one form set pulls away from the top sheet of the next set, leaving padded unit sets. Unit sets are used in place of flat forms because they

1. contain a carbon additive, which increases speed and neatness;
2. are available with page and stub variations to fit different form needs; and
3. produce forms that are always in register.

Salesbooks

Salesbooks are similar to unit sets but have a greater volume of forms. Salesbooks usually contain a cover and either carbonless forms or forms with a reusable carbon sheet. See Figure 15-5.

Salesbooks are bound at the top. The forms are often perforated to facilitate removal. One form in each set of two, three, or four forms is not perforated and remains in the book.

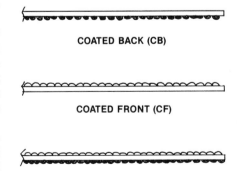

COATED BACK (CB)

COATED FRONT (CF)

COATED FRONT AND BACK (CFB)

Figure 15-4. Carbonless unit sets are coated with a chemical mating agent on the front, back, or front and back.

The remaining form is often used as a record. Salesbooks help businesses save time and the added expense of keeping a record of sales, which are the primary functions of salesbooks. Salesbooks remain a popular form in the small business industry because they

1. are economical and versatile;
2. are inexpensive to produce and may be designed to fit any size or binding requirement;
3. are usually small, easy to store, and simple to use;
4. provide an area on the form for adding sales, which serves as a receipt for the buyer and a record for the seller; and
5. allow consistent recordkeeping and a customized numbering system.

BOUND AT TOP AND PERFORATED

REUSABLE CARBON SHEET

Figure 15-5. Salesbooks are commonly used in small businesses for receipts and records of sales.

Continuous Forms

Continuous forms are forms that are drilled or punched along the outer margin, allowing the forms to be fed through a machine on a sprocket gear. See Figure 15-6. With increased computer use in business, continuous forms, or computer forms, are quickly replacing all other forms. Continuous

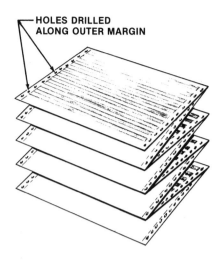

Figure 15-6. Continuous forms are drilled along the outer margins, which allows the forms to be fed through various printing devices.

forms allow for automated transcription and produce hard copies for records and receipts. Soft copies of the information are stored on computer disk, which is an added advantage of continuous forms.

Some continuous forms are still completed by hand. Register forms are an example of handwritten, mechanically driven forms. Register forms allow one form to be used as a receipt and a duplicate form to be used as a record. On some register form machines, the record form is stored in a compartment in the machine.

Continuous forms are designed to fit business needs and mechanized or automated requirements. Before any continuous form is designed, the designer must determine printer specifications, size limitations, transcription space (computer and hand) and multipage limitations.

Advantages of continuous forms are that they
1. can be adapted to fit hand-operated or automated systems;
2. provide accurately aligned forms and computer controlled printing, bursting, sorting, and mailing in high volume systems such as credit card and telephone billings;
3. are easily customized to fit the needs of the machine and the user; and

4. are available in many styles and layouts, which allows the user to seek competitively priced forms.

FORMS PRODUCTION

Forms production includes all of the processes required to assemble and print a form. Following the specifications designated by the user, the designer creates a layout for a form. The properties of a form require specialized tools, formats, graphics, typestyles and sizes, and stock and inks to be used. A designer considers all of the user specifications and production requirements before beginning the forms layout.

Forms Layout

A *forms layout* is a detailed draft of the proposed form. A forms layout, unlike most conventional comprehensive layouts, is drawn on graph paper. Graph paper is ruled specifically for forms designed to promote accurate layout measurements. The designer creates a forms layout that is easily understood. The most common forms layout uses the "zone system." The

zone system separates the form into the logical categories of identification, instructions, introduction, body, and closing. See Figure 15-7.

In addition to the zone system, form designers use sequencing and grouping to make the form easier to follow and enter information. *Sequencing* is the natural or familiar flow of information, for example, "Name" before "Address" or "Area Code" before "Phone Number." Usually the space for the "Date" is near the top of the form, and the space for a "Signature" is at the bottom of the form.

The use-sequence of the form is also considered when the flow of the data on the form is planned. When a form is to be used in more than one department of a company, the logical sequence of information follows the sequence of use. *Grouping* is the arrangement of like data on a form, for example, customer information, project information, billing information, and shipping information.

Once the general flow of information on a form is planned, the designer formats, or spaces the data. The designer utilizes user specifications and forms tools to format the layout. In addition, many computer software pro-

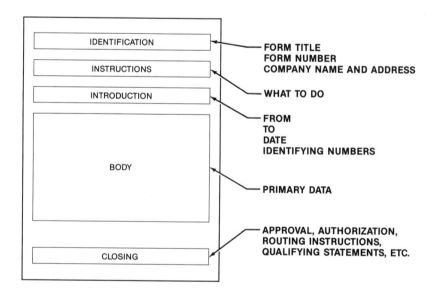

ZONE SYSTEM—BASIC CATEGORIES

Figure 15-7. The forms layout is commonly separated into categories according to the zone system.

grams are used today to design and format the layout.

Spacing Format. The *spacing format* of a form is the spacing of the elements on the form. The spacing format is determined by the amount of information required on the form and the manner in which the user fills in the information. The spacing format of a form is determined horizontally and vertically. Horizontal spacing is character spacing, while vertical spacing is linespacing. *Character spacing* is the amount of space allowed for each character on a line. *Linespacing* is the amount of space between lines of type and is measured from the baseline of one line of type to the baseline of the next line of type. See Figure 15-8.

The amount of character space and linespace formatted on a form directly relates to the manner in which the form is to be filled in. Forms are filled in on a computer, typewriter, handwritten, or a combination of both. Forms that are designed to be handwritten are not easily filled in by machine. In turn, forms that are designed to be filled in using a computer or a typewriter are virtually impossible to fill in neatly by hand. Nothing decreases the efficiency of a form more than an improper spacing format. The spacing format is derived by the average amount of space required by a character horizontally and vertically. The spacing format is chosen to meet the transcription requirements of the user. See Figure 15-9.

A 6 - 10 spacing format has six lines per inch linespacing and 10 characters per inch character spacing. This spacing format is equivalent to most machines, including a pica typewriter.

A 6 - 12 spacing format has six lines per inch linespacing and 12 characters per inch character spacing. This spacing format is equivalent to some machines, including an elite typewriter.

A 4 - 5 spacing format has four lines per inch linespacing and five characters per inch character spacing. This spacing format represents the minimum amount of space allotted for completing a form by hand. This spacing

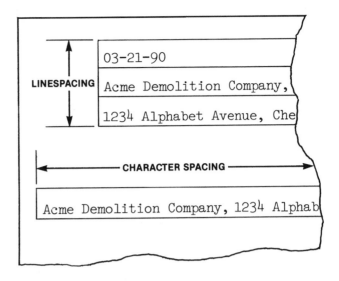

Figure 15-8. Character spacing and linespacing on forms are the amount of horizontal and vertical space allowed to accommodate typed information.

format is often called the ¼″ spacing format because ¼″ is allotted between lines of space.

A 3 - 5 spacing format has three lines per inch linespacing and five characters per inch character spacing. This broad spacing format is known as multimedia spacing or all-purpose spacing because it allows for double-spaced typewritten and handwritten data. A 3 - 5 spacing format is found on a variety of forms, for example, application forms, medical forms, and accident reports.

Entry Format. The *entry format* is the layout of each data entry space on a form. Entry formats include box design, on-line, under-line, columning, and ballot box. See Figure 15-10.

Box design is effective for most entry requirements. The box design entry area is defined by horizontal and vertical rules. The box design entry format uses the upper left corner of the box for the entry caption. The entry caption is a request for data. The box design is clear as to the requested data, does not require the user to search for the caption, and uses space that does not interfere with data entry space.

On-line entry format has the caption on the same line as the data entry space. On-line entry format is less efficient than the box design because it uses entry space for the caption.

Under-line entry format has the caption under the data entry line space. Under-line entry format is less efficient than both the box design and the on-line entry formats. Under-line entry format is time-consuming because the user often has to search to find the caption and decipher whether the entry belongs on the line above or below the caption. When used on a typewriter the caption of an under-line entry format falls below the carriage and requires the user to adjust, read, readjust, and then type.

The columning entry format groups similar items. Each column has a caption that is centered in a box at the top of the column. When the column width is narrower than the space necessary for the column caption, the column caption is written vertically. Two-line column captions are inverted to avoid confusion.

Ballot box entry format is the simplest and most efficient format. The user reads the caption for each item and places an "X" in the appropriate ballot box. A ballot box is an outlined box ⅛″ square (common size for machine and hand-completed forms). The box is placed before or under

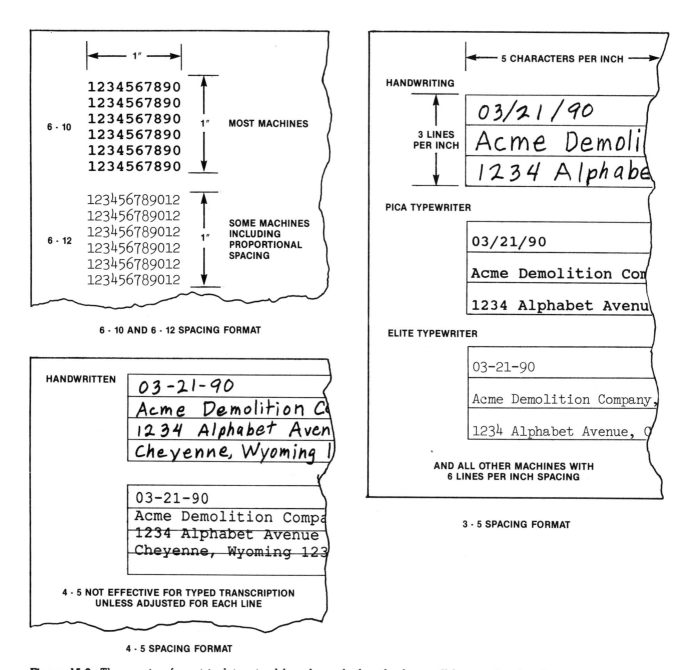

Figure 15-9. The spacing format is determined based on whether the form will be typed or handwritten.

each entry. An appropriate amount of space is placed between each entry so that the user is not confused as to which box belongs with which entry.

Ballot box entry format is efficient because it groups similar entry data, is easier to complete, saves space, and ensures clarity. Ballot box entry format, although not feasible for all data entry, should be used whenever possible.

Form Typography. *Form typography* is the typestyles and type sizes used on a form. When choosing typestyles and type sizes for a form, the designer should make the form simple and functional.

Typestyles used on forms are generally sans serif, for example, Helvetica, News Gothic, Optima, Univers, and Futura. A medium weight type is recommended for most entry cap-

tions. Boldface type is used primarily for direct instructions, for example, **RETURN TO SENDER.** An alternate to boldface type is italic type, which may be used in small amounts for emphasis. Serif, script, textletter, decorative, and reverse type are generally avoided in forms except where the typestyle is part of a logo or corporate identity. Entry captions and column captions are easier to read in

BOX DESIGN

NAME | AGE

ON-LINE

NAME: _____ AGE: _____

UNDER-LINE

_____ _____
NAME   AGE

COLUMNING

ORDER DATE	ORDER NO.	SOLD TO	SHIP DATE	ITEM NO.	QUAN.	

BALLOT BOX DATA ENTRY

REGION
☐ NORTH ☐ SOUTH ☐ EAST ☐ WEST

MARITAL STATUS
MARRIED   SINGLE   WIDOWED   DIVORCED   SEPARATED
☐   .   ☐   ☐   ☐   ☐

Figure 15-10. The box design data entry format is more efficient than the on-line or under-line data entry format because the entry caption is highly visible. The columning and ballot box entry formats are also commonly used.

all uppercase letters. Uppercase and lowercase letters are designated when questions or large amounts of text are required.

Type sizes on a form usually range from 6- to 24-point type. Entry captions and column captions range from 6- to 8-point type. Section captions and instructions range from 10- to 12-point type, while forms titles usually range from 12- to 24-point type. The designer chooses type sizes that are readable and use space efficiently. See Figure 15-11.

Form Graphics. *Form graphics* are the elements on a form used to lead the eye along the page. Grouping like entries and separating unlike entries are two functions of form graphics. Graphics used on a form are generally rules, curved corners, tint screens, and textures. Rules used on a form vary in style and function. A hairline rule is the most common rule thickness used on a form. A hairline rule defines areas without distracting the eye. A double hairline rule may be used to separate sections of a form. Bold rules separate and add emphasis to an area. Dashed rules are used to subdivide boxes and columns.

Curved corners are used on a form to soften the appearance of boxed design or columned forms. A designer

uses curved corner boxes cautiously because they are often more time-consuming to produce than square corner boxes and are distracting if overused. See Figure 15-12.

Tint screens are used on a form to emphasize specific areas, to lead the eye, and to enhance instructions.

Screened areas are used to section out portions of a form. For optimum readability a screened area of 5% to 15% is recommended.

Screened rules are used to guide the eye along a column or area without distracting attention from the entry. Screened rules for optimum

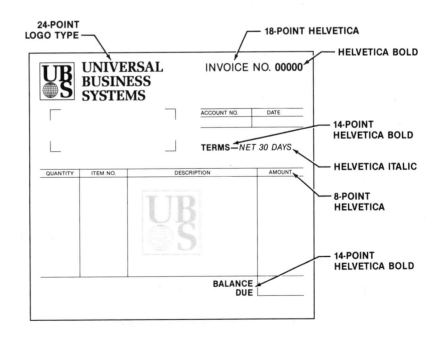

Figure 15-11. Variations of a sans serif typeface are used to emphasize and clarify areas of the form. The type sizes used generally range between 6- to 24-point.

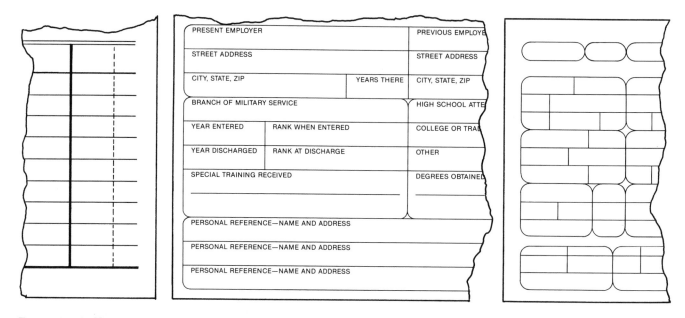

Figure 15-12. Various thicknesses of rules are used to separate areas on a form. Double hairline rules and dashed rules are also used. Rules and curved corners may be used to separate sections of a form. However, overuse of curved corners is distracting and should be avoided.

visibility should range from 30% to 50% depending on the thickness of the rule.

Screened type or illustrations on a form may be used to highlight areas or on the graphics or logo. See Figure 15-13. Screened type is used with caution as it may distract from the function of the form. For optimum readability of completed entry, it is recommended that screened images should range from 5% to 10%.

Texturing is a background printed behind the type on a form. Texturing is usually used on forms for protection from document alteration on checks, bonds, or deeds. Texturing may be solid ink coverage of a light color or a tint screen of a dark color. Texturing may cover the entire form or only a portion of a form.

Form Stock. Form stock varies with each form style. Nearly all forms are printed on a bond paper. Bond paper is a general category of writing papers. The form printer should be consulted before a paper is specified.

Colored stocks are used in forms production to aid in form recognition, ease eye strain, and gain attention. Colored stocks aid in form recognition when a color code system is adopted. A color code system, usually found in unit sets, applies a specified form color to each area or department of a company. For example, a company might use the white copy as the client's receipt; the canary copy as the job ticket, which is attached to the job file; the pink copy for recording client and/or job information, which is filed in the records department; the goldenrod copy for billing; and the green copy for shipping. Although any sequence of colored stock may be used in a color coded multipart form, it is more cost effi-

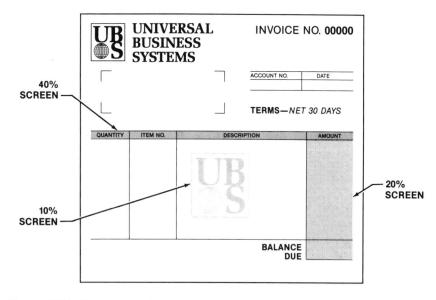

Figure 15-13. Tint screens chosen for optimum readability may be used to emphasize specific areas of a form.

cient to use the paper manufacturer's color sequence. The standard color sequence is white, canary, pink, goldenrod, green, blue, and salmon. Buff or white is a standard color for index stock backing sheets.

Colored stocks are used to reduce eye strain in areas with high light reflectance and in departments that deal with a multitude of paperwork. Colored stocks of light green, buff, ivory, and light blue are generally used to ease eye strain. The light reflected off the colored stock is softer than light reflected off white stock. Dark colored stock is avoided because the low reflectance level between the stock and the ink may cause greater eye strain, especially in dimly lighted areas.

Colored stock is often used to gain attention to a form by using an unusual or high-quality paper. A form sent to preferred customers would better represent the company if printed on an expensive 100% cotton watermark paper, than if produced on a utility grade, white offset paper.

Regardless of the form style or reason for using a colored paper, a form's use must be analyzed before a colored stock is chosen. Colored stock should not be used when copies are to be photocopied, optical character readers (OCRs) are to be used, and/or magnetic inks or colored inks are used.

Form Ink.
Form ink is generally a standard black ink. However, a variety of inks is available to fill the specific requirements of the form, for example, colored ink, magnetic ink, and optical reading ink, and ink used with thermal copiers.

Colored inks of any type may be used for general forms production. Flat color inks, or PMS, are most common, while occasionally 4-color process inks may be used. The color of the ink chosen depends on the use and the desired appearance of the form.

Magnetic ink contains iron oxide, which can be magnetized. The magnetic ink can be read by electronic Magnetic Ink Character Recognition (MICR) machinery. Magnetic ink is available in black, green, red, and brown. Magnetic inks are usually

printed on MICR bond paper, a white stock that accepts ink well. Magnetic inks are used for automated identification and are generally found on direct mail and banking forms.

Optical reading ink or OCR ink is used on forms that are to be read by machine. The most common OCR ink is black ink on white stock. Not all black ink is OCR ink. The OCR ink must absorb a specified percentage of the light reflecting from the stock. When requesting OCR ink, the type of equipment that will read the ink must be determined.

Ink used with thermal copiers has metallic or carbon additives that enable it to be visible to infrared or thermal copiers. All black inks can be used with thermal copiers. All colored inks cannot. Colored inks to be used with thermal copiers must be specified to the printer as such.

Carbonizing.
Carbonizing is the process of creating copies of form entry with carbon and carbonless materials. The three methods of carbonizing are carbon paper, carbon stripe or carbon spot, and carbonless.

Carbon paper is a sheet of thin tissue coated on one side with carbon ink. Carbon ink is a dense, waxy ink that is easily transferred with pressure. Carbon paper is available in a variety of finishes with the most common being hard, medium, and intense. Hard carbon finish needs heavy pressure to transfer, medium carbon finish needs less pressure to transfer, and intense carbon finish needs the least pressure to transfer. The carbon finish required for the form relates to the type of paper on which the form is printed, the number of parts or pages to the form, and the method used to complete the form.

The *carbon stripe* and *carbon spot* are methods of carbonizing the back of the form stock. Carbon ink is applied to the entire page, a section, a stripe, or a spot specified by the designer. See Figure 15-14. A form with a carbonized back is easier to use than carbon sheets because the carbonized back is stationary and does not slip out of position. It is, however, easier to handle since the

individual form sheets carry the carbon with them.

Carbon stripes and spots allow only specific entries to copy onto duplicate forms. Carbon stripes and spots can also be specified for carbon paper. Whether the form stock is carbonized or the carbon paper is treated in carbon patterns (stripes or spots), both methods are costly. Carbon patterns are specially ordered, cost more, and have a longer delivery time than standard carbon paper.

Carbonless paper is paper that transfers entries to duplicate forms without carbon ink. Carbonless paper is treated with encapsulated chemicals. The most common use of carbonless paper is in carbonless unit sets.

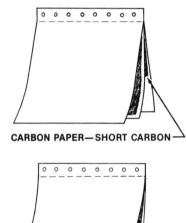

CARBON PAPER—SHORT CARBON

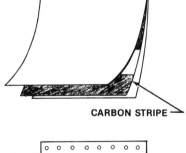

CARBON STRIPE

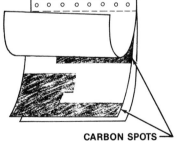

CARBON SPOTS

Figure 15-14. Short carbon, carbon stripes, and carbon spots on the back of unit set forms allow only specific entries to be duplicated on the form or forms beneath.

True-False

T   F   **1.** A flat form can be reproduced through a variety of printing methods.

T   F   **2.** Carbonized pegboard forms are efficient because they are can be stacked and shingled.

T   F   **3.** A unit set is connected at one end to hold all the forms in register.

T   F   **4.** Three chemicals are used to create a carbonless unit set.

T   F   **5.** The last page of a carbonless unit set may be coated only on the front.

T   F   **6.** Salesbooks are similar to unit sets but have a greater volume of forms.

T   F   **7.** Sequencing is the natural or familiar flow of information.

T   F   **8.** The spacing format of a form directly relates to the typestyle used to typeset the form.

T   F   **9.** Typestyles used on forms are usually serif typefaces.

T   F   **10.** Form captions are easier to read in all uppercase letters.

T   F   **11.** All questions on forms should be set in all uppercase letters.

T   F   **12.** The standard sequence of colors for unit sets is white, canary, pink, goldenrod, green, blue, and salmon.

T   F   **13.** All colored inks can be used in thermal copiers, while all black inks cannot.

Multiple Choice

_____   **1.** Poorly organized forms result in lost work hours caused by _____.
A. unnecessary forms
B. poorly spaced and hard to complete forms
C. repetition of forms
D. all of the above

_____   **2.** A _____ form is a one-sheet form.
A. pegboard
B. flat
C. continuous
D. unit set

_____   **3.** A _____ form is a combination of individual forms held in register by pins.
A. pegboard
B. flat
C. continuous
D. unit set

_____ **4.** A _____ is a multipage form in which duplicate forms are completed as the user completes the top form.
A. pegboard
B. flat
C. continuous
D. unit set

_____ **5.** A _____ form is drilled along the outer margin to allow it to be pulled through a machine.
A. pegboard
B. flat
C. continuous
D. unit set

_____ **6.** Character spacing is _____ spacing on a form.
A. vertical
B. horizontal
C. diagonal
D. all of the above

_____ **7.** Linespacing is _____ spacing on a form.
A. vertical
B. horizontal
C. diagonal
D. all of the above

_____ **8.** A box design uses the upper _____ corner of the box for the entry caption.
A. left
B. right
C. middle
D. all of the above

_____ **9.** Form _____ are elements on a form used to lead the eye along the page.
A. rules
B. graphics
C. tint screens
D. all of the above

_____ **10.** Texturing is generally used to protect against document alteration on _____.
A. checks
B. bonds
C. deeds
D. all of the above

Matching

_____ **1.** Flat form

_____ **2.** Pegboard form

_____ **3.** Unit set

_____ **4.** Salesbook

_____ **5.** Continuous form

A. Computer form
B. Multipage form bound with glue
C. One-sheet form
D. Combination of individual forms held by pins
E. Multipage form in large volume

_____ 6. 3 - 5 spacing

_____ 7. 6 - 10 spacing

_____ 8. 6 - 12 spacing

_____ 9. 4 - 5 spacing

A. Spacing format for elite typewriter
B. Spacing format for pica typewriter
C. Spacing format for multimedia entry
D. Spacing format for minimum space alloted for handwritten data

Completion

_____ 1. Forms _____ is the process of creating a business form that will increase communication between the user and the reader.

_____ 2. Before a forms layout is begun, the designer completes a forms _____.

_____ 3. There are _____ basic form styles.

_____ 4. A(n) _____ form is the most common form style.

_____ 5. A photocopier is a common method of producing a(n) _____ form.

_____ 6. The _____ form is usually used for recording ledger information.

_____ 7. With increased computer use in business, the _____ form is quickly replacing all other forms.

_____ 8. Forms _____ includes all of the processes required to assemble and print a form.

_____ 9. The most common forms layout uses the _____ system.

_____ 10. The entry _____ is a request for data.

_____ 11. _____ entry format has the caption on the same line as the data entry space.

_____ 12. _____ entry format has the caption under the data entry line space.

_____ 13. _____ box entry format is the simplest data entry format.

_____ 14. _____ stocks are used to ease eye strain.

_____ 15. _____ ink contains iron oxide, which can be magnetized.

Identification

_____ 1. Pegboard form

_____ 2. Unit set

_____ 3. Continuous form

_____ 4. Flat form

_____ 5. Salesbook

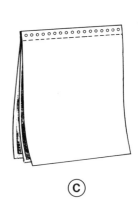

A

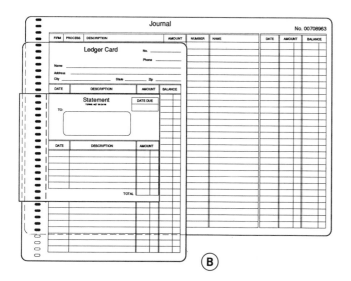

B

C

D

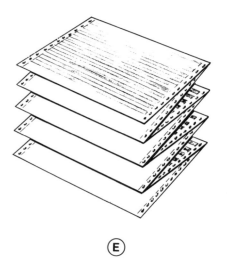

E

ACTIVITIES

Chapter 1 Activities—PRODUCTION OF JOBS

1. Find and label samples of the following type arrangements: justified, flush left, centered, run-around, and artistic.

2. Find and label samples of soft art and mechanical art.

3. Find and label samples of printed jobs from the following printing processes: letterpress/flexography, gravure, photo-offset lithography, and screen printing.

4. Use a T-square to draw a 3″ horizontal line.

5. Use a T-square and triangle to draw 3″ lines at the following angles: 30°, 45°, 60°, and 90°.

6. Use an adjustable triangle to draw 3″ lines at the following angles: 10°, 15°, 35°, 55°, and 75°.

7. Draw a 2″ horizontal line and measure the line in points, picas, and agates.

8. Measure the following typestyles with a type scale to determine the height of the type:
   A. Typestyle
   B. Typestyle
   C. TYPESTYLE

Chapter 2 Activities—COMPREHENSIVE LAYOUT

1. Use eight pieces of 8½″ × 11″ paper to make folding dummies for each of the folds illustrated in Figure 2-3 on page 23.

2. Find printed samples of the following folds:
   A. Letter—6 pages
   B. Accordion—6 pages
   C. French—8 pages

3. Find samples of printed coarse and fine tint screens and label each screen.

4. Preparing an artboard and folding dummy:
   A. Cut an artboard for a job with an 8½″ × 11″ trim size.
   B. Use a T-square to square the artboard to the table.
   C. Find the center of the artboard using the three centering methods: measurement method, centering ruler method, and diagonal corners method.
   D. Make an 8½″ × 11″ trim size guideline in non-photo blue on the artboard.
   E. Use a technical pen to apply trim marks to the artboard.
   F. Apply center marks to the artboard using one of the three methods of indicating center: center marks, marks with C, or register marks.
   G. Use a piece of 8½″ × 11″ paper to make a folding dummy of a letter fold. Measure the depth of each fold and mark the artboard with horizontal fold marks.

Chapter 3 Activities—RULING

1. Measure the weight of the following rules with a rule scale:
   A. _____
   B. _____
   C. _____
   D. _____

2. Draw a 1-point thick, 15-pica long, black horizontal rule using a technical pen.

3. Draw a 1-point thick, 20-pica long, black vertical rule using a technical pen.

4. Draw 1-point thick, 25-pica long rules at the following angles using a technical pen: 30°, 45°, and 60°.

5. Draw 20-point thick, 24½-pica long horizontal rules using a technical pen and a brush and ink.

6. Use white opaque and a brush to shorten by one pica the 1-point horizontal and vertical rules on the artboard.

7. Use white tape or white pressure sensitive paper to make the 20-point rule a 12-point rule on the artboard.

8. Use the scribing and cutting techniques to correct all the angled rules on the artboard.

9. Draw a 2″ × 2″ square on an artboard using a technical pen, T-square, and triangle.

10. Use adhesive tape rules or preprinted adhesive rules to create a 3″ × 3″ square on the artboard. Miter the corners to create a 90° angle using the triangle method and the blade pressure method.

Chapter 4 Activities—SPECIALIZED ART ELEMENTS

1. Draw a 6″ diameter circle using a bow compass with a technical pen adapter.

2. Draw a 10″ diameter circle using a beam compass with a technical pen adapter.

3. Draw a 1″ diameter circle using a circle template and a technical pen.

4. Draw a smooth, irregular-shaped curve using a french curve and technical pen.

5. Create a multi-curved image using a flexible curve and technical pen.

6. Create a 5″ × 5″ border using a preprinted border.

7. Create a 3″ × 4″ curved border using preprinted adhesive rules and elbows.

8. Create a 4″ × 5″ curved border using a technical pen.

9. Create a 6″ × 8″ ornate border using a preprinted adhesive border.

10. Select or draw a line art image, and add texture to the image by applying an adhesive tint screen.

Chapter 5 Activities—TYPOGRAPHY

1. Collect samples of typestyles with a tall x-height and short x-height. Compare the readability of the typestyles.

2. Collect samples of typestyles with shortened, elongated, and moderate length ascenders and descenders. Compare the readability of the typestyles.

3. Collect samples of body copy set in all uppercase characters and in upper- and lowercase characters. Compare the readability of the body copy.

4. Collect samples of good and poor letterspacing. Compare the readability of the copy.

5. Collect samples of good and poor wordspacing. Compare the readability of the copy.

6. Collect samples of kerned copy and copy that is not visibly kerned. Compare the readability of the copy.

7. Collect samples of body copy containing moderate leading, too much leading, and too little leading. Compare the readability of the body copy.

8. Collect samples of body copy containing each of the following type arrangements: justified, flush right, flush left, centered, run-around, and artistic. Compare the readability of the body copy.

9. Collect samples of the following type classifications: serif, sans serif, script or cursive, textletter, and decorative. Compare the readability of each type classification.

Chapter 6 Activities—INKED AND HAND-SET TYPE

1. Set a headline using a template and lettering device.

2. Set two headlines applying adhesive type, one using the headline setter method and one using the headline template method. Note the ease of application of each process.

3. Create one line of adhesive type for each of the following: cut, extended, overlapped, and textured appearances. Note the ease of application of each process.

4. Set a headline using transfer type. Note the ease of application of the process.

Chapter 7 Activities—TYPE AND ILLUSTRATIONS

1. Paste up a block of copy to an artboard using rubber cement. After the rubber cement has dried, remove the block of copy with rubber cement thinner. Note the ease of application and removal of rubber cement.

2. Paste up a block of copy to an artboard using wax. After burnishing the block of copy, remove the block of copy with rubber cement thinner. Note the ease of application and removal of wax.

3. Paste up five blocks of copy to an artboard using the following adhesives: paste, liquid glue, glue stick, dry-mount tissue, and double-sided adhesive material. After each block of copy has dried, remove the copy from the artboard. Note and compare the ease of application and removal of each of the adhesives.

4. Paste up a sheet of 8½″ × 11″ typewritten copy to an artboard using spray adhesive. After burnishing, remove the copy from the artboard. Note the ease of application and removal of the copy from the artboard.

5. Apply column type to an artboard.

6. Apply circular type to an artboard.

7. Apply copy to an artboard and an overlay using the overlay method.

8. Apply reverse type to an artboard.

9. Attach a tissue overlay to an artboard and mark it for production.

Chapter 8 Activities—CAMERA COPY

1. Collect samples of printed halftones. Indicate the highlight, midtone, and shadow dots in each halftone.

2. Collect samples of line copy containing various densities. Reproduce the copy to equalize the density using the photomechanical transfer (PMT) process.

3. Create a fine line copy test board and reproduce it at 100%, 75%, 50%, and 25%. Compare the reproduction quality of the test board of each percentage.

4. Reproduce copy containing multiple cutlines through sidelighting and backlighting. Compare the reproduction quality of each film negative.

5. Create a color test board containing various ink colors. Compare the reproduction quality of each ink.

6. Reproduce a prescreened halftone containing a standard 10% highlight dot and a 90% shadow dot onto negative film. Record the reproduction quality of the dots on the negative in the highlight and shadow areas.

7. Reproduce a manipulated prescreened halftone containing a 20% highlight dot and a 80% shadow dot onto negative film. Record the reproduction quality of the dots on the negative in the highlight and shadow areas.

8. Compare the reproduction quality of the standard prescreened halftone with the reproduction quality of the manipulated prescreened halftone.

Chapter 9 Activities—COLOR AND IMPOSITION

1. Collect samples of printed pieces using flat colors.

2. Collect samples of printed pieces using process colors.

3. Collect samples of printed pieces with color elements in hairline register. Explain how the job would be prepared in the paste-up process.

4. Collect samples of printed pieces with color elements in commercial register. Explain how the job would be prepared in the paste-up process.

5. Collect samples of printed pieces with color elements in nonregister. Explain how the job would be prepared in the paste-up process.

6. Create a folding dummy and imposition layout for an 8-page newsletter. Indicate the printer's spreads and reader's spreads for the dummy and the layout.

7. Collect samples of printed pieces with the following binding methods: saddle stitching, side stitching, adhesive binding, and mechanical binding. Explain the advantages and disadvantages of each binding method.

Chapter 10 Activities—DESIGN SPECIFICATIONS

1. Collect samples of printed pieces that use each of the design principles. Explain the use of the major design principle in each piece.

2. Select a sample of a printed piece containing color. Draw a thumbnail sketch and rough and comprehensive layouts to represent the development of the plan for the printed piece.

3. Collect samples of pieces printed on each of the paper grades. Explain how the job would be prepared in the paste-up process.

4. Collect samples of printed pieces on the four types of coated stocks. Compare the reproduction quality of the type and halftones on each printed piece.

Chapter 11 Activities—PHOTOGRAPHIC DESIGN

1. Collect samples of printed pieces containing photographs representing the following: montage, manipulated image, extended image, textured photograph, anamorphic image, silhouette image, and ghost image.

2. Select a sample printed piece containing one of the photographic enhancement methods. Explain how the job would be prepared for reproduction.

3. Use the diagonal line method to scale a photograph.

4. Use the mathematical method of scaling to calculate the size of an image at 25% of the original size.

Chapter 12 Activities—DESKTOP PUBLISHING SYSTEMS

1. Use a roller mouse and optical mouse to input data and commands. Compare the ease of use of each mouse.

2. Use a keyboard and mouse to input data and commands. Compare the ease of use of the keyboard to the mouse.

3. Use an OCR scanner to scan in text. Compare the quality of the input to the output of the text. Explain the advantages and disadvantages of using an OCR scanner to input text.

4. Scan line art into a computer using a graphics scanner. Output the line art on a laser printer and compare the quality of the output to the original. Explain the advantages and disadvantages of using a graphics scanner to input images.

5. Output an image containing text and graphics on a dot matrix printer, laser printer, and an imagesetter. Compare the quality of the output of each image.

6. Output a line image on a laser printer and pen plotter. Compare the accuracy and quality of each image.

7. Create a document containing a headline, body copy, and graphics using a wordprocessing program, paint program, draw program, and page layout program. Compare the ease of use and output quality of each program.

Chapter 13 Activities—DESKTOP PUBLISHING APPLICATIONS

1. Prepare a layout containing a headline, body copy, and graphics using the traditional paste-up process. Create the same layout using a page layout program on a computer. Compare the steps taken in each process.

2. Produce a tint screen test board from a page layout program by creating seven to 10 boxes containing different tint percentages. Label each box and output the test board on a laser printer, dot matrix printer, and imagesetter. Compare the percentage and dpi of each box.

3. Use a paint program to create textured type. Note the ease of use of the program and the quality of the output.

4. Collect samples of printed pieces produced through a desktop publishing system. Observe and compare the typestyles and size of the text and headlines. Comment on the readability of each.

5. Collect samples of printed pieces produced through a desktop publishing system. Observe and compare the letterspacing and wordspacing. Comment on the readability of each and explain how poor letterspacing and wordspacing are improved.

6. Collect samples of printed pieces produced through a desktop publishing system. Observe the hyphenation of the text. Explain how poor hyphenation is improved.

7. Scan a continuous tone photograph with a graphics scanner and a software with gray-scale image capabilities. Manipulate the image on the screen to match as close to the original as possible. Output the image on a laser printer and comment on the quality of the reproduction as it compares to the original.

8. Color separate a spot color job using a page layout program. Comment on the ease of use and quality of the separation output.

Chapter 14 Activities—POSTAL REGULATIONS

1. Collect samples of correctly and incorrectly addressed mail. Explain how the incorrectly addressed mail should be corrected to comply with postal regulations.

2. Collect samples of a variety of envelopes. Measure each envelope and indicate if it complies with the general mail regulations for envelopes.

3. Collect samples of a variety of self-mailers. Indicate if each self-mailer complies with the self-mailer regulations.

4. Collect samples of a variety of mail pieces containing barcodes for mail sorting. Indicate if each mail piece complies with the regulations regarding barcode positioning.

5. Select a mail piece containing a Zip + 4 system code. Explain the significance of each digit in the Zip + 4 system code.

6. Select a piece of business reply mail. Identify the permit number, facing identification mark, horizontal identification bars, the NO POSTAGE NECESSARY endorsement, the BUSINESS REPLY legend, the POSTAGE WILL BE PAID endorsement, and the address.

Chapter 15 Activities—FORMS DESIGN AND LAYOUT

1. Collect printed samples of each of the following forms: flat form, pegboard, unit set, salesbook, and continuous form. Explain the advantages and disadvantages of each form.

2. Choose a sample form and draw a forms layout indicating the position of the text and graphics and binding information.

3. Choose a sample of a flat form and label the following zones: identification, instructions, introduction, body, and closing.

4. Collect samples of forms containing well-planned character spacing and linespacing, and poorly planned character spacing and linespacing. Explain how each form was planned.

5. Collect samples of forms with the following entry formats: box design, on-line, under-line, columning, and ballot box. Explain how each form was planned.

6. Collect samples of forms with proper and improper typestyles and type sizes. Explain why the typestyles and type sizes of one form are more readable than the other.

7. Collect samples of forms with the following graphic elements: rules, curved corners, tint screens, and textures. Explain how the graphic elements improve the readability of the forms.

8. Collect samples of forms with carbon spots and carbon stripes. Explain the benefits of using carbon spots and stripes.

9. Collect samples of forms using carbonless paper. Explain the benefits of using carbonless paper.

PROJECTS

The twelve projects that follow provide practical, hands-on experience in using tools, materials, equipment, and techniques covered throughout the text. Skills for general paste-up, keylining, applying adhesive type and other graphic elements, inking, copyfitting and proofreading, creating folding dummies, indicating halftones, color separating by the overlay and indicated methods, designing layouts, photo editing, marking mechanicals with production instructions for the printer, etc. are developed by working through these projects. Accuracy, neatness, and cleanness of work must always be considerations when completing each project. A project checklist on page 228 is given as a quality control and self-check measure. Note the various project elements that must be considered before and while doing the projects. Each project element on the project checklist, as it applies to each project, should be checked off to ensure the best quality job possible. The projects are as follows:

1. Grid-Chart
2. Certificate
3. Copyfitting and Proofreading
4. Logo
5. Calendar
6. Halftone Position
7. Flat Color and Imposition
8. Process Color
9. Food Ad
10. Photographic Editing
11. Business Reply Mail
12. Form Design

The following is a list of tools and materials needed for most projects:

1. T-square
2. Ruler
3. Non-photo blue pen or pencil
4. Art knife
5. Masking or drafting tape
6. Rubber cement or wax
7. Tissue for overlays
8. 1-point technical pen and ink
9. Brush and correction fluid
10. Triangle

Also given with each project is a list of tools/materials specifically for that project.

PROJECT CHECKLIST

PROJECT ELEMENTS	PROJECTS CHECKED											
GENERAL	1	2	3	4	5	6	7	8	9	10	11	12
Artboard												
Cleanness												
2″ border all sides												
Guidelines												
Non-photo blue lines												
Straightness												
Accurate measurements												
Inked Rules												
Straightness												
Accurate line weights and lengths												
Correction techniques												
Adhesive Rules												
Straightness												
Accurate line weights and lengths												
Correction techniques												
Headline Copy												
Straightness												
Cleanness of cuts												
Accurate positioning												
Body Copy												
Straightness												
Cleanness of cuts												
Accurate positioning												
Accurate column lengths												
Illustrations												
Cleanness of cuts												
Accurate positioning												
Tissue Overlay												
Securely attached												
Correct instructions												
Overall Condition												
Neatness												
Accuracy												
Cleanness												
SPECIALTY												
Curved Corner Borders												
Corner weight matches rule weight												
Accurate positioning												
Neatness of adhesive												
Curved Type												
Cleanness of cuts												
Accurate positioning												
Neatness												
Design												
Design principles applied												
Quality of thumbnails												
Quality of rough layout												
Quality of comprehensive layout												
Photographs												
Proper cropping and scaling techniques												
Effective photo editing												

Project 1: Grid-Chart

Tools/Materials:

1. Artboard
2. Paintbrush and india ink
3. 3-point adhesive ruling
4. 6-point flexible tape
5. Acetate overlay
6. Register marks

Procedure:

1. Measure the layout for position of elements.
2. Sketch in the grid-chart rules in non-photo blue on the artboard.
3. Ink all the 1-point rules.
4. Ink the block for reversing out "SPECTRA."
5. Apply the 3-point adhesive rules.
6. Create the irregular curve with the 6-point flexible tape.
7. Paste up copy on the artboard.
8. Apply register marks on the artboard.
9. Attach the acetate overlay to the artboard.
10. Apply register marks to the overlay and paste up copy to be reversed out.
11. Attach tissue and write the full production instructions on the tissue.

TRIM SIZE: 8½" × 11"
1 COLOR: BLUE

Spectra Industries

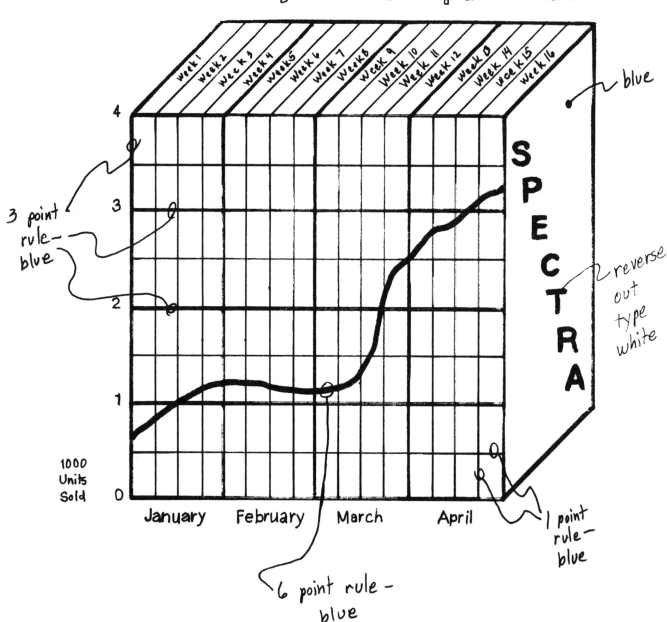

Spectra Industries

Analysis of Computer Sales

S		
P	January	0
E	February	1
C	March	2
T	April	3
R	1000	4
A	Units	
	Sold	

Week 1	Week 2	Week 3	Week 4	Week 5
Week 6	Week 7	Week 8	Week 9	Week 10
Week 11	Week 12	Week 13	Week 14	Week 15	Week 16

Project 2: Certificate

Tools/Materials:

1. Artboard
2. Ornate adhesive border material (if not available, use border copy provided)
3. Compass with 1-point technical pen
4. Coated stock
5. Circle template
6. Adhesive texture screen

Procedure:

1. Measure the layout for position of elements.
2. Sketch in guidelines in non-photo blue on the artboard.
3. Use ornate adhesive border material or border copy provided to create the ornate border.
4. Ink a large circle using the compass.
5. Rule 1-point lines in the circle.
6. Create a rectangular box on the coated stock.
7. Ink a circle using the circle template to create the curved corners for the curved corner box.
8. Cut the circle into quadrants.
9. Paste up the curved corners (quadrants) on the rectangular box.
10. Paste up the rectangular box over the circle as shown in the layout.
11. Apply adhesive texture screens.
12. Paste up copy.
13. Attach tissue and write the full production instructions on the tissue.

TRIM SIZE: 8½" × 11"

GOLD

60%
BLACK

SATERN

SCIENTIFIC

Certificate of Completion
on this day of _____

Awarded to: _____

For the completion of course _____

ALL TYPE
100% BLACK

Certificate of Completion

on the day of _____

Awarded to: _____

For the completion of course _____

SATERN

SCIENTIFIC

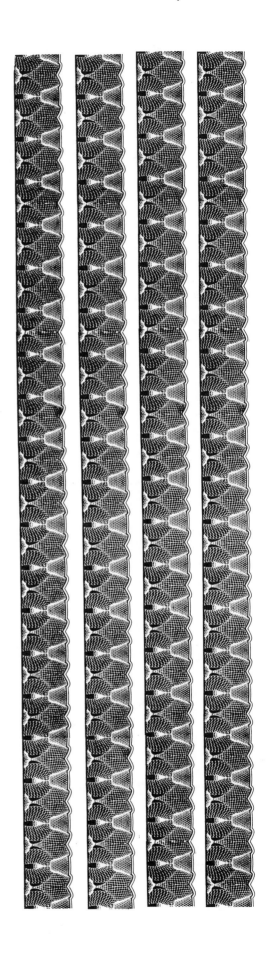

Project 3: Copyfitting and Proofreading

Tools/Materials:

1. Red ink pen
2. Line gauge
3. Paper

Procedure—Copyfitting to fit space:

Note: Refer to the CPP chart given for typestyles and point sizes.

1. Copyfit the given paragraph to fit a space of 20 picas × 12 picas, with a 1-pica margin on all sides.
2. Draw a layout of the space.
3. Select a typestyle, point size, leading, and line length to fit the space.
4. Write type specifications in the margin.

Procedure—Copyfitting to find required space:

1. Copyfit the given paragraph to determine space requirements by using the CPP chart. The typestyle is Times Roman, the point size is 10, leading is 11 point, and line length is 24 picas.
2. Determine linespacing with a line gauge.
3. Indicate point size, typestyle, leading, and line length near the paragraph copy.
4. Draw a layout of the required space on a separate sheet of paper.

Procedure—Proofreading:

1. Proofread the paragraph marked "TYPESET COPY" against the paragraph marked "ORIGINAL COPY."
2. Mark the changes with red ink on the typeset copy using proofreaders' marks.

Typestyle (name)	Characters Per Pica (CPP) of selected typestyle				
Point Size	8	9	10	11	12
Bernhard Modern	3.59		2.99		2.54
Bookman	3.11	2.88	2.60	2.37	2.21
Caledonia	3.12	2.87	2.63	2.44	2.26
Cheltenham	3.56	3.20	2.99	2.72	2.53
Helvetica Medium	3.25	2.90	2.65	2.40	2.26
Helvetica Bold	3.00	2.65	2.43	2.26	2.05
Optima	3.28	2.93	2.66	2.43	2.26
Times Roman	3.47	3.10	2.80	2.62	2.44

COPYFITTING TO FIT SPACE

Unusual effects can be reproduced with flat color in the reproduction of photographs. One ink may be used to print the image, creating a halftone, or two inks may be used, creating a duotone. Even three inks may be used, although not very common, to create a tritone. These photographic images, although creating a range of tone combinations, do not appear as a 4-color process reproduction. Duotones and tritones are used to enhance the density of the reproduction and are a good choice when the budget does not allow for process colors.

COPYFITTING TO FIND REQUIRED SPACE

Metallic inks, fluorescent inks, and opaque inks are all flat colors. These colors and any colors that cannot be reproduced by combining the process colors are chosen from a flat color selector. Process colors can often be combined to create a certain flat color; however, it is costly to produce a certain color by using process colors because four inks instead of one are used.

PROOFREADING COPY

ORIGINAL COPY

The following are basic tools and materials a graphic artist typically needs on a day-to-day basis: light or drafting table, T-square, art knife, compass, circle template, irregular curves, masking or drafting tape, technical pens, india ink, white opaque, non-photo blue pen or pencil, pencil sharpener, triangles--30°-60° and 45° or adjustable, wax or rubber cement, rubber cement thinner dispenser, color markers or pencils, and line and type gauges.

TYPESET COPY

The following are basic tools and materals a graphic artist typically needs in a day-today basics: light, or drafting table, t-square, art knife, compass, circle template, iregular curves masking or drafting tape, technical pens, India ink, white opaque, non-photo blue pen or pencil, pencil sharpener, triangles-30°-60° and 45° or adjustable, wax or rubber cement, rubber cement thinner dispenser, colored markers or pencils, and line and type gauge.

Project 4: Logo

Tools/Materials:

1. Artboard
2. 96-point sans serif adhesive type
3. 18-point serif adhesive type
4. Headline setter
5. Adhesive rules (determine rule weights from layout)

Procedure:

1. Cut and align the sans serif adhesive type on the artboard to create a logo that looks as close as possible to the logo in the layout.
2. Use the headline setter to align the serif adhesive type.
3. Add adhesive rules.
4. Attach tissue and write color instructions on the tissue.

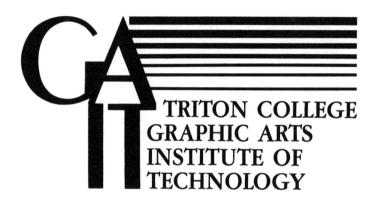

Project 5: Calendar

Tools/Materials:

1. Two artboards
2. Stock for folding dummy
3. Circle template
4. Red ink pen
5. 10%, 20%, 30% tint screens

Procedure:

1. Make a folding dummy according to the layout.
2. Mark all page numbers in non-photo blue on the folding dummy.
3. Lay out front and back artboards, indicating trim, center, and fold marks.
4. Draw concentric circles for the cover, using the circle template and 1-point technical pen.
5. Ink the 1-point rules for "NOTES" for pages 4 through 15, following the comprehensive layout for rule length and number of rules.
6. Indicate reverse color blocks with a red keyline.
7. Center and paste up each month's heading for reversing out.
8. Align and paste up "HOLIDAYS" copy.
9. Paste up "PHONE NUMBERS" copy.
10. Paste up calendar copy.
11. Paste up "NOTES" copy to align with the 1-point rules.
12. Paste up circular type on the cover.
13. Apply adhesive screens to the concentric circles.
14. Attach tissue and write the full production instructions on the tissue.

TRIM SIZE   8" × 7"
FINAL SIZE   2" × 3½"

16 page / parallel fold
2 R/ angles

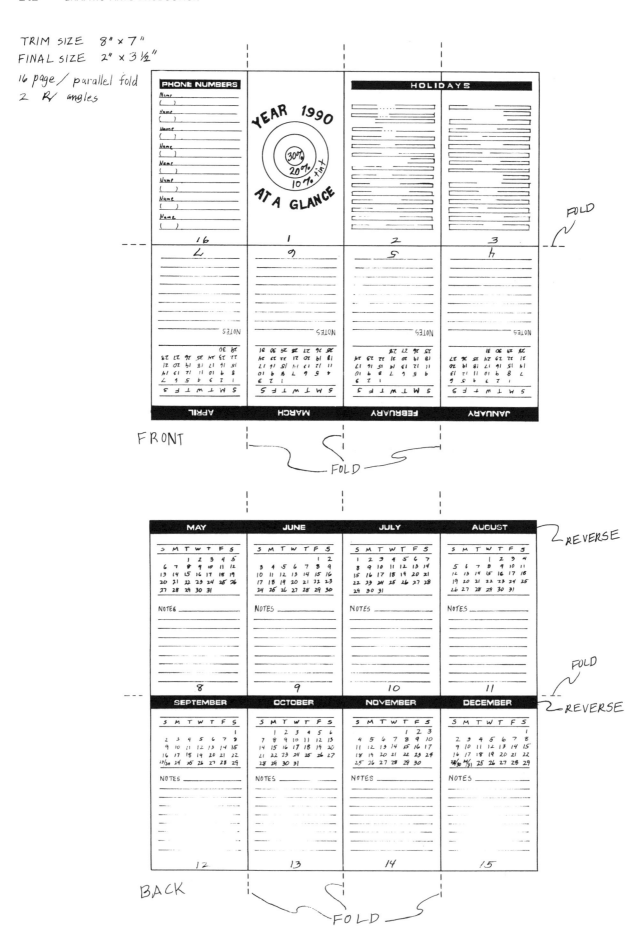

FRONT

FOLD

BACK

FOLD

REVERSE

FOLD

REVERSE

YEAR 1990

AT A GLANCE

HOLIDAYS

PHONE NUMBERS

Name_____
(   )_____

Name_____
(   )_____

Name_____
(   )_____

Name_____
(   )_____

Name_____
(   )_____

Name_____
(   )_____

Name_____
(   )_____

Name_____
(   )_____

January 1 . . . . . . New Year's Day
January 15 . . . Martin Luther King Day (Observed)
February 12 . . Lincoln's Birthday
February 14 . . . . Valentine's Day
February 19 . . . Presidents' Day
February 22 . . . . Washington's Birthday
February 28 . . . . Ash Wednesday
March 17 . . . . . St. Patrick's Day
April 8 . . . . Palm Sunday
April 10 . . . . Passover
April 13 . . . . Good Friday
April 14 . . . . Easter Sunday
May 13 . . . . Mother's Day
May 19 . . . . . Armed Forces Day
May 28 . . . . Memorial Day (Observed)
June 14 . . . . Flag Day
June 17 . . . . Father's Day
July 4 . . . . . . Independence Day
September 3 . . . . Labor Day
September 20 . . Rosh Hashanah
September 29 . . . . . Yom Kippur
October 8 . . . . . . Columbus Day (Observed)
October 31 . . . . Halloween
November 6 . . . . . . Election Day
November 11 . . . . Veterans Day
November 22 . . Thanksgiving Day
December 12 . . . . Hanukkah
December 25 . . . . Christmas

JANUARY

S	M	T	W	T	F	S
	1	2	3	4	5	6
7	8	9	10	11	12	13
14	15	16	17	18	19	20
21	22	23	24	25	26	27
28	29	30	31			

FEBRUARY

S	M	T	W	T	F	S
				1	2	3
4	5	6	7	8	9	10
11	12	13	14	15	16	17
18	19	20	21	22	23	24
25	26	27	28			

MARCH

S	M	T	W	T	F	S
				1	2	3
4	5	6	7	8	9	10
11	12	13	14	15	16	17
18	19	20	21	22	23	24
25	26	27	28	29	30	31

APRIL

S	M	T	W	T	F	S
1	2	3	4	5	6	7
8	9	10	11	12	13	14
15	16	17	18	19	20	21
22	23	24	25	26	27	28
29	30					

MAY

S	M	T	W	T	F	S
		1	2	3	4	5
6	7	8	9	10	11	12
13	14	15	16	17	18	19
20	21	22	23	24	25	26
27	28	29	30	31		

JUNE

S	M	T	W	T	F	S
					1	2
3	4	5	6	7	8	9
10	11	12	13	14	15	16
17	18	19	20	21	22	23
24	25	26	27	28	29	30

JULY

S	M	T	W	T	F	S
1	2	3	4	5	6	7
8	9	10	11	12	13	14
15	16	17	18	19	20	21
22	23	24	25	26	27	28
29	30	31				

AUGUST

S	M	T	W	T	F	S
			1	2	3	4
5	6	7	8	9	10	11
12	13	14	15	16	17	18
19	20	21	22	23	24	25
26	27	28	29	30	31	

SEPTEMBER

S	M	T	W	T	F	S
						1
2	3	4	5	6	7	8
9	10	11	12	13	14	15
16	17	18	19	20	21	22
23/30	24	25	26	27	28	29

OCTOBER

S	M	T	W	T	F	S
	1	2	3	4	5	6
7	8	9	10	11	12	13
14	15	16	17	18	19	20
21	22	23	24	25	26	27
28	29	30	31			

NOVEMBER

S	M	T	W	T	F	S
				1	2	3
4	5	6	7	8	9	10
11	12	13	14	15	16	17
18	19	20	21	22	23	24
25	26	27	28	29	30	

DECEMBER

S	M	T	W	T	F	S
						1
2	3	4	5	6	7	8
9	10	11	12	13	14	15
16	17	18	19	20	21	22
23/30	24/31	25	26	27	28	29

NOTES

NOTES

NOTES

NOTES

NOTES

NOTES

NOTES

NOTES

NOTES

NOTES

NOTES

NOTES

Project 6: Halftone Position

Tools/Materials:

1. Two artboards
2. Stock for folding dummy
3. Red ink pen

Procedure:

1. Make a folding dummy according to the layout.
2. Lay out front and back artboards, indicating trim and fold marks.
3. Paste up halftones in position.
4. Paste up copy.
5. Mark the halftones for position only.
6. Attach tissue and write the full production instructions on the tissue.

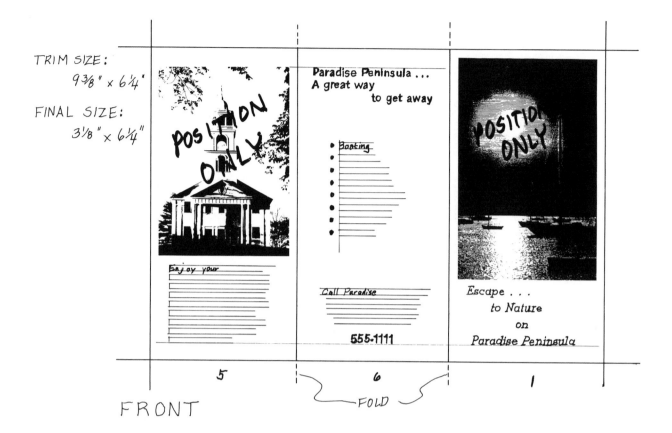

TRIM SIZE:
9⅜" × 6¼"

FINAL SIZE:
3⅛" × 6¼"

Paradise Peninsula...
A great way
to get away

• Boating

Call Paradise

555-1111

Escape . . .
to Nature
on
Paradise Peninsula

5

6

1

FOLD

FRONT

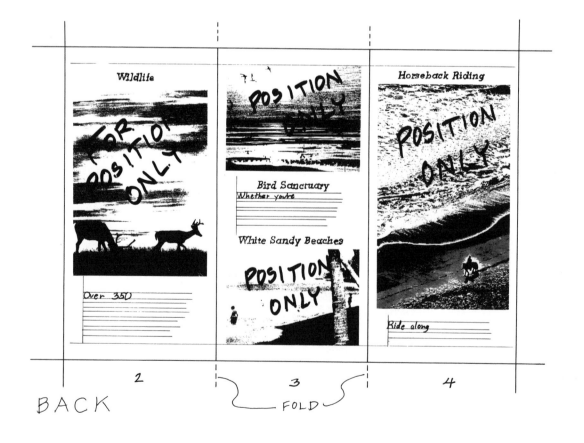

Wildlife

Over 350

Bird Sanctuary
Whether you're

White Sandy Beaches

Horseback Riding

Ride along

2

3

4

FOLD

BACK

Escape . . .
to Nature
on
Paradise Peninsula

Wildlife

Over 350 species of animals live on Paradise Peninsula. Watch the deer feed at sunset and listen to the harmony of the calls of the other wildlife.

Bird Sanctuary

Whether you're a bird-watcher or sunbather, there are miles and miles of blue waterfront and white sandy beaches.

White Sandy Beaches

Horseback Riding

Ride along the 26-mile beach trail in peace and tranquility.

Enjoy your stay at Paradise Peninsula's historic Hideaway Inn. This 36-room inn has all the comforts of home. Each luxurious room has a sauna, king-size waterbed, cable television, refrigerator packed with food and drink, and much, much more.

- Boating
- Swimming
- Waterskiing
- Bird-watching
- Horseback riding
- Scuba diving
- Sunbathing
- Fishing

**Paradise Peninsula . . .
A great way
to get away**

Call Paradise Peninsula today for more information and reservations. Our 24-hour telephone number is

555-1111

Project 7: Flat Color and Imposition

Tools/Materials:

1. Four artboards (for reader's spread)
2. Stock for folding dummy
3. Circle template
4. Ruby film or acetate and masking film
5. Register marks

Procedure:

1. Make a folding dummy according to the layout.
2. Lay out four artboards, indicating trim, center, and fold marks.
3. Rule 1-point boxes with curved corners for pages 2 through 8.
4. Paste up text and line art to print in black on the artboard.
5. Paste up prescreened halftones on the base art, noting position of each halftone for bleeds.
6. Trim halftones to fit rounded corners.
7. Apply register marks on the artboard.
8. Attach ruby film or acetate and masking film.
9. Cut the ruby or masking film for blue tints.
10. Paste up text and line art to print blue on the overlay.
11. Attach tissue and write the full production instructions on the tissue.

Mom...
I'm bored!

Do you hear this from your child?

Put a smile on your child's face with

from the

Village Park District

The Village Park District has programs for every child!

- Infant and Toddler Parent/Child Programs

- Swimming

- Gymnastics

- Horseback Riding

- Family Days

- Gardening

- Cooking

- Supervised Play

- Summer Camp for Infant–12 years

- Field Trips

- Special Holiday Events

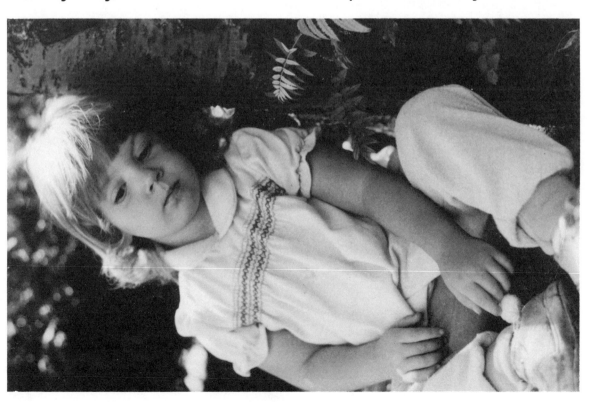

SUMMER PROGRAM

- Summer Day Camp I (3–5 yrs)
- Summer Day Camp II (6–9 yrs)
- Summer Day Camp III (10–15 yrs)
- Overnight Pioneer Camp (10–15 yrs)
- Diving Team (10–18 yrs)
- Swim Team (9–18 yrs)
- Volleyball Team (12–18 yrs)
- Arts and Crafts Fair (3–18 yrs)
- Archery (9–18 yrs)
- Nature Hikes (9–18 yrs)

WINTER PROGRAM

- Parent/Child Gymnastics (2–5 yrs)
- Parent/Child Tumbling (6 mo–2 yrs)
- Ice-skating (7–18 yrs)
- Sledding (7–12 yrs)
- Hockey Team (9–15 yrs)
- Swim Team (9–18 yrs)
- Cooking for Kids (8–15 yrs)
- Holiday Crafts I (5–7 yrs)
- Holiday Crafts II (8–12 yrs)

The Village
Park District
205 West Greenwood
Village, IL 60013

Phone **692-1801**

For more information on
how to make your
child's life happier and
healthier write or call:

SPRING PROGRAM

- Gardening I   (1–6 yrs)
- Gardening II   (7–12 yrs)
- May Day Picnic   (Family)
- Memorial Day Parade   (7–15 yrs)
- Egg Hunt   (3–10 yrs)
- Flower Art I   (3–6 yrs)
- Flower Art II   (7–10 yrs)

FALL PROGRAM

- Pumpkin Hunt   (2–12 yrs)
- Fall Leaf Art   (8–12 yrs)
- Swim Team   (9–18 yrs)
- Horseback Riding   (9–18 yrs)
- Halloween Haunt   (9–18 yrs)
- Halloween Party   (4–6 yrs)
- Thanksgiving Treat   (5–10 yrs)

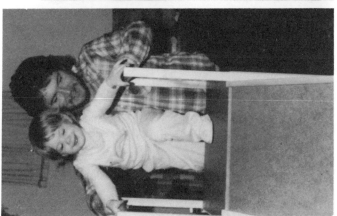

Project 8: Process Color

Tools/Materials:

1. Two artboards
2. Stock for folding dummy
3. Compass
4. Compass with universal attachment
5. Red ink pen
6. Color pencils or markers

Procedure:

Note: Halftone art supplied is for position only. Actual color photographs not supplied in this project, but are supplied to printer in a normal production situation.

1. Make a folding dummy according to the layout.
2. Sketch position of all art on the folding dummy.
3. Sketch position of die cut on the folding dummy.
4. Using the compass with universal attachment, make the die cut on the folding dummy.
5. Make angle cut along top of folding dummy.
6. Lay out artboards, indicating trim and fold marks and bleeds.
7. Mark position of the die cut with red keyline and compass.
8. Paste up text and art on the artboard.
9. Mark halftones for position only.
10. Attach tissue to the artboard.
11. Color in an angled portion on the tissue across page 1.
12. Show details of process color breaks and percentages.
13. Write the full production instructions on the tissue.

TRIM SIZE: 8½" × 11" w/ DIE CUT

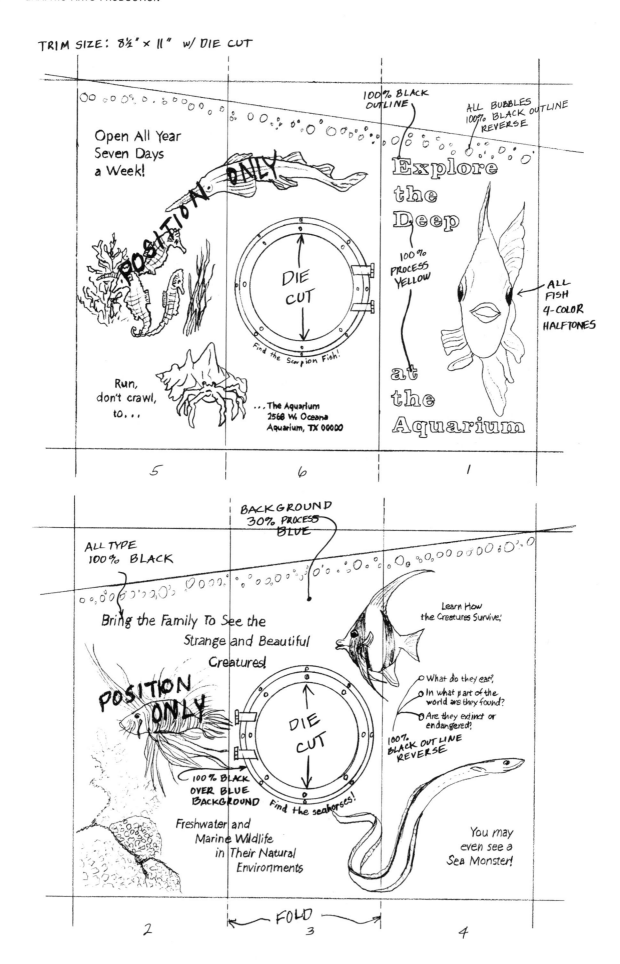

Open All Year
Seven Days
a Week!

POSITION ONLY

100% BLACK
OUTLINE

ALL BUBBLES
100% BLACK OUTLINE
REVERSE

Explore
the
Deep

100%
PROCESS
YELLOW

ALL
FISH
4-COLOR
HALFTONES

DIE
CUT

Find the Scorpion Fish!

Run,
don't crawl,
to...

...The Aquarium
2568 W. Oceana
Aquarium, TX 00000

at
the
Aquarium

5   6   1

BACKGROUND
30% PROCESS
BLUE

ALL TYPE
100% BLACK

Bring the Family To See the
Strange and Beautiful
Creatures!

Learn How
the Creatures Survive!

POSITION
ONLY

DIE
CUT

What do they eat?

In what part of the
world are they found?

Are they extinct or
endangered?

100%
BLACK OUTLINE
REVERSE

100% BLACK
OVER BLUE
BACKGROUND   Find the seahorses!

Freshwater and
Marine Wildlife
in Their Natural
Environments

You may
even see a
Sea Monster!

FOLD

2   3   4

Explore the Deep

at the Aquarium

Open All Year Seven Days a Week!

. . . The Aquarium
2568 W. Oceana
Aquarium, TX 00000

Bring the Family To See the Strange and Beautiful Creatures!

Freshwater and Marine Wildlife in Their Natural Environments

You may even see a Sea Monster!

Run, don't crawl, to. . .

Learn How the Creatures Survive:

⊘ What do they eat?

⊘ In what part of the world are they found?

⊘ Are they extinct or endangered?

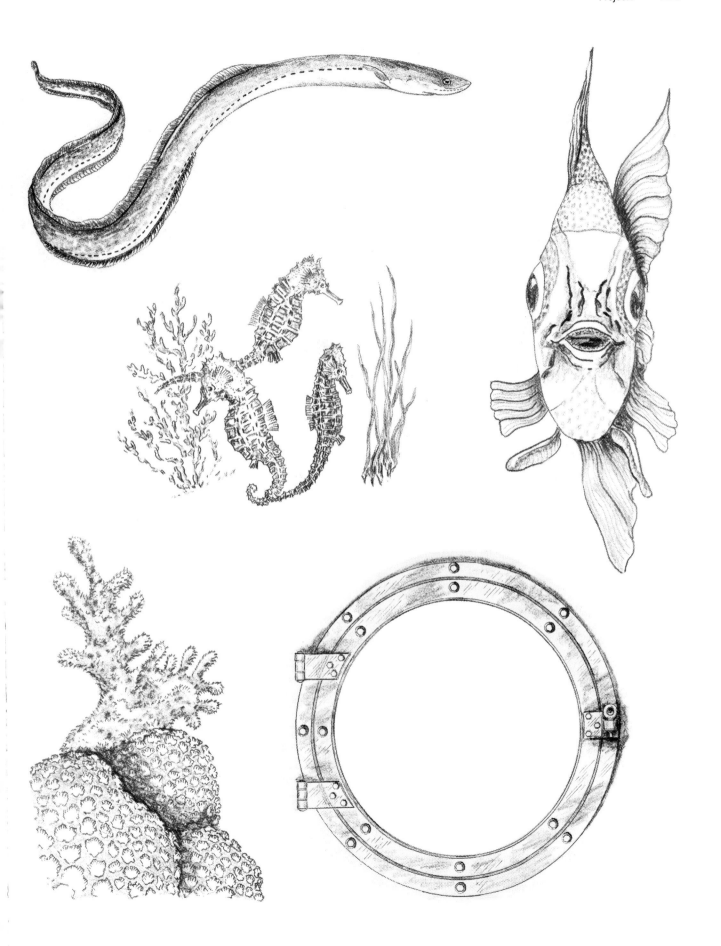

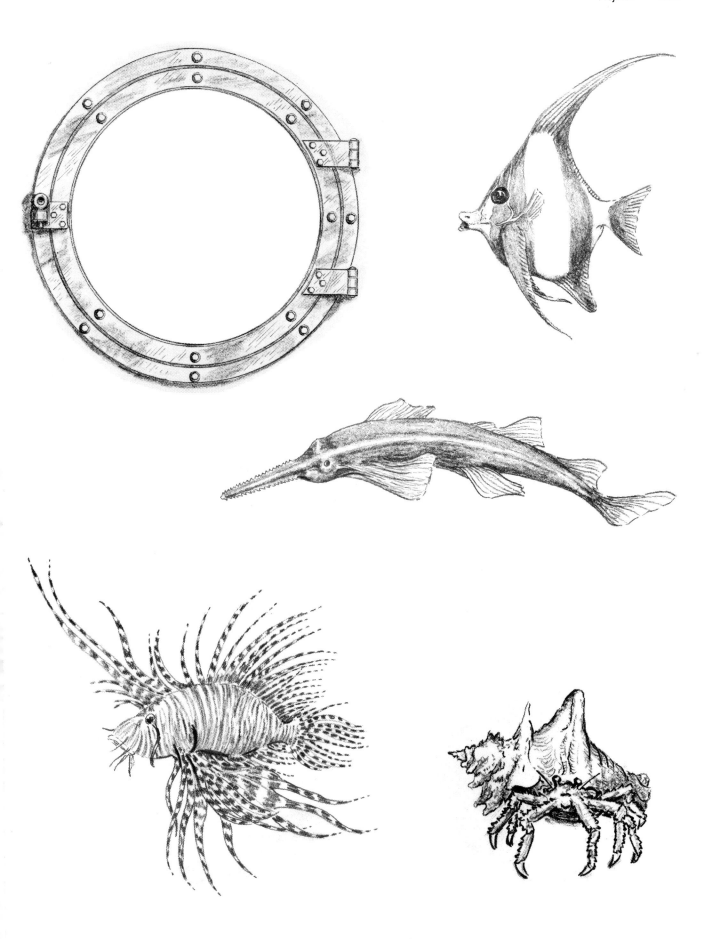

Project 9: Food Ad

Tools/Materials:

1. Artboard for 17″ × 21½″ trim size
2. Paper for thumbnail sketches and rough and comprehensive layouts
3. Color pencils or markers
4. Acetate for overlay
5. Other materials dependent on design

Procedure:

1. Review all copy elements given to create a food ad design. Consider the importance and logical placement of each copy element.
2. Lay out the trim size of the artboard to visualize proportion of page size to elements. Rules and borders may be added if desired.
3. Draw four thumbnail sketches.
4. From the four thumbnail sketches, select the one that would make the most effective ad.
5. Draw a rough layout.
6. Create a comprehensive layout showing color breaks.
7. Ink any rules and borders.
8. Paste up all copy to print in black.
9. Attach acetate to artboard and paste up copy to print in second color on the acetate.
10. Attach tissue and write full production instructions on the tissue.

FROZEN

Whole
Turkeys

lb. **69¢**

Sander's
FINER FOODS

FINEST
QUALITY
MEATS

THE HARVEST IS IN...

Buy at these great

CALIFORNIA
Navel Oranges . . . . 4 lbs. **$1³⁹**

$$\text{CALIFORNIA Navel Oranges} \dots \text{4 lbs.} \quad \$1^{39}$$

MICHIGAN
Blueberries . . . . pt. 1^{29}

FREESTONE
Peaches . . . . lb. 69¢

LARGE BING
Cherries . . . . lb. 89¢

SANTA ROSA
Plums . . . . lb. 98¢

Canada Dry Ginger Ale OR **Tonic Water** . . . . NO RETURN 6-pack 1^{99}

7-UP . . . . NO RETURN 6-pack 2^{19}

RC Cola . . . . NO RETURN 6-pack 1^{99}

Mountain Dew . . . . 12 oz. 6-pack 1^{59}

16 oz. Pop Special

Save 17¢	Save 12¢	Save 32¢	Save 36¢

prices!

This Week's Special

FRESH BAKED
Apple Pie **$2⁶⁹**

SANDER'S OWN
Hot Dog Buns . . . . 8-pack **49¢**

SANDER'S OWN
Sandwich Buns . . . . 6-pack **49¢**

DELI FRESH
Onion Rolls 6-pack **$1¹⁹**

FROM OUR BUTCHER SHOP

DELI SPECIAL
Canadian Bacon .... lb. $2¹⁹

Grade A
Whole Fryers .... CUT UP lb. 69¢

CATCH OF THE DAY

NORTHERN
White Fish .... lb. $1⁵⁹

FRESH
Lake Trout .... lb. $3⁴⁹

QUALITY PRODUCE

Sweet Corn .... ear **12¢**

Cherry Tomatoes .... lb. **89¢**

Cucumbers .... lb. **39¢**

Green Beans .... lb. **79¢**

Spinach .... lb. **89¢**

Yellow Onions ...... 3-lb. bag **$1²⁹**

Acorn Squash .... lb. **99¢**

YOUNG
Asparagus ... lb. $1⁷⁹

FROM OUR BAKERY

Check THESE PRICES!

70% LEAN
Ground Beef .... 3 lbs. or more $1²⁹

LOIN CUT
Porterhouse Steak .... lb. $3⁵⁹

LARGE FRESH
Lamb Shoulder Chops .... lb. $3²⁹

GRAIN FED
Sirloin Steak .... lb. $2⁸⁹

We just can't wait to save you money.

Project 10: Photographic Editing

Tools/Materials:

1. Proportional scale
2. Other materials dependent on photographic editing

Procedure:

1. For photographs A and B, select two of the following three images to create: montage, manipulated image, and extended image. If creating a montage, other photographs or line art may be used.
2. Crop and scale photograph C to fit a head and shoulders image of the girl in a 2⅛″ × 3″ keyline.

PHOTOGRAPH A

National Aeronautics and Space Administration

PHOTOGRAPH B

PHOTOGRAPH C

Project 11: Business Reply Mail

Tools/Materials:

1. Two artboards
2. Stock for folding dummy
3. Red ink pen

Procedure:

1. Make a folding dummy according to the layout.
2. Lay out front and back artboards, indicating trim, fold, and perforation marks.
3. Draw keylines for color bars and bleeds.
4. Paste up text and line art. Be very accurate to ensure that the job conforms to postal regulations.
5. Attach tissue and indicate second color on the tissue as well as the full production instructions.

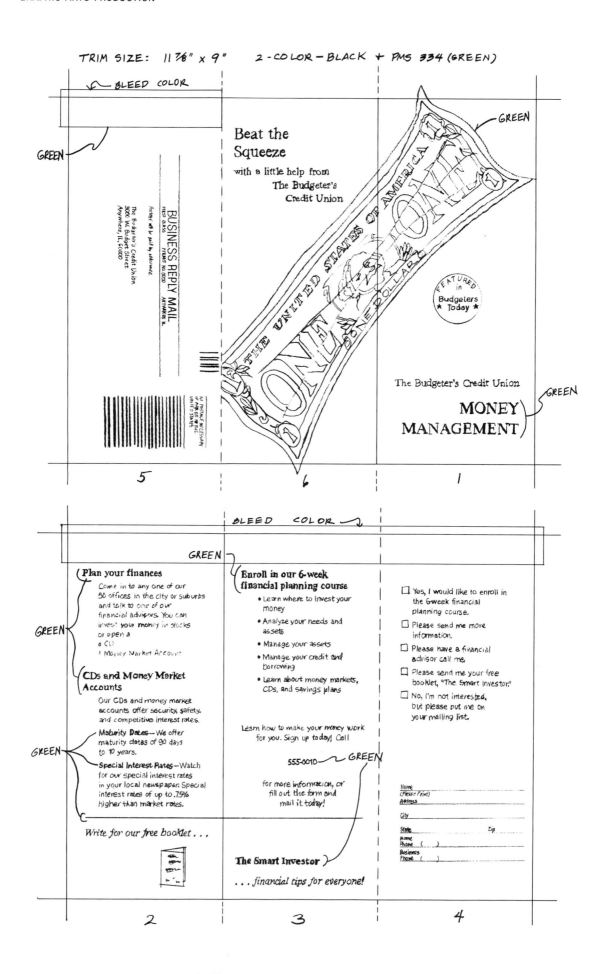

Beat the Squeeze

with a little help from
The Budgeter's
Credit Union

The Budgeter's Credit Union

MONEY MANAGEMENT

Plan your finances

Come in to any one of our 50 offices in the city or suburbs and talk to one of our financial advisors. You can invest your money in stocks or open a
- CD
- Money Market Account

CDs and Money Market Accounts

Our CDs and money market accounts offer security, safety, and competitive interest rates.

Maturity Dates—We offer maturity dates of 90 days to 10 years.

Special Interest Rates—Watch for our special interest rates in your local newspaper. Special interest rates of up to .75% higher than market rates.

Enroll in our 6-week financial planning course

- Learn where to invest your money
- Analyze your needs and assets
- Manage your assets
- Manage your credit and borrowing
- Learn about money markets, CDs, and savings plans

Learn how to make your money work for you. Sign up today! Call

555-0010

for more information, or fill out the form and mail it today!

Write for our free booklet . . .

The Smart Investor

. . . financial tips for everyone!

☐ Yes, I would like to enroll in the 6-week financial planning course.

☐ Please send me more information.

☐ Please have a financial advisor call me.

☐ Please send me your free booklet, "The Smart Investor."

☐ No, I'm not interested, but please put me on your mailing list.

Name
(*Please Print*)
Address

City

State   Zip

Home
Phone   (   )

Business
Phone   (   )

The Smart Investor

BUSINESS REPLY MAIL
FIRST CLASS   PERMIT NO 0000   ANYWHERE IL

Postage will be paid by addressee

FEATURED
in

**Budgeters
Today**

The Budgeter's Credit Union
3000 W. Budget Street
Anywhere, IL 60000

NO POSTAGE NECESSARY
IF MAILED IN THE
UNITED STATES

THE UNITED STATES OF AMERICA

ONE DOLLAR

ONE

Project 12: Form Design

Tools/Materials:

1. Artboard
2. 4-point adhesive ruling
3. Circle template
4. Ink and brush
5. Adhesive type (type size to fit layout) for "JOB ESTIMATE"
6. Circular headline template

Procedure:

1. Sketch in all guidelines for rules and copy according to the layout.
2. Ink 1-point grid rules.
3. Ink all curved corner boxes. Use the $3/8''$ diameter circle on the circle template for the curved corners.
4. Ink 18-point rule.
5. Use adhesive ruling to create 4-point rules.
6. Paste up all copy.
7. Set the headline in a semicircle using adhesive type and the circular headline template according to the layout.
8. Attach tissue and write the full production instructions on the tissue.

TRIM SIZE 8½" x 11"
1/C 100% BLACK

↕ 9/16"

CUSTOMER ADDRESS

BOXES 3½" x 1¼"

5/8"

PRINTER ADDRESS

JOB ESTIMATE

Estimate Number _____
Date of Estimate _____
Prepared By _____
RE: ☐ Day Work   ☐ Contract   ☐ Extra
    Explanation _____
Job Name/Number _____
Job Location _____
Job Phone _____ Exten. _____
Start Date _____ End Date _____

LEAVE AT
LEAST 1/8"
MARGIN
AT ALL
EDGES.

1 pt.
rule

ADDITIONAL WORK AUTHORIZATION

3/16"

#	MATERIAL	QTY	PRICE EACH	TOTAL PRICE	#	LABOR	RATE	HRS.	TOTAL AMOUNT
1	2 3/16"	3/8"	3/4"	9/16"	3/16"	1 5/8"	7/16"	7/16"	1 3/16"
2									
3									
4									
5	↕ ¼"								
6									
7									
8									
9									
10									
11									
12									
13									
14									
15									
16									

4 pt.
rule

1 pt.
rule

#	MISC OTHER ITEMS	TOTAL AMOUNT
1		
2		
3		
4		
5		

Your Order No. _____ Date _____
Work Ordered By _____
Explanation _____
_____

Estimate Approved By _____

Signature Approval For Quotation Release

ADDITIONAL WORK SUMMARY	
TOTAL MATERIALS	
TOTAL LABOR	
TOTAL MISC.	
TOTAL TAX/PERMIT/INS.	

TOTAL COST	
TAX	
TOTAL BILLING	

CUSTOMER ADDRESS   PRINTER ADDRESS

Estimate Number _____

Date of Estimate _____

Prepared By _____

RE: ☐ Day Work   ☐ Contract   ☐ Extra

   Explanation _____

Job Name/Number _____

Job Location _____

Job Phone _____ Ext. _____

Start Date _____ End Date _____

Your Order No. _____ Date _____

Work Ordered By _____

Explanation _____

_____

_____

_____

Estimate Approved By _____

_____
Signature Approval For Quotation Release

1
2
3
4
5
6
7
8
9
10
11
12
13
14
15
16
1
2
3
4
5

ADDITIONAL WORK SUMMARY

TOTAL MATERIALS

TOTAL LABOR

TOTAL MISC.

TOTAL TAX/PERMIT/INS.

TOTAL COST

TAX

TOTAL BILLING

MATERIAL

QTY.

LABOR

RATE

HRS.

MISC. OTHER ITEMS

\#   \#   \#

PRICE EACH	TOTAL PRICE	TOTAL AMOUNT	TOTAL AMOUNT

ADDITIONAL WORK AUTHORIZATION

GLOSSARY

A

accordion fold: Two or more folds made parallel to each other, but not over and over.

accordion fold

acetate: Transparent sheet made of clear plastic; frequently used to make overlays.

acetate base: Transparent plastic sheet used as a base for photographic films.

across the grain: The direction 90°, or at a right angle, to the paper grain.

adhesive binding: Binding that uses glue to hold the pages of a book together. Signatures are rough-trimmed at the bind margin to improve adhesion.

adhesive type: Pressure-sensitive type printed on transparent sheets of adhesive acetate. Applied by positioning type on the artboard and burnishing it in place.

against the grain: Folding paper at right angles to the direction in which fibers of the sheets tend to lie; also called across-the-grain folding or cross-grain folding. Folding with, not against, the grain is recommended.

American Standard Code for Information Interchange (ASCII): Standard code for raw text to be input or imported into additional computer software programs.

anamorphic image: Photograph enlarged or reduced disproportionately horizontally or vertically.

artboard: Dull white stock that copy elements are pasted up on. May vary in thickness but should be stiff enough to accept copy elements without buckling. Should be cut at least 2″ larger on all sides than final trim size of finished job.

art director: Individual responsible for the development and assembly of elements according to the designer's specifications.

artwork: General term for photographs, drawings, paintings, hand letterings, etc. that are prepared to illustrate printed matter.

ascender: Portion of a lowercase character that extends above the x-height (body) of the letter, for example, b, d, and f.

B

backlight: To illuminate copy from behind the copyboard.

back margin: Space between pages of a job that allows for folding and binding. Size of back margin is generally determined by size of book and method of binding.

barcode: Vertical rules printed on the face of mail to facilitate automated sorting.

baseline: In composition, the line on which the bottom of letters rest, exclusive of descenders that fall below the baseline.

batch program: Computer program that uses coding in the text to define page layout commands. Batch programs do not allow viewing of the page layout before the final output.

beam compass: Instrument that consists of a horizontal beam with two adjustable legs that can be positioned at any point along the beam; used to draw circles larger than 10″ in diameter.

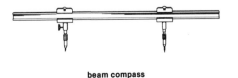

beam compass

benday: Screen pattern (dots, lines, and other textures) on artwork or plates laid in such a way as to obtain various tones and shadings. See *mapping*.

bind: To join pages of a book together with thread, wire, adhesive, or other means; to enclose them in a cover when so specified.

binder: **1.** One who binds books. **2.** Detachable cover into which loose pages or bound books or pamphlets are inserted on rings or posts; contents are easily removed.

bindery: Establishment where books are bound.

bind margin: Gutter or inner margin from the binding to the beginning of the printed area.

black printer: Black negative or plate made for color reproductions to give proper emphasis to neutral tones and detail, as well as print the black copy.

bleed: **1.** Any part of the printed area (usually a photograph or other artwork; never headlines or copy) that extends beyond the trim edge of the page. **2.** Lithographic ink pigment that dissolves in the fountain etch and causes tinting.

body type: Type that is 13 points or smaller and used for the text matter, as distinguished from the headings and display type.

boldface: Heavy-faced type.

border: Printed line or design surrounding an illustration or other printed matter.

bow compass: Instrument that consists of two legs joined at a pivot point, a handle, and an adjustment mechanism; used to draw circles from 3″ to 10″ in diameter.

breakacross image: Elements of a facing page that align across the gutter.

brightness: **1.** The light being reflected by copy to the lens of the process camera. **2.** In paper, the reflectance or brilliance of the paper.

bump exposure: Exposure of white light reflecting off copy, through the lens, and directly onto the film that adds detail in the highlight areas of the halftone.

burnisher: Flat, dull plastic instrument used to transfer letters or rules from pressure-sensitive acetate or to adhere material using a rubbing pressure.

byte: Computer storage unit.

C

calendered paper: Paper that has been glazed during manufacture by passing it through a stack of polished metal rollers, or calenders.

calender rolls: Set or stack of horizontal cast iron rollers at the end of a papermaking machine. The paper is passed between the rolls to increase the smoothness and gloss of its surface.

camera copyboard: The part of a process camera on which copy to be photographed is placed. Usually has a hinged glass cover to hold copy flat and can be tilted to a horizontal position for placing copy.

camera setting: Percentage of reduction or enlargement at which copy is to be photographed to achieve desired size.

carbonizing: Process of creating copies of form entries with carbon and carbonless materials. Three methods include carbon paper, carbon stripe or carbon spot, and carbonless.

caret: Symbol ($\wedge$) used in writing or in proofreading that indicates where a change is to be inserted.

case bound: Book bound with a stiff or hard cover.

cast coating: Paper coating with a high-gloss enamel finish. Cast coated paper is dried under pressure against a polished cylinder.

cast off: To estimate the number of finished pages a given amount of manuscript will be, or the number of characters that will be typeset.

centered type: Type that is mathematically centered on each line, usually headline type.

center marks: Thin, dense black lines approximately $1/2''$ in length placed on mechanical $1/16''$ outside the image area to indicate the center of the trim margin of a page or a form; also used for registration.

center spread: Facing pages in the center of a signature, also called natural spread.

central processing unit (CPU): Part of the computer system that controls the interpretation and execution of instructions (codes).

certified mail: Mail that provides for a record of delivery to be maintained by the post office from which the mail is delivered. The carrier delivering the item obtains a signature from the addressee. There is a charge for certified mail. If a return receipt is requested, an additional fee is charged.

characters per pica (CPP): Decimal value indicating the number of characters that fit into a pica. CPP of a typestyle is used to determine size specifications for a predetermined space. See *copyfit.*

character spacing: Amount of space allowed horizontally for each character on a line.

circle template: Thin piece of plastic or metal with circles of various sizes cut in it; edges of circles should be beveled to prevent ink from bleeding under template.

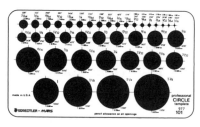

circle template

clay coating: Paper coating that improves the quality of the printing surface. One or both sides of the paper are coated with clay.

close register: Register with little trap allowance, requiring more press printing position accuracy; also called tight register.

coated paper: Paper surfaced with white clay or an acrylic substance to provide a smooth printing sur-face. Coated paper is usually glossy but can also be dull.

coating: 1. Mineral substances such as china clay, blanc fixe, or satin white used to cover the surface of paper, making the coated surface of enameled papers. **2.** In photography and photomechanics, application of varnishes and other mixtures to plates and negatives. **3.** Application of light-sensitive solutions to plate surfaces.

cold type: Text composition prepared for photomechanical reproduction with a computer printer, by hand-lettering, or by photocomposition, not requiring the use of metal lead to form the type. All typesetting not using molten lead is cold type.

color bar: Control strip printed on the edge of a press sheet for visual and densitometer checking of ink color and density.

color separation: 1. In photography, the division of colors of a continuous-tone full color original, each of which is reproduced by a separate printing plate carrying a color. **2.** In lithographic platemaking, separation of colors by handwork performed directly on the printing surface. **3.** Preseparation of colors by using a separate overlay for each color.

compass: Instrument used to draw circles of varying sizes. See *bow compass* and *beam compass.*

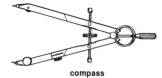

compass

composition: Assembling of characters into words, lines, and paragraphs of text for print reproduction.

comprehensive layout: Rendition of the printed piece in full size, made to look as close to the final printed piece as possible with art and head-line elements drawn in position. Photographs and copy blocks are usually indicated with lines showing size and position of elements.

contact screen: Photographically made halftone film screen approximately .007″ thick and having a dot structure of graded density used in vacuum contact with photographic film.

continuous forms: Forms drilled or punched along outer margin, allowing the forms to be fed through a machine on a sprocket gear.

continuous tone copy: Photographic image that has not been screened and contains gradient tones from black to white.

copy: Photograph, paste-up, art, or other material furnished for reproduction to be copied in printing. Also called *original* because it is from this material that reproduction originates.

copy density: Darkness or light-absorbing ability of copy.

copy dot: To photograph dot for dot; to exactly match previously screened originals.

copyfit: To adjust typeset copy to the space allotted; done by changing space allotment, copy length, and/or type size. See *characters per pica (CPP).*

copywrite: To write a clear, concise message for a job.

cover sheet: Heavy piece of paper used to protect the mechanical.

crop: To opaque, mask, cut, or trim an illustration, or its reproduction, to the required size to fit a specified area.

crop marks: Marks along the margins of an illustration, used to indicate the portion of the illustration to be reproduced.

D

darkroom: Room without white light in which film may be handled without being exposed. Darkrooms have red, green, or yellow safelights, depending on the type of film or paper being processed.

deckle edge: Untrimmed feather edge of a sheet of paper formed where the pulp flows against the deckle.

delete: Instruction to remove a character, word, or other designated matter from copy or film. The delete mark ($\mathscr{S}$) is used to designate the material to be removed.

density: 1. Specific gravity of paper or weight per unit volume. 2. Measure of the degree of blackness. 3. Blackness and weight of type set in phototypesetting.

descender: Portion of a lowercase character that extends below the x-height (body) of the letter, for example, g, j, p, q, and y.

descender

designing: Process in which the job takes on its visual form.

desktop publishing system: Page layout system used to create pages on a personal computer (PC); composed of hardware and software used to produce pages of text and graphics.

die: Design, letters, or pattern cut in metal for stamping book covers or for embossing.

die cut: Special shape cut made from sharp steel rules from printed or unprinted material. Die cuts are used for labels, boxes, containers, etc. Die cutting can be done on flatbed or rotary presses. Die cuts are indicated on mechanical with dashed red keylines.

digitizing: Electronically dividing an image into dark and light points by creating codes that a computer can use. See *scanner.*

direct input: To input data manually into a computer; may be done through use of a keyboard, mouse, stylus, or light pen.

display type: Type that is 14 points or larger.

dot: Individual element of a halftone.

draw program: Computer software program using vector system; creates geometric shapes and a few tint screens.

dummy: 1. Preliminary drawing or layout showing the position of illustrations and text as they are to appear in the final reproduction. 2. Set of blank pages made up in advance to show the size, shape, form, and general style of a printed piece.

duotone: Two-color halftone reproduction from a one-color original, requiring two halftone negatives, for opposite ends of the gray scale, laid at proper screen angles. One plate usually is printed in dark ink, the other in a lighter ink.

E

em (space): Unit of space measurement equal in width to the selected type size; also used as an abbreviation of "pica-em," where the em is equivalent to a 12-point (approximately $\frac{1}{6}$″) em space.

en (space): One-half the width of an em space.

estimate: To compute the approximate cost of a job.

exposure: 1. In platemaking, the exposing of the plate and negative together by a source of light. This hardens the light-sensitive plate coating, which then becomes receptive to ink. 2. In photography, the length of time the camera shutter or diaphragm remains open to admit light for reflecting the image on the film.

F

facing images: Elements on facing pages that mirror each other in position.

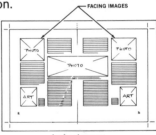

facing images

family: All sizes and weights of one type design; the type may vary in weight, width, or other treatment. For example, a family may include roman, italic, and boldface variations of a typeface.

film: Thin, transparent plastic sheet that is coated with a photographic emulsion. After exposure, it is developed and processed to produce either a negative or a positive.

fine line copy: Type, line illustrations, and rules of 1-point thickness or less.

finish: Surface property of a sheet of paper determined by its contour and gloss.

flash exposure: Exposure of dim yellow light through the contact screen that adds density to shadow areas of the halftone negative.

flat: **1.** In lithography, the assembly of photographic negatives or positives on goldenrod paper, glass, or vinyl acetate from which the printing plate is made. **2.** In photographs, the quality of lacking in contrast.

flat color: Printing two or more colors without overlaying color dots; individual color matching. This differs from process color, which is a blending of four colors to produce a broad range of colors.

flat color inks: Premixed inks used to create a variety of colors, which are selected by the client or designer from a sample book. See *Pantone® Matching System* (*PMS*).

flat form: One-sheet form style; most common and economical form, which is produced using various presses or a photocopier.

flexible curve: Flexible ruler consisting of a lead bar encased in smooth plastic used as a guide to trace curves.

flexible curve

floppy disk: Flat, circular plate with a magnetic surface on which data can be stored by selective polarization of portions of the surface; available as 5¼″ and 3½″ disks. See *hard disk.*

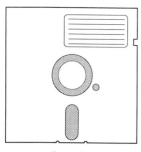

floppy disk

flush left type: Typeset copy that begins evenly along the left margin and ends unevenly along the right margin; ragged right.

flush paragraph: A paragraph with no indention.

flush right type: Typeset copy that begins unevenly along the left margin and ends evenly along the right margin; ragged left.

folding dummy: Sheet of stock folded and marked to indicate how pages are to be arranged. Stock used is recommended to be the same stock selected for the job.

fold marks: Marks added to a negative flat along the margins of a press sheet as a guide for folding.

folio: Page number; may be placed next to the running head or foot.

font: Complete assortment of one typestyle, containing all of the characters needed for general composition.

foot: Bottom of a column, page, or book.

foreign mail: Mail destined for a foreign country.

fourth-class mail: Class of mail that includes domestic parcel post and special catalog mailing, book, and library rates.

french fold: Printing arrangement in which all of the pages are printed on one side or both sides of the sheet; the back side is folded inward before the other folds are made.

full bleed: Image that extends to all four edges of a printed sheet.

G

galley: Typeset material from the typesetter before it has been arranged into final page form.

ghost image: Reproduction of a continuous tone at a lighter percentage of ink coverage.

gloss: Surface quality of paper that reflects light.

goldenrod: Opaque paper used for positioning film to create flats.

goldenrod paper: Specially coated masking paper of yellow or orange color used to assemble and position negatives for exposure onto press plates.

grade: Means of ranking various kinds of paper and cloth.

grain: **1.** In paper, the machine direction in papermaking along which the majority of fibers are aligned. This governs some paper properties such as increased size change with relative humidity across the grain, and better folding qualities along the grain. **2.** In photography, grain is an indication of the relative particle size forming the photographic image, such as fine grain and coarse grain. **3.** Roughened or irregular surface of an offset printing plate.

grain long: Grain stock aligned parallel to the press gripper margin.

grain short: Grain stock aligned perpendicular to the press gripper margin.

graphic arts: In common usage, all components of the printing industry.

graphics software: Software used to produce computer illustrations and line art. See *draw program* and *paint program.*

gravure: Method of intaglio printing using a sunken or depressed surface for the image. The image area consists of wells etched into a copper cylinder of a wrap-around plate. The surface of the cylinder rotates in a bath of ink. Excess ink is wiped off by a flexible steel doctor blade. Ink remaining in the recessed wells forms the image by direct transfer to the image as it passes between the plate and impression cylinders. Gravure is generally used for long press runs because of high platemaking costs.

gray scale: Strip of standard gray tones, ranging from white to black, placed at the side of original copy during photography or beside the negative or positive during plate exposure to measure the tonal range obtained.

gripper: Bar of mechanical fingers on a press that grab the press sheet.

gripper edge: **1.** Leading edge of paper as it passes through a printing press or folding machine. No printing can take place on ³⁄₈″ of the paper on the gripper edge. It is the longer edge of the sheet. **2.** Front edge of a wrap-around plate that is secured to the front clamp of the plate cylinder.

gripper margin: Area at the lead edge of the sheet allotted for the press grippers to hold the sheet. This area is usually not printed on since the grippers smear ink; generally a ³⁄₈″ space.

guidelines: Thin, non-photo blue lines drawn on artboard for reference by a paste-up artist.

guide marks: Cross marks on the offset press plate that indicate trim, center of sheet, or center of plate; sometimes called register marks.

gutter: 1. Space between columns of copy on a page in multi-column composition. **2.** Short for gutter margin.

H

hairline register: Register by joining or butting of two or more colors with no color overlapping.

halftone: Reproduction of a continuous tone original, such as a photograph, in which the image is represented by a series of evenly spaced dots of varying sizes and shapes. Dot areas vary in direct proportion to the intensity of the tones they represent. A halftone screen is placed in front of the negative during photography.

handset type: Type that has been assembled by hand.

hard copy: Any output from a computer, wordprocessor, or typewriter that is readable copy on paper or film.

hard disk: Round platter that electronically stores software program data files; permanent part of the computer system. Hard disk has larger memory capacity than floppy disk. See *floppy disk.*

hardware: In computers, all physical units of a computer, including the keyboard, monitor, and disk drive. See *software.*

head: 1. Top of a page or form. **2.** Heading in text composition.

headline setter: Thin plastic ruler with a series of guidelines used to align type characters; helps in letterspacing or wordspacing adhesive type before it is applied to artboard.

headline setter

headline template: Headline setter with a curved or an irregular shape.

head margin: White space above the first line on a page.

highlight dots: Halftone dots that range from 5% to 30%.

I

imagesetter: Output device that outputs high-resolution type and images (line art and halftones). Creates highest quality reproduction of all output devices used in desktop publishing.

imposition: Alignment of images for press and binding. Laying out of pages in a press form so that they will be in correct sequence after the printed sheet is folded.

india ink: Dense black ink that can be applied with a brush, technical pen, ruling pen, or special fountain pen; used in artwork preparation.

indicia: Mailing permit imprint that is preprinted on the envelope, mailing carton, or directly on the publication if it is not inserted in an envelope or other container.

indirect input: Inputting data electronically into a computer; most common indirect input device in desktop publishing is the scanner.

ink holdout: Paper's ability to resist ink absorption.

input: 1. Data (files or tapes) to be processed by a computer. **2.** Process of transferring data from external storage to internal storage.

input device: Device that allows operator to enter information, or data, into the computer. Input devices include keyboard, mouse, stylus, light pen, and scanner.

in-register: Proper alignment of elements.

intaglio printing: Method of printing from plates or cylinders in which the image is etched or sunken below the surface, such as in steel and copper engraving or gravure. Printing areas on an intaglio printing plate are depressed so that when the entire plate is flooded with ink and then wiped, ink remains in these depressed areas in proportion to their depth.

interactive program: Computer program that allows the user to see the page layout on the computer screen exactly as it will be output as the page is designed.

interface: Computer program that allows two incompatible pieces of computer hardware to communicate with each other.

irregular curve: Clear plastic instrument with a variety of curves along the edges; used to draw curves or irregular shapes.

irregular curve

J

justified type: Lines of type spaced so that the right and left margins are aligned.

justify: To set type or prepare text composition to a specified width or measure so that the left- and right-hand margins of the printed matter are aligned; may be accomplished by adjusting the spacing between words or between words and characters (letterspacing) so as to fill the measure with each full line of type.

K

kern: In typesetting, to adjust the spacing between two characters so they are closer than normal, usually so that part of one letter shape overhangs the following character.

keyline: 1. To paste up copy from galleys, along with illustrations and tables, into finished pages. **2.** Thin black or red lines used to indicate position of elements not directly pasted to the mechanical. **3.** Technique used in copy preparation to handle copy for some simple types of color separation, or for indicating reverses or outlines of background. Artist prepares a tissue overlay outlining different color areas or special effects, which is used as a guide in making the necessary negative flat or flats.

L

layout: 1. Drawing or sketch of a proposed printed piece; the working diagram for a printer to follow. **2.** Short for layout sheet.

leading: Amount of space between lines of type, measured from baseline to baseline; always expressed in points. For example, 8/9 is 8-point type and 9-point leading. This may also be expressed as 8-point type, 1-point leading.

lens: Device, usually glass or quartz, used to focus light in a camera.

lettering pen: Broad, flat tip pen generally used for calligraphy.

letterspacing: Space between type characters; sometimes used to help spread a line of type to fill the measure for justification.

light pen: Hand-held device shaped like a pen used to input information manually into a computer through coordinates and programmed commands.

line copy: Any copy suitable for reproduction without using a halftone screen; copy composed of lines or dots as distinguished from continuous tones. Lines or dots may be small and close together to simulate tones, but are still regarded as line copy if they can be reproduced without a halftone screen.

line drawing: Drawing containing no grays or middletones. In general, any drawing that can be reproduced without the use of halftone techniques.

line gauge: Gauge used to determine the number of lines of a particular leading or the leading between lines of type.

line gauge

line length: In typesetting and desktop publishing, the length of a line of type measured in picas and points.

linespace: Amount of space between lines of type, measured from the baseline of one line of type to the baseline of the next line of type.

logo: Graphic and/or letters used to represent a company or a product as an advertising trademark or symbol.

logotype: Name of a company or product in a specific typestyle, color, or other configuration; used as a trademark.

lowercase characters: Small letters, as distinguished from uppercase characters (capital letters).

M

magenta: Subtractive color, minus green, used in 4-color printing; also called process red. Visual color is red, but magenta acts to filter green out of white light.

main exposure: Exposure of white light reflecting off the copy, through the lens, penetrating the contact screen and exposing the film. It exposes the broadest range of tones, the middletones.

mapping: Defining areas of an illustration by using a variety of tint screen patterns; tint screen patterns are usually separated by rules.

margin: White space around the printed matter on a page.

mark up: To prepare a manuscript for typesetting with standard markings for the typesetter.

mask: 1. In color separation photography, an intermediate photographic negative or positive used in color correction. 2. In offset lithography, opaque material used to protect open or selected areas of printing plates during exposure.

matte finish: 1. Flat, nonreflecting surface on a photograph; generally not as good for reproduction as a glossy surface. 2. Dull paper finish without gloss or luster.

mechanical: Camera copy showing exact placement of every element and carrying actual or simulated type and artwork.

megabyte: In data processing, one million bytes.

memory: Part of the computer in which data is stored.

middletone dots: Halftone dots between highlight dots and shadow dots of a halftone, ranging from 30% to 70%.

mirror: Reflection of elements or entire pages to another page.

modem: Computer device that sends and receives data over telephone lines.

moiré: Undesirable pattern occurring when reproductions are made from halftones, caused by conflict between the ruling of the halftone screen and the dots or lines of the original; caused by incorrect overlapping of screen angles.

montage: Combination of photographs, parts of photographs, and/or pieces of copy to create one image.

mouse: Hand-held electromechanical or optical device used for direct input of computer coordinate-based data (horizontal and vertical locations on the screen) and programmed commands.

mouse

N

negative: Photographic image on film in which black values in the original subject are transparent and white values are opaque; light grays are dark, and dark grays are light.

nonimage area: Portion of the printing plate that does not accept ink. Also called nonprinting area.

O

off-register: 1. Improper alignment of elements. 2. Two or more colors not in the proper position when printed.

offset: Wet ink transferred from one sheet to another in a load of freshly printed sheets.

offset lithography: Lithography produced on an offset lithographic press. A right-reading plate is used and an intermediate rubber-covered offset cylinder transfers the image from the plate cylinder to the paper, cloth, metal, or other material being printed.

opacity: The property of paper that minimizes the show-through of printing from the back side or the next sheet. The ability to stop light from passing through is a material's opacity.

opaque: 1. Area or material that completely blocks out unwanted light; a filter may be opaque to only certain colors. 2. Red or black liquid used to block out or cover unwanted clear or gray areas on a negative. **3.** White liquid used to cover unwanted black images on an original copy (on white paper). **4.** To paint out areas on a negative that are not to print. **5.** In paper, the property that makes it less transparent.

opaque ink: Ink that does not allow the light to pass through it and has good hiding power. It does not permit the paper or previous printing to show through.

optical character reader (OCR): Automated machinery that reads characters on a page and translates the information to sort mail.

output: Product of computer processing, usually hard copy.

outside margin: See *trim margin.*

overlay: In artwork, a clear acetate sheet with color separations marked. Sometimes confused with tissue overlay.

P

page description language: Computer language that describes layout of the page.

page proof: Proof of type and art in page form.

pagination: The numbering of pages of a book.

paint program: Bit-mapped graphics program that produces free-form images, textures, and type pixel by pixel.

Pantone® Matching System (PMS): Ink color system widely used in graphic arts. There are approximately 500 basic colors for both coated and uncoated paper. The color number and formula for each color are shown beneath the color swatch.

parallel fold: Any series of folds in sequence, made in parallel fashion.

parallel fold

paste-up: Assembling of type elements, illustrations, and other copy elements into final page form, ready for photographing.

pegboard form: Form style that has individual forms held together by pegs or pins.

perforate: To make slits in the paper during folding, at the fold, to prevent wrinkles and allow air to escape.

perforation marks: Marks made to indicate where small, evenly spaced cuts are to be made in stock to facilitate hand-tearing.

permit mailing: Method of paying for movement of mail at rates that are dependent upon the specific permit, such as Second Class, Third Class, or Nonprofit Second Class.

photography: Use of light to produce an image on light-sensitive material, either by projection or contact exposure.

photomechanical transfer (PMT) print: Camera-generated positive print used for paste-up and for making paper contacts without a negative.

phototypesetting: Process of setting type via a photographic process directly onto film or paper.

pica: Unit of measure for line lengths and depth of type pages. One pica equals .1666″; 6 picas equal approximately 1″.

plastic comb binding: Mechanical binding using a piece of rigid vinyl plastic sheeting die cut in the shape of a comb or rake and rolled to make a cylinder of any thickness. The book is punched with slots along the binding edge, through which this comb is inserted.

point: Unit of measure used for designating type sizes and leading. Twelve points equal 1 pica; 72 points equal approximately 1″.

point size: Size of type. Point size indicates the approximate height of the type in points when measured from the bottom of the descenders to the top of the ascenders.

position stat: Line image of a continuous tone copy produced on high-contrast paper, such as a photomechanical transfer print, in the size needed for reproduction. Used to indicate the position of the halftone only.

posterization: Continuous tone photograph reproduced without a halftone contact screen by single exposure line photography.

prescreened halftone: Continuous tone copy broken into dots through the halftone process and reproduced on paper rather than film; pasted up directly on the mechanical and reproduced along with line copy on one sheet of film.

pressure-sensitive paper: Paper with an adhesive coating protected by a backing sheet until used, which will stick without moistening.

primary colors: In printing inks, yellow, magenta (process red), and cyan (process blue).

printer's spread: Spread of two pages based on signature imposition.

process camera: Camera designed specifically for a process lens; usually a large camera.

process colors: Yellow, magenta (red), cyan (blue), and black. When these colors are used in various strengths and combinations, thousands of colors can be produced with minimal photography, platemaking, and presswork.

process inks: Yellow, magenta (red), cyan (blue), and black transparent inks for process color printing that print over one another to create a variety of colors.

proof: Trial print from type, negatives, or plates.

proofreader: One who reads copy and marks errors for corrections.

proofreader's marks: Conventional signs and abbreviations used by a proofreader in the correction of copy.

proofreading: Procedure of checking a job to correct errors as it progresses through all phases of production.

proportional scale: Scale used to calculate enlargement and reduction percentages of an element, such as a photograph.

proportional scale

R

random access memory (RAM): Working memory of the computer; temporarily stores information from software programs and data while a job is being worked on.

reader's spread: Two facing pages as they would appear in an assembled book.

read only memory (ROM): Permanent memory stored in the computer by the manufacturer; contains instructions for the computer on how software programs and data are to be used.

reflectance quality: Difference between the light reflecting off the stock and the ink absorbing a portion of the reflected light.

register: 1. Exact correspondence in the position of pages or other printed matter on both sides of a sheet or in relation to other matter already ruled or printed on the same side of the sheet. 2. In photo reproduction and color printing, the correct relative position of two or more colors so that no color is out of its proper position.

register mark: 1. Small cross, guide, or pattern placed on original before reproduction; used for positioning negatives for stripping or for color register. 2. Similar mark added to a negative flat to print along the margin of a press sheet; used as a guide for correct alignment, backing, and color register in printing.

reverse: Type appearing in white on a black or color background or in a dark area of a photograph.

reverse overlay: Copy pasted on an overlay that is to be reversed.

right-angle fold: In binding, two or more folds each at 90° angles to the preceding fold.

rough layout: Full-size pencil drawing of the printed page used for visualizing size and position of elements before the comprehensive layout is made.

ruby film: Separable two-layer acetate film of red or amber emulsion on a clear base. Most often used for color separation by hand.

run-around type: Type that follows the perimeter of an illustration or photograph.

Typographical layout is the manner in which type is placed on the printed piece. Typographical layout includes the type and the space surrounding the characters, words, and sentences. Good typographical layout improves the readability of a printed piece while poor typographical layout reduces the readability. A designer determines the typographical layout and the typesetter fits the typographical layout to the comprehensive layout. A paste-up artist occasionally is required to hand set or paste-up type according to a specified typographical layout. Letterspacing is the space

run-around type

running foot: Type placed at the bottom of each page of a book, usually giving the main title of the work on the left-hand (verso) page and the title of the chapter or other subdivision on the right-hand (recto) page.

running head: Type placed at the top of each page of a book, usually giving the main title of the work on the left-hand (verso) page, and the title of the chapter or other subdivision on the right-hand (recto) page.

S

saddle stitching: Binding method in which sections are inserted into sections, then fastened with wires (stitches) through the middle fold of the sheets.

salesbook: Form style that contains a great volume of multipage forms bound at the top and often perforated to facilitate removal. One form in each set of two, three, or four is not perforated and remains in the book.

sans serif: Typeface distinguished by the absence of serifs, which are smooth, pointed, or rounded strokes on the ends of letters.

scale: To determine the proper size for an image that is to be reduced or enlarged.

scanner: Device that reads an image and electronically digitizes the image. See *digitizing.*

score: To compress the fiber of heavy paper along a line, either to facilitate folding or tearing. Scoring with a dull rule actually increases the folding endurance. Scoring with a sharp rule partially breaks the paper fibers and is similar to perforating.

score marks: Marks made to indicate where stock is to be indented to facilitate folding or tearing by easing the tension of the stock.

screen: 1. Short for halftone screen. Glass halftone screens consist of a pattern of fine, engraved and opaque crossed lines on the inside of two plates of cemented glass. 2. Halftone contact screen prepared photographically as a uniform pattern of fine magenta-colored (or gray) vignetted (variable-density) dots.

screen ruling: Number of lines per inch on a contact screen or ruled glass halftone screen.

scribe: To etch or remove part of the emulsion on a negative or to scratch the clay coating from an artboard.

scriber: Pencil-like tool with a steel point; used to remove the emulsion of a negative, for engraving rules, or for adding other fine detail.

script: Typestyle that has connecting characters and resembles fine handwriting.

self-mailer: One or more pages of folded and bound stock that are bound by a staple, an adhesive, or a label tab for mailing without an envelope.

serif: Typeface distinguished by smooth, pointed, or rounded strokes crossing or projecting from the ends of the lines or strokes of a letter.

set solid: Type composed without extra leading between lines, where the leading used equals the type size.

shadow dots: Halftone dots that range from 70% to 95% in the darkest area.

sidesewing: Binding method in which an entire block is sewn together along the binding edge without sewing of individual sections. A side-sewn book does not lie open flat.

side stitching: Binding method in which the folded signatures or cut sheets are stitched with wire along and through the side, close to the gutter margin. Pages cannot be fully opened to a flat position.

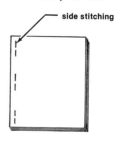

side stitching

signature: Folded, printed sheet forming one section of a book.

silhouette: To opaque out the background around a subject on a halftone negative.

silhouette image: Photographic halftone image that has its background removed; dots surrounding any part of the image have been cut away or removed prior to printing.

silhouette image

small caps (SC): Small capital letters available in most typefaces, approximately the size of the x-height of lowercase characters.

soft copy: Readable information not in a form that is printed on paper or film, but rather in an electronic image of characters or other graphic display, such as images on a video display terminal.

software: Program that runs the personal computer (PC) system; distributes information to all areas of the PC and directs each area to complete various functions.

solid leading: In typesetting, type set so the space from baseline to baseline is the same as the point size specified for the typeface used; expressed, for example, as 8/8.

spiral binding: Mechanical binding method that uses a continuous wire of corkscrew or spring coil form that is run through round holes punched in the binding edge; can be exposed, semiconcealed, or concealed.

spread: Photographic thickening of type characters or other printing detail that will provide a color or tint overlap and allow for slight off-register in successive printings.

stepped image: Job printed more than once on the same press sheet; it may be printed on one- or two-sided pages.

stet: Proofreader's term signifying that copy marked for corrections should remain as it was.

stock: Paper or other material on which a job is printed.

straightedge: Tool for drawing or establishing a straight line.

stylus: Hand-held device shaped like a pen used to input information manually into a computer through coordinates and programmed commands. See *light pen.*

surprint: To print copy over the design areas of previously printed matter (for example, over a tint screen, photograph, or an illustration).

T

thumbnail sketch: Small, proportional sketch with minimal detail that allows the designer to put initial ideas on paper.

tint screen: Various tones (strengths) of color; sometimes handled on the original copy by pasting down a piece of stock shading sheet that is photographed as line copy. Photographic (halftone) tint screens are stock developed film (negative and positive) in various strengths of tone (24%, 50%, etc.) used to generate tone values photographically. A dot pattern is generally used, although line, circle, triangle, square, and texture patterns are also available.

tissue overlay: Thin, translucent paper placed over artwork for protection; also may be used to indicate instructions, color breaks, and corrections.

tone: 1. Shade, hue, or degree of a color. **2.** Short for screen tone.

transfer type: Dry transfer type printed in dense ink on frosted acetate. Applied by removing the character from the backing sheet and applying it to an artboard.

transparent ink: Ink that lacks hiding power and permits light to pass through.

transpose: To exchange the position of a letter, work, line, or negative with another letter, work, line, or negative.

trap: Overlap allowed for two colors to print on the same sheet; used to compensate for off-register and to avoid white space between colors.

trim: To cut away the folded or uneven edges to form a smooth even edge and permit all pages to open.

trim margin: Margin of the open side, away from the bind; also called thumb, face, or outside margin.

trim marks: Thin, dense black lines approximately $1/2''$ in length placed on mechanical $1/16''$ outside the image area to indicate trim size of a job; also used for registration.

trim size: Final size of the job after waste has been removed.

tritone: Halftone printed using three colors.

typeface: Style or design of type encompassing shape, weight, and proportions that make it distinct from other typestyles.

type family: Group of typefaces that are similar in style, usually differing only in boldness and whether characters are straight (roman) or inclined slightly (italic).

type gauge: Measuring tool calibrated in picas; used to measure the various dimensions of typesetting.

type scale: Measuring tool used to determine type size.

type scale

type specification: Indicating type requirement for typesetting.

typo: Short for typographical error.

U

uncoated paper: Paper generally made on a conventional Fourdrinier machine and machine-dried.

unit set: Form style that has a multipage form duplicated throughout the set. All forms are connected at one end to hold forms in register.

uppercase characters: Capital letters. Uppercase characters rest on a baseline and extend upward.

V

vertical camera: Process camera that has a vertically mounted lens.

vignette: Illustration in which the background fades gradually away until it blends into the unprinted paper.

vignette dots: Series of equally spaced dots of varying densities, clear in center and gradually become darker toward the edges.

W

watermark: In papermaking, a name or design impressed on paper by the raised pattern of the dandy roller during manufacture; mark faintly shows when the paper is held to light.

web offset: Offset press in which paper is fed from a roller and printed on both sides in one continuous web, as opposed to sheetfed presses.

widow: 1. Short single line at the top of a page or column, usually the last line of a paragraph; to be avoided in good typesetting. **2.** One word or syllable standing alone as the last line of a paragraph.

window: Open or clear area on a negative used by the stripper to position halftone.

wordprocessing software: Computer program used to process (produce) words (text).

wordspacing: In typesetting, the space between words. Each typestyle requires a different amount of wordspacing.

wrong font (wf): Proofreader's mark that indicates the wrong typeface was used.

X

x-height: Body or area between the baseline and approximately one-half the height of an uppercase character.

INDEX

A

Adhesive binding, 134–135, *135*
Adhesive rules, 45–50, *46*
  and corners, 47–49, *48*, *49*, *50*
  removing, 46, *46*
Adhesives, 97–98
  applying, 99
  miscellaneous, 98
  rubber cement, 97
  spray, 98
  wax, 98
Adhesive type, 85–93
  altering, 88, 91, *92*
  artistically aligning, 88, *91*
    curved rule method, 88
    headline template method, 88, *91*
  creating headline with, 86, 88, 89, 90, 91
    guideline method, 86, 88, *89*
    headline setter method, 88, *90*
  letterspacing guidelines for, 86, *87*
  shelf life of, 86
Agate, 12
Art
  mechanical, 4, *5*
  soft, 4, *5*
Artboard, 25–30
  centering image on, 26–27, *28*, *29*, *30*
    centering ruler method, 26, *29*
    diagonal corners method, 26–27, *30*
    measurement method, 26, *28*
  coated, 44
  preparing for reproduction, 27–29, 31–34
  size, 25, *26*
  squaring, 25–26, *27*
  stock for, 25
Art director, 2
Artistic type, 72, *73*
Art knife, 44
Art table, 9, *10*
Ascender, 69, *69*, *70*

B

Backlighting, 113, *113*
Barcode sorters, 197–198
Baselines, 21
Beam compass, 53, *54*
Benday. *See* Mapping
Binder's creep, 133, *134*
Bindery
  operations, 8–9
  specifications, 21

Binding methods, 132–136
  adhesive, 134–135, *135*
  mechanical, 135, *136*
  saddle stitching, 133, *134*
  side stitching, 133–134, *135*
Black box, for halftone position, 114, *115*
Bleed, 21, 125–126, *126*
  full, 125, *126*
  margin, 125, *126*
  standard, 125, *126*
Bleeding, ink, 31
Body type, 21
Borders, 56–59, 60
  curved, 57–58, *58*, *59*
  mitered, 57
  ornate, 58–59, *60*
  preprinted adhesive, 56–57, *57*
Bow compass, 53, *54*
Breakacross images, 132, *133*
Brushes, for liquid white opaque, 42–43
Bump exposure, 110
Burnisher, 46
Business reply mail, 200, *202*

C

CAD. *See* Computer-aided design
Calender stack, 146, *146*
Calligraphy, 85
Camera copy, 109–116
  continuous tone, 109
  halftone, 113–116
  line, 109–113
Camera exposures, 110
Camera, process, 109, *109*
Centered type, 72, *73*
Center marks, 32–33, *34*
Central processing unit, 170
Character count formula, 76, 77
Character per pica number, 76, 77
Circles, 53–54, *54*
Circle template, 53–54, *55*
Circular type, pasting up, 99, *101*
Clip art, 4
Colors
  flat, 21, 119
  on mechanicals, 113
  paste-up for, 120–125
  process, 21
  and register, 119–125
Color separation, 110, 120
  and desktop publishing, 188–189
Commercial register, 120, *122*, *124*, 125

Compass, 53, *54*
Comprehensive layout, 2, *3*, 19–34, *20*, 144, *145*
  altering, 25
  bindery specifications indicated on, 21
  elements of, 19–24
  measurements on, 25, *25*
  using to create mechanical, 24–27
Computer-aided design, 172
Computer-aided illustration, 4, *5*
Computer hardware. *See* Hardware
Computers, 11
Computer software. *See* Software
Continuous tone copy, 7, 109, 110
Copy, pasting up
  printed, 99, *102*
  typewritten, 99, *102*
Copy dotting, 116
Copyfitting, 76–78
  determining number of typeset lines, 77
  determining space for manuscript copy, 77–78
  to fit fixed space, 76–77
Copy-free illustration, 4
Copywriting, 1
Cover sheet, 5
CPP number. *See* Character per pica number
CPU. *See* Central processing unit
Crepe tape, 88, *90*
Cross-hatching, on comprehensive layout, 24, *25*
Cursive type, 75–76, *76*
Curves, 53, 54–56
  creating with
    flexible curve, 56, *57*
    flexible tape, 49, *50*
    irregular curve, 54–55, *56*
  irregular, 54–56, *55*, *56*
Cutlines, 112, 113
Cutting, as correction technique, 44–45, *46*

D

Decorative type, 76, *76*
Descender, 69, *69*, *70*
Designing, 1–2
Design principles, 141–143
  balance, 141–142, *142*
  contrast, 142, *142*
  harmony, 143, *144*
  proportion, 141, *141*
  rhythm, 142, *143*

unity, 142–143, *143*
white space, 142, *143*
Design specifications, 141
Desktop publishing, 120
    applications, 179–189
    and color work, 180
    graphics, 185–188
        charts, 186–187, *187*
        graphs, 186–187, *187*
        line art, 185–186, *186*
        photographs, 187–188, *188*
    ruling, 181, *184*
    systems, 167–174
    textures, 181, *183*
    tint screens, 181, *182*
    type, 181, 183–185, *185*
Diameter, 53
Die cuts, 21, 127, *127*, *128*
Disks, computer, 170, *170*
Display type, 21, *23*
Dot gain, 115
Dot matrix printers, 171, *171*
Double-dot reproduction, 119
Drafting table. *See* Art table
Drill marks, 21
Duotones, 119, *121*
Dry-transfer type. *See* Transfer type

E

Envelopes, 196, *197*
Equipment, graphic arts, 9–14
E scale. *See* Type scale
Estimating, 2
Exposures, camera, 110

F

Facing images, 132, *133*
Facing pages layout, 132, *133*
Filigree, 76
Film tint screens, 63
Fine line copy, 111–112
    test boards, 112, *112*
Fixative, 99, 102
Flash exposure, 110
Flat colors, 21, 119, 120
    and commercial register paste-up, 120, *124*, 125
Flats, 7, *7*
    stripping, 7
Flexible curve, 54, *55*
Flexible tape, 49, *50*, 88, *90*
Flexography, 8
Floppy disk, 170, *170*
Flush left type, 72, *73*
Flush right type, 72, *73*
Folding dummy, 19, *20*, 126
    for saddle stitched book, 134
Fold marks, 33, *34*, 126, *127*, *128*
Folds, 21, *23*
    on stepped image imposition, 129
    on two-sided, one-up imposition, 126, *127*
Folios, 19, 132
Font, 73, *74*, 79

Footers, 132, *132*
Forms, 207–215
    carbonizing, 215, *215*
    continuous, 209–210, *210*
    entry format on, 211–212
    flat, 207, *208*
    graphics, 213–214, *214*
    ink for, 215
    layout, 210–215
    pegboard, 207, *208*
    salesbooks, 209, *209*
    spacing on, 211, *211*, *212*
    stock for, 214–215
    typography, 212–213, *213*
    unit sets, 207–209, *209*
Forms, pasting up, 102–103, *103*
4-color jobs, 120, *123*. *See also* Process colors
French curve. *See* Irregular curve

G

Galley, 3
    and proofreaders' marks, 79
Goldenrod, 7
Grain long, 129, *132*
Grain short, 129, *132*
Graphics software, 173
    draw, 173, *173*
    paint, 173, *174*
Gray-scale images, 187–188, *188*, *189*
Grids, 13, 14, *14*
Gripper margin, 125, *125*, 127
Guidelines, non-photo blue
    on artboard, 26
    for inking rules, 39
Gutters, 21, *22*

H

Hairline register, 120, *122*, *123*
Halftone dots, 110, *110*
    in prescreened halftones, 115–116, *115*, *116*
Halftone photography, 7
Halftones, 7, 109–110, *110*, 113–116
    and flat color inks, 119
    position on mechanical, 113–115, *115*
    prescreened, 115–116, *115*, *116*
    and stock colors, 119, *121*
Hand-set type, 85–93
    adhesive, 86, 88–91, *92*
    layout of, 86–93
    transfer, 91–93
Hard disk, 170
Hardware, 167–172
    central processing unit, 170
    input devices, 167–169
        keyboard, 167, *168*
        light pen, 167–168
        mouse, 167, *168*
        scanner, 168–169
        stylus, 167–168, *168*
    output devices, 170–172
        dot matrix printer, 171, *171*

imagesetter, *171*, 172
    laser printer, 171–172, *171*, 179, 180
    pen plotter, *171*, 172
Headers, 132, *132*
Headline setter, 88, *90*
Headline template, 88, *90*, *91*
Headline type. *See* Display type
Highlight dots, 110, *110*
    in prescreened halftones, 115, *115*

I

Illustrations, 3–4
    on comprehensive layout, 23
Image area, on image carrier, 7
Image carrier, 7–8, *8*
    image area on, 7
    non-image area on, 7
Images
    breakacross, 132, *133*
    facing, 132, *133*
Imagesetters, *171*, 172
Imposition, 125–136
    back-to-back, 127–129, *128*, *130*, *131*
        back-to-front, 129, *130*
        master grid, 129, *131*
        side-by-side, 127, *128*, 129
    binding, 132–136
        adhesive, 134–135, *135*
        mechanical, 135, *136*
        saddle stitching, 133, *134*
        side stitching, 133–134, *135*
    one-sided, one-up, 125–126
    signature, 129–132
        facing pages, 132, *133*
        printer's spread, 132, *134*
        reader's spread, 132, *133*
    stepped image, 129
        folds, scores, and perforations, 129
        trim and retrim, 129
    two-sided, one-up, 126–127
Inch, 11, 12
Ink
    bleeding, 31
    holdout, 146
    sneak, 126
    for technical pens, 31
Input devices, computer, 167–169
Intaglio image carrier, 7, 8, *8*
Irregular curve, 54–56, *55*
    used as headline template, 88, *90*, *91*

J

Job ticket, 19, *20*
Justified type, 72, *73*

K

Kerning, 71, *71*, 184
    for hand-set type, 86, *87*
Keyboard, 167, *168*
Keylines, 5
    black, 114
    for bleeds, 125

and color separation, 120, *123*
for halftone position, 114, *115*
red, 63, *63*, 114

L

Laser printers, 171–172, *171*
  paper for, 180
  and paper sizes, 179
Layout
  comprehensive, 2, *3*, 19–34, *20*, 144, *145*
  elements, 21, 23–24
  rough, 2, *3*, 143, *144*
  specifications, 19, 21
Layout development, 143–144
Leading, 12, 71, *72*, 184–185
Lettering device, and template, 85, *86*
Lettering pen, 85, *86*
Letterpress image carrier, 8
Letterspacing, 71, *71*
  for hand-set type, 86, *87*
Light pen, 167–168
Light table, 9, *10*
Line copy, 5, 7, *7*, 109–113
  density, 111
  fine, 111–112
  size, 111, *112*
Line gauge, *13*, 14
Line length, 185
Line photography, 5, 7, 109, *110*
Logo, 91, *92*
Loose-leaf binding, 135, *136*
Lowercase characters, 69

M

Mail
  automated, 197–202
  general, 195–197
Main exposure, 110
Make-ready time, 5
Manuscript copy, 1, *2*
Mapping, with tint screens, 61, 63, *63*
Margins, 21, *22*
  column alignment, 126
  nonprinting, 125, *125*, 126, *127*
Measurement devices, 13–14
Measurement systems, 11–13, *13*
Mechanical art, 4, *5*
Mechanical binding, 135–136
  loose-leaf, 135, *136*
  plastic comb, 135, *136*
  spiral, 135, *136*
Mechanicals, 5, *6*, *22*
  and desktop publishing, 188–189
  negative of, 114
Middletone dots, 110, *110*
  in prescreened halftones, 115, *115*
Moiré, 61, *62*
Mouse, 167, *168*

N

Negative
  base, 114, *114*
  halftone, 114, *114*

Non-image area, on image carrier, 7
Non-photo blue lines, 26. *See also* Guide-
  lines, non-photo blue
Nonprinting margins, 125, *125*, 126, *127*
Nonregister, 120, *122*
  paste-up for, 125

O

Opaque
  black, 112
  liquid white, 42–43
    brush used with, 42–43
    technical pen used with, 43
Opaquing, 7
Optical character readers, 197
Overlay, tissue, 19, 63, *63*
Overlay method, of paste-up, 99–105

P

Page description language, 172
Page makeup system, 11, *12*, 173, *174*
PANTONE® Color and Black Selector, 119
PANTONE® Matching System, 21, 119. *See
  also* PMS colors
Paper, 21. *See also* Stock
  bond, 149
  book, 149
  coatings, 146–149
  cover, 149
  finishing, 146, *146*
  grades, 149
  making, 145–146, *146*
  manufacturing, 144–146
    pulp processing in, 144–145
  specialty, 149
  specifications, 148
  text, 149
Paste-up, 5
Paste-up techniques, 99–105
  for circular type, 99, 101
  for color, 120, 122–125
  for forms, 102–103, *103*
  for nonregister, 125
  overlay method, 99, 102–105
  for printed and typewritten copy, 99, *102*
  for register, 120, 122–125
Pen
  lettering, 85, *86*
  technical. *See* Technical pen
Pen plotters, *171*, 172
Perforation marks, 33, *34*, *127*, *128*
Perforations, 21
  on stepped image imposition, 129
  on two-sided, one-up imposition, 126, *127*
Photographs, 4–5
  on comprehensive layout, 23, *24*
  and desktop publishing, 187–188, *188*,
    189
  keying, 23, *24*
  reproduction of, 5, 7
  treatment on mechanicals, 5
Photography, line, 5, 7
Photomechanical transfer, 111

Photo-offset lithographic printing, 7–8
Picas, 11, 12
Pixel, 169
Planographic image carrier, 7–8, *8*
Plastic comb binding, 135, *136*
Plate, black, 119
Platemaking, 7–8
PMS colors, 21
PMT. *See* Photomechanical transfer
Points, 11, 12
Point size. *See* Type size
Position stat, 114, *115*
Postal regulations, 195–202
  automated mail, 197–202
  general mail, 195–197
Postcards, 196
PostScript®, 172
Prescreened halftones, 115–116, *115*, *116*
Presses, 8, *9*
Press proof, 8
Press sheet, 8
  same-size, 125
Presswork, 8
Printer, black, 119, *123*
Printers, computer, 171–172, *171*
Printer's spread, 132, *134*
Printing, photo-offset lithographic, 7–8
Printing presses. *See* Presses
Process camera, 109, *109*
  exposures, 110
Process colors, 21, 110, 120, *121*, *123*
  and hairline register paste-up, 120, *122*,
    123
Production process, 1–9
Production techniques, 99–105
Proofreaders' marks, 79, *79*
Proofreading, 1, 78, 79
Proportional scale, *13*, 14, *14*, 163, *163*

Q

Quadrant, 53

R

Radius, 53
RAM. *See* Random access memory
Random access memory, 170
Reader's spread, 132, *133*
Read only memory, 170
Reflectance quality, 199
Register, 8, 120–125
  commercial, 120, *122*, *124*, 125
  and desktop publishing, 188
  hairline, 120, *122*, *123*
  nonregister, 120, *122*
  off, 120, *122*
  paste-up for, 120–125
Register marks, 99, 102, *102*
  used as center marks, 32, *34*
Relief image carrier, 7, 8, *8*
Reversing type, 104–105, *105*
ROM. *See* Read only memory
Rosette, 61, *62*
Rotogravure printing, 8

Rough layouts, 2, *3*, 143, *144*
Rubber cement, 97–98
Ruby film box, for halftone position, 114, *115*
Rubylith. *See* Ruby film box
Rulers, 13–14, *13*
Rules
  adhesive, 45–50, *46*
    removing, 46, *46*
  correcting, 42–45, *46*
  drawing
    horizontal, 40, *41*
    inclined, 40–41, *43*
    vertical, 40, *42*
    wide, 39, 41–42, *44*
  weights, 39, *39*
Rule scale, 39, *40*
Ruling, 39–50
  with adhesive material, 45–50
  and desktop publishing systems, 181, *184*
  with ink, 39–45
  technical pen for, 39
  techniques, 39–42
  tools used for, 39–42
Run-around type, 72, *73*
Running foot, 132, *132*
Running head, 132, *132*

S

Saddle stitching, 133, *134*
Sans serif type, 75, *75*
Scales, 13, 14, *14*
Scanners, 168–169
  flatbed, 168, *169*
  graphics, 169
  hand-held, 168, *169*
  OCR, 169
  overhead, 168–169, *169*
  sheetfed, 168, *169*
Score marks, 33, *34*, *127*, *128*
Scores, 21
  on stepped image imposition, 129
  on two-sided, one-up imposition, 126, *127*
Screens. *See* Tint screens
Scribing, 44–45, *46*
Script type, 75–76, *76*
Self-mailers, 197, *198*
Serif type, 75, *75*
Shadow dots, 110, *110*
  in prescreened halftones, 115, *115*
Shadowing, on film, 112–113
Side stitching, 133–134, *135*
Signature imposition, 129, 132
  facing pages, 132, *133*
  printer's spread, 132, *134*
  reader's spread, 132, *133*
Signatures, 129, 132
Software, 172–174
  graphics, 173
    draw, 173, *173*
    paint, 173, *174*
  page layout, 173, *174*
  wordprocessing, 173
Spiral binding, 135, *136*

Spray adhesive, 98
Stat, position, 114, *115*
Stencil image carrier, 7, 8, *8*
Stock, 21, 144–149. *See also* Paper
  for artboards, 21
  coatings, 146–149
    cast, 147–148, *148*
    dull, 147, *147*
    gloss, 147, *148*
    matte, 147, *147*
  color, 148
  surface, 148–149
    finish, 149
  weight, 148
Stylus, 167–168, *168*
Substrate, 7
Surprinting, 103–104, *104*

T

Tape, used for corrections, 43–44, *45*
Technical pen, 27–29, *30*, 31
  cleaning, 29, 31, 43
  for inking rules, 39
  inks for, 31
  nibs, 28–29
  parts of, 28–29, *30*
  sizes, 28–29
Template and lettering device, 85, *86*
Test boards
  color, 113, *113*
  fine line copy, 112, *112*
Textletter type, 76, *76*
Text type. *See* Body type
Textures, and desktop publishing systems, 181, *183*
Texturing, with tint screens, 61, 63, *63*
Thumbnail sketches, 2, *3*, 143, *144*
Tint screens, 23–24, *24*, 59, 61–63, *61*
  applying, 61, *62*
  on comprehensive layout, 24, *25*
  and desktop publishing systems, 181, *182*
  film, 63
  line value of, 23–24, 61
  mapping with, 61, 63, *63*
  percent value of, 23
  ruling, 59
  texturing with, 61, 63, *63*
Tissue overlay, 19, 63, *63*, 128
Tools, graphic arts, 9–14
Trade shop, 2
Transfer type, 85, 91–92, *92*
  creating headline with, 91–92, *93*
  shelf life, 91
Triangles, 10–11, *11*, *12*
Trim lines, 31, *31*
Trim marks, 31–32, *31*, *33*
Trim size, 21
  and artboard size, 25, *26*
  and bleeds, 125, *126*
  laying out, 31, *32*
Tritone, 119
T-square, 10
Tweezers, 47

Type, 21, 23
  adhesive, 85–93
  ascender, 69, *69*, *70*
  circular, pasting up, 99, *101*
  descender, 69, *69*, *70*
  and desktop publishing systems, 181, 183–185, *185*
  hand-set, 85–93
  inked, 85, *86*
  kerning, 71, *71*
  leading, 71, *72*
  legibility, 69–76
  letterspacing, 71, *71*
  lowercase characters, 69
  pasting up, 99–102
  readability, 69–76
  reversing, 104–105, *105*
  size, 70, *71*, 183–184
  transfer, 85, 91–92, *92*
  uppercase characters, 69
  wordspacing, 71, *72*
  x-height, 69, *70*
Type arrangement, 3, *4*, 72, *73*, 79, 185. *See also* Typographical layout
  artistic, 72, *73*
  centered, 72, *73*
  flush left, 72, *73*
  flush right, 72, *73*
  justified, 72, *73*
  run-around, 72, *73*
Type classifications, 73, 75–76
  cursive, 75–76, *76*
  decorative, 76, *76*
  sans serif, 75, *75*
  script, 75–76, *76*
  serif, 75, *75*
  textletter, 76, *76*
Type scale, 13, 14, *14*
Typesetter, 3, *4*
Typesetting, 2–3
Type specifications, 72–73, 78–79, *78*
  family, 73, *74*, 79
  font, 73, *74*, 79
  layout, 73, *74*
  series, 73, *74*
Typographical layout, 70–72. *See also* Type arrangement
Typography, 69–79

U

Uppercase characters, 69

V

Vignette dots, 110

W

Watermark, 149, *149*
Wax, 98
Windows, on negatives, 114
Wordspacing, 71, *72*

X

X-acto knife. *See* Art knife